A HISTORY OF OUR TIME

A HISTORY
OF OUR TIME
Readings on Postwar America

Second Edition

Edited by

William H. Chafe
DUKE UNIVERSITY

Harvard Sitkoff
UNIVERSITY OF NEW HAMPSHIRE

New York   Oxford
OXFORD UNIVERSITY PRESS
1987

Oxford University Press

Oxford New York Toronto
Delhi Bombay Calcutta Madras Karachi
Petaling Jaya Singapore Hong Kong Tokyo
Nairobi Dar es Salaam Cape Town
Melbourne Auckland

and associated companies in
Beirut Berlin Ibadan Nicosia

Library of Congress Cataloging-in-Publication Data
A history of our time.
  Bibliography: p.
  1. United States—History—1945–
I. Chafe, William Henry. II. Sitkoff, Harvard.
F742.H57 1986 973.92 86-18084
ISBN 0-19-504204-2

9 8 7 6 5 4 3 2 1
Printed in the United States of America

Preface

One of the ironies of learning about history is that we often know more about events hundreds of years ago than we do about the recent past. Even when it comes to the United States, students are likely to have a clearer sense of the Dred Scott decision of 1857 (when the Supreme Court ruled that a slave remained legally a slave even in free territory) than of the Brown v. Board of Education decision of 1954 that ruled segregation in the public schools unconstitutional. Thus, to many of the students who read this book, the American Revolution will seem more familiar, tangible, and immediate than the Montgomery bus boycott or McCarthyism.

Yet to a remarkable extent, the history we live today is a direct product of recent changes—those that have transpired *since* the beginning of World War II. In 1940 the nation had not yet emerged from the Great Depression, and permanent economic stagnation seemed just as likely as prosperity. Barely 15 percent of all young people attended college. American foreign policy was based on a commitment to neutrality, with a majority of Americans intent on avoiding involvement in any foreign ventures, even against Hitler. Black Americans lived predominantly in the South, could not vote, were denied access to restaurants, theaters, and other public accommodations, except on a segregated basis, and suffered systematic brutality, with no recourse before the law. Women—at least middle-class, white women—were expected to marry, raise children, and devote themselves to homemaking. The idea of pursuing a career as well as marriage was frowned on, and most professional schools—especially those in law and medicine—accepted only a token number of women, usually less than 5 percent of the entering class.

Today, that world has, in many ways, been transformed. Nearly

50 percent of young people attend some institution of post-secondary education. Despite an alarming persistence of poverty, especially among children and women, the two-car family has become typical, with ribbons of four-lane highways linking regions that fifty years ago seemed worlds apart. American foreign policy is now premised on active involvement everywhere in the world, with antipathy to the Soviet Union providing a rationale for U.S. engagement in a variety of regional and multilateral alliances. In the 1950s and 1960s, the civil rights movement—arguably the greatest insurgent movement in our history—both demanded equal justice for the children of all races, and set in motion parallel movements for social reform among women, young people, Indians, Chicanos, and gay Americans. In family life the norm for most households has become two wage earners; women apply in nearly equal numbers with men to many professional schools; and in theory, at least, most Americans now subscribe to the idea of sex equality. During the post-World War II era, Americans even had the experience of losing a war and seeing a president resign in disgrace.

Clearly, not every development since World War II has involved a departure from the past. Many of the political and social themes discussed in this book have origins that go far back in our history. McCarthyism, for example, bears a strong resemblance to the Red Scare after World War I, the nativism of the 1850s, and the xenophobia of the 1790s. Despite major changes in legislation, black Americans (and other minorities) continue to suffer from discrimination that eludes correction under the law. Nevertheless, it seems accurate to conclude that the period since 1940 represents a distinctive era in our history, shaping in a new way the lives of those who will assume leadership in the next century.

This book represents an effort to come to grips with some of the major themes and issues of the postwar period. Although we have presented these issues in a chronological framework, the organizational structure is thematic. Such issues as the Cold War, civil rights, and changes in sex roles—extending over more than one decade—can best be viewed as a coherent whole, rather than being parceled out into different sections depending on who happened to be president at a given time. The selections we have chosen also reflect an emphasis on developments in social history, although traditional political history is not ignored. For this new edition, we have also included material from recently published works on civil rights, politics, the New Right, poverty, and the counterculture, hoping to give readers the most up-to-date scholarship available.

The book is structured so that students will have a basis for asking critical questions and arriving at independent judgments on major issues. It is our belief that the best learning occurs when different points of view are presented and individuals have the means for comparison. Consequently, each section of the book contains historical interpretations of a given problem, plus at least one primary document from an involved participant. In this way, we hope that students can achieve an understanding of, and empathy with, those who influenced the events being discussed, as well as the retrospective view of scholars.

We hope that readers of this volume will come away from it with a new understanding of the developments that have brought us where we are today, as well as sensitivity to the unresolved questions that confront us as we face the next century.

Durham, N.C.   W.H.C.
Durham, N.H.   H.S.
June, 1986

Contents

A HISTORY OF OUR TIME

Part One

THE SOURCES
OF THE COLD WAR

Probably no event has been more decisive in shaping the world of postwar Americans than the Cold War. Prior to the 1940s, the United States had studiously refrained from involvement in international alliances. World War I represented an exception to that policy. Inspired by the apocalyptic rhetoric of Woodrow Wilson that this would be a war "to end all wars" and to "make the world safe for democracy," Americans had participated with fervor in a European war. But in the aftermath of that experience—particularly the sense of betrayal that wartime ideals were abandoned at Versailles—Americans had retreated again to isolationism.

World War II brought a permanent end to that phenomenon. For reasons of both self-interest and moral commitment, fascism had to be fought. But even as the wartime alliance between Great Britain, the Soviet Union, and the United States successfully attacked Hitler's tyranny, there were questions as to how the postwar world would be organized. Americans had traditionally expressed a bitter hostility toward Bolshevism. Russia, in turn, resented America's refusal to acknowledge the Soviet regime through diplomatic recognition, and believed that western failure to join in a collective pact against Germany prior to 1939 represented a not so subtle effort to make the Soviet government vulnerable to German aggression.

These problems of suspicion and division continued even during the war. Russia bore the brunt of the battle, losing over twenty million lives. A second front in western Europe was crucial to her own survival, and Roosevelt and Churchill repeatedly promised that such a front would be initiated, first in 1942, then in 1943. Resentment that the Normandy invasion did not occur until June

1944 clearly provided an ongoing source of tension. Similarly, Russia and her western allies split over who would control occupation governments in Italy, Rumania, and other conquered territory. Underlying all of these problems was a basic conceptual conflict over the purposes for which the war was being fought. The primary goal of the Soviet Union was security on her borders and control over those governments closest to Russia. The United States, in contrast, articulated the more universalistic principles of the Atlantic Charter, insisting that the war was fought for self-determination, democracy, territorial integrity, and traditional western freedoms. This underlying conflict of sphere of influence versus universalist principles during the war meant conflict over priorities and values in a postwar world.

These problems came to a head over five specific issues. The Polish question—the first—symbolized to both sides the primary purpose for which they had fought the war. A friendly Polish government meant everything to the Soviet Union since, on three occasions, the Polish corridor had been the path through which invasions of Russia had occurred. Self-determination for Poland was also the immediate pretext why Britain had gone to war, and a democratically elected government there represented, in the purest possible form, a test of the principles of the Atlantic Charter. Who would control Poland thus constituted a profound point of contention for both sides. A second issue involved the fate of other occupied nations. American wishes for democratic elections clashed with the division of authority that Churchill and Stalin had agreed upon for Greece, Rumania, and other occupation governments.

The fate of Germany presented a third point of conflict, with the allies divided over reparations from Germany, whether that country should remain industrialized, and whether it should be permanently divided. Control over atomic energy constituted a fourth point of division, with many Russians believing that the U.S. monopoly over atomic weaponry represented an effort to intimidate the world. America, in turn, insisted that only after everyone else had agreed to United States proposals would she turn over control of nuclear secrets. Fifth, and finally, was the conflict over economic reconstruction of Europe, and particularly, whether the United States would provide loans to eastern as well as western Europe for the purpose of rehabilitation. What form

European economies would take was clearly an underlying source of stress.

The following selections address major questions of the origins of the Cold War. Martin Sherwin carefully analyzes the intertwining of atomic bomb policies and diplomatic objectives during the Roosevelt and Truman administrations, and shows how wartime assumptions and decisions contributed to the emergence of the Cold War. Similarly emphasizing the consequences of wartime problems and policies, John Gaddis examines the development of the American strategy of containment toward the Soviet Union and provides a valuable perspective on the inevitability of Cold War conflicts. Henry Wallace takes a different view in his plea to Truman for cooperation with the Soviet Union and an understanding of Soviet motives and drives. Clark Clifford, Truman's closest personal aide, summarizes the views of most American foreign policy officials in his confidential memorandum to the President in September 1946. Based largely upon George F. Kennan's diplomatic cables from Moscow, Clifford's report reflects the assumptions behind the steadily developing "get tough" containment policy in Washington.

Students examining this period will want to consider such questions as: Was the Cold War inevitable? If so, what made it a necessity? Were the primary differences ideological? Economic? Political? If the Cold War was not inevitable, how could it have been avoided? Was there room for compromise in eastern Europe along the lines of the Churchill/Stalin agreement? What diplomatic considerations affected the decision to drop the atomic bomb on Japan, and what were the diplomatic consequences of that decision? Would it have made any difference if Roosevelt had lived? Finally, are we perpetual victims of the Cold War, or does there remain any posibility of finding the basis for mutual accommodation?

The Atomic Bomb and the Origins of the Cold War

Martin J. Sherwin

The deaths from incineration and radiation of some 200,000 residents of Hiroshima and Nagasaki in August 1945 dramatically ushered in the atomic age, surely one of the most significant developments in recorded history. Among its more profound consequences, the destruction of these two cities contributed to the origins of the Cold War. The American possession of a monopoly on atomic power and the subsequent effort of Secretary of State James F. Byrnes to practice atomic diplomacy rapidly catalyzed Soviet-American disagreements into an implacable confrontation.

Assessments of the motives behind the decision to drop the bombs have tended to cluster diplomatic historians into opposing camps. Those labeled "traditionalist" or "orthodox" echo Secretary of War Henry L. Stimson's contention that the use of the bomb was militarily necessary to force Japan's surrender as quickly as possible and with the least possible loss of American lives. Contrarily, "revisionists" generally argue that the bombs were not vital to defeating Japan but were utilized to influence Soviet behavior.

Martin J. Sherwin forges a synthesis of these clashing interpretations. In the article from which this selection is excerpted, and in greater detail in his A World Destroyed: The Atomic Bomb and the Grand Alliance *(New York, 1975), Sherwin contends that the bombs were dropped to bring a speedy conclusion to the war with Japan, but also that American leaders understood the potential diplomatic value of the bombs and viewed them as a lever against the Soviet Union. He particularly stresses the implications of Franklin D. Roosevelt's wartime atomic policy decisions. The President recognized the bomb both as a legitimate weapon of war against the Axis and as a possible diplomatic weapon against the*

Soviet Union. Perhaps most fatefully, Roosevelt permitted the British a junior partnership in the Manhattan Project but totally excluded the Russians.

During the Second World War the atomic bomb was seen and valued as a potential rather than an actual instrument of policy. Responsible officials believed that its impact on diplomacy had to await its development and, perhaps, even a demonstration of its power. As Henry L. Stimson, the secretary of war, observed in his memoirs: "The bomb as a merely probable weapon had seemed a weak reed on which to rely, but the bomb as a colossal reality was very different." That policymakers considered this difference before Hiroshima has been well documented, but whether they based wartime diplomatic policies upon an anticipated successful demonstration of the bomb's power remains a source of controversy. Two questions delineate the issues in this debate. First, did the development of the atomic bomb affect the way American policymakers conducted diplomacy with the Soviet Union? Second, did diplomatic considerations related to the Soviet Union influence the decision to use the atomic bomb against Japan?

These important questions relating the atomic bomb to American diplomacy, and ultimately to the origins of the cold war, have been addressed almost exclusively to the formulation of policy during the early months of the Truman administration. As a result, two anterior questions of equal importance, questions with implications for those already posed, have been overlooked. Did diplomatic considerations related to Soviet postwar behavior influence the formulation of Roosevelt's atomic-energy policies? What effect did the atomic legacy Truman inherited have on the diplomatic and atomic-energy policies of his administration?

To comprehend the nature of the relationship between atomic-energy and diplomatic policies that developed during the war, the bomb must be seen as policy makers saw it before Hiroshima, as a weapon that might be used to control postwar diplomacy. For this task our present view is conceptually inadequate. After more than a quarter century of experience we understand, as wartime policy

Walter S. Dickson Professor of History and Director of the History & Humanities Center for Nuclear Age Studies, Tufts University.

makers did not, the bomb's limitations as a diplomatic instrument. To appreciate the profound influence of the unchallenged wartime assumption about the bomb's impact on diplomacy we must recognize the postwar purposes for which policy makers and their advisers believed the bomb could be used. In this effort Churchill's expectations must be scrutinized as carefully as Roosevelt's, and scientists' ideas must be considered along with those of politicians. Truman's decision to use the atomic bomb against Japan must be evaluated in the light of Roosevelt's atomic legacy, and the problems of impending peace must be considered along with the exigencies of war. To isolate the basic atomic-energy policy alternatives that emerged during the war requires that we first ask whether alternatives were, in fact, recognized.

What emerges most clearly from a close examination of wartime formulation of atomic-energy policy is the conclusion that policy makers never seriously questioned the assumption that the atomic bomb should be used against Germany or Japan. From October 9, 1941, the time of the first meeting to organize the atomic-energy project, Stimson, Roosevelt, and other members of the "top policy group" conceived of the development of the atomic bomb as an essential part of the total war effort. Though the suggestion to build the bomb was initially made by scientists who feared Germany might develop the weapon first, those with political responsibility for prosecuting the war accepted the circumstances of the bomb's creation as sufficient justification for its use against any enemy.

Having nurtured this point of view during the war, Stimson charged those who later criticized the use of the bomb with two errors. First, these critics asked the wrong question: it was not whether surrender could have been obtained without using the bomb, but whether a different diplomatic and military course from that followed by the Truman administration would have achieved an earlier surrender. Second, the basic assumption of these critics was false: the idea that American policy should have been based primarily on a desire not to employ the bomb seemed as "irresponsible" as a policy controlled by a positive desire to use it. The war, not the bomb, Stimson argued, had been the primary focus of his attention; as secretary of war his responsibilities permitted no alternative.

Stimson's own wartime diary nevertheless indicates that from

1941 on, the problems associated with the atomic bomb moved steadily closer to the center of his own and Roosevelt's concerns. As the war progressed, the implications of the weapon's development became diplomatic as well as military, postwar as well as wartime. Recognizing that a monopoly of the atomic bomb gave the United States a powerful new military advantage, Roosevelt and Stimson became increasingly anxious to convert it to diplomatic advantage. In December 1944 they spoke of using the "secret" of the atomic bomb as a means of obtaining a *quid pro quo* from the Soviet Union. But viewing the bomb as a potential instrument of diplomacy, they were not moved to formulate a concrete plan for carrying out this exchange before the bomb was used. The bomb had "this unique peculiarity," Stimson noted several months later in his diary; "Success is 99% assured, yet only by the first actual war trial of the weapon can the actual certainty be fixed." Whether or not the specter of postwar Soviet ambitions created "a positive desire" to ascertain the bomb's power, until that decision was executed "atomic diplomacy" remained an idea that never crystallized into policy.

Although Roosevelt left no definitive statement assigning a postwar role to the atomic bomb, his expectations for its potential diplomatic value can be recalled from the existing record. An analysis of the policies he chose from among the alternatives he faced suggests that the potential diplomatic value of the bomb began to shape his atomic-energy policies as early as 1943. He may have been cautious about counting on the bomb as a reality during the war, but he nevertheless consistently chose policy alternatives that would promote the postwar diplomatic potential of the bomb if the predictions of scientists proved true. These policies were based on the assumption that the bomb could be used effectively to secure postwar diplomatic aims; and this assumption was carried over from the Roosevelt to the Truman administration.

Despite general agreement that the bomb would be an extraordinarily important diplomatic factor after the war, those closely associated with its development did not agree on how to use it most effectively as an instrument of diplomacy. Convinced that wartime atomic-energy policies would have postwar consequences, several scientists advised Roosevelt to adopt policies aimed at achieving a postwar international control system. Churchill, on the other hand, urged the president to maintain the Anglo-American atomic monopoly as a diplomatic counter against the postwar ambitions of other nations—particularly against the Soviet Union. Roosevelt fashioned his atomic-energy policies from the choices he made between these conflicting recommendations. In 1943 he rejected the counsel of his science advisers and began to consider the diplomatic component of atomic-energy policy in consultation with Churchill alone. This decision-making procedure and Roosevelt's untimely death have left his motives ambiguous. Nevertheless it is clear that he pursued policies consistent with Churchill's monopolistic, anti-Soviet views.

The findings of this study thus raise serious questions concerning generalizations historians have commonly made about Roosevelt's diplomacy: that it was consistent with his public reputation for cooperation and conciliation; that he was naive with respect to postwar Soviet behavior; that, like Wilson, he believed in collective security as an effective guarantor of national safety; and that he made every possible effort to assure that the Soviet Union and its allies would continue to function as postwar partners. Although this article does not dispute the view that Roosevelt desired amicable postwar relations with the Soviet Union, or even that he worked hard to achieve them, it does suggest that historians have exaggerated his confidence in (and perhaps his commitment to) such an outcome. His most secret and among his most important long-range decisions—those responsible for prescribing a diplomatic role for the atomic bomb—reflected his lack of confidence. Finally, in light of this study's conclusions, the widely held assumption that Truman's attitude toward the atomic bomb was substantially different from Roosevelt's must also be revised.

Like the grand alliance itself, the Anglo-American atomic-energy partnership was forged by the war and its exigencies. The threat of a German atomic bomb precipitated a hasty marriage of convenience between British research and American resources. When scientists in Britain proposed a theory that explained how an atomic bomb might quickly be built, policymakers had to assume that German scientists were building one. "If such an explosive were made," Vannevar Bush, the director of the Office of Scientific Research and Development, told Roosevelt in July 1941, "it would be thousands of times more powerful than existing explosives, and its use might be determining." Roosevelt assumed nothing less. Even before the atomic-energy project was fully organized he assigned it the highest priority. He wanted the program "pushed not only in regard to development, but also with due regard to time. This is very much of the essence," he told Bush in March 1942. "We both felt painfully the dangers of doing nothing," Churchill recalled, referring to an early wartime discussion with Roosevelt about the bomb.

The high stakes at issue during the war did not prevent officials in Great Britain or the United States from considering the postwar implications of their atomic-energy decisions. . . .

It can be argued that Roosevelt, the political pragmatist, renewed the wartime atomic-energy partnership to keep relations with the British harmonious rather than disrupt them on the basis of a postwar issue. Indeed it seems logical that the president took this consideration into account. But it must also be recognized that he was perfectly comfortable with the concept Churchill advocated—that military power was a prerequisite to successful postwar diplomacy. As early as August 1941, during the Atlantic Conference, Roosevelt had rejected the idea that an "effective international organization" could be relied upon to keep the peace; an Anglo-American international police force would be far more effective, he told Churchill. By the spring of 1942 the concept had broadened: the two "policemen" became four, and the idea was added that every other nation would be totally disarmed. "The Four Policemen" would have "to build up a reservoir of force so powerful that no aggressor would dare to challenge it," Roosevelt told Arthur Sweetser, an ardent internationalist. Violators first would be quarantined, and, if they persisted in their disruptive activities, bombed at the rate of a city a day until they agreed to behave. The president told Molotov about this idea in May, and in November he repeated it to Clark Eichelberger, who was coordinating the activities of the American internationalists. A year later, at the Teheran Conference, Roosevelt again discussed his idea, this time with Stalin. As Robert A. Divine has noted: "Roosevelt's concept of big power domination remained the central idea in his approach to international organization throughout World War II."

Precisely how Roosevelt expected to integrate the atomic bomb into his plans for keeping the peace in the postwar world is not clear. However, against the background of his atomic-energy policy decisions of 1943 and his peace-keeping concepts, his actions in 1944 suggest that he intended to take full advantage of the bomb's potential as a postwar instrument of Anglo-American diplomacy. If Roosevelt thought the bomb could be used to create a more peaceful world order, he seems to have considered the threat of its power more effective than any opportunities it offered for international cooperation. If Roosevelt was less worried than Churchill about Soviet postwar ambitions, he was no less determined than the prime minister to avoid any commitments to the Soviets for the international control of atomic energy. There could still be four policemen, but only two of them would have the bomb.

Harry S. Truman inherited a set of military and diplomatic atomic-energy policies that included partially formulated intentions, several commitments to Churchill, and the assumption that the bomb would be a legitimate weapon to be used against Japan. But no policy was definitely settled. According to the Quebec Agreement the president had the option of deciding the future of the commercial aspects of the atomic-energy partnership according to his own estimate of what was fair. Although the policy of "utmost secrecy" had been confirmed at Hyde Park the previous September, Roosevelt had not informed his atomic-energy advisers about the *aide-mémoire* he and Churchill signed. Although the assumption that the bomb would be used in the war was shared by those privy to its development, assumptions formulated early in the war were not necessarily valid at its conclusion. Yet Truman was bound to the past by his own uncertain position and by the prestige of his predecessor. Since Roosevelt had refused to open negotiations with the Soviet government for the international control of atomic energy, and since he had never expressed any objection to the wartime use of the bomb, it would have required considerable political courage and confidence for Truman to alter these policies. Moreover it would have required the encouragement of his advisers, for under the circumstances the most serious constraint on the new president's choices was his dependence upon advice. So Truman's atomic legacy, while it included several options, did not necessarily entail complete freedom to choose from among all the possible alternatives.

"I think it is very important that I should have a talk with you as soon as possible on a highly secret matter," Stimson wrote to Truman on April 24. It has "such a bearing on our present foreign relations and has such an important effect upon all my thinking in this field that I think you ought to know about it without further delay." Stimson had been preparing to brief Truman on the atomic bomb for almost ten days, but in the preceding twenty-four hours he had been seized by a sense of urgency. Relations with the Soviet Union had declined precipitously during the past week, the result, he thought, of the failure of the State Department to settle the major problems between the Allies before going ahead with the San Francisco Conference on the United Nations Organization. The secretary of state, Edward R. Stettinius, Jr., along with the department's Soviet specialists, now felt "compelled to bull the thing through." To get out of the "mess" they had created, Stimson wrote in his diary, they were urging Truman to get tough with the Russians. He had. Twenty-four hours earlier the president met with the Soviet foreign minister, V. M. Molotov, and "with rather brutal frankness" accused his government of breaking the Yalta Agreement. Molotov was furious. "I have never been talked to like that in my life," he told the president before leaving.

With a memorandum on the "political aspects of the S-1 [atomic bomb's] performance" in hand and General Groves in reserve, Stimson went to the White House on April 25. The document he carried was the distillation of numerous decisions already taken, each one the product of attitudes that developed along with the new weapon. The secretary himself was not entirely aware of how various forces had shaped these decisions: the recommendations of Bush and Conant, the policies Roosevelt had followed, the uncertainties inherent in the wartime alliance, the oppressive concern for secrecy, and his own inclination to consider long-range implications. It was a curious document. Though its language revealed Stimson's sensitivity to the historic significance of the atomic bomb, he did not question the wisdom of using it against Japan. Nor did he suggest any concrete steps for developing a postwar policy. His objective was to inform Truman of the salient problems: the possibility of an atomic arms race, the danger of atomic war, and the necessity for international control if the United Nations Organization was to work. "If the problem of the proper use of this weapon can be solved," he wrote, "we would have the opportunity to bring the world into a pattern in which the peace of the world and our civilizations can be saved." To cope with this difficult challenge Stimson suggested the "establishment of a select committee" to consider the postwar problems inherent in the development of the bomb. If his presentation was the "forceful statement" of the problem that historians of the Atomic Energy Commission have described it as being, its force inhered in the problem itself, not in any bold formulations or initiatives he offered toward a solution. If, as another historian has claimed, this meeting led to a "strategy of delayed showdown," requiring "the delay of all disputes with Russia until the atomic bomb had been demonstrated," there is no evidence in the extant records of the meeting that Stimson had such a strategy in mind or that Truman misunderstood the secretary's views.

What emerges from a careful reading of Stimson's diary, his memorandum of April 25 to Truman, a summary by Groves of the meeting, and Truman's recollections is an argument for over-all caution in Amercan diplomatic relations with the Soviet Union: it was an argument against any showdown. Since the atomic bomb was potentially the most dangerous issue facing the postwar world and since the most desirable resolution of the problem was some form of international control, Soviet cooperation had to be secured. It was imprudent, Stimson suggested, to pursue a policy that would preclude the possibility of international cooperation on atomic-energy matters after the war ended. Truman's overall impression of Stimson's argument was that the secretary of war was "at least as much concerned with the role of the atomic bomb in the shaping of history as in its capacity to shorten the war." These were indeed Stimson's dual concerns on April 25, and he could see no conflict between them.

Despite the profound consequences Stimson attributed to the development of the new weapon, he had not suggested that Truman reconsider its use against Japan. Nor had he thought to mention the possibility that chances of securing Soviet postwar cooperation might be diminished if Stalin did not receive a commitment to international control prior to an attack. The question of why these alternatives were overlooked naturally arises. Perhaps what Frankfurter once referred to as Stimson's habit of setting "his mind at one thing like the needle of an old victrola caught in a single groove" may help to explain his not mentioning these possibilities. Yet Bush and Conant never raised them either. Even Niels Bohr had made a clear distinction between the bomb's wartime use and its postwar impact on diplomacy. "What role it [the atomic bomb] may play in the present war," Bohr had written to Roosevelt in July 1944, was a question "quite apart" from the overriding concern: the need to avoid an atomic arms race.

The preoccupation with winning the war obviously helped to create this seeming dichotomy between the wartime use of the bomb and the potential postwar diplomatic problems with the Soviet Union raised by its development. But a closer look at how Bohr and Stimson each defined the nature of the diplomatic problem created by the bomb suggests that for the secretary of war and his advisers (and ultimately for the president they advised) there was no dichotomy at all. Bohr apprehended the meaning of the new weapon even before it was developed, and he had no doubt that scientists in the Soviet Union would also understand its profound implications for the postwar world. He was also certain that they would interpret the meaning of the development to Stalin just as scientists in the United States and Great Britain had explained it to Roosevelt and Churchill. Thus the diplomatic problem, as Bohr analyzed it, was not the need to convince Stalin that the atomic bomb was an unprecedented weapon that threatened the life of the world but the need to assure the Soviet leader that he had nothing to fear from the circumstances of its development. By informing Stalin during the war that the United States intended to co-operate with him in neutralizing the bomb through international control, Bohr reasoned that its wartime use could be considered apart from postwar problems.

Stimson approached the problem rather differently. Although he believed that the bomb "might even mean the doom of civilization or it might mean the perfection of civilization" he was less confident than Bohr that the weapon in an undeveloped state could be used as an effective instrument of diplomacy. Until its "actual certainty [was] fixed," Stimson considered any prior approach to Stalin as premature. But as the uncertainties of impending peace became more apparent and worrisome, Stimson,

Truman, and the secretary of state-designate, James F. Byrnes, began to think of the bomb as something of a diplomatic panacea for their postwar problems. Byrnes had told Truman in April that the bomb "might well put us in a position to dictate our own terms at the end of the war." By June, Truman and Stimson were discussing "further *quid pro quos* which should be established in consideration for our taking them [the Soviet Union] into [atomic-energy] partnership." Assuming that the bomb's impact on diplomacy would be immediate and extraordinary, they agreed on no less than "the settlement of the Polish, Rumanian, Yugoslavian, and Manchurian problems." But they also concluded that no revelation would be made "to Russia or anyone else until the first bomb had been successfully laid on Japan." Truman and Stimson based their expectations on how they saw and valued the bomb; its use against Japan, they reasoned, would transfer this view to the Soviet Union.

Was an implicit warning to Moscow, then, the principal reason for deciding to use the atomic bomb against Japan? In light of the ambiguity of the available evidence the question defies an unequivocal answer. What can be said with certainty is that Truman, Stimson, Byrnes, and several others involved in the decision consciously considered two effects of a combat demonstration of the bomb's power: first, the impact of the atomic attack on Japan's leaders, who might be persuaded thereby to end the war, and second, the impact of that attack on the Soviet Union's leaders, who might then prove to be more cooperative. But if the assumption that the bomb might bring the war to a rapid conclusion was the principal motive for using the atomic bomb, the expectation that its use would also inhibit Soviet diplomatic ambitions clearly discouraged any inclination to question that assumption. . . .

Thus by the end of the war the most influential and widely accepted attitude toward the bomb was a logical extension of how the weapon was seen and valued earlier—as a potential instrument of diplomacy. Caught between the remnants of war and the uncertainties of peace, scientists as well as policy makers were trapped by the logic of their own unquestioned assumptions. By the summer of 1945 not only the conclusion of the war but the organization of an acceptable peace seemed to depend upon the success of the atomic attacks against Japan. When news of the successful atomic test of July 16 reached the president at the

Potsdam Conference, he was visibly elated. Stimson noted that Truman "was tremendously pepped up by it and spoke to me of it again when I saw him. He said it gave him an entirely new feeling of confidence." The day after receiving the complete report of the test Truman altered his negotiating style. According to Churchill the president "got to the meeting after having read this report [and] he was a changed man. He told the Russians just where they got on and off and generally bossed the whole meeting." After the plenary session on July 24 Truman "casually mentioned to Stalin" that the United States had "a new weapon of unusual destructive force." Truman took this step in response to a recommendation by the Interim Committee, a group of political and scientific advisers organized by Stimson in May 1945 to advise the president on atomic-energy policy. But it is an unavoidable conclusion that what the president told the premier followed the letter of the recommendation rather than its spirit, which embodied the hope that an overture to Stalin would initiate the process toward international control. In less than three weeks the new weapon's destructive potential would be demonstrated to the world. Stalin would then be forced to reconsider his diplomatic goals. It is no wonder that upon learning of the raid against Hiroshima Truman exclaimed: "This is the greatest thing in history."

As Stimson had expected, as a colossal reality the bomb was very different. But had American diplomacy been altered by it? Those who conducted diplomacy became more confident, more certain that through the accomplishments of American science, technology, and industry the "new world" could be made into one better than the old. But just how the atomic bomb would be used to help accomplish this ideal remained unclear. Three months and one day after Hiroshima was bombed Bush wrote that the whole matter of international relations on atomic energy "is in a thoroughly chaotic condition." The wartime relationship between atomic-energy policy and diplomacy had been based upon the simple assumption that the Soviet government would surrender important geographical, political, and ideological objectives in exchange for the neutralization of the new weapon. As a result of policies based on this assumption American diplomacy and prestige suffered grievously: an opportunity to gauge the Soviet Union's response during the war to the international control of atomic energy was missed, and an atomic-energy policy for dealing with the Soviet government after the war was ignored. Instead of promoting American postwar aims, wartime atomic-energy policies made them more difficult to achieve. As a group of scientists at the University of Chicago's atomic-energy laboratory presciently warned the government in June 1945: "It may be difficult to persuade the world that a nation which was capable of secretly preparing and suddenly releasing a weapon as indiscriminate as the [German] rocket bomb and a million times more destructive, is to be trusted in its proclaimed desire of having such weapons abolished by international agreement." This reasoning, however, flowed from alternative assumptions formulated during the closing months of the war by scientists far removed from the wartime policy-making process. Hiroshima and Nagasaki, the culmination of that process, became the symbols of a new American barbarism, reinforcing charges, with dramatic circumstantial evidence, that the policies of the United States contributed to the origins of the cold war.

Containment Before Kennan

John Lewis Gaddis

Similar to the conflicting interpretations of the decision to drop the atomic bombs, the historical debate on the causes of the Cold War has largely followed the disagreements voiced by the leading actors in the drama. Whether stressing Communist ideology, Russian expansionism, Soviet totalitarianism, or Stalin's paranoia, "traditionalists" tend to restate the official explanations of the Truman Administration. They place responsibility for the conflict squarely in Moscow and suggest that the United States did only what was prudent and necessary in the face of Soviet aggression and intransigence. Heeding the criticism of such Administration foes as Walter Lippmann and Henry Wallace, most "revisionists" focus on the rigidity of American policy, its rejection of legitimate Soviet needs, and its hypocritical employment of a double standard of international behavior. While they differ on the selective importance of various cultural, economic, personal, and political determinants, "revisionists" largely agree that the United States sought to use its overwhelming power after the Second World War to establish a Pax Americana.

Like Sherwin, John Lewis Gaddis in this selection seeks to circumvent the simplistic dualism of this debate on Cold War origins. His interpretation synthesizes what is best in the opposing arguments. Moreover, Gaddis also strongly emphasizes the consequences of wartime decisions and developments. Rather than seeking to apportion or assign "blame," he depicts an intricate web of interrelated phenomena over an extended period of time. After reading the selection one may well reflect on the implications of a theory of historical inevitability, on how to assign weight to assorted causative factors, and on what it means to seek the "origin" of an historical event.

Excerpted from *Strategies of Containment: A Critical Appraisal of Postwar American National Security Policy* by John Lewis Gaddis. Copyright © 1982 by Oxford University Press, Inc. Reprinted by permission.

Footnotes omitted.

"My children, it is permitted you in time of grave danger to walk with the devil until you have crossed the bridge." It was Franklin D. Roosevelt's version of an old Balkan proverb (sanctioned by the Orthodox Church, no less), and he liked to cite it from time to time during World War II to explain the use of questionable allies to achieve unquestionable objectives. In all-out war, he believed, the ultimate end—victory—justified a certain broad-mindedness regarding means, nowhere more so than in reliance on Stalin's Russia to help defeat Germany and Japan. Allies of any kind were welcome enough in London and Washington during the summer of 1941; still the Soviet Union's sudden appearance in that capacity could not avoid setting off Faustian musings in both capitals. Winston Churchill's willingness to extend measured parliamentary accolades to the Devil if Hitler should invade Hell is well-known; less familiar is Roosevelt's paraphrase of his proverb to an old friend, Joseph Davies: "I can't take communism nor can you, but to cross this bridge I would hold hands with the Devil."

The imagery, in the light of subsequent events, was apt. Collaboration with the Soviet Mephistopheles helped the United States and Great Britain achieve victory over their enemies in a remarkably short time and with surprisingly few casualties, given the extent of the fighting involved. The price, though, was the rise of an even more powerful and less fathomable totalitarian state, and, as a consequence, an apparently perpetual condition of precarious uncertainty that has now many times outlasted the brief and uneasy alliance that brought it about.

"Containment," the term generally used to characterize American policy toward the Soviet Union during the postwar era, can be seen as a series of attempts to deal with the consequences of the World War II Faustian bargain: the idea has been to prevent the Soviet Union from using the power and position it won as a result of that conflict to reshape the postwar international order, a prospect that has seemed, in the West, no less dangerous than what Germany or Japan might have done had they had the chance. George F. Kennan coined the term in July 1947, when he called publicly for a "long-term, patient but firm and vigilant containment of Russian expansive tendencies," but it would be an injustice to wartime policy-makers to imply, as has too often been done, that they were oblivious to the problem. In fact, "containment" was much on the minds of Washington officials from 1941 on; the difficulty was to mesh that long-term concern with the more immediate imperative of defeating the Axis. What Roosevelt, Truman, and their advisers sought was a way to win the war without compromising the objectives for which it was being fought; it was out of their successive failures to square that circle that Kennan's concept of "containment" eventually emerged.

One way to have resolved the dilemma would have been to devise military operations capable of containing the Russians while at the same time enlisting their help to the extent necessary to subdue the Axis. Truman himself had suggested a crude way of doing this after Hitler attacked the Soviet Union in June 1941: "If we see that Germany is winning the war we ought to help Russia, and if Russia is winning we ought to help Germany and in that way let them kill as many as possible." But Truman at the time was an obscure Missouri senator; his somewhat brutal flash of geopolitical cynicism attracted little attention until he unexpectedly entered the White House four years later. By that time, and with increasing frequency in the months that followed, questions were being raised as to whether the United States had not in fact relied on the Russians too heavily to defeat the Germans too thoroughly. William C. Bullitt, former ambassador to the Soviet Union and now one of its most vociferous critics, said it best in a 1948 *Life* magazine article entitled: "How We Won the War and Lost the Peace."

Bullitt himself had advocated an alternative strategy five years earlier in a series of top secret memoranda to Roosevelt. Stalin's war aims were not those of the West, he had insisted: those who argued that participation in an anti-fascist coalition had purged the Soviet dictator of his autocratic and expansionist tendencies were assuming, on the basis of no evidence, a conversion "as striking as [that] of Saul on the road to Damascus." The fact was that a Europe controlled from Moscow would be as dangerous as one ruled from Berlin, and yet "if Germany is to be defeated without such cost in American and British lives that victory might well prove to be a concealed defeat (like the French victory in the war of 1914), the continued participation of the Red Army in the war against Germany is essential." The problem, then, was to prevent "the domination of Europe by the Moscow dictatorship without losing the participation of the Red Army in the war against the Nazi dictatorship." Bullitt's answer, put forward long before Winston Churchill had explicitly advocated a similar but better-known solution, was to introduce Anglo-American forces into Eastern Europe and the Balkans, for the purpose, first, of defeating the Germans, but second, to bar the Red Army from Europe. "War is an attempt to achieve political objectives by fighting," he reminded Roosevelt in August 1943, "and political objectives must be kept in mind in planning operations."

There are hints that Roosevelt did, from time to time, consider using military forces to achieve something like the political results Bullitt had in mind. The President showed more than polite interest in Churchill's subsequent schemes for Anglo-American military operations in the Balkans, despite the horrified reactions of Secretary of War Henry Stimson and the Joint Chiefs of Staff. He emphasized, at least twice in 1943, the need to get to Berlin as soon as the Russians did in the event of a sudden German collapse. And in April 1945, less than a week before his death, he countered Churchill's complaints about Soviet behavior by pointing out that "our armies will in a very few days be in a position that will permit us to become 'tougher' than has heretofore appeared advantageous to the war effort."

But Roosevelt generally resisted efforts to deploy forces for the dual purposes of defeating the Germans and containing the Russians. He did not do this, though, in a geopolitical vacuum: there were, in his mind, powerful reasons other than a single-minded concentration on victory for holding hands with the Devil to cross the bridge.

One had to do with Roosevelt's conception of the balance of power. American security, he thought, lay chiefly in preventing the coming together of potentially hostile states. He had extended diplomatic recognition to the Soviet Union in 1933 partly to counter-balance, and attempt to keep separate, the growing military power of Germany and Japan. When the Kremlin backed out of that role in 1939, F.D.R., sensitive to the unnatural character of the Nazi-Soviet alignment, carefully left the way open for an eventual reconciliation with Moscow, despite his intense personal revulsion at the Russians' behavior. He moved swiftly when the events of June 1941 made it possible to reconstitute his strategy, even though collaboration with Russia was more difficult to sell in a still ostensibly neutral United States than in embattled England. After Pearl Harbor, one of his persistent concerns was to prevent any new "deal" between Hitler and Stalin, and simultaneously to secure the latter's cooperation in the war against Japan. The geopolitical requirements of keeping adversaries divided, therefore, constituted one powerful argument against military deployments directed against Russia as well as Germany.

Coupled with this was an appreciation of the nature of American power. Roosevelt was an early and firm believer in the "arsenal of democracy" concept—the idea that the United States could most effectively contribute toward the maintenance of international order by expending technology but not manpower. Long before Pearl Harbor, he had sought to enlist the productive energies of American industry in the anti-fascist cause: the United States, he thought, should serve as a kind of privileged sanctuary, taking advantage of its geographical isolation and invulnerable physical plant to produce the goods of war, leaving others to furnish the troops required to fight it. Even after active belligerency became unavoidable, Roosevelt and his chief military strategist, General George C. Marshall, retained elements of the earlier approach, limiting the American army to 90 divisions instead of the 215 that had been thought necessary to defeat both Germany and Japan. As Marshall admitted, though, it could not have been done without Soviet manpower. The United States, in this sense, was as dependent on the Red Army as the Russians were on American Lend-Lease—perhaps more so. That fact, too, precluded military operations aimed at containing the Russians while defeating the Germans.

There was yet a third consideration involved, most often attributed to Churchill but very much present in Roosevelt's mind as well: the need to minimize casualties. Averell Harriman has best summarized the President's concern in this regard:

> Roosevelt was very much affected by World War I, which he had, of course, seen at close range. He had a horror of American troops landing again on the continent and becoming involved in the kind of warfare he had seen before—trench warfare with all its appalling losses. I believe he had in mind that if the great armies of Russia could stand up to the Germans, this might well make it possible for us to limit our participation largely to naval and air power.

The United States was new at the business of being a world power, Roosevelt must have reasoned. If the sacrifices involved became too great, especially in a war in which its own territory did not seem directly threatened, then pressures for a reversion to a "fortress America" concept, if not outright isolationism, might still prevail. Letting allies bear the brunt of casualities was a way of ensuring internationalism for the future.

Finally, there was the fact that the United States had another war to wage in the Far East—one in which it was bearing a far heavier share of the burden than in Europe. To be sure, American strategy, even before Pearl Harbor, had been to defeat Germany first. But Roosevelt recognized that support for a major effort against Germany required progress in the war against Japan as well: the American people would not tolerate indefinite defeats in the Pacific while arming to cross the Atlantic. Hence, F.D.R.'s strategy evolved by subtle stages into one of taking on Germany and Japan at the same time; the war in the Pacific became more than just the holding action that had originally been planned. The effects were benefcial in one sense: few would have anticipated that wars against both Germany and Japan could have been brought to roughly simultaneous conclusions with so few casualties. But the price, again, was reliance on Soviet manpower to carry the main burden of the struggle in Europe; had the atomic bomb not worked, the Russians might have been called upon to play a similar role in the Far East as well after Germany's surrender.

It will not do, then, to see Roosevelt's strategy as totally insulated from political considerations. A war plan aimed at making careful use of American resources to maintain a global balance of power without at the same time disrupting the fabric of American society hardly fits that characterization. It is true that Roosevelt did not orient wartime strategy toward the coming Cold War—he foresaw that possibility, but hoped, indeed trusted, that it would not arise. Instead he concentrated on winning the war the United States was in at the time as quickly as possible and at the least possible cost. Given those objectives, it would be hard to have improved on the strategy Roosevelt actually followed.

It is interesting, as a corrective to those who have criticized Roosevelt for ignoring political considerations, to see how Soviet scholars view his conduct of the war. The emphasis here is on the wholly political nature of his strategy: one recent account even has it that F.D.R. in fact adopted Truman's 1941 recommendation to let Russians and Germans kill each other off. Certainly, on the basis of statistical indices, this would appear to have been the effect: for every American who died in the war, fifteen Germans and fifty-three Russians died. It is worth asking whether something like this might not have been a crafty way of ensuring both full Russian participation in the war and the postwar containment of the Soviet Union, not by denying that country territory or resources, but by forcing it to exhaust itself?

With the elusive Roosevelt, one can never be sure. Few statesmen guarded their own counsel more jealously than the deceptively loquacious F.D.R.; if this had been his strategy, it is unlikely that he would have told anyone about it. There is, though, a more plausible and less sinister explanation. To have done what the Russians wanted—create an early second front—or what his domestic critics wanted—deploy forces against both Russians and Germans—would have violated Roosevelt's fundamental aversion to the use of American manpower to bring about major geopolitical shifts in world affairs. The President fully intended to have an impact, but he sought to do it in such a way as to neither demoralize nor debilitate the nation. In short, he wanted to keep means from corrupting ends. It is easy to write off this approach as naive, as some of Roosevelt's American detractors have done, or as self-serving, as the Russians have done. What seems more probable, though, is that Roosevelt's strategy reflected the rational balance of objectives and resources any wise statesman will try to achieve, *if he can.* It was Stalin's misfortune, largely as a result of his errors of strategy between 1939 and 1941, to have denied himself that opportunity.

Another reason for doubting that Roosevelt set out deliberately to contain the Russians by exhausting them is that his postwar plans seemed to lean in a wholly different direction—that of containment by integration. F.D.R. sought to ensure a stable postwar order by offering Moscow a prominent place in it; by making it, so to speak, a member of the club. The assumption here—and it is a critical one for understanding Roosevelt's policy—was that Soviet hostility stemmed from insecurity, but that the sources of that insecurity were external. They lay, the President thought, in the threats posed by Germany and Japan, in the West's long-standing aversion to Bolshevism, and in the refusal, accordingly, of much of the rest of the world to grant the Russians their legitimate position in international affairs. "They didn't know us, that's the really fundamental difference," he commented in 1944. "They are friendly people. They haven't got any crazy ideas of conquest, and so forth; and now that they have got to know us, they are much more willing to accept us." With the defeat of the Axis, with the West's willingness to make the Soviet Union a full partner in shaping the peace to come, the reasons for Stalin's suspicions, Roosevelt expected, would gradually drop away.

The President had never seen in the ideological orientation of the Soviet state a reason not to have cooperative relations at the interstate level. As a liberal, he lacked the visceral horror with which American conservatives regarded the use of state authority to bring about social change. As a self-confident patrician, he discounted the appeal communism might have inside the United States. As a defender of the international balance of power, he distinguished between fascism's reliance on force to achieve its objectives, and what he saw as communism's less dangerous use of subversion and propaganda. But, most important, as an intelligent observer of the international scene, he recognized the significance of a trend in the evolution of the Soviet state many experts on that country were only beginning to grasp: the fact that considerations of national interest had come to overshadow those of ideology in determining Stalin's behavior.

It was within this context that Roosevelt developed his idea of integrating the Soviet Union into a postwar security structure. F.D.R. had long advocated some form of great-power condominium to maintain world order. He was, it has been argued, a "renegade Wilsonian," seeking Wilson's goals by un-Wilsonian means. Chief among these was his conviction that the peace-loving states should band together to deter aggression, first by isolating the perpetrators, and then, if necessary, by using force against them. As early as 1935, Roosevelt had begun talking about an arrangement along those lines to blockade Nazi Germany; two years later he was proposing similarly vague plans for collective resistance against Japan. Nothing came of either initiative, but it is worth noting that Roosevelt had counted on the Soviet Union's cooperation in both of them. It was not too surprising, then, that after June 1941. when Moscow was again in a position to cooperate with the West, F.D.R. should have revived his plan, this time in the form of the "Four Policemen"—the United States, Great Britain, the Soviet Union, and China—who would, as the President described it, impose order on the rest of the postwar world, bombing anyone who would not go along.

The "Four Policemen" concept, it has been argued, reflected an unrealistic assumption on Roosevelt's part that the great powers would always agree, an expectation that seemed painfully at odds with the obviously antagonistic nature of the international system. Again, though, surface manifestations were deceiving. "When there [are] four people sitting in a poker game and three of them [are] against the fourth," F.D.R. told Henry Wallace late in 1942, "it is a little hard on the fourth." Wallace took this to mean the possibility of American, Russian, and Chinese pressures against the British, and indeed the President did make efforts subsequently to impress both Stalin and Chiang Kai-shek with his own anti-imperial aspirations. But Roosevelt was telling others, at roughly the same time, that he needed China as one of the "Four Policemen" to counter-balance Russia. And certainly Churchill, without even being asked, could have been counted upon to join in any such enterprise, should it have become necessary. The picture is hardly one of anticipating harmony, therefore; rather, it is reminiscent, as much as anything else, of Bismarck's cold-blooded tactic of keeping potential rivals off balance by preventing them from aligning with each other.

It is also the case that Roosevelt was not above using what a later generation would call "linkage" to ensure compliance with American postwar aims. His employment of economic and political pressure to speed the dismantling of the British Empire has recently been thoroughly documented. No comparably blatant requirements were imposed on the Russians, probably because Roosevelt feared that the relationship, unlike the one with London, was too delicate to stand the strain. Still, he did keep certain cards up his sleeve for dealing with Moscow after the war, notably the prospect of reconstruction assistance either through Lend-Lease or a postwar loan, together with a generous flow of reparations from Western-occupied Germany, all of which Washington would have been able to control in the light of Soviet behavior. Also, intriguingly, there was Roosevelt's refusal, even after learning they knew of it, to tell the Russians about the atomic bomb, perhaps with a view to postwar bargaining. This combination of counter-weights and linkages is not what one would expect from a statesman assuming a blissfully serene postwar environment: although Roosevelt certainly hoped for such an outcome, he was too good a poker player to count on it.

But Roosevelt's main emphasis was on trying to make the Grand Alliance survive Hitler's defeat by creating relationships of mutual trust among its leaders. The focus of his concern—and indeed the only allied leader not already in some position of dependency on the United States—was Stalin. F.D.R. has been criticized for thinking that he could use his personal charm to "get through" to the Soviet autocrat, whose resistance to such blandishments was legendary. But, as with so much of Roosevelt's diplomacy, what seems at first shallow and superficial becomes less so upon reflection. The President realized that Stalin was the only man in the Soviet Union with the authority to modify past attitudes of hostility; however discouraging the prospect of "getting through," there was little point in dealing with anyone below him. . . .

Like any statesman, though, Roosevelt was pursuing multiple objectives; building a friendly peacetime relationship with the Soviet Union was only one of them. As often happens, other priorities got in the way. For example, Roosevelt's second front strategy, designed not so much to weaken Russia as to avoid weakening the United States, could not help but create suspicions in Moscow that Washington was in fact seeking containment by exhaustion. These dark misgivings survived even the D-Day landings: as late as April 1945 Stalin was warning subordinates that the Americans and British might yet make common cause with the Germans; that same month the Red Army began constructing *defensive* installations in Central Europe.

Another of Roosevelt's priorities was to win domestic support for his postwar plans, and thereby to avoid Wilson's repudiation of 1919–1920. To do this, he became convinced of the need to moderate his own somewhat harsh approach to the task of peacekeeping: the country was not ready, Speaker of the House Sam Rayburn told him late in 1942, for a settlement to be enforced through blockades and bombing. Roosevelt sought, accordingly, to integrate the great power condominium his strategic instincts told him would be necessary to preserve world order, on the one

hand, with the ideals his political instincts told him would be necessary at home to overcome objections to an "unjust" peace, on
the other. Idealism, in Roosevelt's mind, could serve eminently
realistic ends.

It would be a mistake, then, to write off Roosevelt's concern
for self-determination in Eastern Europe as mere window-dress-
ing. Although prepared to see that part of the world fall within
Moscow's sphere of influence, he expected as well that as fears
of Germany subsided, the Russians would moderate the severity
of measures needed to maintain their position there. Otherwise,
he was convinced, it would be impossible to "sell" the resulting
settlement to the American people. But, like Henry Kissinger in
somewhat different circumstances thirty years later, Roosevelt
thus found himself in a situation in which domestic support for
what he had negotiated depended upon the exercise of discretion and restraint in the Kremlin. Those tendencies were no
more prevalent then than later; as a consequence, a gap developed between what F.D.R. thought the public would tolerate and
what the Russians would accept—a gap papered over, at Yalta,
by fragile compromises.

Competing priorities therefore undercut Roosevelt's efforts to
win Stalin's trust: to that extent, his strategy was flawed. And even
if that had not happened, there is reason to wonder whether
F.D.R.'s approach would have worked in any event, given the
balefully suspicious personality of the Soviet autocrat. But there
are, at times, justifications for directing flawed strategies at inaus-
picious targets, and World War II may have been one of these.
Certainly alternatives to the policies actually followed contained
difficulties as well. And there are grounds for thinking that Roosevelt might not have continued his open-handed approach once
the war had ended: his quiet incorporation of counter-weights
and linkages into his strategy suggests just that possibility. One is
left, then, where one began: with the surface impression of casual,
even frivolous, superficiality, and yet with the growing realization
that darker, more cynical, but more perceptive instincts lay not far
beneath.

Whatever Roosevelt's intentions were for after the war, though,
dissatisfaction with the strategy he was following during it had

become widespread within the government by the end of 1944. American military chiefs and Lend-Lease administrators resented the Russians' increasingly importunate demands on their limited resources, made with little understanding of supply problems or logistics, and with infrequent expressions of gratitude. Career diplomats had always maintained a certain coolness toward the U.S.S.R.; now, with the State Department excluded by Roosevelt from any significant dealings with that country, they brooded in relative isolation over the gap they saw emerging between Stalin's postwar aims and the principles of the Atlantic Charter. But it was officials with direct experience of service in the Soviet Union who developed the strongest and most influential reservations about Roosevelt's open-handedness. Attempts to win Stalin's trust through generosity and good will would not work, they argued: the Soviet dictator was too apt to confuse those qualities with weakness. What was needed instead was recognition of the fact that the Soviet Union was neither going to leave nor lose the war, and that if its Western allies did not soon begin to apply such leverage as they had available, the Kremlin would shape its own peace settlement, without regard to their aspirations or interests. . . .

F.D.R.'s death cleared the way for a revision of strategy he himself would probably have executed in time, but not in as abrupt and confused a manner as was actually done. Harry S. Truman, totally unbriefed as to what Roosevelt had been trying to do, did the natural thing and consulted the late President's advisers. But those most directly associated with Soviet affairs, notably Harriman, had been trying to stiffen Roosevelt's position; now, with a new and untutored chief executive in the White House, they redoubled their efforts at "education." Eager to appear decisive and in command, Truman accepted this instruction with an alacrity that unsettled even those providing it, lecturing the Soviet foreign minister in person, and his distant master by cable, in a manner far removed from the graceful ambiguities of his predecessor. The result was ironic: Truman embraced a *quid pro quo* approach in the belief that he was implementing Roosevelt's policy, but in doing so he convinced the Russians that he had changed it. F.D.R.'s elusiveness continued to bedevil Soviet-American relations even after his death.

In fact (and despite his 1941 remark about letting Germans

and Russians kill each other off), Truman was no more prepared
to abandon the possibility of an accommodation with Moscow
than were Harriman and Deane. He firmly rejected Churchill's
advice to deploy Anglo-American military forces in such a way as
to keep the Russians out of as much of Germany as possible. He
sent Harry Hopkins to Moscow in May of 1945 in part to repair
the damage his own brusqueness had done. Long after relations
with Stalin went sour, he continued to seek the counsel of those
sympathetic to the Soviet Union, notably Henry Wallace and Joseph E. Davies. The new President harbored a healthy skepticism
toward all totalitarian states: ideology, he thought, whether communist or fascist, was simply an excuse for dictatorial rule. But,
like Roosevelt, he did not see totalitarianism in itself as precluding
normal relations. Not surprisingly in the light of his own background, the analogy of big city political bosses in the United States
came most easily to mind: their methods might not be delicate or
fastidious, but one could work with them, so long as they kept
their word.

Truman found a kindred spirit in James F. Byrnes, whom he
appointed Secretary of State shortly after taking office. An individual of vast experience in domestic affairs but almost none in
diplomacy, Byrnes believed in applying to this new realm an assumption that had worked well for him at home: nations, he
thought, like individuals or interest groups, could always reach
agreement on difficult issues if a sufficient willingness to negotiate
and to compromise existed on both sides. A *quid pro quo* strategy
was as natural for Byrnes as for Truman, then; the new Secretary
of State observed that dealing with the Russians was just like dealing with the United States Senate: "You build a post office in their
state and they'll build a post office in our state."

The new administration thought it had leverage over the Russians in several respects. Harriman himself had stressed the importance of postwar reconstruction assistance, which the United
States would be able to control, whether through Lend-Lease, a
rehabilitation loan, or reparations shipments from its occupation
zone in Germany. Roosevelt had been leaning toward use of this
leverage at the time of his death; Truman quickly confirmed that
unconditional aid would not be extended past the end of the
fighting. Lend-Lease would be phased out, and postwar loans and
reparations shipments would be tied, at least implicitly, to future

Soviet political cooperation. Publicity was another form of leverage: the administration assumed that the Kremlin was still sensitive to "world opinion," and that by calling attention openly to instances of soviet unilateralism, it could get the Russians to back down. Then there was the ultimate sanction of the atomic bomb: Byrnes, though not all his colleagues in the administration, apparently believed that the simple presence of this awesome weapon in the American arsenal would make the Russians more manageable than in the past; at a minimum, he wanted to hold back commitments to seek the international control of atomic energy as a bargaining chip for use in future negotiations.

But none of these attempts to apply leverage worked out as planned. The Russians were never dependent enough on American economic aid to make substantial concessions to get it: intelligence reports had long indicated that such aid, if extended, would have speeded reconstruction by only a matter of months. Another difficulty was that key Congressmen, whose support would have been necessary for the passage of any loan, quickly made it clear that they would demand in return nothing less than free elections and freedom of speech inside the Soviet Union, and the abandonment of its sphere of influence in Eastern Europe. Publicity, directed against Soviet violations of the Yalta agreements in that part of the world, produced no greater success: when Byrnes warned that he might have to make public a report on conditions in Rumania and Bulgaria prepared by the American publisher, Mark Ethridge, Stalin, with understandable self-confidence, threatened to have his own "impartial" observer, the Soviet journalist Ilya Ehrenburg, prepare and release his own report on those countries. The Russians dealt effectively with the atomic bomb by simply appearing to ignore it, except for a few heavyhanded cocktail party jokes by a tipsy Molotov. In the meantime, domestic pressures had forced Truman to commit the United States to the principle of international control before Byrnes had even attempted to extract a *quid pro quo* from Moscow.

By the time of the Moscow foreign ministers' conference in December 1945, Byrnes had come to much the same conclusion that Roosevelt had a year earlier: that the only way to reconcile the American interest in self-determination with the Soviet interest in security was to negotiate thinly disguised agreements designed to cloak the reality of Moscow's control behind a facade of democratic procedures. But that approach, manifested in the form of token concessions by the Russians on Bulgaria and Rumania, came across at home as appeasement: as a result, Byrnes found himself under attack from both the President and Congress, upon his return, for having given up too much. The *quid pro quo* strategy, by early 1946, had not only failed to produce results; it had become a domestic political liability as well.

The *quid pro quo* approach proved unsuccessful for several reasons. One was the difficulty of making "sticks" and "carrots" commensurate with concessions to be demanded from the other side. The "sticks" the United States had available were either unimpressive, as was the case with publicity, or unusable, as in the case of the atomic bomb. The major "carrot," economic aid, was important to the Russians, but not to the point of justifying the concessions that would have been required to obtain it. Another difficulty with the strategy was the problem of coordination. Bargaining implies the ability to control precisely the combination of pressures and inducements to be applied, but that in turn implies central direction, something not easy to come by in a democracy in the best of circumstances, and certainly not during the first year of an inexperienced and badly organized administration. Extraneous influences—Congress, the press, public opinion, bureaucracies, even personalities—tended to intrude upon the bargaining process, making the alignment of conditions to be met with incentives to be offered awkward, to say the least.

But the major difficulty was simply the Soviet Union's imperviousness to external influences. The *quid pro quo* strategy had assumed, as had Roosevelt's, that Soviet behavior could be affected from the outside: the only difference had been over method and timing. In fact, though, experience showed that there was remarkably little the West could do, in the short term, to shape Stalin's decisions: the Soviet dictator maintained tight control in a mostly self-sufficient country, with little knowledge or understanding of, much less susceptibility to, events in the larger world. It was this realization of impermeability—the fact that neither trust nor pressure had made any difference—that paved the way for the revision of strategy set off by George Kennan's "long telegram" of February 1946. . . .

"Patience and firmness" became the watchword for dealings

with the Soviet Union over the next year—if anything, the emphasis, as the Joint Chiefs of Staff had recommended, was primarily on the "firmness." The new approach showed up in the Eastern Mediterranean and the Near East, where the administration not only induced the Russians to withdraw troops from Iran and to give up demands for boundary concessions and base rights from Turkey, but in addition committed itself to support the government of Greece against an externally supplied communist insurgency and to make the presence of the Sixth Fleet in waters surrounding the latter two countries a permanent fixture of the postwar world. It showed up in the Far East, where Washington continued to resist any substantive role for the Russians in the occupation of Japan, while at the same time making clear its determination to prevent a Soviet takeover of all of Korea. It showed up in Germany, where the United States cut off reparations shipments from its zone and began moving toward consolidating it with those of the British and the French, while at the same time offering the Russians a four-power treaty guaranteeing the disarmament of Germany for twenty-five years. It showed up in the Council of Foreign Ministers, where Byrnes firmly resisted Soviet bids to take over former Italian territories along the Mediterranean, while at the same time patiently pursuing negotiations on peace treaties for former German satellites. Finally, and most dramatically, the new strategy manifested itself in the Truman Doctrine, in which the administration generalized its obligations to Greece and Turkey into what appeared to be a world-wide commitment to resist Soviet expansionism wherever it appeared.

Truman's March 12, 1947, proclamation that "it must be the policy of the United States to support free peoples who are resisting attempted subjugation by armed minorities or outside pressures" has traditionally been taken as having marked a fundamental point of departure for American foreign policy in the Cold War. In fact, though, it can more accurately be seen as the ultimate expression of the "patience and firmness" strategy that had been in effect for the past year. Decisions to aid Greece and Turkey, as well as other nations threatened by the Soviet Union, had been made months before. What was new, in early 1947, was Great Britain's abrupt notice of intent to end its own military and financial support to those countries, and the need that imposed for quick Congressional approval of aid to replace it. It was that requirement, in turn, that forced the administration to justify its request in globalist terms; even so, that rhetoric was consistent with the assumption, underlying the "patience and firmness" strategy for almost a year, that the United States could afford no further gains in territory or influence for the Soviet Union anywhere.

Are We Only Paying Lip Service to Peace

Henry A. Wallace

The Truman Administration's stiffened resistance to Russian demands in 1945 and 1946 greatly disturbed Henry Wallace. The Secretary of Commerce, who had served as Secretary of Agriculture from 1933 to 1941 and Vice-President from 1941 to 1945, feared the consequences of what appeared to be a reversal of President Roosevelt's policy of wartime cooperation with the Soviet Union. In his private letter to the president in July 1946, he urged Truman to act to diminish Soviet distrust and to avoid a catastrophic arms race. The president rejected Wallace's counsel for a more conciliatory attitude toward the Russians, and fired his Secretary of Commerce in September 1946 when Wallace publicly opposed the administration's policies toward the Soviet Union.

Wallace's views anticipate many of the arguments made by "revisionist" historians. Note particularly his emphasis on the Soviet fears over their own security, how American actions seem to be aggressive, the dangers of intensifying the public's anxieties, and the possibility of coexistence between competing ideologies. Wallace's interpretation of postwar events, as well as his recommendations to the president, should be carefully compared with the preceding historical analysis by Gaddis and with the strikingly different private memorandum for Truman prepared by Clark Clifford in the following selection.

I have been increasingly disturbed about the trend of international affairs since the end of the war, and I am even more trou-

Excerpted from a letter sent by Henry Wallace to President Truman, July 23, 1946, in Harry Truman Papers, Harry S. Truman Library, Independence, Missouri.

bled by the apparently growing feeling among the American people that another war is coming and the only way that we can head it off is to arm ourselves to the teeth. Yet all of past history indicates that an armaments race does not lead to peace but to war. The months just ahead may well be the crucial period which will decide whether the civilized world will go down in destruction after the five or ten years needed for several nations to arm themselves with atomic bombs. Therefore I want to give you my views on how the present trend toward conflict might be averted. . . .

How do American actions since V-J Day appear to other nations? I mean by actions the concrete things like $13 billion for the War and Navy Departments, the Bikini tests of the atomic bomb and continued production of bombs, the plan to arm Latin America with our weapons, production of B-29s and planned production of B-36s, and the effort to secure air bases spread over half the globe from which the other half of the globe can be bombed. I cannot but feel that these actions must make it look to the rest of the world as if we were only paying lip service to peace at the conference table.

These facts rather make it appear either (1) that we are preparing ourselves to win the war which we regard as inevitable or (2) that we are trying to build up a predominance of force to intimidate the rest of mankind. How would it look to us if Russia had the atomic bomb and we did not, if Russia had 10,000-mile bombers and air bases within a thousand miles of our coastlines, and we did not?

Some of the military men and self-styled "realists" are saying: "What's wrong with trying to build up a predominance of force? The only way to preserve peace is for this country to be so well armed that no one will dare attack us. We know that America will never start a war."

The flaw in this policy is simply that it will not work. In a world of atomic bombs and other revolutionary new weapons, such as radioactive poison gases and biological warfare, a peace maintained by a predominance of force is no longer possible.

Why is this so? The reasons are clear:

FIRST. Atomic warfare is cheap and easy compared with old-fashioned war. Within a very few years several countries can have atomic bombs and other atomic weapons. Compared with the cost of large armies and the manufacture of old-fashioned weapons, atomic bombs cost very little and require only a relatively small part of a nation's production plant and labor force.

SECOND. So far as winning a war is concerned, having more bombs—even many more bombs—than the other fellow is no longer a decisive advantage. If another nation had enough bombs to eliminate all of our principal cities and our heavy industry, it wouldn't help us very much if we had ten times as many bombs as we needed to do the same to them.

THIRD. And most important, the very fact that several nations have atomic bombs will inevitably result in a neurotic, fear-ridden, itching-trigger psychology in all the peoples of the world, and because of our wealth and vulnerability we would be among the most seriously affected. Atomic war will not require vast and time-consuming preparations, the mobilization of large armies, the conversion of a large proportion of a country's industrial plants to the manufacture of weapons. In a world armed with atomic weapons, some incident will lead to the use of those weapons.

There is a school of military thinking which recognizes these facts, recognizes that when several nations have atomic bombs, a war which will destroy modern civilization will result and that no nation or combination of nations can win such a war. This school of thought therefore advocates a "preventive war," an attack on Russia *now* before Russia has atomic bombs.

This scheme is not only immoral, but stupid. If we should attempt to destroy all the principal Russian cities and her heavy industry, we might well succeed. But the immediate countermeasure which such an attack would call forth is the prompt occupation of all Continental Europe by the Red Army. Would we be prepared to destroy the cities of all Europe in trying to finish what we had started? This idea is so contrary to all the basic instincts and principles of the American people that any such action would be possible only under a dictatorship at home. . . .

Our basic distrust of the Russians, which has been greatly intensified in recent months by the playing up of conflict in the press, stems from differences in political and economic organization. For the first time in our history defeatists among us have raised the fear of another system as a successful rival to democracy and free enterprise in other countries and perhaps even our own. I am convinced that we can meet that challenge as we have in the past by demonstrating that economic abundance can be achieved without sacrific-

ing personal, political and religious liberties. We cannot meet it as
Hitler tried to by an anti-Comintern alliance.

It is perhaps too easy to forget that despite the deep-seated
differences in our cultures and intensive anti-Russian propaganda
of some twenty-five years' standing, the American people reversed their attitudes during the crisis of war. Today, under the
pressure of seemingly insoluble international problems and continuing deadlocks, the tide of American public opinion is again turning against Russia. In this reaction lies one of the dangers to
which this letter is addressed.

I should list the factors which make for Russian distrust of the
United States and of the Western world as follows. The first is
Russian history, which we must take into account because it is the
setting in which Russians see all actions and policies of the rest of
the world. Russian history for over a thousand years has been a
succession of attempts, often unsuccessful, to resist invasion and
conquest—by the Mongols, the Turks, the Swedes, the Germans
and the Poles. The scant thirty years of the existence of the Soviet
Government has in Russian eyes been a continuation of their historical struggle for national existence. The first four years of the
new regime, from 1917 through 1921, were spent in resisting
attempts at destruction by the Japanese, British and French, with
some American assistance, and by the several White Russian
armies encouraged and financed by the Western powers. Then, in
1941, the Soviet State was almost conquered by the Germans after
a period during which the Western European powers had apparently acquiesced in the rearming of Germany in the belief that the
Nazis would seek to expand eastward rather than westward. The
Russians, therefore, obviously see themselves as fighting for their
existence in a hostile world.

Second, it follows that to the Russians all of the defense and
security measures of the Western powers seem to have an aggressive intent. Our actions to expand our military security system—
such steps as extending the Monroe Doctrine to include the arming of the Western Hemisphere nations, our present monopoly of
the atomic bomb, our interest in outlying bases and our general
support of the British Empire—appear to them as going far beyond the requirements of defense. I think we might feel the same
if the United States were the only capitalistic country in the world,
and the principal socialistic countries were creating a level of

armed strength far exceeding anything in their previous history. From the Russian point of view, also, the granting of a loan to Britain and the lack of tangible results on their request to borrow for rehabilitation purposes may be regarded as another evidence of strengthening of an anti-Soviet bloc.

Finally, our resistance to her attempts to obtain warm-water ports and her own security system in the form of "friendly" neighboring states seems, from the Russian point of view, to clinch the case. After twenty-five years of isolation and after having achieved the status of a major power, Russia believes that she is entitled to recognition of her new status. Our interest in establishing democracy in Eastern Europe, where democracy by and large has never existed, seems to her an attempt to re-establish the encirclement of unfriendly neighbors which was created after the last war, and which might serve as a springboard of still another effort to destroy her.

If this analysis is correct, and there is ample evidence to support it, the action to improve the situation is clearly indicated. The fundamental objective of such action should be to allay any reasonable Russian grounds for fear, suspicion and distrust. We must recognize that the world has changed and that today there can be no "One World" unless the United States and Russia can find some way of living together. For example, most of us are firmly convinced of the soundness of our position when we suggest the internationalization and defortification of the Danube or of the Dardanelles, but we would be horrified and angered by any Russian counterproposal that would involve also the internationalizing and disarming of Suez or Panama. We must recognize that to the Russians these seem to be identical situations. . . .

We should make an effort to counteract the irrational fear of Russia which is being systematically built up in the American people by certain individuals and publications. The slogan that communism and capitalism, regimentation and democracy, cannot continue to exist in the same world is, from a historical point of view, pure propaganda. Several religious doctrines, all claiming to be the only true gospel and salvation, have existed side by side with a reasonable degree of tolerance for centuries. This country was for the first half of its national life a democratic island in a world dominated by absolutist governments.

We should not act as if we too felt that we were threatened in today's world. We are by far the most powerful nation in the world, the only Allied nation which came out of the war without devastation and much stronger than before the war. Any talk on our part about the need for strengthening our defenses further is bound to appear hypocritical to other nations. . . .

This proposal admittedly calls for a shift in some of our thinking about international matters. It is imperative that we make this shift. We have little time to lose. Our postwar actions have not yet been adjusted to the lessons to be gained from experience of Allied cooperation during the war and the facts of the atomic age.

It is certainly desirable that, as far as possible, we achieve unity on the home front with respect to our international relations; but unity on the basis of building up conflict abroad would prove to be not only unsound but disastrous. I think there is some reason to fear that in our earnest efforts to achieve bipartisan unity in this country we may have given way too much to isolationism masquerading as tough realism in international affairs.

The real test lies in the achievement of international unity. It will be fruitless to continue to seek solutions for the many specific problems that face us in the making of the peace and in the establishment of an enduring international order without first achieving an atmosphere of mutual trust and confidence. The task admittedly is not an easy one.

There is no question, as the Secretary of State has indicated, that negotiations with the Russians are difficult because of cultural differences, their traditional isolationism, and their insistence of a visible quid pro quo in all agreements. But the task is not an insuperable one if we take into account that to other nations our foreign policy consists not only of the principles that we advocate but of the actions we take.

Fundamentally, this comes down to the point discussed earlier in this letter, that even our own security, in the sense that we have known it in the past, cannot be preserved by military means in a world armed with atomic weapons. The only type of security which can be maintained by our own military force is the type described by a military man before the Senate Atomic Energy Commission— a security against invasion after all our cities and perhaps 40 million of our city population have been destroyed by atomic weapons. That is the best that "security" on the basis of armaments has to offer us. It is not the kind of security that our people and the people of the other United Nations are striving for.

American Firmness vs. Soviet Aggression

Clark Clifford

To understand history requires an attitude of historical mindedness. Students must put themselves in the position of other people in other times. They must try to be aware of the frame of reference of others, of the pressures on them, and of the nature of their understanding of a particular problem or development. An analysis of President Harry Truman's actions in the Cold War needs to be rooted in an examination of how he and his closest advisors viewed American relations with the Soviet Union.

This private memorandum for the President, prepared by his Special Counsel, Clark Clifford, just a year after V-J Day, summarizes the attitudes and outlook of the Joint Chiefs of Staff, the Secretaries of State, War, and Navy, and other high level officials, especially George F. Kennan's diplomatic cables from Moscow. It wholly blames the Soviet Union for the emerging Cold War. It urges the President to arm the United States for possible war, to negotiate reluctantly with the Russians, to never compromise for fear that it might be interpreted as weakness, to utilize American economic power to force Soviet concessions, and to employ foreign aid to build a "barrier to communism." Students may wish to compare Clifford's interpretation of Soviet behavior with that of Gaddis, and Clifford's "get tough" recommendations with the reconsideration of Cold War assumptions offered by George Kennan in 1981 (reprinted here in Part IX).

It is perhaps the greatest paradox of the present day that the leaders of a nation, now stronger than it has ever been before,

Excerpted from a Clark Clifford memorandum to President Truman, September 24, 1946, in Clark Clifford Papers, Harry S. Truman Library, Independence, Missouri.

should embark on so aggressive a course because their nation is "weak." And yet Stalin and his cohorts proclaim that "monopoly capitalism" threatens the world with war and that Russia must strengthen her defenses against the danger of foreign attacks. The USSR, according to Kremlin propaganda, is imperilled so long as it remains within a "capitalistic encirclement." This idea is absurd when adopted by so vast a country with such great natural wealth, a population of almost 200 million and no powerful or aggressive neighbors. But the process of injecting this propaganda into the minds of the Soviet people goes on with increasing intensity.

The concept of danger from the outside is deeply rooted in the Russian people's haunting sense of insecurity inherited from their past. It is maintained by their present leaders as a justification for the oppressive nature of the Soviet police state. The thesis, that the capitalist world is conspiring to attack the Soviet Union, is not based on any objective analysis of the situation beyond Russia's borders. It has little to do, indeed, with conditions outside the Soviet Union, and it has risen mainly from basic inner-Russian necessities which existed before the Second World War and which exist today. . . .

The Kremlin acknowledges no limit to the eventual power of the Soviet Union, but it is practical enough to be concerned with the actual position of the USSR today. In any matter deemed essential to the security of the Soviet Union, Soviet leaders will prove adamant in their claims and demands. In other matters they will prove grasping and opportunistic, but flexible in proportion to the degree and nature of the resistance encountered.

Recognition of the need to postpone the "inevitable" conflict is in no sense a betrayal of the Communist faith. Marx and Lenin encouraged compromise and collaboration with non-Communists for the accomplishment of ultimate communistic purposes. The USSR has followed such a course in the past. In 1939 the Kremlin signed a nonaggression pact with Germany and in 1941 a neutrality pact with Japan. Soviet leaders will continue to collaborate whenever it seems expedient, for time is needed to build up Soviet strength and weaken the opposition. Time is on the side of the Soviet Union, since population growth and economic development will, in the Soviet view, bring an increase in its relative strength. . . .

A direct threat to American security is implicit in Soviet foreign policy which is designed to prepare the Soviet Union for war with the leading capitalistic nations of the world. Soviet leaders recognize that the United States will be the Soviet Union's most powerful enemy if such a war as that predicted by Communist theory ever comes about and therefore the United States is the chief target of Soviet foreign and military policy. . . .

The most obvious Soviet threat to American security is the growing ability of the USSR to wage an offensive war against the United States. This has not hitherto been possible, in the absence of Soviet long-range strategic air power and an almost total lack of sea power. Now, however, the USSR is rapidly developing elements of her military strength which she hitherto lacked and which will give the Soviet Union great offensive capabilities. Stalin has declared his intention of sparing no effort to build up the military strength of the Soviet Union. Development of atomic weapons, guided missiles, materials for biological warfare, a strategic air force, submarines of great cruising range, naval mines and mine craft, to name the most important, are extending the effective range of Soviet military power well into areas which the United States regards as vital to its security. . . .

The primary objective of United States policy toward the Soviet Union is to convince Soviet leaders that it is in their interest to participate in a system of world cooperation, that there are no fundamental causes for war between our two nations, and that the security and prosperity of the Soviet Union, and that of the rest of the world as well, is being jeopardized by the aggressive militaristic imperialism such as that in which the Soviet Union is now engaged.

However, these same leaders with whom we hope to achieve an understanding on the principles of international peace appear to believe that a war with the United States and the other leading capitalistic nations is inevitable. They are increasing their military power and the sphere of Soviet influence in preparation for the "inevitable" conflict, and they are trying to weaken and subvert their potential opponents by every means at their disposal. So long as these men adhere to these beliefs, it is highly dangerous to conclude that hope of international peace lies only in "accord," "mutual understanding," or "solidarity" with the Soviet Union.

Adoption of such a policy would impel the United States to make sacrifices for the sake of Soviet-U.S. relations, which would only have the effect of raising Soviet hopes and increasing Soviet demands, and to ignore alternative lines of policy, which might be much more compatible with our own national and international interests.

The Soviet government will never be easy to "get along with." The American people must accustom themselves to this thought, not as a cause for despair, but as a fact to be faced objectively and courageously. If we find it impossible to enlist Soviet cooperation in the solution of world problems, we should be prepared to join with the British and other Western countries in an attempt to build up a world of our own which will pursue its own objectives and will recognize the Soviet orbit as a distinct entity with which conflict is not predestined but with which we cannot pursue common aims.

As long as the Soviet government maintains its present foreign policy, based upon the theory of an ultimate struggle between communism and capitalism, the United States must assume that the USSR might fight at any time for the two-fold purpose of expanding the territory under Communist control and weakening its potential capitalist opponents. The Soviet Union was able to flow into the political vacuum of the Balkans, Eastern Europe, the Near East, Manchuria and Korea because no other nation was both willing and able to prevent it. Soviet leaders were encouraged by easy success and they are now preparing to take over new areas in the same way. The Soviet Union, as Stalin euphemistically phrased it, is preparing "for any eventuality."

Unless the United States is willing to sacrifice its future security for the sake of "accord" with the USSR now, this government must, as a first step toward world stabilization, seek to prevent additional Soviet aggression. . . . This government should be prepared, while scrupulously avoiding any act which would be an excuse for the Soviets to begin a war, to resist vigorously and successfully any efforts of the USSR to expand into areas vital to American security.

The language of military power is the only language which disciples of power politics understand. The United States must use that language in order that Soviet leaders will realize that our government is determined to uphold the interests of its citizens and the rights of small nations. Compromise and concessions are considered, by the Soviets, to be evidences of weakness and they are encouraged by our "retreats" to make new and greater demands.

The main deterrent to Soviet attack on the United States, or to attack on areas of the world which are vital to our security, will be the military power of this country. It must be made apparent to the Soviet government that our strength will be sufficient to repel any attack and sufficient to defeat the USSR decisively if a war should start. The prospect of defeat is the only sure means of deterring the Soviet Union.

The Soviet Union's vulnerability is limited due to the vast area over which its key industries and natural resources are widely dispersed, but it is vulnerable to atomic weapons, biological warfare, and long-range power. Therefore, in order to maintain our strength at a level which will be effective in restraining the Soviet Union, the United States must be prepared to wage atomic and biological warfare. A highly mechanized army, which can be moved either by sea or by air, capable of seizing and holding strategic areas, must be supported by powerful naval and air forces. A war with the USSR would be "total" in a more horrible sense than any previous war and there must be constant research for both offensive and defensive weapons.

Whether it would actually be in this country's interest to employ atomic and biological weapons against the Soviet Union in the event of hostilities is a question which would require careful consideration in the light of the circumstances prevailing at the time. The decision would probably be influenced by a number of factors, such as the Soviet Union's capacity to employ similar weapons, which can not now be estimated. But the important point is that the United States must be prepared to wage atomic and biological warfare if necessary. The mere fact of preparedness may be the only powerful deterrent to Soviet aggressive action and in this sense the only sure guaranty of peace.

The United States, with a military potential composed primarily of [highly] effective technical weapons, should entertain no proposal for disarmament or limitation of armament as long as the possibility of Soviet aggression exists. Any discussion on the limitation of armaments should be pursued slowly and carefully with the knowledge constantly in mind that proposals on outlawing atomic warfare and long-range offensive weapons would greatly limit United States strength, while only moderately affecting the Soviet Union. The Soviet Union relies primarily on a large infantry and artillery force and the result of such arms limitation would be to deprive the United States of its most effective weapons without impairing the Soviet Union's ability to wage a quick war of aggression in Western Europe, the Middle East or the Far East. . . .

In addition to maintaining our own strength, the United States should support and assist all democratic countries which are in any way menanced or endangered by the USSR. Providing military support in case of attack is a last resort; a more effective barrier to communism is strong economic support. Trade agreements, loans and technical missions strengthen our ties with friendly nations and are effective demonstrations that capitalism is at least the equal of communism. The United States can do much to ensure that economic opportunities, personal freedom and social equality are made possible in countries outside the Soviet sphere by generous financial assistance. Our policy on reparations should be directed toward strengthening the areas we are endeavoring to keep outside the Soviet sphere. Our efforts to break down trade barriers, open up rivers and international waterways, and bring about economic unification of countries, now divided by occupation armies, are also directed toward the reestablishment of vigorous and healthy non-Communist economies.

In conclusion, as long as the Soviet government adheres to its present policy, the United States should maintain military forces powerful enough to restrain the Soviet Union and to confine Soviet influence to its present area. All nations not now within the Soviet sphere should be given generous economic assistance and political support in their opposition to Soviet penetration. Economic aid may also be given to the Soviet government and private trade with the USSR permitted provided the results are beneficial to our interests. . . .

Even though Soviet leaders profess to believe that the conflict between Capitalism and Communism is irreconcilable and must eventually be resolved by the triumph of the latter, it is our hope that they will change their minds and work out with us a fair and equitable settlement when they realize that we are too strong to be beaten and too determined to be frightened.

Part Two

THE COLD WAR AT HOME

There has always been a close connection between American foreign policy and American domestic politics. In a democracy, it is difficult to pursue diplomatic positions that do not have broad popular support. Given the distinctive image America has had of its role in the world, that has almost always meant posing foreign policy issues in moralistic or universal terms. During World War I, for example, Woodrow Wilson would not have been able to justify American involvement simply on the basis of economic or military self-interest. Rather, drawing upon America's traditional image as being a beacon of hope, morality, and freedom, Wilson portrayed the war as a crusade to "make the world safe for democracy."

When the Truman administration found itself at loggerheads with the Soviet Union after World War II, it too resorted to a rhetoric of moralism as a means of justifying the massive economic and military aid it deemed necessary to combat the perceived Soviet threat. In 1947 the administration decided to ask Congress for a major program of assistance to Greece and Turkey in what became the Truman doctrine. The Secretary of State and other officials briefing congressional leaders met with a cool response when they simply presented the issue in terms of self-interest. Only when Dean Acheson invoked the specter of Russian tyranny spreading throughout the world in a direct assault on freedom did the congressmen respond. As Arthur Vanderburg, Republican leader of the Senate foreign relations committee, told the President, Truman would have to "scare hell" out of the American people if he wished their support for his program. Consequently, Truman presented the Cold War to Congress as an

issue of freedom against tryanny, democracy against totalitarianism, a struggle between those who believed in God and those who
were atheists.

Eventually, this kind of rhetoric created its own logic—a logic
that inhibited freedom of discussion and amounted to a form of
domestic tyranny at home. Anyone who dared question the wisdom of America's Cold War policies was portrayed as a sympa-
thizer of communism and part of a "fifth column" beholden to
the Soviet Union. If one's own policy was defined as moral, anyone opposing that policy was inevitably immoral. Indeed, when
Truman ran for re-election in 1948, he followed a strategy of
defining his left-wing opponent, Henry Wallace of the Progressive
Party, as pro-communist and hence disloyal.

It was out of such a framework that the phenomenon we call
McCarthyism grew. Many Americans felt beleaguered and threatened in the immediate postwar years, as the Soviet Union asserted
control over eastern Europe, tested an atomic bomb, and put
forward her own rhetoric of ideological confrontation with the
United States. When Chinese communists took over China in
1949, many Americans saw events in the world moving against
them. The fact that Soviet spies had secured atomic energy secrets
from the United States, and that some State Department officials
had predicted the victory of the Chinese communists, gave rise to
a sense, on the part of some, that a communist conspiracy existed
within the ranks of the United States government itself. Responding to such fears, Truman himself instituted a security program to
impose a test of loyalty on government employees. Not satisfied
with that response, the House Committee on Un-American Activities and others in Congress launched what became a witch hunt,
seeking to ferret out anyone and everyone who might be
accused—fairly or unfairly—of less than one hundred percent
loyalty to the most conservative program of patriotism. Those
who had been part of Soviet-American Friendship Societies during World War II while America and Russia were allies, or who
had flirted with communism in the 1930s, or who had participated in various progressive causes including advocacy of civil
rights for blacks or national health insurance, were brought before congressional committees, subjected to harrassing questioning, and treated as pariahs. Hundreds of lives were destroyed by
the insinuation—often never justified—that at some point in the

past, they had said something or belonged to an organization that could be construed as friendly to the Soviet Union or to social democratic policies.

When Senator Joseph McCarthy announced in Wheeling, West Virginia, in 1950 that he had a list of 207 card-carrying communists in the State Department, he simply carried to a new height the hysteria that was already rampant in the country. McCarthy had no such list and most of his charges were made of whole cloth. Nevertheless, he succeeded through the technique of the big lie and the red smear in intimidating the American people in and outside of Congress, as well as destroying careers and lives. So powerful was McCarthy, and so out of control were his charges, that even people as established and invulnerable as President Dwight David Eisenhower refused to attack him or challenge his credibility. McCarthyism cast a pall over the land, chilling political debate for a decade and making it virtually impossible for many Americans to actively espouse any cause, domestic or international, that could be distorted as sympathetic to socialism or communism.

The following selections analyze and illustrate the impact of the Cold War at home. Robert Griffith's assessment indicates that although McCarthy did not represent a new or powerful political force, he was able to impose his own political tyranny due to partisan Republicanism and the agitation of conservative interest groups. The senator's demagoguery is best exemplified by the words which launched his personal crusade against the Democrats for their alleged "softness" on communism. The "Declaration of Conscience" by seven Republican senators and the comments of Margaret Chase Smith represent both a courageous effort to stand up to McCarthy by moderates within his own party and a principled statement against the selfish exploitation of fear and intolerance. Finally, Lillian Hellman, who risked going to jail by taking the position that she would inform the House Un-American Activities Committee about herself but would say nothing about other people, describes her thoughts while being interrogated and the devastating personal consequences of McCarthyism for those who sought to carry forward the American principles of freedom of speech and independent thought.

Among the questions that remain from the McCarthy period are the extent to which Truman himself paved the way for

McCarthyism by his definition of Cold War issues; whether other political leaders could have acted in concert to put a stop to the reckless charges of the anti-communist Right; and how it was possible for such a poison to spread through the body politic in the name of democratic principle. The McCarthy period had a disastrous impact on American political discussion for a generation, and it is imperative to come to grips with that heritage in order to understand the history of the postwar period.

American Politics and the Origins of "McCarthyism"

Robert Griffith

At the height of McCarthyism many critics pictured the junior Senator from Wisconsin as a charismatic demagogue with a special flair for arousing the darkest instincts of the American public. Some compared him to Hitler. Others emphasized the irrationality of the Senator's popular following. Still others, borrowing the insights and terminology of social psychology, described McCarthyism as a mass movement rooted in the status resentments of the lower-middle and working-class Americans. Most commentators on McCarthyism today, however, concentrate on politics rather than social pathology. They stress the role of political institutions and interest groups. They emphasize the actions and inactions of both conservative and liberal elites, down-playing the fears and discontents of the mass of Americans.

Fundamentally, they depict Senator McCarthy as an outgrowth, not the origin, of the Second Red Scare. McCarthy, they aver, was the consequence of an already formed anti-Communist consensus, not its cause. In the following selection, Robert Griffith, winner of the Frederick Jackson Turner Award of the Organization of American Historians for his brilliant analysis of McCarthyism as a political phenomenon, The Politics of Fear, Joseph R. McCarthy and the Senate (1970), succinctly summarized the views of these historians who interpret McCarthyism not as "mass" but as "interest group" politics. If there is any truth to the dictum "The study of history is the best guarantee against repeating it," the roots and repercussions of McCarthyism ought to be carefully pondered.

For nearly two decades American scholars and journalists have described "McCarthyism" in terms of a popular uprising, a mass movement of the "radical right" that threatened the very fabric of American society. Inchoate, irrational, it swept across the political landscape like an elemental force of nature carrying all before it. Its sources, these scholars maintained, lay not so much in the emergent cold war, but in the "social strains" and status tensions produced by a century of modernization. McCarthyism, like populism, was seen as an attack by paranoid provincials upon the educated and the wealthy. Politicians, in this view, were but the passive instruments of the popular will, reflecting the hysteria that welled up from the grass roots. McCarthy himself, of course, was something of an exception. Indeed, he was credited with a demonic talent for probing "the dark places of the American mind." He was "the most gifted" demagogue in American history, succeeding where others had failed in arousing the American masses and inciting them to action "outside of and against the established channels of constitutional government."

But was McCarthyism really a popular movement? Probably not. To be sure, anti-Communism was an element in the American polical culture, and popular attitudes toward Communism, conditioned as they were by several decades of misinformation and strident propaganda, were mostly negative. It is also true that public opinion polls showed a rather high level of support for McCarthy (around 35 percent for most of 1953–54), combined with frequently intolerant attitudes toward nonconformists and dissenters. But popular intolerance and anti-Communism, however important, have tended to be constants. Even in the supposedly radical thirties, for example, most Americans seemed to favor denying freedom of speech, press, and assembly to native Communists. What needs to be explained, therefore, is not the mere existence of such attitudes, but how, during the late 1940's and early 1950's, they were mobilized and became politically operational.

Second, as even Seymour Martin Lipset and other proponents of the "radical right" thesis admit, intense negative feelings about McCarthy were usually more common than strongly favorable ones. McCarthy aroused more opposition than support. Third, as

Nelson Polsby has suggested in a critique of the radical right thesis, the most common characteristic of McCarthy supporters was not class, religion, or ethnicity, but political affiliation. Support for McCarthy was strongest among Republicans. Socioeconomic factors were not unimportant—when party affiliation was held constant, those with lower status, less education, and of the Catholic faith tended to support McCarthy disproportionately. But these last factors seem clearly less significant than party. There was, moreover, no continuity between populism and McCarthyism, as some historians have argued. Indeed, as Michael Paul Rogin has shown, nearly the reverse was true—agrarian radicalism, where cohesive, contributed not to the Republican right, but to the constituency of Democratic liberalism.

Fourth, while the polls did show substantial support for McCarthy and extremely negative feelings about Communism, as well as a low level of support for the civil liberties of Communists and other political dissidents, the intensity of these feelings was apparently not very strong. When people were asked, for example, whether they favored allowing Communists to teach in their schools, the response (both in the thirties and in the fifties) was largely and unsurprisingly negative. But in 1953, at the height of the McCarthy era, when people were asked a simple, nondirective question ("What kinds of things do you worry about most?"), less than 1 percent listed the threat of Communism as a major concern and only 8 percent mentioned the tangentially related area of world problems. Even when the interviewer sought to lead the respondent ("Are there other problems you worry about or are concerned about, especially political or world problems?"), the level of concern was not great. The number expressing anxiety about Communism increased only from 1 percent to 6 percent. The number concerned over international affairs rose more substantially, from 8 percent to 30 percent. Significantly, more than half of those so questioned added nothing to their initial response. Thus, as Samuel Stouffer concluded in his 1954 study, *Communism, Conformity and Civil Liberties,* Americans were not very deeply concerned over domestic Communism. The "picture of the average American as a person with the jitters, trembling lest he find a Red under the bed, is clearly nonsense."

Finally, what is all too often overlooked is the congruence between popular attitudes toward Communism and the attitudes of

influential public figures. Many prominent Republicans, for example, were constantly accusing the Roosevelt and Truman Administrations of selling out to Communism at home and abroad.
Nor were such charges limited to conservatives. Some liberal Republicans, such as Senator Ralph Flanders of Vermont who would
later lead the movement to censure McCarthy, believed that "our
late departed saint Franklin Delano Roosevelt was soft as taffy on
the subject of Communism and Uncle Joe." Even Democrats such
as Massachusetts Congressman John F. Kennedy attacked the
Truman Administration's foreign policies, charging that "what
our young men saved [in World War II], our diplomats and our
President have frittered away." The Truman Administration itself
used the Red issue against Henry Wallace and the Progressives
and occasionally even against the Republicans. McCarthy, the
President charged at one point, was the Kremlin's "greatest asset."
In denouncing Communism, then, Joe McCarthy, despite his occasional attacks on "the bright young men who are born with
silver spoons in their mouths," was adopting a political issue already sanctioned by much of the nation's political leadership.

The commonly accepted portrait of McCarthyism as a mass
movement and McCarthy as a charismatic leader is, thus, badly
overdrawn. People were less concerned about the threat of Communism and less favorably inclined toward McCarthy than is generally thought. Support for McCarthy, moreover, was closely identified with partisan Republicanism. Finally, popular attitudes about
Communism generally mirrored the views of many prominent political leaders, and McCarthy's use of the issue was unexceptional.

But if McCarthyism is not to be understood primarily in terms of
popular passion, then how do we explain the contentious and
tumultuous politics of the mid-twentieth century? A partial
answer to this problem involves a political definition of McCarthyism and, as Michael Paul Rogin has suggested, the actions and
inactions of political elites. McCarthyism may not have been only a
political phenomenon; it may indeed have reflected the "social
strains" of modern American society, as Talcott Parsons and
others have maintained. But it was primarily a product of the
political system and its leaders. The latter did not simply respond

to popular protest, but rather helped to generate the very sense of concern and urgency that came to dominate the decade.

This is not to argue that the politics of McCarthyism was born solely of the postwar period. There was a long history of anti-radicalism in America, a history produced both by conservative resistance to social change and by nativist fears of strangers in the land. It was not a history created by protean mass movements, however, but by the complicated interplay of political manipulation and popular myth and stereotype. . . .

The cold war transformed the climate of American politics, overlaying traditional political issues with a new and emotionally charged set of concerns. The growing power of the Soviet Union and its challenge to American supremacy served to focus previously diffuse fears and anxieties over Communism. So did the arrest of men and women accused of spying for the U.S.S.R. But the anti-Communist protest of the late 1940's was more than a simple response to external events. It also sprang from the goals that American leaders set for postwar foreign policy, the manner in which they perceived the Soviet challenge to that policy, and the methods they chose to meet that challenge.

For a variety of reasons—idealism, self-interest, the hubris of the very powerful—American leaders defined United States policy in sweeping terms: the creation of a global system of stability, peace, and prosperity. The Soviet challenge to this new order was seen as a threat to world peace and to American security, a threat to which the United States was compelled to respond. The character of this response, in turn, helped to create a climate in which anti-Communist politics gained a vastly heightened potency and appeal. In part, this was because the Truman Administration itself couched its policies in a rhetoric of crusading anti-Communism, which stressed American innocence, Soviet depravity, and the necessity for confrontation.

Such views, of course, were scarcely unique to the Truman Administration. Rather they were shared by a broad segment of America's political leadership—liberal and conservative, Democratic and Republican. Both Truman and his conservative critics were influenced to a great extent by the legacy of prewar anti-Communism. Both shared illusions concerning the limits of American power and the nature of Soviet foreign policy. Truman's critics, however, generally proposed more drastic policies and justified them with greater militance than did the Administration. Even Robert Taft, a frequently incisive critic of containment, denounced the Administration for being "soft on Communism," advocated greater assistance for Chiang Kai-shek, and supported General Douglas MacArthur in the controversy over the Korean War. The Truman Administration, committed to an interventionist policy abroad, stressed anti-Communism as a means of winning support from such nationalistic but fiscally cautious conservatives. As a result, most conservatives joined the Administration in a bipartisan anti-Communist consensus, while the rest, including Taft, were left isolated and impotent. A second, and unintended consequence of this tactic, however, was the generation of a new and conservative political climate, resistant to social change at home and to negotiation and compromise abroad.

The new political climate inspired conservative businessmen, organized veterans, patriotic societies, and other zealous anti-Communists and made their efforts appear more plausible and relevant. The Chamber of Commerce, for example, through its Committee on Socialism and Communism, prepared and distributed a series of pamphlets designed to expose Communists in government and labor, to discredit New Deal social legislation, and to help businessmen reassert themselves at the community level. The American Legion was even more active. Led by its Americanism Division and active at both the state and federal levels, the Legion campaigned vigorously to arouse the nation to the perils of Communism. The Legion played an important role in creating and sustaining the Special House Committee on Un-American Activities and in the establishment of "little Dies Committees" in the states. The Legion lobbied hard for new anti-Communist legislation, supporting the Mundt-Nixon Communist registration bill as well as a wide variety of restrictive measures at the state level. Finally, the Legion became deeply involved in the colorful crusade against Communism in Hollywood and in the subsequent spread of blacklisting in the film, radio, and television industries.

The Legion and the Chamber of Commerce were only two among a welter of anti-Communist organizations, which included patriotic societies such as the Daughters of the American Revolution, Catholic groups such as the Knights of Columbus and the

Catholic War Veterans, ethnic groups such as the Polish-American Congress, and a host of smaller right-wing organizations. The activities of these groups included lobbying, propaganda, and on occasion picketing and other forms of public protest. The concerns of such groups were amplified by the press. The conservative McCormick, Hearst, and Gannett chains were especially active in this undertaking, though overwrought anti-Communism was not limited to them alone. As early as 1945, for example, *Life* magazine complained that "The 'fellow traveler' is everywhere, in Hollywood, on college faculties, in government bureaus, in publishing companies, in radio offices, even on the editorial staffs of eminently capitalistic journals." From here it was but a short step to the demand that such "fellow travelers" be purged from American life.

This was not, of course, "mass" politics but "interest group" politics, a typical expression of the American political culture and not an aberrational one. The group base of American politics was not aligned, as earlier scholars have suggested, against a mass politics of anti-Communism. Instead, interest groups themselves lay at the heart of the anti-Communist politics of the era.

The aggressive actions of right-wing interest groups were not, moreover, met by countervailing pressures from the left. Instead, the same broad forces that lent strength and legitimacy to the postwar right served to undermine and destroy the postwar left. In 1945 the American left was a relatively large and potentially powerful movement, which included a wide assortment of liberals, socialists, and Communists. Though scarred by the memory of past betrayals and sharply divided among themselves, these leftists nevertheless shared a consensus on two fundamental points: the necessity for radical social change at home and for a conciliatory and pacific foreign policy abroad. The rise of the cold war and the resurgence of conservatism, however, led to bitter divisions within the left over American policy toward the Soviet Union and over the role of Communism in American life. The precarious unity of the popular front was shattered, both by the Communists who repudiated the wartime leadership of Earl Browder and by cold-war liberals who supported the foreign policies of the Truman Administration and sought to purge Communists from labor unions, political parties, and other voluntary associations. The overwhelming rejection of Henry Wallace in the 1948 campaign and the emergence of Americans for Democratic Action (ADA) marked the beginning of a new political era in which the left was in virtual eclipse and in which the distinction between liberals and conservatives became one of method and technique, not fundamental principle. Divided, demoralized, and after 1948 led by men who shared many of the anti-Communist assumptions of the right, the American left was unable to withstand the mounting demands of McCarthyite conservatives.

The political climate of postwar America was thus shaped by the cold war, by the agitation of conservative interest groups, and by the disintegration of liberalism. It remained, however, for politicians to mobilize the support necessary for a politics of anti-Communism. Foremost among such politicians were those Republican and Democratic conservatives who had championed the anti-Communist issues since the thirties and who had maintained all along that Democratic liberalism was leading the country down the road to Communism. After 1945, however, this anti-reformist impulse was joined with the new foreign policy and internal security issues bred by the cold war. Congressional conservatives now charged that the Roosevelt and Truman Administrations were "soft" on Communism abroad and tolerant of subversion and disloyalty at home; and beginning in 1945 they launched a series of investigations in Communist activities designed in part to embarrass the government.

The frequency of such investigations was one measure of the rise of the Communist issue in American politics. There were four investigations during the 79th Congress (1945–47); twenty-two during the Republican 80th Congress (1947–49); twenty-four during the 81st Congress (1949–51); thirty-four during the 82nd Congress (1951–53); and fifty-one, an all-time high, during the Republican 83rd Congress (1953–55). Throughout the forties most of these investigations were conducted by the House Committee on Un-American Activities, led, following the retirement of Martin Dies, by J. Parnell Thomas (Republican-New Jersey) and by John S. Wood (Democrat-Georgia). More important, the focus and character of these investigations changed. Before December 1948 most of HUAC's investigations seemed to be linked to domestic concerns—the committee's primary targets were left-wing

New Deal personnel, New Deal agencies such as the Federal Theatre Project and the Office of Price Administration, trade unions whose leadership included Communists, and Hollywood. But after 1948, the year in which Whittaker Chambers accused Alger Hiss first of having been a Communist and then, later, of having spied for the Soviet Union, the committee began increasingly to emphasize the internal security issues of espionage, subversion, and "Communists in government."

The Communist issue was injected into the 1946 elections and was apparently a factor in the Republican triumph, especially among urban Catholics. In 1947–48 the Truman Administration responded to these pressures by justifying its foreign policies with a crusading anti-Communist rhetoric, by instituting a federal loyalty-security program, by prosecuting Communist party leaders under the Smith Act, and in general by stressing its own firm anti-Communist credentials. Indeed, by 1948 the Administration had succeeded, if only temporarily, in using the Communist issue to its own advantage against both the Progressives and the Republicans. Crusades, however, are more easily begun than halted, and by early 1950 those conservative politicians whom Truman had sought to outflank once again held the initiative, now denouncing the Administration for the "loss" of China and demanding a sweeping purge within the government.

The rise of anti-Communism as an issue in national politics was accompanied by the growth of a derivative anti-Communist politics at the state and local levels. In part this was because many of the organizations that had agitated for restrictive measures at the federal level were also active in the states and in the communities. Some of these groups, the Chamber of Commerce and the American Legion, for example, labored not only to arouse others to the menace of Communism, but also to popularize techniques and methods for combating it. The Chamber sponsored anti-Communist seminars for local businessmen, while the American Legion held conferences for state legislators anxious to learn what the federal government and other states were doing to safeguard the Republic. Catholic Church groups and the conservative Hearst press also helped agitate the issue, as did the coterie of staff and witnesses that surrounded the House Committee on Un-American Activities.

More important, state legislatures responded almost slavishly to

t₁e force of federal law and precedent and to the anxieties
aroused by national leaders. Anti-radical legislation was not, of
course, new to most states. Yet what was remarkable about the
great outpouring of the late forties was that so many legislatures
acted at the same time and in the same way. In 1949, for example,
the Maryland legislature passed a Subversive Activities Act, popularly known as the Ober Law. There was little original in the new
law, however, for it had been drawn from the Smith Act of 1940,
from Truman's Loyalty Program of 1947, and from portions of
the Mundt-Nixon bill then pending before Congress. The Ober
Law was in turn copied in part or entirely by the states of Mississippi, New Hampshire, Washington, and Pennsylvania. In the
case of Pennsylvania, the legislature in 1951 established as the
criteria for dismissing state employees not the Ober Law's standard—"reasonable grounds . . . to believe that any person is a
subversive person"—but instead "reasonable doubt as to the loyalty of the person involved." The Maryland law had followed the
criteria set forth in Truman's March 1947 loyalty order (Ex.
Order 9835); the Pennsylvania legislature incorporated a generally unheralded but highly significant change in that criteria, in
effect reversing the burden of proof, which Truman had ordered
in April 1951 (Ex. Order 10241).

During the late forties, nearly thirty states enacted laws seeking
to bar from public employment those who advocated the violent
overthrow of the government, or who belonged to organizations
which so advocated. In only one instance did such a state statute
predate the Truman loyalty order; all of them, of course, came
after the 1939 Hatch Act, which had provided such restrictions for
federal employment. The Attorney General's list, institutionalized
by Truman's 1947 loyalty order, was quickly adopted as a test of
loyalty by states (including Arizona, New York, Michigan, Texas,
Oklahoma), by municipalities (among them Detroit and New York
City), and even by private employers (including the Columbia
Broadcasting System). Following the passage in September 1950 of
the McCarran Internal Security Act, more than a half dozen states
rushed to enact so-called Communist Control Laws. Even cities
passed municipal ordinances directed against Communists.

Thus state and local anti-Communist legislation, though widespread, is best understood as a reflection, not a cause, of national
priorities. Unlike populism, the impact of which was felt first at

the local and state level and only later at the national level, the politics of anti-Communism originated at the national level and then spread to the states.

By 1950, then, political leaders had succeeded through the manipulation of popular myths and stereotypes, in creating a mood conducive to demagogues such as Joseph R. McCarthy. The Wisconsin senator's crude attacks on American policy and policy-makers resonated through the political system not because of their uniqueness, but because of their typicality. To call this political impulse "McCarthyism," however, is to exaggerate the senator's importance and to misunderstand the politics that he came to symbolize. McCarthy was the product of anti-Communist politics, not its progenitor. Had he never made that speech in Wheeling, West Virginia, had his name never become a household word, what people came to call "McCarthyism" would nevertheless have characterized American politics at the mid-century.

Speech at Wheeling, West Virginia

Joseph McCarthy

Whatever the deeper causes of the Second Red Scare, few doubt that Senator Joseph R. McCarthy did more than any other individual to turn the concern about domestic disloyalty and security into a form of national hysteria. His name still stirs violent emotions in those who lived through that turbulent period. The words McCarthyism *and* McCarthyite *have become a part of our language.*

"A man without moral perceptions," in the words of one recent biographer, "one who will break all the rules because for him there are none," McCarthy had floundered through four years in the Senate and was desperately searching for an issue that would increase his visibility and would aid his plans for reelection when he appeared before the Ohio County Women's Republican Club in Wheeling, West Virginia, on February 9, 1950. Following the outline of speeches by other Republican anticommunists, McCarthy charged that the United States had lost ground in the world not as a result of foreign aggression, but "because of the traitorous actions of those who have been treated so well by this nation." He claimed, according to press reports of the address, to have in his hands a list of 205 members of the Communist Party and members of a spy ring currently employed by "and shaping the policy of the State Department." When later challenged to produce evidence for his charges McCarthy maintained that he was referring to Communist "party loyalists" or "bad risks" in the State Department, and in the moderated version of the Wheeling speech introduced into the Congressional Record *on February 20, reprinted below, he reduced the number of alleged Communists to 57.*

McCarthy had no list at all. But it didn't matter. In an atmosphere charged by the Communist victory in China, the successful explosion of an A-bomb by the Soviet Union, the Hiss-Chambers confrontations, the Tru-

man Administration's own campaign against subversion, and soon the outbreak of war in Korea, McCarthy had a winning issue which dominated news headlines and the Republican Party had a potent weapon which pummeled the Democrats.

Five years after a world war has been won, men's hearts should anticipate a long peace, and men's minds should be free from the heavy weight that comes with war. But this is not such a period—for this is not a period of peace. This is a time of the "cold war." This is a time when all the world is split into two vast, increasingly hostile armed camps—a time of a great armaments race. . . .

Today we are engaged in a final, all-out battle between communistic atheism and Christianity. The modern champions of communism have selected this as the time. And, ladies and gentlemen, the chips are down—they are truly down. . . .

Six years ago, at the time of the first conference to map out the peace—Dumbarton Oaks—there was within the Soviet orbit 180,000,000 people. Lined up on the antitotalitarian side there were in the world at that time roughly 1,625,000,000 people. Today, only 6 years later, there are 800,000,000 people under the absolute domination of Soviet Russia—an increase of over 400 percent. On our side, the figure has shrunk to around 500,000,000. In other words, in less than 6 years the odds have changed from 9 to 1 in our favor to 8 to 5 against us. This indicates the swiftness of the tempo of Communist victories and American defeats in the cold war. As one of our outstanding historical figures once said, "When a great democracy is destroyed, it will not be because of enemies from without, but rather because of enemies from within." . . .

The reason why we find ourselves in a position of impotency is not because our only powerful potential enemy has sent men to invade our shores, but rather because of the traitorous actions of those who have been treated so well by this Nation. It has not been the less fortunate or members of minority groups who have been selling this Nation out, but rather those who have had all the

From *Congressional Record*, 81 Congress, 2nd Session, 1954–57.

benefits that the wealthiest nation on earth has had to offer—the
finest homes, the finest college education, and the finest jobs in
Government we can give.

This is glaringly true in the State Department. There the bright
young men who are born with silver spoons in their mouths are
the ones who have been the worst. . . . In my opinion the State
Department, which is one of the most important government departments, is thoroughly infested with Communists.

I have in my hand 57 cases of individuals who would appear to
be either card carrying members or certainly loyal to the Communist Party, but who nevertheless are still helping to shape our
foreign policy. . . .

I know that you are saying to yourself, "Well, why doesn't the
Congress do something about it?" Actually, ladies and gentlemen, one of the important reasons for the graft, the corruption,
the dishonesty, the disloyalty, the treason in high Government
positions—one of the most important reasons why this continues
is a lack of moral uprising on the part of the 140,000,000 American people. In the light of history, however, this is not hard to
explain.

It is the result of an emotional hang-over and a temporary
moral lapse which follows every war. It is the apathy to evil which
people who have been subjected to the tremendous evils of war
feel. As the people of the world see mass murder, the destruction
of defenseless and innocent people, and all of the crime and lack
of morals which go with war, they become numb and apathetic. It
has always been thus after war.

However, the morals of our people have not been destroyed.
They still exist. This cloak of numbness and apathy has only
needed a spark to rekindle them. Happily, this spark has finally
been supplied.

As you know, very recently the Secretary of State proclaimed
his loyalty to a man guilty of what has always been considered as
the most abominable of all crimes—of being a traitor to the
people who gave him a position of great trust. The Secretary of
State in attempting to justify his continued devotion to the man
who sold out the Christian world to the atheistic world, referred
to Christ's Sermon on the Mount as a justification and reason
therefore, and the reaction of the American people to this would
have made the heart of Abraham Lincoln happy.

When this pompous diplomat in striped pants, with a phony British accent, proclaimed to the American people that Christ on the Mount endorsed communism, high treason, and betrayal of a sacred trust, the blasphemy was so great that it awakened the dormant indignation of the American people.

He has lighted the spark which is resulting in a moral uprising and will end only when the whole sorry mess of twisted, warped thinkers are swept from the national scene so that we may have a new birth of national honesty and decency in government.

Republican Declaration of Conscience

Margaret Chase Smith

Not all Republicans applauded the accusations of treason that McCarthy hurled at the Democratic Administration. On June 1, 1950, Margaret Chase Smith of Maine presented to the Senate the Declaration of Conscience that she penned and that six other moderate Republican senators had cosigned. Evenhandedly, it criticized the Democratic Administration's "complacency to the threat of communism here at home" while refusing to countenance Republicans who sought party victory "through the selfish political exploitation of fear, bigotry, ignorance, and intolerance." Such a view, however, did not represent a majority of the GOP. In the immediate years ahead Republican red-baiting increased in volume and virulence.

Mr. President, I would like to speak briefly and simply about a serious national condition. It is a national feeling of fear and frustration that could result in national suicide and the end of everything that we Americans hold dear. It is a condition that comes from the lack of effective leadership either in the legislative branch or the executive branch of our Government. That leadership is so lacking that serious and responsible proposals are being made that national advisory commissions be appointed to provide such critically needed leadership.

I speak as briefly as possible because too much harm has already been done with irresponsible words of bitterness and selfish political opportunism. I speak as simply as possible because the

From *Congressional Record*, 81 Congress, 2nd Session, 1954–57.

issue is too great to be obscured by eloquence. I speak simply and briefly in the hope that my words will be taken to heart.

Mr. President, I speak as a Republican. I speak as a woman. I speak as a United States Senator. I speak as an American.

The United States Senate has long enjoyed world-wide respect as the greatest deliberative body in the world. But recently that deliberative character has too often been debased to the level of a forum of hate and character assassination sheltered by the shield of congressional immunity.

It is ironical that we Senators can in debate in the Senate, directly or indirectly, by any form of words, impute to any American who is not a Senator any conduct or motive unworthy or unbecoming an American—and without that non-Senator American having any legal redress against us—yet if we say the same thing in the Senate about our colleagues we can be stopped on the grounds of being out of order.

It is strange that we can verbally attack anyone else without restraint and with full protection, and yet we hold ourselves above the same type of criticism here on the Senate floor. Surely the United States Senate is big enough to take self-criticism and self-appraisal. Surely we should be able to take the same kind of character attacks that we "dish out" to outsiders.

I think that it is high time for the United States Senate and its Members to do some real soul searching and to weigh our consciences as to the manner in which we are performing our duty to the people of America and the manner in which we are using or abusing our individual powers and privileges.

I think it is high time that we remembered that we have sworn to uphold and defend the Constitution. I think it is high time that we remembered that the Constitution, as amended, speaks not only of the freedom of speech but also of trial by jury instead of trial by accusation.

Whether it be a criminal prosecution in court or a character prosecution in the Senate, there is little practical distinction when the life of a person has been ruined.

Those of us who shout the loudest about Americanism in making character assassinations are all too frequently those who, by our own words and acts, ignore some of the basic principles of Americanism—

The right to criticize.

The right to hold unpopular beliefs.

The right to protest.

The right of independent thought.

The exercise of these rights should not cost one single American citizen his reputation or his right to a livelihood nor should he be in danger of losing his reputation or livelihood merely because he happens to know someone who holds unpopular beliefs. Who of us does not? Otherwise none of us could call our souls our own. Otherwise thought control would have set in.

The American people are sick and tired of being afraid to speak their minds lest they be politically smeared as Communists or Fascists by their opponents. Freedom of Speech is not what it used to be in America. It has been so abused by some that it is not exercised by others. . . .

As members of the minority party, we do not have the primary authority to formulate the policy of our Government. But we do have the responsibility of rendering constructive criticism, of clarifying issues, of allaying fears by acting as responsible citizens.

As a woman, I wonder how the mothers, wives, sisters, and daughters feel about the way in which members of their families have been politically mangled in Senate debate—and I use the word "debate" advisedly.

As a United States Senator, I am not proud of the way in which the Senate has been made a publicity platform for irresponsible sensationalism. I am not proud of the reckless abandon in which unproved charges have been hurled from this side of the aisle. I am not proud of the obviously staged, undignified countercharges which have been attempted in retaliation from the other side of the aisle.

I do not like the way the Senate has been made a rendezvous for villification, for selfish political gain at the sacrifice of individual reputations and national unity. I am not proud of the way we smear outsiders from the floor of the Senate and hide behind the cloak of congressional immunity and still place ourselves beyond criticism on the floor of the Senate.

As an American, I am shocked at the way Republicans and Democrats alike are playing directly into the Communist design of "confuse, divide, and conquer." As an American, I do not want a

Democratic administration white wash or cover up any more than I want a Republican smear or witch hunt.

As an American, I condemn a Republican Fascist just as much as I condemn a Democrat Communist. I condemn a Democrat Fascist just as much as I condemn a Republican Communist. They are equally dangerous to you and me and to our country. As an American, I want to see our Nation recapture the strength and unity it once had when we fought the enemy instead of ourselves. . . .

STATEMENT OF SEVEN REPUBLICAN SENATORS

1. We are Republicans. But we are Americans first. It is as Americans that we express our concern with the growing confusion that threatens the security and stability of our country. Democrats and Republicans alike have contributed to that confusion.

2. The Democratic administration has initially created the confusion by its lack of effective leadership, by its contradictory grave warnings and optimistic assurances, by its complacency to the threat of communism here at home, by its oversensitiveness to rightful criticism, by its petty bitterness against its critics.

3. Certain elements of the Republican party have materially added to this confusion in the hopes of riding the Republican Party to victory through the selfish political exploitation of fear, bigotry, ignorance, and intolerance. There are enough mistakes of the Democrats for Republicans to criticize constructively without resorting to political smears.

4. To this extent, Democrats and Republicans alike have unwittingly, but undeniably, played directly into the Communist design of "confuse, divide, and conquer."

5. It is high time that we stopped thinking politically as Republicans and Democrats about elections and started thinking patriotically as Americans about national security based on individual freedom. It is high time that we all stopped being tools and victims of totalitarian techniques—techniques that, if continued here unchecked, will surely end what we have come to cherish as the American way of life.

Scoundrel Time

Lillian Hellman

"I cannot and will not cut my conscience to fit this year's fashions,"
playwright Lillian Hellman wrote to the chairman of the House Committee
on Un-American Activities when called to testify in 1952. Her refusal to
imitate the behavior of the "scoundrels" of the title of her book, who ruined
the lives of others in their groveling appearances before the Committee,
came at a particularly grim moment in the Second Red Scare. Alger Hiss
had been sent to jail and the Rosenbergs condemned to death. With impu-
nity, Joe McCarthy implicated Democratic officials for every manner of
infamous behavior. And the stalemated war in Korea ground on with little
hope for victory. Fear and hatred of communism were paramount. In an
ugly mood, the American people apparently would brook no interference
with the congressional search for spies and scapegoats. Thus, Hellman's
offer to answer all questions about herself but refusal to name others—"to
bring bad trouble to people"—had an extraordinary impact at the time.
Her moral courage in choosing not to hurt innocent people to save herself
made it easier for others to deny the demand to name names and inspired
still others to speak out for freedom of speech and thought. Although
Congress, to the surprise of many, did not cite Hellman for contempt, the
author paid dearly for her defiance, as her autobiographical account,
Scoundrel Time, makes painfully clear.

DEAR MR. WOOD:

As you know, I am under subpoena to appear before your
Committee on May 21, 1952.

I am most willing to answer all questions about myself. I have nothing to hide from your Committee and there is nothing in my life of which I am ashamed. I have been advised by counsel that under the Fifth Amendment I have a constitutional privilege to decline to answer any questions about my political opinions, activities, and associations, on the grounds of self-incrimination. I do not wish to claim this privilege. I am ready and willing to testify before the representatives of our Government as to my own opinions and my own actions, regardless of any risks or consequences to myself.

But I am advised by counsel that if I answer the Committee's questions about myself, I must also answer questions about other people and that if I refuse to do so, I can be cited for contempt. My counsel tells me that if I answer questions about myself, I will have waived my rights under the Fifth Amendment and could be forced legally to answer questions about others. This is very difficult for a layman to understand. But there is one principle that I do understand: I am not willing, now or in the future, to bring bad trouble to people who, in my past association with them, were completely innocent of any talk or any action that was disloyal or subversive. I do not like subversion or disloyalty in any form, and if I had ever seen any, I would have considered it my duty to have reported it to the proper authorities. But to hurt innocent people whom I knew many years ago in order to save myself is, to me, inhuman and indecent and dishonorable. I cannot and will not cut my conscience to fit this year's fashions, even though I long ago came to the conclusion that I was not a political person and could have no comfortable place in any political group.

I was raised in an old-fashioned American tradition and there were certain homely things that were taught to me: to try to tell the truth, not to bear false witness, not to harm my neighbor, to be loyal to my country, and so on. In general, I respected these ideals of Christian honor and did as well with them as I knew how. It is my belief that you will agree with these simple rules of human decency and will not expect me to violate the good American tradition from which they spring. I would, therefore, like to come before you and speak of myself.

I am prepared to waive the privilege against self-incrimination and to tell you everything you wish to know about my views or actions if your Committee will agree to refrain from asking me to name other people. If the Committee is unwilling to give me this assurance, I will be forced to plead the privilege of the Fifth Amendment at the hearing.

A reply to this letter would be appreciated.

Sincerely yours,
LILLIAN HELLMAN

The answer to the letter is as follows:

DEAR MISS HELLMAN:

Reference is made to your letter dated May 19, 1952, wherein you indicate that in the event the Committee asks you questions regarding your association with other individuals you will be compelled to rely upon the Fifth Amendment in giving your answers to the Committee questions.

In this connection, please be advised that the Committee cannot permit witnesses to set forth the terms under which they will testify.

We have in the past secured a great deal of information from persons in the entertainment profession who cooperated wholeheartedly with the Committee. The Committee appreciates any information furnished it by persons who have been members of the Communist Party. The Committee, of course, realizes that a great number of persons who were members of the Communist Party at one time honestly felt that it was not a subversive organization. However, on the other hand, it should be pointed out that the contributions made to the Communist Party as a whole by persons who were not themselves subversive made it possible for those members of the Communist Party who were and still are subversives to carry on their work.

The Committee has endeavored to furnish a hearing to each person identified as a Communist engaged in work in the entertainment field in order that the record could be made clear as to whether they were still members of the Communist Party. Any persons identified by you during the course of Committee hearings will be afforded the opportunity of appearing before the Committee in accordance with the policy of the Committee.

Sincerely yours,
JOHN S. WOOD, *Chairman*

... The room suddenly began to fill up behind me and the press people began to push toward their section and were still piling in when Representative Wood began to pound his gavel. I hadn't seen the Committee come in, don't think I had realized that they were to sit on a raised platform, the government having learned from the stage, or maybe the other way around. I was glad I hadn't seen them come in—they made a gloomy picture. Through the noise of the gavel I heard one of the ladies in the rear cough very loudly. She was to cough all through the hearing. Later I heard one of her friends say loudly, "Irma, take your good cough drops."

The opening questions were standard: what was my name, where was I born, what was my occupation, what were the titles of my plays. It didn't take long to get to what really interested them: my time in Hollywood, which studios had I worked for, what periods of what years, with some mysterious emphasis on 1937. (My time in Spain, I thought, but I was wrong.)

Had I met a writer called Martin Berkeley? (I had never, still have never, met Martin Berkeley, although Hammett told me later that I had once sat at a lunch table of sixteen or seventeen people with him in the old Metro-Goldwyn-Mayer commissary.) I said I must refuse to answer that question. Mr. Tavenner said he'd like to ask me again whether I had stated I was abroad in the summer of 1937. I said yes, explained that I had been in New York for several weeks before going to Europe, and got myself ready for what I knew was coming: Martin Berkeley, one of the Committee's most lavish witnesses on the subject of Hollywood, was now going to be put to work. Mr. Tavenner read Berkeley's testimony. Perhaps he is worth quoting, the small details are nicely formed, even about his "old friend Hammett," who had no more than a bowing acquaintance with him.

MR. TAVENNER: ... I would like you to tell the committee when and where the Hollywood section of the Communist Party was first organized.

MR. BERKELEY: Well, sir, by a very strange coincidence the section was organized in my house. . . . In June of 1937, the middle of June, the meeting was held in my house. My house was picked because I had a large living room and ample parking facilities. . . . And it was a pretty good meeting. We were honored by the presence of many functionaries from downtown, and the spirit was swell. . . . Well, in addition to Jerome and the others I have mentioned before, and there is no sense in going over the list again and again. . . . Also present was Harry Carlisle, who is now in the process of being deported, for which I am very grateful. He was an English subject. After Stanley Lawrence had stolen what funds there were from the party out here, and to make amends had gone to Spain and gotten himself killed, they sent Harry Carlisle here to conduct Marxist classes. . . . Also at the meeting was Donald Ogden Stewart. His name is spelled Donald Ogden S-t-e-w-a-r-t. Dorothy Parker, also a writer. Her husband Allen Campbell, C-a-m-p-b-e-l-l; my old friend Dashiell Hammett, who is now in jail in New York for his activities; that very excellent playwright, Lillian Hellman . . .

And so on.

When this nonsense was finished, Mr. Tavenner asked me if it was true. I said that I wanted to refer to the letter I had sent. I would like the Committee to reconsider my offer in the letter.

> MR. TAVENNER: In other words, you are asking the committee not to ask you any questions regarding the participation of other persons in the Communist Party activities?

I said I hadn't said that.

Mr. Wood said that in order to clarify the record Mr. Tavenner should put into the record the correspondence between me and the Committee. Mr. Tavenner did just that, and when he had finished Rauh sprang to his feet, picked up a stack of mimeographed copies of my letter, and handed them out to the press section. I was puzzled by this—I hadn't noticed he had the copies—but I did notice that Rauh was looking happy.

Mr. Tavenner was upset, far more than the printed words of my hearing show. Rauh said that Tavenner himself had put the letters in the record, and thus he thought passing out copies was proper. The polite words of each as they read on the page were not polite as spoken. I am convinced that in this section of the testimony, as in several other sections—certainly in Hammett's later testimony before the Senate Internal Security Subcommittee—either the court stenographer missed some of what was said and filled it in later, or the documents were, in part, edited. Having read many examples of the work of court stenographers, I have never once seen a completely accurate report.

Mr. Wood told Mr. Tavenner that the Committee could not be

"placed in the attitude of trading witnesses as to what they will testify to" and that thus he thought both letters should be read aloud.

Mr. Tavenner did just this, and there was talk I couldn't hear, a kind of rustle, from the press-section. Then Mr. Tavenner asked me if I had attended the meeting described by Berkeley, and one of the hardest things I ever did in my life was to swallow the words, "I don't know him, and a little investigation into the time and place would have proved to you that I could not have been at the meeting he talks about." Instead, I said that I must refuse to answer the question. The "must" in that sentence annoyed Mr. Wood—it was to annoy him again and again—and he corrected me: "You might refuse to answer, the question is asked, do you refuse?"

But Wood's correction of me, the irritation in his voice, was making me nervous, and I began to move my right hand as if I had a tic, unexpected, and couldn't stop it. I told myself that if a word irritated him, the insults would begin to come very soon. So I sat up straight, made my left hand hold my right hand, and hoped it would work. But I felt the sweat on my face and arms and knew that something was going to happen to me, something out of control, and I turned to Joe, remembering the suggested toilet intermission. But the clock said we had only been there sixteen minutes, and if it was going to come, the bad time, I had better hang on for a while.

Was I a member of the Communist Party, had I been, what year had I stopped being? How could I harm such people as Martin Berkeley by admitting I had known them, and so on. At times I couldn't follow the reasoning, at times I understood full well that in refusing to answer questions about membership in the Party I had, of course, trapped myself into a seeming admission that I once had been.

But in the middle of one of the questions about my past, something so remarkable happened that I am to this day convinced that the unknown gentleman who spoke had a great deal to do with the rest of my life. A voice from the press gallery had been for at least three or four minutes louder than the other voices. (By this time, I think, the press had finished reading my letter to the committee and were discussing it.) The loud voice had been answered by a less loud voice, but no words could be distin-

guished. Suddenly a clear voice said, "Thank God somebody finally had the guts to do it."

It is never wise to say that something is the best minute of your
life, you must be forgetting, but I still think that unknown voice
made the words that helped to save me. (I had been sure that not
only did the elderly ladies in the room disapprove of me, but the
press would be antagonistic.) Wood rapped his gavel and said
angrily, "If that occurs again, I will clear the press from these
chambers."

"You do that, sir," said the same voice.

Mr. Wood spoke to somebody over his shoulder and the somebody moved around to the press section, but that is all that happened. To this day I don't know the name of the man who spoke,
but for months later, almost every day I would say to myself, I
wish I could tell him that I had really wanted to say to Mr. Wood:
"There is no Communist menace in this country and you know it.
You have made cowards into liars, an ugly business, and you
made me write a letter in which I acknowledged your power. I
should have gone into your Committee room, given my name and
address, and walked out." Many people have said they liked what
I did, but I don't much, and if I hadn't worried about rats in jail,
and such. . . . Ah, the bravery you tell yourself was possible when
it's all over, the bravery of the staircase.

In the Committee room I heard Mr. Wood say, "Mr. Walter
does not desire to ask the witness any further questions. Is there
any reason why this witness should not be excused from further
attendance before the Committee?"

Mr. Tavenner said, "No, sir."

My hearing was over an hour and seven minutes after it began.
I don't think I understood that it was over, but Joe was whisper-
ing so loudly and so happily that I jumped from the noise in my
ear.

He said, "*Get up. Get up.* Get out of here immediately. Pollitt will
take you. Don't stop for any reason, to answer any questions from
anybody. Don't run, but walk as fast as you can and just shake
your head and keep moving if anybody comes near you."

Life had changed and there were many people who did not call
me. But there were others, a few friends, a few half-strangers,
who made a point of asking me for dinner or who sent letters.

That was kind, because I knew that some of them were worried about the consequences of seeing me.

But the mishmash of those years, beginning before my congressional debut and for years after, took a heavy penalty. My belief in liberalism was mostly gone. I think I have substituted for it something private called, for want of something that should be more accurate, decency. And yet certain connecting strings have outworn many knives, perhaps because the liberal connections had been there for thirty years and that's a long time. There was nothing strange about my problem, it is native to our time; but it is painful for a nature that can no longer accept liberalism not to be able to accept radicalism. One sits uncomfortably on a too comfortable cushion. Many of us now endlessly jump from one side to another and endlessly fall in space. The American creative world is not only equal but superior in talent to their colleagues in other countries, but they have given no leadership, written no words of new theory in a country that cries out for belief and, because it has none, finds too many people acting in strange and aimless violence.

But there were other penalties in that year of 1952: life was to change sharply in ordinary ways. We were to have enough money for a few years and then we didn't have any, and that was to last for a while, with occasional windfalls. I saw that coming the day the subpoena was first served. It was obvious, as I have said, the farm had to be sold. I knew I would now be banned from writing movies, that the theatre was as uncertain as it always had been, and I was slow and usually took two years to write a play. Hammett's radio, television and book money was gone forever. I could have broken up the farm in small pieces and made a fortune—I had had an offer that made that possible—and I might have accepted it except for Hammett, who said, "No, I won't have it that way. Let everybody else mess up the land. Why don't you and I leave it alone?", a fine sentiment with which I agree and have forever regretted listening to. More important than the sale of the farm, I knew that a time of my life had ended and the faster I put it away the easier would be an altered way of living, although I think the sale of the farm was the most painful loss of my life. It was, perhaps, more painful to Hammett, although to compare the pains of the loss of beloved land one has worked oneself, a house that fits because you have made it fit thinking you would live in it forever, is a foolish guess-game.

Part Three

THE POLITICS OF
THE AFFLUENT SOCIETY

The 1950s and 1960s are generally seen as very different eras in American history. Under the calm, beneficent, paternal leadership of Dwight Eisenhower, America in the 1950s appeared to be enjoying a time of equanimity. After the immediate postwar tensions of inflation, strikes, and foreign policy conflicts, the era of Eisenhower seemed remarkable for its stability. The first Republican to be elected in twenty years, Eisenhower pledged moderation, peace, and an end to corruption in government. While not extending New Deal social welfare programs, neither did Eisenhower attempt to reverse them. Rather, his was an administration of consolidation. The country appeared prosperous, and happy to have a respite from conflict.

The 1960s, by contrast, represented a new cycle of reform and insurgency. Led by the presidencies of John F. Kennedy and Lyndon B. Johnson, the nation set forth to allieviate persistent inequities of racial discrimination, to combat poverty, and to create a new and improved society. "We can do better," Kennedy had said in 1960. "We *will* do better," Johnson promised in 1964. At least on the surface, the two postwar eras seemed radically different, one given to complacency, quietude, and stability, the other to activism, challenge, and change.

In fact, the appearances were as deceptive as they were accurate. The struggles that brought reform in the 1960s were already emerging throughout the "quiet years of the 1950s." Moreover, the policies of the 1960s represented continuity with the past as well as an effort to generate new programs. Both eras, in fact, reflected what Godfrey Hodgson has called the "liberal consensus" in America—the belief that improvement is always possible within a fundamentally sound economic and social system, that right-minded and intelligent people can create a healthy and viable social system, that moderation is preferable to extremism, and that an economy committed to growth will provide the basis for eliminating almost all social problems while assuring prosperity for the middle class.

The selections included here paint in broad strokes the similarities as well as discontinuities in these two eras. Alonzo Hamby recounts the achievements and failures of President Eisenhower, and the appeal of his moderation. Despite his apparent complacency, Eisenhower recognized the long-range dangers in a society where technology and corporate control could work together with the military to shape and define the options available to the society. His plea for awareness of, and control over, the military-industrial complex voiced his concern about the dangers of the new forces taking control of the society. The meaning of, and reasons for, the "liberal consensus" are detailed by Hodgson, and President Kennedy's proposal to land a man on the moon forcefully exemplifies that ideology. Even more, President Johnson's Great Society reflected the almost limitless belief in the promises of American capitalism and democracy. Frederick Siegel discusses Johnson's electoral and legislative successes, and the president expresses his belief that a nation willing and able to harness the forces of technology and economic growth could go on to create a quality existence for virtually everyone.

Among the questions raised by these selections are the extent to which we are controlled by impersonal economic and social forces beyond our ability to shape; whether political leaders are capable of directing these forces; and how and whether it is possible to achieve our goals within the constraints of the existing social and economical order, based as it is on significant class and income differences. One ought to ponder, moreover, why such a false complacency existed in American life and thought, the assumptions of modern American liberalism, and the causes of its successes and failures.

Eisenhower: Holding the Line

Alonzo L. Hamby

Virtually unique in the high level of popularity he maintained during his two terms in office, Dwight D. Eisenhower was perceived by most Americans as a man of integrity and humane instincts who presided wisely over an era of peace and prosperity. Liberal intellectuals, however, viewed him critically, and in the 1960s historians compared him unfavorably with his immediate Democratic predecessors and successors. They downgraded him for refusing to battle publicly with Senator Joseph McCarthy, for failing to speak out in favor of the Supreme Court's Brown *decision against segregated public education and to lead in the struggle for black rights, and for being more concerned with a balanced budget than with the nation's prestige and military power. Then in the late 1960s, the war in Vietnam, the riots in the cities and upheaval on college campuses, soaring inflation, and bitter partisanship caused many historians to reevaluate Eisenhower. He was now given high marks for his restraint in exercising executive power, caution about becoming involved in Vietnam, calm quest for better relations with the Soviet Union, and shrewd "hidden-hand" leadership when it was warranted.*

Alonzo Hamby synthesizes both approaches in stressing the flaws as well as the strengths of Eisenhower in the context of his times. Students may well ask what is omitted in Hamby's portrait of Eisenhower's domestic policies and how that affects his evaluation of the president, as well as how changing circumstances may alter the interpretations of historians in the future.

From *Liberalism and Its Challenges: F.D.R. to Reagan* by Alonzo L. Hamby. Reprinted by permission of publisher (New York: Oxford University Press, 1985).

Dwight D. Eisenhower was the last of the twentieth-century American presidents to be nurtured in the Victorian climate of opinion that had produced Roosevelt and Truman. He was also the only twentieth-century president, other than Theodore Roosevelt, to have experienced public celebration as a military hero, and he possessed a more tangible democratic touch than any of his predecessors save Truman. These attributes coalesced to make his administration an oasis of placidity between eras of extraordinary turbulence in American politics. Eisenhower's espousal of the values of a cherished past provided Americans with a sense of continuity in a troubled, changing time. His status as a hero blended with his image as a democrat to secure him a combination of reverence and trust that made him all but invulnerable to political sniping.

Eisenhower's career as a politician, even more than his career as a soldier, was one of almost storybook individual success, as measured by landslide election victories and remarkable popularity ratings. His larger goals, however, were much more elusive. He sought the presidency because he felt a duty to save his party and his country from forces of irrational extremism. Ultimately, he gave the nation a badly needed breathing spell and time of adjustment to the realities of the post-New Deal, postatomic, postcolonial world, and he made a modest beginning in his more ambitious objective of establishing a moderate-to-conservative political tradition and a cadre of political leaders who could carry on after him. If less than creative, his leadership may have served a useful purpose in times that did not demand creativity.

In 1952, Eisenhower acquiesced to the political draft he had rebuffed in 1948, primarily because he was determined to stop a takeover of the Republican party by Taft and McCarthy. He succeeded Willkie and Dewey as the candidate of the party's "Northeastern establishment"—leaders of the world of finance, corporate business, and communications, moderate to conservative in their domestic outlooks, internationalist in diplomacy, and supported by a broad constituency that perceived far greater cultural and ethnic ties to Europe than did the American heartland. He was the last but also the best hope of a group that had lost three consecutive presidential elections and had no other viable candidate to offer against Taft.

More was involved in the establishment's choice than a sense of political expediency; its leaders must have instinctively seen in the Old Hero a man of kindred sentiments. Eisenhower's outlook, which Robert Griffith has labeled "the corporate commonwealth," was markedly similar to that of the executive elite of the country. He had respect for efficiency and organization, a generally concealed contempt for politics and politicians, a well-hidden distrust of popular democracy and mass emotions, and a commitment to duty and disinterested public service. To this he added a highly developed talent for compromise and conciliation, an intuitive skill in public relations, and a remarkable capacity for dealing with the press. He represented the idea of the organization man at the highest point of its development.

Eisenhower's campaign for the nomination, undertaken in the beginning without his assent, demonstrated both the smooth efficiency of the group with which he had aligned himself and the enduring depth of his own appeal. Throwing together a drive at the last moment without an active candidate, the Eisenhower Republicans scored victories in some key primaries and ran strongly in most others. Polls demonstrated that Ike was the overwhelming choice of the independent voters, whom the Republicans needed in order to win an election. Impressed by the primary results, convinced that the call of duty was genuine, warned by his backers that he had to work actively for the Republican nomination, Eisenhower resigned his NATO post and his army commission and returned to America.

By the time Ike opened his campaign on June 4, Taft, although ahead in committed delegates, was on the defensive; he was, the general and his forces charged, attempting to steamroll the convention. The final weeks before the Republican meeting amounted to a political blitz worthy of a Patton. Having thoroughly intimidated undecided delegates, Eisenhower successfully challenged the credentials of Taft delegations from three Southern states and took the Republican nomination on the first ballot. He was almost sixty-two years old, still loved by the country, still vigorous, and more capable than ever of simultaneously projecting auras of fatherly warmth and stern authority. Upon meeting him for the first time, Emmet John Hughes was impressed by the strength of his presence and by one feature especially: "the blue eyes of a force and intensity singularly deep, almost disturbing, above all commanding."

Although he had been nominated as an alternative to Taftism and McCarthyism, Eisenhower found himself heading a campaign that demonstrated the inroads that McCarthyism had made among Republicans of all varieties. His vice-presidential candidate, Senator Richard Nixon, had built a national reputation as a militant anti-Communist conservative. Leading Republicans from the Eisenhower segment of the party routinely threw charges of Communist sympathies at their Democratic opponents. The general's advisers persuaded him to behave almost with deference toward McCarthy and to omit from an important speech words of praise for George Marshall, one of McCarthy's most prominent targets.

In part, such moves were a matter of political tactics. The most telling issue the Republicans had was frustration with the Korean War in particular and with what appeared to be a larger pattern of Cold War reverses in general. Neither the tepid inflation that had attended Korea nor the small-bore corruption that had marred the Truman administration constituted compelling reasons for voting against Adlai Stevenson. Politics aside, however, even moderate Republicans had found the fall of China stunning, demoralizing, and ultimately inexplicable. They tended to resent the Truman-Acheson effort to put the best possible face on such setbacks and to work for an accommodation with Maoist China. The unhappy course of the Korean War had confirmed all their worst fears, convincing them that U.S. foreign policy shapers were, if not quite traitors, at least blundering fools who deserved the attacks they had sustained and who should be purged from the State Department. From that perspective, it was easy to give McCarthy some tolerance while deploring his ham-handedness, and even to engage in a little bit of McCarthyism. Without fully sharing such prejudices, Eisenhower allowed himself to be carried along with them. He was too inexperienced in politics to be able to form the sound judgment that McCarthyism was not necessary for victory; thus, he was willing to swallow hard and tolerate it. After all, to acquiesce in an occasional smear was distasteful but hardly as terrible as the duty of sending men to their deaths.

Still, the Republicans would have won without McCarthyite tactics. Against one of the most revered figures of the Western world, the Democrats had been able only to come up with Adlai Stevenson, a man of unusual competence and eloquence but lacking both a well-established national reputation and mass political appeal. He had no chance of defeating Eisenhower, especially after the general delivered the necessary reassurances about preserving the New Deal and all but promised to end the Korean War by visiting the battle zone himself. After the turmoil—domestic and foreign—of the Roosevelt and Truman administrations, the nation elected an Old Hero, perhaps in the hope of gaining a lost sense of stability and confidence.

Eisenhower's presidential objectives have been well summarized by the titles of two historical works on his administration: Charles C. Alexander's *Holding the Line* and Gary W. Reichard's *The Reaffirmation of Republicanism*. He and the people around him wanted to preserve the essence of traditional Republicanism and at the same time make it palatable to mid-twentieth-century America. They wanted to impart a fresh tone to old values, produce policies that would somehow reconcile the needs of the present with the outlook of the past, and eventually develop the new personalities that would carry their effort into the future. They hoped to use his administration as the spring-board for a viable new conservative tradition that would assimilate much of the accomplishment of the New Deal-Fair Deal tradition while drawing a line against its extension.

Eisenhower's management of the presidency reflected this larger aspiration. Conditioned by Roosevelt and Truman—and before that by the earlier Roosevelt and Woodrow Wilson—both contemporary observers and scholars since have been most impressed by the weak, passive, negative character of the Eisenhower leadership. Generally liberal-Democratic in their orientation, they have assumed that activism in the pursuit of social change is a commendable norm and that words such as *weak*, *passive*, and *negative* may be used almost as synonyms. Whatever the merits of this outlook, it is useful more as a point of departure for criticism than in aiding understanding.

Eisenhower's handicaps as president are obvious. His political experience was severely limited, and he had little working knowledge of the civilian Washington bureaucracy. What he eventually gained in experience may have been more than countered by the deterioration of his health through a heart attack, a stroke, and a major abdominal operation; there can be little question that he had lost substantial vigor and capacity for work by the end of his second term. Moreover, his well-established distaste for detail no doubt served him less well in the White House than it had in the military. He handled the presidency in the role of a supreme commander, reserving only the larger issues for his personal attention and engaging in compromise and conciliation as the major tools of leadership. If one accepts him and his objectives on his own terms, however, it really is not meaningful to characterize him, as does James David Barber, as a "passive-negative" president. He moved with vigor against excessive social activism when the occasion demanded and worked hard to remake the Republican party. Ultimately more successful than Taft, he nevertheless fell short of establishing Republicanism as a credible alternative to New Deal-Fair Deal Democracy.

However much he rejected vigorous Roosevelt-Truman-style leadership in some areas, Eisenhower never doubted that the presidency was a post that called for vigorous moral leadership. By preachment and deed, he sought to bring America back to the values of his youth—pietistic religion and self-help. Although he never before had displayed signs of having absorbed the devout faith of his parents, he assuredly had absorbed their broader outlook. He presented his political campaign as a "crusade." He took formal membership in the Presbyterian church. He began his inaugural address with a prayer and opened cabinet meetings in the same way. The custom spread quickly throughout the conformist atmosphere of the executive branch. (Soon a joke was making the rounds to the effect that a high-level official had exclaimed in the midst of an important meeting: "Dammit! We forgot the prayer!")

The religion that Eisenhower projected was the religion of a conservative, the classical—if misnamed—"Protestant ethic" with its connection between piety and worldly success, its affirmation of individualism and self-help as keys to salvation as well as riches. It provided both a sense of continuity with the past and a moral alternative to liberal welfarism. It also had a heavy dose of nationalistic patriotism, stemming from the assumption that the United States was a nation favored by God and that the atheistic Soviet Union represented a force that God's Nation had to crusade against. From the mouths of vulgar, right-wing demagogues, such assumptions had appeared ludicrous. Expressed in a benign, fatherly way by a beloved hero, they took on respectability.

The Eisenhower years witnessed a superficial religious revival of impressive proportions. Its most representative leaders were moderately conservative ministers, such as Reverend Norman Vincent Peale or Bishop Fulton J. Sheen, who doubled as personal advice writers and connected religion to getting ahead in the world. The result—when compared to the high philosophy of the theologians or the intense quest for salvation that had once characterized American Protestantism—was little more than a bland affirmation of faith, a homogenized, bloodless American religion that perfectly suited the yearnings of Eisenhower and of much of the American middle class in the fifties. In the end, it was less a search for redemption than a form of national self-congratulation.

This reassuring vision was only a small part of the new political appeal that Eisenhower attempted to develop. He must have understood that his presidency was a national tribute to him as an individual, not to the appeal of his party. The Republicans had won control of Congress only by a hairbreadth in 1952, lost it in 1954, and never regained it. The old values of individualism and self-help had been grievously discredited by Herbert Hoover and could never be resuscitated in their starkest form. Eisenhower seems instinctively to have realized that a public willing to pay homage to the old values was unwilling to accept them in undiluted form.

He never was foolish enough to advocate a return to the 1920s and was apt to be curt with those who did. A sharp, private reprimand to his right-wingish brother, Edgar, vividly illustrates his grasp of reality:

> Should any political party attempt to abolish social security and eliminate labor laws and farm programs, you would not hear of that party again in our political history. There is a tiny splinter group, of course, that believes that you can do those things. Among them are H. L. Hunt, . . . a few other Texas oil millionaires, and an occasional politician and businessman from other areas. Their number is negligible and they are stupid.

He was even careful about applying the term *conservative* to himself, more often using such words as *moderate* or *middle-of-the-road*, and at times adopting the phrase *dynamic conservatism*. Not a theoretician, he could do little more than grope for ways to express a new mood.

The most conspicuous administration intellectual was Arthur Larson, a presidential speechwriter and subcabinet official with an academic background. In his widely read book *A Republican Looks at His Party* (1956), Larson set forth the principles of a "New Republicanism." He described it as a mean between the political principles of 1896 (McKinley Republicanism) and those of 1936 (Rooseveltian Democracy), based upon the ideological and tactical premise that "in politics—as in chess—the man who holds the center holds a position of almost unbeatable strength." The New Republicanism aimed at the preservation of the federal-state balance in American federalism, encouraged business enterprise as a legitimate, progressive force in American life, extended the same tolerance to labor (whether organized or unorganized), and accepted broad government responsibility for the general welfare. It professed a belief in God and a divine order of things. It cited the special American historical and political experience of national development without revolution or intense class conflict. Larson's thinking appealed strongly to Eisenhower, but the task of translating it into political experience and a usable political tradition was more formidable than either could have realized at the euphoric midpoint of Ike's reign.

In his personal values and preferences on most specific domestic issues, Eisenhower was actually a bit more conservative than Taft (with whom he developed a cordial relationship before Taft's sudden death in 1953). Yet the political tradition that Roosevelt and Truman had built emerged from his [Eisenhower's] administration largely unscathed, cut back a bit here and there perhaps, but also advanced in other areas. This occurred even though the administration openly aligned itself with the only group in American life that had opposed Roosevelt and Truman with near unanimity—the business community. The counterrevolution never came and was never even attempted.

One can find no single answer for the smooth emergence of the New Republicanism and the widespread GOP acceptance of the works of the party's political enemies. Several considerations appear important. The New and Fair Deals were too woven into the fabric of society to be torn out; moreover, it was obviously unwise to contemplate such a step. The dispensing of benefits throughout society, whether or not it was just and enlightened, had surely been politically popular; any effort to take them away would be doubly unpopular. It was in any case conservatism at its simplest and most elemental to accept social and political arrangements much as they existed and to assume that change in any direction had to be a slow process. The New Republicanism reflected Eisenhower's well-developed style of leadership with its emphasis upon realism, accommodation, and compromise. It also reflected the changed character of American business, at least at the level of elite leadership.

The corporate tone of the Eisenhower administration was never in doubt. The president surrounded himself with successful financiers, corporate lawyers, and high-level business executives; those of his advisers who did not fit those categories usually possessed the values of the people who did. There were, to be sure, some characters in this group. Secretary of Defense Charles Wilson, the former president of General Motors, compared advocates of social welfare spending to kennel dogs that bayed for food rather than hunting dogs that worked for it; he announced to the world that the interests of GM were those of the United States.[1] Secretary of the Treasury George M. Humphrey, a vehement fiscal conservative, in a moment of dismay at a substantial Eisenhower budget deficit predicted in public that continued large-scale spending would lead to a "hair-curling" depression.

But whatever the occasional tendency of a Wilson or a Humphrey to sound like political primitives, the Eisenhower business executives actually tended to represent the values and aspirations of the mid-twentieth-century corporate executive suite. They were torn between the inner-directed, individualistic ethos of the entrepreneurial past and the other-directed, adaptive values of the managerial present, capable of feeling nostalgia for Herbert Hoover while making the compromises necessary to run an organization in the real world. The new corporate outlook and experience mirrored Eisenhower's to a remarkable degree, gave coherence to his politics, and more than anything else accounted for his choice of the Republican party and the importance of the "millionaires" in his administration.

[1]Wilson's remark was actually a statement that what was good for the country would be good for General Motors and vice versa. Critics of the administration rather misleadingly rephrased it as "What's good for General Motors is good for the country."

Much like executives who had learned to live with labor unions and government regulations even while grumbling about them, the president and those around him resignedly adapted themselves to the social-political structure of a new America. They reflected the values of both the managerial subclass and much of the broader middle class by working hard to govern efficiently, control costs, and thereby contain inflation. Within these limits, they displayed little resistance to government activism, social welfarism, or the continuing prosperity of those who had reaped benefits from the New Deal.

No group had received more from Roosevelt and Truman than organized labor; union spokesmen were thus persistently critical of the Eisenhower administration, just as they were of individual managements from whom they nonetheless received recognition and with whom they engaged in negotiations. Yet Eisenhower never posed the slightest threat to the position that the trade unions had achieved; like the American corporate elite, he had no foolish hope of turning back the clock. It is inevitably recalled that his first secretary of labor, Martin Durkin, resigned in protest against the administration's failure to recommend major changes in the Taft-Hartley Act. It is often forgotten that Durkin's successor, James P. Mitchell, a former personnel executive with vast business and government experience, enjoyed the respect of the labor establishment and much of the liberal community. The administration's only significant move in labor legislation, the Landrum-Griffin Act, was a mild, barely effective regulatory measure aimed primarily at mobster infiltration of unions. In general, Eisenhower and his team dealt with labor much as the management of a large, mature organization might deal with a well-established bargaining agent.

Farmers, the beneficiaries of increasingly expensive and decreasingly effective price support programs, fared less well for several reasons. They were a declining segment of the population, lacked organizational solidarity, and had failed to establish a home in either party. They never had achieved an ideological consensus about their own identity, thinking of themselves at times as the neglected, downtrodden yeoman backbone of America, and at times as entrepreneurs engaged in a business enterprise. Democratic liberalism, predominantly urban in its orientation and offended by the general failure of the farm community to support trade union objectives, became ever cooler to agricultural subsidies as the fifties progressed. The corporate managerial outlook of the Eisenhower administration rather naturally responded negatively to petty entrepreneurs who demanded government aid rather than practice self-help.

Eisenhower and his secretary of agriculture, Ezra Taft Benson, were able to secure legislation establishing ever lower price support levels. Although the program remained horrendously expensive, its cost grew at a much lower rate than would have been the case with the continuance of high supports. One result was the liquidation of many marginal farmers and the augmentation of urban social problems by a rural migration to the cities. Benson expressed the hope that the federal government could extricate itself entirely from agriculture, but neither he nor Eisenhower actually proposed withdrawal as anything more than a long-term objective. Instead they moved cautiously back from what they considered an overextended position.

Social welfarism as such did not give the Eisenhower administration grave difficulties so long as it met the tests of efficiency and reasonable costs. It was Eisenhower who obtained the creation of the Department of Health, Education and Welfare, an objective Truman had failed to achieve. He went along with a higher minimum wage (not a cost to the government), extensive increases in Social Security (a self-funded program), a limited program of medical care for the indigent elderly (a vital social duty with carefully controlled costs), and the National Defense Education Act (a response to Sputnik wrapped in the protective cloak of national security). Such positions, of course, pleased neither liberal Democrats nor hard-core conservative Republicans, a fact that doubtless confirmed the administration's faith in the rightness of its course.

Governmental activism held few terrors for Eisenhower so long as it met the same tests. His administration, for example, acceded to the St. Lawrence Seaway project (self-funded) and the interstate highway system (underwritten by a trust fund financed by new taxes). Both were monumental public works projects that spendthrift New Dealers would have envied, but established in such a way that neither would put a drain on the budget. When pressed to state some sort of philosophical principle, the president and most of his associates would declare themselves states' righters and deplore the size of the federal bureaucracy. From time to time, as in the return of the Tidelands oil claims to the states, they acted upon this intuition; in other cases, when the need for federal action appeared established and the expense could be managed, they ignored it.

Eisenhower's moderation had a powerful appeal to a nation ready for a period of peace and tranquility after years of domestic change and bitterness. But it also was a style of leadership incapable almost by definition of dealing with extreme situations that required something more than bland, moderate treatment. Perhaps the two major failures of the domestic side of Ike's administration were his treatments of McCarthyism and the black revolution.

In McCarthy, Eisenhower faced a nihilist and verbal terrorist for whom immersion in the administration atmosphere of compromise and moderation would have been akin to political suffocation. Having achieved fame and a sizable following with charges of Communism in government, McCarthy had no intention of disappearing from public attention just because his own party had won the White House. Like all terrorists, he had to be handled forcefully; this Eisenhower was unwilling to do, in part because the president himself had sanctioned the continued use of the Communist issue against the Democrats by high officials of his own administration, in part because a strong denunciation of McCarthy would have conflicted with his own concept of party and national leadership. He did not want to alienate McCarthy's disciples on the Republican Right, and he wanted to avoid an unseemly public fight with one of the most accomplished bare-knuckle brawlers. Unopposed by the one public leader who could have discredited him, McCarthy ran amok for almost two years, harassing and embarrassing his own party while the Democrats looked on in mingled delight and dismay. Finally, the Senate disciplined him with covert encouragement from the White House, and he slipped into a well-deserved obscurity.

However grievous, the damage that McCarthy had been permitted to cause was not irreparable; but it is hard to make the same statement about Eisenhower's indifference to the black revolution. In order to understand his attitude toward the American Negro, one must recall the narrowness of his professional experience. He had spent almost his entire life as a career soldier, breathing an atmosphere in which blacks were universally considered inferior, segregated, and kept in their very low place. He rarely, if ever, dealt with blacks on his own level; and unlike the professional politician who must build coalitions, he never had to negotiate with black leaders and discuss their aspirations. Intellectually and socially, he was about as unprepared for the explosion of the civil rights movement as a president could have been.

As the Supreme Court pondered its decision in the school desegregation case in 1954, the president invited the new chief justice, Earl Warren, to dinner at the White House. He expressed his personal hope that the Court's decision would not result in any fundamental change. At no time after the Court had ruled against "separate but equal" educational facilities did Eisenhower speak out in support of the decision. He saw the presidency as a place of moral leadership, but he clearly did not conceive of segregation as a moral issue. Moreover, any strong advocacy of civil rights might have damaged growing Republican strength in the South. His support of black objectives was quite limited and resulted mostly from the urgings of his Department of Justice; its most tangible fruits were two civil rights bills universally recognized as ineffective as soon as they were passed. It is often remembered that Eisenhower sent federal troops to Little Rock to enforce a desegregation order, but it is also frequently forgotten that he took no action in other cases, such as the expulsion of black student Autherine Lucy from the University of Alabama, a situation in which defiance was more subtle and hence more capable of being ignored.

Eisenhower was of course hardly the first political leader to temporize on the position of blacks in American life—and scarcely the last. His inaction was consistent with the entire tenor of his presidency, and it is perhaps foolish to assume that any political leaders will grasp the banner of a social revolution unless they are forced to make a choice. One may nevertheless regret that finding himself at a turning point in American history, Eisenhower could do no more than retreat from positions staked out by his predecessor.

Eisenhower's greatest failure by his own lights was his inability to make the New Republicanism into a movement of the American majority. As a hero, he enjoyed immunity from political defeat, but his status as a hero also blinded the public to both his partisan affiliation and to the ideological perspective he sought to advance. Moreover, his presidency demonstrated anew the old, sound political axiom that popularity is very hard to transfer. Even during the headiest days of the Eisenhower ascendancy, the New Republicanism as a doctrine had to stand on its own merits. However interesting it might have been as a social-intellectual phenomenon, politically it was a flop, incapable of producing the numbers of legislators, governors, and congressmen it needed to establish itself as an enduring force. Neither Eisenhower nor his partisans could persuade the public that the New Republicanism really differed from the Old.

The central problem was the uninspiring performance of the economy in the 1950s—slow economic growth, periodic recession, creeping inflation. The nation never approached a disaster akin to that of the 1930s; most Americans, in fact, perceptibly bettered their lot. Still, the lackluster performance of the economy generated a substantial upward trend in unemployment and created considerable apprehension in a nation not that far from the trauma of the Depression. The persistence of inflation, albeit at a modest rate that would have been welcomed as a salvation two decades later, added both to public irritation and to the problems of the administration. From the perspective of Eisenhower and his aides, inflation was the worst danger; they fought it relentlessly with conservative fiscal and monetary policies that contributed to the prolonged economic slowdown of the fifties and cast doubt upon their argument that the Republicans could bring the country prosperity as well as peace.

This doubt received considerable reinforcement from the failure of the New Republicanism to produce fresh new moderate faces on a national basis. The Old Hero, like Roosevelt or Truman, could do little to speed up the slow pace of change at the state and local levels of party organization; consequently, whatever the desires of the White House, the GOP faces before the electorate usually appeared a bit more reminiscent of Herbert Hoover than Arthur Larson. Here and there, the administration achieved a breakthrough. In the Illinois of the late fifties, Charles Percy, a successful young corporate executive, emerged as the up-and-coming figure in the Republican party of the appropriately named Everett McKinley Dirksen; the White House saw to it that Percy achieved maximum visibility by making him chairman of the platform committee at the 1960 Republican convention. An achiever in business, moderate in ideology, articulate, and handsome, Percy was the New Republicanism personified.

Unfortunately, few like him had emerged by the end of Eisenhower's second term, and fewer still (Percy included) had won election to major offices. The face of Republicanism was more typically that of an Everett Dirksen, a John Bricker, a William Jenner, a Bourke Hickenlooper—visages scarcely calculated to assure a nervous electorate that the party as a whole had entered a new era. Gradually, of course, the old generation would give way to the inexorable certainties of death or defeat, thereby clearing the path for younger moderates. In the meantime, it could fairly be said that Eisenhower had most clearly succeeded in bringing to a position of fame and strength only a dynamic young Republican whose moderation was questionable and about whom he seems to have entertained periodic doubts—Richard M. Nixon.

The Military–Industrial Complex

Dwight D. Eisenhower

As a consequence of World War II and the Cold War, the military, once a small part of American life, waxed increasingly influential and powerful. The armed forces, moreover, developed vital ties with the giant corporations and thousands of subcontractors heavily dependent upon government defense spending. Joined by such organizations as the Air Force Association, the Navy League, and the Association of the United States Army, military and industrial leaders campaigned together for the production of more and newer weapons. Abetted by veterans and labor groups, by university scientists eager for a slice of the military's R and D budget, and by congressmen representing districts laden with defense plants and bases, the "military-industrial complex" rarely had difficulty in exerting the pressure on the government necessary for increased defense funds.

In the late 1950s, however, President Eisenhower grew alarmed at the vast enlargement of government spending and its impairment of the economic health of the United States. He sought to curtail the mushrooming power of the "conjunction of an immense military establishment and a large arms industry." As a part of his effort to control its "unwarranted influence," the retiring President issued this fateful warning in his farewell address. Students can surmise what the General might say two decades later as the annual defense budget soars over $200 billion.

We now stand ten years past the midpoint of a century that has witnessed four major wars among great nations. Three of these

From *Public Papers of the Presidents of the United States: Dwight D. Eisenhower, 1960–1961* (Washington, 1961), pp. 1036–1040.

involved our own country. Despite these holocausts, America is today the strongest, the most influential and most productive nation in the world. Understandably proud of this pre-eminence, we yet realize that America's leadership and prestige depend, not merely upon our unmatched material progress, riches and military strength, but on how we use our power in the interests of world peace and human betterment. . . .

Our military organization today bears little relation to that known by any of my predecessors in peacetime, or indeed by the fighting men of World War II or Korea.

Until the latest of our world conflicts, the United States had no armaments industry. American makers of plowshares could, with time and as required, make swords as well. But now we can no longer risk emergency improvisation of national defense; we have been compelled to create a permanent armaments industry of vast proportions. Added to this, three and a half million men and women are directly engaged in the defense establishment. We annually spend on military security more than the net income of all United States corporations.

This conjunction of an immense military establishment and a large arms industry is new in the American experience. The total influence—economic, political, even spiritual—is felt in every city, every State house, every office of the Federal government. We recognize the imperative need for this development. Yet we must not fail to comprehend its grave implications. Our toil, resources and livelihood are all involved; so is the very structure of our society.

In the councils of government, we must guard against the acquisition of unwarranted influence, whether sought or unsought, by the military-industrial complex. The potential for the disastrous rise of misplaced power exists and will persist.

We must never let the weight of this combination endanger our liberties or democratic processes. We should take nothing for granted. Only an alert and knowledgeable citizenry can compel the proper meshing of the huge industrial and military machinery of defense with our peaceful methods and goals, so that security and liberty may prosper together.

Akin to, and largely responsible for, the sweeping changes in our industrial-military posture has been the technological revolution during recent decades.

In this revolution, research has become central; it also becomes more formalized, complex, and costly. A steadily increasing share is conducted for, by, or at the direction of, the Federal government.

Today, the solitary inventor, tinkering in his shop, has been overshadowed by task forces of scientists in laboratories and testing fields. In the same fashion, the free university, historically the fountainhead of free ideas and scientific discovery, has experienced a revolution in the conduct of research. Partly because of the huge costs involved, a government contract becomes virtually a substitute for intellectual curiosity. For every old blackboard there are now hundreds of new electronic computers.

The prospect of domination of the nation's scholars by Federal employment, project allocations, and the power of money is ever present—and is gravely to be regarded.

Yet, in holding scientific research and discovery in respect, as we should, we must also be alert to the equal and opposite danger that public policy could itself become the captive of a scientific-technological elite.

It is the task of statesmanship to mold, to balance, and to integrate these and other forces, new and old, within the principles of our democratic system—ever aiming toward the supreme goals of our free society.

Down the long lane of the history yet to be written America knows that this world of ours, ever growing smaller, must avoid becoming a community of dreadful fear and hate, and be, instead, a proud confederation of mutual trust and respect.

Such a confederation must be one of equals. The weakest must come to the conference table with the same confidence as do we, protected as we are by our moral, economic, and military strength. That table, though scarred by many past frustrations, cannot be abandoned for the certain agony of the battlefield.

Disarmament, with mutual honor and confidence, is a continuing imperative. Together we must learn how to compose differences, not with arms, but with intellect and decent purpose. Because this need is so sharp and apparent I confess that I lay down my official responsibilities in this field with a definite sense of disappointment. As one who has witnessed the horror and the lingering sadness of war—as one who knows that another war could utterly destroy this civilization which has been so slowly and painfully built over thousands of years—I wish I could say tonight that a lasting peace is in sight.

Happily, I can say that war has been avoided. Steady progress toward our ultimate goal has been made. But, so much remains to be done. As a private citizen, I shall never cease to do what little I can to help the world advance along that road.

The Ideology of the Liberal Consensus

Godfrey Hodgson

One of the central themes of America In Our Time, *Hodgson's probing examination of the crisis of the mind and the spirit of the United States between the inauguration of John F. Kennedy and the resignation of Richard M. Nixon, is the ideology of the liberal consensus. In the chapter from which this selection is excerpted he analyzes the main assumptions of this system of ideas and beliefs and the reasons for its widespread acceptance. Understanding its roots and the factors that enabled it to go virtually unchallenged should illuminate many aspects of American history in the 1950s and 1960s.*

It is worth considering how this consensus affected the presidencies of Eisenhower, Kennedy, and Johnson, and how its existence should inform an historical interpretation of those presidencies. It is also important to examine the accuracy of the component parts of the consensus. Did they reflect or distort the realities of the age? One may, moreover, speculate on what new myths have supplanted the old, and how erroneous assumptions today affect current ideologies.

It is always risky to try to draw the portrait of the ideas and beliefs of a society at any point in its evolution. Contradictions and cross-currents defy generalization. Too much survives from the past, and too much anticipates the future. Usually, perhaps, the attempt is doomed to end either in superficiality or in intellectual dishonesty. But the period from the middle of the 1950s in the

United States up to the impact of the crisis of the 1960s was not usual in this respect. It was an age of consensus. Whether you look at the writings of intellectuals or at the positions taken by practicing politicians or at the data on public opinion, it is impossible not to be struck by the degree to which the majority of Americans in those years accepted the same system of assumptions. Official and semiofficial attempts were even made to codify these assumptions in such works as the report of President Eisenhower's Commission on National Goals or in the Rockefeller Brothers Fund panel reports. The crisis of the late 1960s was caused partly by the mistakes and shortcomings of this system of assumptions and partly by a series of attacks upon it.

. . . At the end of the 1950s, Americans worried about their own personal lives—about health and status. At the other end of the scale of immediacy, they worried about the danger of nuclear war. But few of them doubted the essential goodness and strength of American society.

Four times between 1959 and 1961, the Gallup poll asked its sample what they regarded as the "most important problem" facing the nation. Each time, the most frequent answer (given in each case by at least close to half of the respondents and sometimes by far more than half) was "keeping the peace," sometimes glossed as "dealing with Russia." No domestic issue came anywhere close to challenging that outstanding concern.

In the presidential campaign of 1960, only two types of domestic issues were rated as critical by either candidate or by his advisers: on the one hand, atavistic ethnic issues—the Catholic vote, or Martin Luther King's arrest—and on the other hand, the behavior of the economy. And the latter, to Kennedy, at least, seemed important mainly as a prerequisite of foreign policy.

Kennedy built his appeal around the call to get the country moving again. He left a strong impression that his main reason for doing so was in order to recover lost prestige in the competition with the Soviet Union. Summing up his campaign, in Hartford, Connecticut, on the eve of polling, Senator Kennedy listed three major differences between his opponent and himself:

> first a different view of the present state of the American economy; secondly a different view of our prestige in the world, and there-

fore, our ability to lead the free world; and thirdly, whether the balance of power in the world is shifting in our direction or that of our adversaries.

Nixon, too, had three themes. First, that Kennedy was running America down; second, that the Democrats would cause inflation; and third, that he, Richard Nixon, could speak better for America in confrontation with the Soviet leader.

When it came to sensing the issues that had a gut appeal to the electorate as a whole, that is, each candidate chose to stress foreign dangers (and glories) over domestic problems in the proportion of two to one.

The various American elites took more complicated views. A good deal of concern was expressed by intellectuals in the late 1950s about the lack of excellence in American education (especially in the context of an alleged inferiority to Soviet achievements in space science and missile technology), about the (temporarily) lagging growth rate of the economy, and in diffuse and cloudy jeremiads about the materialism of mass culture. But in the most ambitious contemporary analyses, the same dualism was the recurrent major theme: never so much hope in America, never so much danger abroad.

It was in 1956 that the Rockefeller brothers organized their special studies project to "meet and examine the most critical problems facing the nation over the next ten to fifteen years." Never before had such a prestigious team of dignosticians gathered at the national bedside. Bipartisan and interdisciplinary, it was a roster of those men who had expounded the conventional wisdom since World War II and would remain its champions until the bitter end of the 1960s: Adolf Berle of the New Deal and John Gardner of Common Cause, Chester Bowles and Charles Percy, Edward Teller and David Sarnoff, Lucius Clay and Dean Rusk, Henry Luce and Henry Kissinger.

The reports of the various panels were published separately between January 1958 and September 1960 and as a single volume, *Prospect for America,* in 1961. Together they form a handbook of the shared assumptions of the American governmental and business elite: the two had become hard to distinguish. These were the assumptions that governed the policies of the Kennedy administration, and no one can doubt that they would have guided the Republicans if they had won in 1960.

It would not be fair to call the tone of *Prospect for America* complacent in any vulgar way. It has a muscular Christian strenuousness, rather reminiscent of Kipling's *If,* or of the sermons on the social question preached at expensive boarding schools:

> The number and the depth of the problems we face suggests that the very life of our free society may be at stake, [the report began by saying]. We are concerned that there has not been . . . enough sense of urgency throughout our nation about the mortal struggle in which we are engaged.

Yet all may not yet be lost:

> America has a notable record of responding to challenges and making the most of opportunities. With our growing population, our extraordinary record of rising productivity, the inherent dynamism in our free enterprise economy, there is every reason to face the future with all confidence.

The panel reports contained very able discussion of particular issues such as strategic policy or economic growth. But essentially they saw all the various challenges to America in terms of one big challenge: "the mortal struggle in which we are engaged," the "basic underlying Soviet danger."

The central dualism of the reports' philosophy was baldly, almost naïvely, spelled out right at the beginning in a preface signed by the Rockefellers themselves:

> This project grew out of a belief that the United States in the middle of the twentieth century found itself in a critical situation.
> As a nation we had progressed in our domestic development to an extent hardly imaginable a few short decades ago. . . .
> Throughout this world alive with hope and change stalks the Communist challenge.

"Stalks" is a nice Manichaean touch. It was this very feeling that the hosts of Midian were on the prowl, that the United States was wrestling with the Evil One, and therefore needed to match the messianic beliefs of the adversary with an equivalent dogma, that made it so fashionable in the late 1950s to define the grand purposes of America. The official report on the national goals produced by the Eisenhower administration in 1960 was strikingly similar in tone and conclusions to that of the Rockefeller brothers and their experts.

The extremely distinguished panel of economists, for example—it included Paul Samuelson and Milton Friedman, Herbert Stein and Charles L. Schultze—drew almost exactly the same picture of a perfectible America threatened from without by the Communist serpent. "The American economy works well," they pronounced; "the system is highly responsive to the demands of the people." Yet, even in a discussion of the economy they felt it appropriate to add, "America and the civilization to which it belongs stand at an historic turning-point. They confront a critical danger and inspiring opportunities. The danger is indicated by the phrase 'Cold War.' "

The introduction to the National Goals report gave an official imprimatur to this same dualism. It was signed by, among others, the head of DuPont and the head of the AFL/CIO, the head of the University of California and the head of the First National City Bank of New York. At home, these Olympians thundered in unison, "We have achieved a standard of individual realization new to history." Abroad, "The nation is in grave danger, threatened by the rulers of one third of mankind."

One eminent historian was so carried away by this mood that he even projected it back into an indefinite past: "In this favored country," wrote Clinton Rossiter, "we have always found more things on which to agree than to disagree." Always? In the 1860s? Still, there could be no dissent from his next proposition: "The early 1960s appear to be a time of broad consensus on fundamentals." Looking back to the same period, the late Fred Freed, one of the most thoughtful of television producers, came to much the same conclusion (it was his habit never to use capital letters):

when i began doing my documentaries at nbc in 1961 we lived in a consensus society. those were the days of the cold war. there was an enemy outside, the communists, nikita khrushchev, the red chinese . . . back then there was general agreement in the united states about what was right and what was wrong about the country. nobody really questioned the system. . . . we had a common set of beliefs and common values.

... For some seven years after 1955, few fundamental disagreements, foreign or domestic, were aired in either presidential or Congressional politics. That the United States should in principle seek better relations with the Soviet Union while keeping its guard up and seeking to contain communism—this was common ground. Disagreement was relegated to issues of the second order of importance: the extent to which the United States should support the United Nations, the level of foreign aid, the speed of space development. The main lines of domestic policy were equally beyond controversy. The Eisenhower administration accepted that the federal government must continue social security and such other New Deal programs as had stood the test of public popularity. It was ready to enforce due compliance with the law in civil rights, though reluctantly and with caution. And it was prepared to use fiscal and monetary measures to maintain full employment and economic growth. Not much more, and no less, could be said of the Kennedy administration in its first two years.

The political process, it was taken for granted throughout that period, was a matter of emphasizing one nuance or another of this generally agreed program. A "liberal" congressman, as the word was then used, was one who might be expected to speak up for the particular interests of organized labor; a "conservative" would voice the reservations of corporate business or of the armed services.

Not only in Washington but in the press, on television, and— with few exceptions—in the academic community, to dissent from the broad axioms of consensus was to proclaim oneself irresponsible or ignorant. That would risk disqualifying the dissenter from being taken seriously, and indeed often from being heard at all.

A strange hybrid, liberal conservatism, blanketed the scene and muffled debate. It stretched from Americans for Democratic Action—which lay at the leftward frontiers of respectability and yet remained safely committed to anti-communism and free enterprise—as far into the board rooms of Wall Street and manufacturing industry as there could be found a realistic willingness to accept the existence of labor unions, the rights of minorities, and some role in economic life for the federal government. Since the consensus had made converts on the Right as well as on the Left, only a handful of dissidents were excluded from the Big Tent: southern diehards, rural reactionaries, the more *farouche* and paranoid fringes of the radical Right, and the divided remnants of the old, Marxist, Left. Together, they hardly added up to a corporal's guard. And they were of course never together.

The lack of clearly opposed alternative policies was revealed, to the point of parody, by the most emotional foreign-policy issue of the time: Cuba.

"For the first and only time" in the presidential campaign of 1960, Richard Nixon wrote in *Six Crises,* he "got mad at Kennedy— personally," when Kennedy advocated support for the anti-Castro rebels. Nixon was not angry because Kennedy's position was a recipe for disaster (though it was). He was angry because Kennedy was saying in public what Nixon had been saying in private but felt bound by the obligations of national security not to reveal. He had reason to believe that Kennedy knew all along that the Eisenhower administration was secretly planning the invasion that Kennedy now, by implication, criticized it for not mounting!

After the venture duly ended in fiasco at the Bay of Pigs, Arthur M. Schlesinger, then a White House aide, was sent a cable by his former Harvard graduate students: "KENNEDY OR NIXON," it read, "DOES IT MAKE A DIFFERENCE?" The question was an unkind reference to a pamphlet with that exact title which Schlesinger had felt moved to dash off during the 1960 campaign.

Schlesinger was right, of course; it did make a difference. But this was hardly because any very distinct issues of basic policy or any sharply divergent visions of the world then lay between John Kennedy and Richard Nixon. They represented the aspirations of different categories of Americans. Their symbolic meaning—vital in the presidency—was almost antithetical. By experience and temperament, they were very different men.

The fact remains that they did share the same basic political assumptions: the primacy of foreign over domestic issues, the paramount importance of containing communism, the reign of consensus in domestic affairs, the need to assert the supremacy of the White House as the command post of a society mobilized to meet external danger. So did their staff and advisers. And so, too, did their running mates and closest rivals: Lyndon Johnson and Henry Cabot Lodge, Hubert Humphrey and Nelson Rockefeller, and everyone else who might conceivably have been nominated as a presidential candidate in that year either by the Democrats or by the Republicans. Kennedy and Nixon, wrote Eric Sevareid, Establishment liberal *par excellence* at the time, were the first two completely packaged products of the managerial revolution in politics. In politics, as in business, it was the era of imperfect competition, with candidates not just for the presidency but for most major offices hardly more different than a Chevy and a Ford, or a Pepsi and a Coke.

. . . Confident to the verge of complacency about the perfectibility of American society, anxious to the point of paranoia about the threat of communism—those were the two faces of the consensus mood. Each grew from one aspect of the experience of the 1940s: confidence from economic success, anxiety from the fear of Stalin and the frustrations of power.

Historical logic made some form of consensus likely. It was natural that the new prosperity should calm the class antipathies of the depression years. It was normal that the sense of an enemy at the gate should strengthen national unity. And a reaction was predictable after the lacerating politics of the McCarthy period. But the basis for the consensus was something more than a vague mood or a reaction to passing events. The assumptions on which it was built had an intellectual life and coherence of their own. In barest outline, they can be summarized in the following set of interrelated maxims:

1. The American free-enterprise system is different from the old capitalism. It is democratic. It creates abundance. It has a revolutionary potential for social justice.
2. The key to this potential is production: specifically, increased production, or economic growth. This makes it possible to meet people's needs out of incremental resources. Social conflict over resources between classes (which Marx called "the locomotive of history") therefore becomes obsolete and unnecessary.
3. Thus there is a natural harmony of interests in society. American society is getting more equal. It is in process of abolishing, may even have abolished, social class. Capitalists are being superseded by managers. The workers are becoming members of the middle class.
4. Social problems can be solved like industrial problems: The problem is first identified; programs are designed to

solve it, by government enlightened by social science;
money and other resources—such as trained people—are
then applied to the problem as "inputs"; the outputs are
predictable: the problems will be solved.

5. The main threat to this beneficent system comes from the
deluded adherents of Marxism. The United States and its
allies, the Free World, must therefore expect a prolonged
struggle against communism.

6. Quite apart from the threat of communism, it is the duty
and destiny of the United States to bring the good tidings
of the free-enterprise system to the rest of the world.

The germ of this intellectual system, which by about 1960 had
emerged as the dominant American ideology, was a simple yet
startling empirical discovery. Capitalism, after all, seemed to
work.

In the early 1940s, the economist Joseph Schumpeter, at work
on his last book, *Capitalism, Socialism and Democracy,* reluctantly
came to the conclusion that socialism—a system about which he
cherished so few illusions that he expected it to resemble fascism
when it came—was inevitable. Capitalism was doomed, he feared.
Schumpeter was a conservative, though a highly original one, and
he had arrived at this conclusion by his own line of argument.
The modern corporation would "socialize the bourgeois mind,"
destroy the entrepreneurial motivation that was the driving force
of capitalism, and thus "eventually kill its own roots." He was at
pains to distinguish this position from what he saw as the almost
universal vulgar anticapitalism of his time. "Every writer or
speaker hastens to emphasize . . . his aversion to capitalist and his
sympathy with anticapitalist interests."

Well under ten years later, the exact opposite would have been
closer to the truth. In the United States (though nowhere else in
the world), socialism was utterly discredited. The same transformation could be observed in popular attitudes and in intellectual
fashion. In 1942 (the year that Schumpeter's book was published),
a poll by Elmo Roper for *Fortune* found that only 40 percent of
respondents opposed socialism, 25 percent said they were in favor
of it, and as many as 35 percent had an open mind. By 1949, a
Gallup poll found that only 15 percent wanted "to move more in
the direction of socialism"; 61 percent wanted to move in the

opposite direction. Making all due allowance for the respondents' possibly vague notion of what socialism means, it was a startling shift, yet not more startling than that of the intellectuals. . . .

At the root of this optimistic new political philosophy, there lay an appropriately optimistic new economic doctrine. It came to be known as the New Economics, though by the time of its triumph, in the 1960s, when its licensed practitioners monopolized the President's Council of Economic Advisers, many of its leading ideas were going on thirty years old.

There were many strands to the New Economics. But the essence of it was the acceptance in the United States of the ideas of John Maynard Keynes, *not* as first received in the 1930s but as modified by American economists in the light of the success of the American economy in the 1940s.

The nub of Keynes' teaching was that, contrary to the tenets of classical economics, savings did not necessarily become investment. This was the cause of cyclical depression and of unemployment: left to itself, the capitalist system contained forces that would tend to produce stagnation. To that extent his position was pessimistic. But Keynes was a political economist. He did not think that things should be left to themselves. He believed that governments could cure the kind of deflation that had caused the Great Depression by spending, and if necessary by deficit spending. He actually wrote a long letter to FDR, in early 1938, pleading with him to spend his way out of the recession. The letter was ignored. But after 1945 the university economists succeeded in persuading the more enlightened businessmen, and some politicians, that Keynes was right. Capitalism could be *made* to work. Depression and unemployment were avoidable, and it was up to government to avoid them.

From a conservative viewpoint, Schumpeter introduced ideas that matched the new Keynesian orthodoxy better than he would have liked. He stressed the unique character of American capitalism. He emphasized productivity and technological change. He argued that concentration and oligopoly, which most economists had wanted government to destroy by trust busting, actually favored invention and innovation.

Unlike Schumpeter, John Kenneth Galbraith was a Keynesian, and it was he who attempted the inevitable synthesis in *American*

Capitalism, published in 1952. Galbraith also started from the observed fact that competition in American corporate capitalism was imperfect. He propounded the theory of what he called "countervailing power." Competition had been supposed to limit private economic power. Well, it didn't. But private power was held in check "by the countervailing power of those who are subject to it." The concentration of industry had brought into existence strong buyers—Sears Roebuck, A & P—to match strong sellers. It had also brought strong unions into existence to match strong employers.

Galbraith and Schumpeter had many disagreements. Their analyses were drawn from different premises and tended toward different conclusions. Yet they shared one common perception: the empirical observation that American capitalism was a success. "It works," said Galbraith shortly on his first page, "and in the years since World War II, quite brilliantly."

> There is another fact about the social situation in the United States that has no analogue anywhere else in the world, said Schumpeter in his second edition, published in 1946, . . . namely the colossal industrial success we are witnessing.

And a few pages later, he italicized a passage that condensed the gist of the new hope and the new pride:

> In the United States alone there need not lurk, behind modern programs of social betterment, that fundamental dilemma that everywhere paralyzes the will of every responsible man, the dilemma between economic progress and immediate increase of the real income of the masses.

In practical terms, the gospel of the New Economics could be translated into exciting propositions. Government can manage the economy by using fiscal and monetary policy. The tyranny of the business cycle, which had brought economic catastrophe and the specter of political upheaval, need no longer be tolerated. Depressions could be a thing of the past.

By changing interest rates and by increasing or decreasing the money supply—technical matters that had the added advantage of being remote from the scrutiny of everyday politics—government could flatten out fluctuations in economic activity.

The economists were emboldened to maintain that these fiscal and monetary controls could be manipulated with such precision—"fine tuning" was the phrase used—that in effect they would be able to fly the economy like an airplane, trimming its speed, course and altitude with tiny movements of the flaps and rudder. That was a later claim. The essential promise of the Keynesian system was that it would allow government to guarantee low and diminishing unemployment without inflation. It could thus banish at a stroke the worst terrors of both liberals and conservatives. At the same time, thus managed, the economy would also be able to deliver growth.

Growth was the second key concept of the new intellectual system, and the link between its strictly economic and its social and political ideas.

We are so accustomed to the idea of economic growth that it comes as a surprise to learn that it was a newer idea than Keynes' discovery of the way to beat the business cycle. Just as modern biology had to wait for the invention of the microscope and modern astronomy for the perfection of the telescope, the idea of economic growth developed only after precise techniques for measuring the gross national product became available. These were perfected only in the late 1930s, by Professor Simon Kuznets, of the University of Pennsylvania.

It is hardly possible to exaggerate the importance that the new concept assumed in the intellectual system of American liberals in the 1950s. It became the test, the aim, even the justification of free enterprise—the race, the runner and the prize.

The economic historian W. W. Rostow offered an interpretation of modern history as a contest in terms of economic growth—and called it an "anti-Communist manifesto."

The political scientist Seymour Martin Lipset came close to making it the chief criterion for judging a political system. "Prolonged effectiveness over a number of years," he suggested in his book *Political Man*, "may give legitimacy to a political system. In the modern world, such effectiveness means primarily constant economic development."

But perhaps the most lyrical description came from Walter Heller, chairman of the Council of Economic Advisers under

Presidents Kennedy and Johnson. He called economic growth "the pot of gold and the rainbow."

The liberals did not worship economic growth merely as a golden calf. They saw in it the possibility of solving social problems with the incremental resources created by growth. That will be done, they hoped, without the social conflict that would be inevitable if those resources had to be found by redistributing existing wealth.

This was the hope that both Schumpeter and Galbraith had seen. Brushing aside the pessimists, Schumpeter had dared to predict in 1942 that GNP would reach $200 billion by 1950. (In the event, he was a pessimist himself: GNP in current dollars reached $284 billion by 1950.) "The huge mass of available commodities and services that this figure . . . represents," he wrote, "promises a level of satisfaction of economic needs even of the poorest members of society . . . that would eliminate anything that could possibly be described as suffering or want." And of course Schumpeter was fully aware of the ideological implications. Such a massive creation of new resources could be the key to his central dilemma. It might "annihilate the whole case for socialism so far as it is of a purely economic nature."

What Schumpeter had described as a theoretical possibility in the 1940s had become by the end of the 1950s the "conventional wisdom," and in the 1960s it was to be the foundation of public economic policy.

"Production has eliminated the more acute tensions associated with inequality," Galbraith wrote in *The Affluent Society,* a book whose title was to become a cliché to an extent that did little credit to the subtlety of its argument. "Increasing aggregate output is an alternative to redistribution."

The same idea was spelled out in the stonecutter's prose of the Rockefeller Brothers Fund's drafting committee:

A healthy and expanding private economy means far more in terms of individual and family well-being than any reasonable expansion of government service and social programs.

No tenet of the consensus was more widely held than the idea that revolutionary American capitalism had abolished the working class, or—as approximately the same thought was sometimes expressed—that everybody in America was middle class now or that American society was rapidly approaching economic equality.

A small encyclopedia of statements to this effect can be garnered from the historians, the social scientists and the journalists of the time.

"The organizing concept of American society," wrote Peter Drucker, "has been that of social mobility . . . which denies the existence of classes."

"The union," said the editors of *Fortune,* "has made the worker, to an amazing degree, a middle class member of a middle class society."

"New Dealism," said historian Eric Goldman, ". . . found that it had created a nation of the middle class."

Yet another historian, Samuel Eliot Morison, boldly dated the abolition of the proletariat rather earlier than some would say the proletariat came into existence. He cited the observations of a Polish Communist visitor to confirm "a fact that has puzzled socialists and communists for a century: the American workman is an expectant capitalist, not a class-conscious proletarian."

Frederick L. Allen, on the other hand, wrote a best seller to prove that "the big change" in American life between 1900 and 1950 was the "democratization of our economic system."

One's first reaction is to yield to the cumulative weight of so many impassioned opinions and to conclude . . . what? For even the most cursory reading of such a miscellany raises questions. Had class stratification never existed in the United States, as Drucker seemed to think? But, then, can one imagine social mobility without class? Mobility between what? Had there never been an American proletariat, as Professor Morison seemed to believe? Or had there been a "big change"? Perhaps the proletariat had ceased to exist. But, then, which agency had earned the credit for this transformation? "Industrial enterprise," as some claimed? *Fortune*'s unions? Or Goldman's "New Dealism"? Corporate business, labor and government may work in harmony. But they are hardly synonyms.

A second reading of this miscellany of texts and of the other evidence suggests two more-modest conclusions:

1. A great many Americans, moved by the ideal of equality but perhaps also by reluctance to admit what was seen as

a Marxist analysis of their own society, passionately wanted to believe that the concept of class was alien to the United States.

It suited business to believe this. It suited labor. It suited intellectuals, and it suited the press. It suited liberals, and it suited conservatives. Who was left to argue otherwise?

2. Nevertheless, something *had* happened. In the profound transformations of the 1940s the class structure of American society and its implications for politics had changed in complex and confusing ways—though not to the point of making "everybody middle class," still less of invalidating class analysis.

The mood of the country may have been relatively complacent in the late fifties and the early sixties. But this was not, as the liberal analysis assumed, because the condition of the American people left so little to be desired. It was because a number of historical factors had weakened the political unity and consciousness of the working class and deprived it of the means to perceive its own interests and to defend them.

One of these factors was the way the idea of equality had evolved in the United States. Historically, the actual condition of American society—with the two major exceptions of black and red Americans—had probably always more closely approached a condition of equality than European society. The availability of land, the unexploited resources of a "new" country of continental extent, the absence—or near absence—of an established feudal upper class with a vested interest in maintaining inequality, all tended to minimize inequality in practice. Yet in theory Americans had always been less concerned than Europeans with equality of condition. The paradox is only apparent. Because of the relative abundance of their environment, Americans could afford to think equality of condition less important than equality of opportunity. In most other cultures, people knew all too well that there would never be enough opportunities to go round.

There was a second group of reasons why American politics failed to reflect class interests or class consciousness. It is true, as Arthur

Schlesinger has written, that "in spite of the current myth that class conflicts in America were a fiendish invention of Franklin Roosevelt, classes have, in fact, played a basic part in American political life from the beginning." But the horizontal class lines in American society have always been crosshatched by deep-cut vertical divisions: ethnic, sectional, and racial. Ultimately, these can be traced back to two of the great facts that set American history apart from that of all the other developed Western nations: slavery and immigration. But there were also reasons why their combined impact blurred the reality of class conflict at this particular moment in American history.

One reason was obvious.

The American working class was divided, because the feeling of belonging to a particular ethnic group often took priority over an individual's economic interests or over any sense of class solidarity. In political terms, this frequently meant that the votes of ethnically conscious low-income voters could be recruited to support politicians who, once in office, only fitfully defended the social and economic interests of their constituency. This was notoriously true of the big-city machines, which, in a decadent form, were still one of the typical forms of political organization in the fifties and, for example, played a part in the election of President Kennedy in 1960. But by the fifties the machine no longer fought for the bread-and-butter interests of its immigrant supporters as it had in its classic phase. Instead, traditional ethnic loyalties were played upon at election time to enlist the support of ethnic blocs on behalf of policies that frequently countered the real interests of lower-class voters. Ethnic antics at election time only briefly interrupted the politicians' eager cooperation with the dominant business interests.

The historical fact of immigration had another, less obvious effect. To the extent that Americans are a self-chosen people, their patriotism has always been a more self-conscious emotion than the more visceral tribal feelings of other nations. The immigrant's patriotism has tended to be compounded in roughly equal proportions of status anxiety—the desire to be assimilated as a good American—and of gratitude for his share in the abundance of American life.

Both the abundance and the anxiety were far more visible in the fifties than they had been in the thirties. In the immigrant, this desire to prove oneself a good American had often been in conflict with the impulse to protect the social and economic interests of the lower class. By the fifties, a full generation after the end of mass immigration, the drive for full assimilation was as strong as ever in second- and third-generation Americans; economic needs, as a result of the postwar prosperity, seemed far less urgent. Again, the effect was to increase the conservatism of that considerable proportion of the working class that came of relatively "new" immigrant descent. For this large group, the free-enterprise system was seen as Americanism; social criticism, class solidarity and radical politics were rejected as "un-American."

If ethnic factors dating back to the days of mass immigration, and the preoccupation with equality of opportunity, both helped to obscure the working class's interests from its own members, the sectional and racial basis of the political system derived from the struggle over slavery was responsible for the fact that no great party of the Left was available to represent those interests. In so far as working-class interests were to be effectively represented within the two-party system, they must be represented by the Democrats. But the Democratic Party under Harry Truman and Adlai Stevenson was no party of the Left: It was not only the party of the immigrant, the Negro, the Roman Catholic, the Jew, the city dweller, and the industrial worker; it was also the party of the rural, conservative, nativist South, an element that not only accounted for a third and more of its strength in Congress but held the balance of power in presidential elections.

During the Depression, the New Deal had come closer to being a party of the Left, because the contradiction at the heart of the Democracy was partially concealed by the sheer economic need of the South. Southern Democrats could vote for and work with Roosevelt because they knew the South desperately needed the federal government's economic help. Southerners in Congress might be racial and therefore constitutional conservatives, willing to fight the national Democratic leadership if they must in defense of the South's peculiar social system; but in the New Deal period, that system was not under direct attack. The immediate issues for the South were economic. So long as that remained true, southern "economic liberals"—which often meant men who were not liberals at all except when it came to accepting federal largess—could work happily enough with northern Democrats.

The prosperity of the years after 1941, and in particular the improvement in the economic situation of the southern white working class as a result of industrialization, diminished this incentive for southern Democrats to cooperate with the national party. In spite of much picturesque mythology about their populist fervor and the wool-hats and galluses of their disciples, most of the leading Southerners in Congress in the fifties were essentially responsive to the business elites of the South. While they continued to support some liberal programs, they were not about to allow the Democratic Party to evolve into a national party of the Left. The more racial issues supplanted economic ones in the forefront of their constituents' concern, as they did increasingly after the *Brown* decision in 1954, the more the sectional dilemma made any such evolution of the Democratic Party unlikely.

The Left, in short, had by the late 1950s virtually ceased to count in American political life. But this fateful eclipse was masked by the triumph of the liberals.

To draw a distinction between the Left and the liberals may sound sectarian or obscure. It is not. It is vital to understanding American politics in the age of the consensus, and therefore to understanding what happened after it.

When I say that the Left had almost ceased to exist, I am not thinking of the socialist Left, though that had indeed withered into insignificance long before the collapse of Henry Wallace's Progressive Party, in 1948.

What I mean by the "Left" is any broad, organized political force holding as a principle the need for far-reaching social and institutional change and consistently upholding the interests of the disadvantaged against the more powerful groups in the society. The liberals were never such a force.

What I mean by the liberals is those who subscribed to the ideology I have described: the ideology that held that American capitalism was a revolutionary force for social change, that economic growth was supremely good because it obviated the need for redistribution and social conflict, that class had no place in American politics. Not only are those not the ideas of the Left; at the theoretical level, they provide a sophisticated rationale for avoiding fundamental change. In practice, the liberals were almost always more concerned about distinguishing themselves from the Left than about distinguishing themselves from conservatives.

The confusion between the liberals and the Left arose partly, perhaps, because, in the 1950s, "liberal" was often used as a euphemism for "Left." In the McCarthy era, to call someone a man of the Left carried a whiff of treason with it; to call him a liberal was a graceful alternative.

A deeper reason for the confusion lay in the fact that in the very parts of American society that might have been expected to hold out as the bastions of the Left, the liberals had triumphed. Organized labor, the intelligentsia, and the universities had become the citadels of what was in effect a conservative liberalism.

There were three important developments in the American labor movement in the 1940s, said the editors of *Fortune:* First was the renaissance of the craft-based, politically conservative American Federation of Labor. Fighting back after a period in which it had seemed destined to be swamped by the industrial unions, the AFL doubled its membership in the 1940s and almost recovered parity with the CIO. The second was the "anti-ideological" trend in the CIO, as *Fortune* put it, in the Daniel Bell sense, meaning the trend toward the liberal ideology. And the third was the decline of the left wing in the labor movement generally. . . .

By the mid-1960s, the AFL-CIO was showing itself a good deal more adventurous and active in fighting communism abroad than it was in organizing unorganized workers in the U.S.A. But George Meany had always belonged to the more conservative wing of the movement. What is more surprising is that anti-communism became the shibboleth of the originally militant CIO wing to almost the same extent. At the time of the merger, Walter Reuther, the most radical and socially conscious labor leader of his generation, allowed the AFL to take the two top places in the new organization, confident that he would be the ultimate legatee of unity. Reuther had started on the left of the United Auto Workers. He was a socialist, and he spent a year in the Soviet Union in the early thirties. But when he finally emerged as the leader of the union, in the 1947 union elections, it was as the leader of the anti-communist faction, and his victory was generally reported, with approval, as "a swing to the Right." By 1948 Reuther was attacking leftist trade union officials as "colonial agents of a foreign government." At this same time, the future Supreme Court justice and member of the Johnson Cabinet Arthur Goldberg replaced the leftist Lee Pressman as general counsel of the CIO—an archetypal liberal, who was to end up defending the Vietnam War to the United Nations, replacing a man of the Left. It is striking how many of the most prominent liberals of the fifties and sixties—Reuther, Goldberg, Hubert Humphrey—first came to prominence by attacking not the Right but the Left.

"Though intellectuals have not created the labor movement," wrote Joseph Schumpeter, "they have worked it up into something that differs substantially from what it would have been without them." He was right. But in the fifties the role of the intellectual was not so much to radicalize the labor movement, as Schumpeter supposed, as to divert a considerable proportion of its energies and those of what would otherwise have been the American Left, from the feelings and needs of union members and the real though complex problems of American society to a crusade against communism.

It may be that this optimistic nationalism had a special appeal to intellectuals who were, in such notable proportion, themselves the second- and third-generation children of immigrants, inheritors of the dream. It may be that, like other Americans of the same generation, they felt a need to assimilate under the pressure of the great nativist rebellion that was McCarthyism, to prove themselves good Americans and better than the book burners.

Whatever the exact causes, the intellectual ballast shifted. In 1932 those who endorsed the Communist Party's candidate for President of the United States included Ernest Hemingway, John Dos Passos, James T. Farrell, Langston Hughes, Theodore Dreiser, Erskine Caldwell, Lincoln Steffens, Richard Wright, Katherine Anne Porter, Edmund Wilson, Nathanael West and Malcolm Cowley. Twenty years later, scarcely an intellectual with a shred of reputation could be found even to raise a voice against the outlawing of that same party. The change is measured, too, by the trajectory, in hardly more than a decade, of *Partisan Review,* the most admired highbrow periodical of the time, from dutiful Stalinism through Trotskyite heresy to the bleakest Cold War anti-communist orthodoxy.

Yet it is striking, in retrospect, how central to that supposedly apolitical culture anti-communism became. The formation of Americans for Democratic Action, excluding Communists, Arthur Schlesinger thought, marked "the watershed at which American liberalism began to base itself once again on a solid conception of man and of history." Of American history? No: for Schlesinger, liberalism had virtually been created by anti-communism, apparently. "The growing necessity of checking Communism," he wrote, "by developing some constructive alternative speeded the clarification of liberal ideas in 1947 and 1948."

After World War II, in almost every department of intellectual life, the doctrine of "American exceptionalism" revived. At the same time, utilitarian doctrines, stressing that morality in politics was an illusion, undercut the moralistic basis of left-wing politics. Sociology, history, economics, political science, even theology in the hands of Reinhold Neibuhr, for example, followed parallel paths, rejecting those who argued for radical change and emphasizing the virtues of "the American way."

What role remains for the men of the Left? Seymour Martin Lipset asked in *Political Man.* Not to advocate change in the society of his own country, if he lived in "the West." Even socialists must agree, Lipset thought, that complete socialism was dangerous and that Marxism was an outmoded doctrine.

Did it follow that the Left was totally obsolete? Lipset thought not. "The leftist intellectual, the trade union leader, and the socialist politician" could still make themselves useful—abroad, where society had not yet evolved to such a fortunate state of perfection as in the United States. Such disaffected persons, no longer required at home, could "communicate and work with non-Communist revolutionaries in the Orient and Africa at the same time that they accept the fact"—it sounds like a polite way of saying "on the condition that they accept the fact"—"that serious ideological controversies have ended at home."

In the culminating chapter, that is, of one of the most admired works of political science that the age of the liberal consensus produced, it was argued as a conclusion of high academic seriousness that the only use for dissenters from the liberal ideology was as its propagandists abroad. . . .

In the great American universities, the twenty years after World War II are beginning to be remembered with nostalgia as a Golden Age. Enrollments were multiplying. Endowments were accumulating. Funds from the federal and state governments and from private foundations were becoming available on a scale undreamed of. The salaries and the social status of professors were rising. They were certainly higher, both absolutely and in relation to those of the business world, than they had been since before World War I, and perhaps higher than they had ever been, at least for men sensible enough to have specialized in some useful subject that would earn them consultancy fees from large corporations, from government, or from the armed services. At a time when the U.S. Air Force was paying (through the RAND Corporation) for a sociological study of the toilet training of the French, even that qualification need not stand in the way of a man of imagination.

But the essential reason for the intellectual excitement that blossomed in the best American universities in the late fifties was neither academic influence nor increased competition. It came from the feeling that, for the first time, the academic world seemed thoroughly integrated into the life and purposes of the nation.

To begin with, this may have owed something to the achievement of the atomic scientists. When the mightiest arm of American power was the product of research science, it was hard to dismiss any research as impractical dreaming. Physicists, mathematicians, engineers, were among the first to be accepted by government. But the social scientists were not far behind. (Indeed, one branch of social science, economics, had long moved with assurance in the world of business as well as in Washington.) The earliest big government research contracts dealt with such "nuts-and-bolts" questions as the design of unmanned satellites or the nose cones of missiles. But as early as 1948 Nathan Leites was calling on the academic techniques of textual and literary criticism to describe "The Operational Code of Politburo." It was not long before sociologists, political scientists, even historians, were being called into service by the government—all of the social sciences received from the relationship an injection of adrenalin, as well as of money.

This was the broader context in which the system of thought I have called the liberal ideology was fitted together and came to predominate not only in the universities but in government and to some extent in politics. The interaction, however, was reciprocal. The intellectuals tended to be influential only in proportion as their ideas fitted in with the needs, fears or preconceptions of their new patrons. They tended to be forced into the role of technicians. The "hot" topics of specialization were those most immediately related to the government's most urgent perplexity, or at best to the tactics of its political opponents. Either way, that generally recommended those studies which assumed the permanence and the paramountcy of the Cold War.

"It is remarkable," wrote Henry Kissinger in 1962, "that during a decade of crisis few fundamental criticisms of American policy have been offered. We have not reached an impasse because the wrong alternative was chosen in a 'Great Debate.' The alternatives have rarely been properly defined." It was indeed remarkable. The Pentagon Papers are a sustained commentary on that observation. Yet it is strange that Henry Kissinger, the future virtuoso of the Carrot and the Stick, should find it hard to understand why the alternatives did not get defined. For if the fear of being investigated had shown the intellectuals the stick during the first half of the fifties, the hope of being consulted had shown them the carrot in the second. Alternatives were not what the government wanted. It wanted solutions. It expected to get them from men who displayed a maximum of technical ingenuity with a minimum of dissent.

The liberal ideology equipped the United States with an elaborately interrelated structure of coherent and plausible working assumptions, all poised like an inverted pyramid on two fundamental assumptions, both of which happened to be diametrically wrong.

American capitalism had not, it turned out, eliminated the possibility of serious social conflict at home. Nor was the most urgent danger to the nation from communism abroad. On the contrary, the United States stood on the eve of exceptional social turmoil.

Abroad, unified Communist power was breaking up, confronting the world with all the dangers of a period of fragmentation and "détente."

This error was to be pitilessly exposed, and that soon enough. Yet the effect of the liberal consensus was to be even more disastrous than the particular mistaken assumptions on which it was based. It condemned the United States to face the real dangers for too long without any fundamental debate. Thanks to the liberal triumph, the powerful emotions and interests that always work for conservative policies were not balanced by equally powerful forces and principles of the Left. Instead, they were opposed by a liberalism that was in effect hardly to be distinguished from a more sophisticated and less resolute conservatism.

The New Frontier in Space

John F. Kennedy

Campaigning for the presidency, John Kennedy insisted that it was time to get the country moving again. He expressed the "quest for national purpose" and new-found sense of crisis that marked the late 1950s and early 1960s. He promised to provide more vigorous leadership to the United States than Eisenhower had provided and upon entering the White House, Kennedy injected a new spirit into national affairs, a feeling that anything was possible.

In his acceptance speech at the Democratic nominating convention, Kennedy termed "uncharted areas of science and space" as part of "the New Frontier." In May 1961 he went before Congress to urge that the United States commit itself to land an American on the moon before the end of the decade. Note the emphasis on crisis and challenge in this excerpt and the connection between the space program and foreign policy. Note, too, the aspects of what Hodgson calls the "liberal consensus" contained in this speech. Although Kennedy's rhetoric was strikingly different than Eisenhower's, his programs were often similar. An assessment of the Kennedy presidency requires careful distinctions between style and substance.

The great battleground for the defense and expansion of freedom today is the whole southern half of the globe—Asia, Latin America, Africa and the Middle East—the lands of the rising peoples. Their revolution is the greatest in human history. They

From *Public Papers of the Presidents of the United States: John F. Kennedy,* 1961 (Washington, 1962), 396–398, 403–405.

seek an end to injustice, tyranny, and exploitation. More than an end, they seek a beginning.

And theirs is a revolution which we would support regardless of the Cold War, and regardless of which political or economic route they should choose to freedom.

For the adversaries of freedom did not create the revolution; nor did they create the conditions which compel it. But they are seeking to ride the crest of its wave—to capture it for themselves.

Yet their aggression is more often concealed than open. They have fired no missiles; and their troops are seldom seen. They send arms, agitators, aid, technicians and propaganda to every troubled area. But where fighting is required, it is usually done by others—by guerrillas striking at night, by assassins striking alone—assassins who have taken the lives of four thousand civil officers in the last twelve months in Vietnam alone—by subversives and saboteurs and insurrectionists, who in some cases control whole areas inside of independent nations.

With these formidable weapons, the adversaries of freedom plan to consolidate their territory—to exploit, to control, and finally to destroy the hopes of the world's newest nations; and they have ambition to do it before the end of this decade. It is a contest of will and purpose as well as force and violence—a battle for minds and souls as well as lives and territory. And in that contest, we cannot stand aside.

We stand, as we have always stood from our earliest beginnings, for the independence and equality of all nations. This nation was born of revolution and raised in freedom. And we do not intend to leave an open road for despotism.

There is no single simple policy which meets this challenge. Experience has taught us that no one nation has the power or the wisdom to solve all the problems of the world or manage its revolutionary tides—that extending our commitments does not always increase our security—that any initiative carries with it the risk of a temporary defeat—that nuclear weapons cannot prevent subversion—that no free people can be kept free without will and energy of their own—and that no two nations or situations are exactly alike.

Yet there is much we can do—and must do. The proposals I bring before you are numerous and varied. They arise from the host of special opportunities and dangers which have become increasingly clear in recent months. Taken together, I believe that they can mark another step forward in our effort as a people. I am here to ask the help of this Congress and the nation in approving these necessary measures. . . .

Finally, if we are to win the battle that is now going on around the world between freedom and tyranny, the dramatic achievements in space which occurred in recent weeks should have made clear to us all, as did the Sputnik in 1957, the impact of this adventure on the minds of men everywhere, who are attempting to make a determination of which road they should take. Since early in my term, our efforts in space have been under review. With the advice of the Vice President, who is Chairman of the National Space Council, we have examined where we are strong and where we are not, where we may succeed and where we may not. Now it is time to take longer strides—time for a great new American enterprise—time for this nation to take a clearly leading role in space achievement, which in many ways may hold the key to our future on earth.

I believe we possess all the resources and talents necessary. But the facts of the matter are that we have never made the national decisions or marshalled the national resources required for such leadership. We have never specified long-range goals on an urgent time schedule, or managed our resources and our time so as to insure their fulfillment.

Recognizing the head start obtained by the Soviets with their large rocket engines, which gives them many months of lead-time, and recognizing the likelihood that they will exploit this lead for some time to come in still more impressive successes, we nevertheless are required to make new efforts on our own. For while we cannot guarantee that we shall one day be first, we can guarantee that any failure to make this effort will make us last. We take an additional risk by making it in full view of the world, but as shown by the feat of astronaut Shepard, this very risk enhances our stature when we are successful. But this is not merely a race. Space is open to us now; and our eagerness to share its meaning is not governed by the efforts of others. We go into space because whatever mankind must undertake, free men must fully share.

I therefore ask the Congress, above and beyond the increases I have earlier requested for space activities, to provide the funds which are needed to meet the following national goals:

First, I believe that this nation should commit itself to achieving the goal before this decade is out, of landing a man on the moon and returning him safely to the earth. No single space project in this period will be more impressive to mankind, or more important for the long-range exploration of space; and none will be so difficult or expensive to accomplish. We propose to accelerate the development of the appropriate lunar space craft. We propose to develop alternate liquid and solid fuel boosters, much larger than any now being developed, until certain which is superior. We propose additional funds for other engine development and for unmanned explorations—explorations which are particuary important for one purpose which this nation will never overlook: the survival of the man who first makes this daring flight. But in a very real sense, it will not be one man going to the moon—if we make this judgment affirmatively, it will be an entire nation. For all of us must work to put him there. . . .

Let it be clear—and this is a judgment which the Members of the Congress must finally make—let it be clear that I am asking the Congress and the country to accept a firm commitment to a new course of action—a course which will last for many years and carry very heavy costs: 531 million dollars in fiscal '62—an estimated seven to nine billion dollars additional over the next five years. If we are to go only half way, or reduce our sights in the face of difficulty, in my judgment it would be better not to go at all. . . .

This decision demands a major national commitment of scientific and technical manpower, material and facilities, and the possibility of their diversion from other important activities where they are already thinly spread. It means a degree of dedication, organization and discipline which have not always characterized our research and development efforts. It means we cannot afford undue work stoppages, inflated costs of material or talent, wasteful interagency rivalries, or a high turnover of key personnel.

New objectives and new money cannot solve these problems. They could in fact, aggravate them further—unless every scientist, every engineer, every serviceman, every technician, contractor, and civil servant gives his personal pledge that this nation will move forward, with the full speed of freedom, in the exciting adventure of space. . . .

Johnson: Triumphant Liberalism

Frederick F. Siegel

Yearning desperately to be as great a president as his idol Franklin Roose-
velt, Lyndon Johnson succeeded in guiding through Congress the most
impressive array of domestic reforms since the New Deal. He sought to
achieve racial justice, to expand opportunities for medical care and educa-
tion, to control environmental abuses, to end poverty and urban blight—
indeed, to improve majestically the quality of American life and make the
United States a Great Society.

In this selection from Troubled Journey, *a fascinating interpretation*
of American politics as a running duel between the heirs and enemies of
the "Roosevelt Revolution," Frederick Siegel traces Johnson's legislative
and electoral successes. Yet his presidency, like Kennedy's, would be filled
with irony and tragedy, much of it rooted in Johnson's own actions. Uto-
pian hopes would be transformed into diminished expectations, and the
man who sought to be "President of all the people" would end his term
discredited and unable to seek reelection.

On November 22, 1963, in the same plane that carried the slain
chief executive's body back to Washington, Lyndon Baines Johnson was sworn in as the thirty-sixth President of the United States.
Lyndon Johnson was a Rabelaisian, larger-than-life figure. A tall
man from Texas, a state with a reputation for producing outsized
characters, Johnson had the face of a riverboat gambler and the

political skills of a master politician. He was only ten years older than Kennedy, but he came from a different generation and a different world. A product of Depression era poverty, Johnson's political views had been shaped in part by his political hero, Franklin Delano Roosevelt. Styling himself after FDR, Johnson liked to be called LBJ. If Kennedy had been born with a silver spoon in his mouth, Johnson grew up with the taste of dirt in his. He came from the desperately poor hill country of West Texas. "When I was young," Johnson told reporters, "poverty was so common that we didn't know it had a name."

A self-made man, Johnson fought his way to the top of the Texas political heap. A man of wildly conflicting impulses, he was driven on the one hand by greed and an unquenchable thirst for success and on the other by a genuine concern for the plight of those who had shared his childhood poverty. Johnson's Texas was a one-party state. The Democratic Party in Texas was a circus tent organization that included everyone from right to left, from business big and little to labor, blacks, and Mexican-Americans. The key to success in that situation was to create a consensus everyone could live with. Johnson became a master of using his extraordinary persuasive skills to engineer agreement between diverse interests. Elected to Congress in 1937, he made his mark bringing together within the Democratic Party rapacious nouveau riche Texas oil millionaires and conscious-striken Northern liberals whose political divisions paralleled those of his own vast personality. He was elected to the Senate in 1948 by the narrowest of margins, leading his detractors to joke about "Landslide Lyndon." But once there, he rose, with the support of his fellow Texan and mentor, Speaker of the House Sam Rayburn, to become Majority Leader of the Senate in 1955 after serving only one term.

Johnson became one of the most powerful and effective Majority Leaders the Hill has ever known. He was an overpowering figure with the psychic energy of a natural phenomenon. When a congressman was asked why he had changed his mind on a key vote, he answered: "Well, it's this way. Lyndon got me by the lapels and put his face on top of mine and talked and talked and talked. I figured it was either getting drowned or joining." Extremely intelligent without being an intellectual, he was a reader of men, not books. Johnson, as an English reporter described it, "comes into a room slowly and warily, as if he means to smell out the allegiances of everyone in it." He combined a rare ability to look inside his fellow politicians with a near-photographic memory for details, so that, as one aide put it, "not a sparrow falls on Capitol Hill" without LBJ knowing.

The Kennedy loyalists and intellectuals were among the few who seemed totally immune to his political sway. They viewed the roughhewn Johnson as a boor and a usurper, much as FDR's retinue looked down on the man from Missouri, Harry S. Truman. For the Kennedyites, brother Bobby was the true heir to the throne, so that the Johnson presidency was simply an unfortunate interregnum. Kennedy's intellectual camp followers were exhilarated by a president who brought taste to the White House and recognition for them. Enthralled by the magic of Camelot, "they received his words and images," said literary critic Alfred Kazin, "as children 'read' the pictures in a storybook." Johnson, on the other hand, reminded intellectuals of what the rest of the country was like." He reminded us of who we were—and some, said Richard Whalen, conceived their dislike of him in that moment.

For his part, Johnson brushed aside the snubs and moved quickly to calm the nation by proclaiming his intent to carry on Kennedy's noble mission. As powerful as he was, Johnson was somewhat in awe of his Ivy League advisers, something that worried Rayburn. After an obviously impressed Johnson recited the extraordinary academic credentials of his Cabinet, the Speaker snorted, "I just wish one of them had been elected anything, even deputy sheriff."

To prove he was worthy of the office and not just another parochial Southerner, Johnson moved quickly to push Kennedy's civil rights legislation, long blocked by his fellow Dixie politicians. As Johnson explained it: "If I didn't get out in front on this issue" the liberals "would get me . . . I had to produce a civil rights bill that was even stronger than the one they'd have gotten if Kennedy had lived." And produce he did. Defying all the writers, politicians, and analysts who spoke of the "deadlock of democracy," Johnson used his unparalleled skills to break the Southern filibuster. He pushed through Congress the most sweeping civil rights legislation since the end of the First Reconstruction. The 1964 Civil Rights Act, described by Supreme Court Justice Arthur Goldberg as "the vindication of human dignity," became the cornerstone of civil rights law. It provided legal and financial support for cities desegregating their schools, banned discrimination by businesses and unions, created an Equal Opportunities Commission to enforce that ban, and outlawed discrimination in places of public accommodation.

With the Civil Rights Act passed and his own legitimacy established, Johnson turned to putting his own stamp on the presidency. Declaring, "We are not helpless before the iron law of [traditional] economics," Johnson called for a "War on Poverty" as Kennedy had called for a war on communism.

The "War," wrote *Time* magazine, reflected the "uniquely American belief" that "evangelism, money and organization can lick just about anything." Americans generally believed that "a rising tide lifts all boats," but a spate of books on poverty, particularly Michael Harrington's powerful *The Other America*, showed that a substantial number of Americans, black and white, silently suffered from such serious deprivation that they would be unaided by the general prosperity. The very poor, argued anthropologist Oscar Lewis, were trapped in a culture of poverty, a culture which, in the words of Harrington, meant that "the poor are not like us. . . . They are a different kind of people."

Social science promised a way to reach the culturally distant world of severe poverty. On assuming the presidency Johnson inherited an economic growth rate that had more than doubled from 2.1 percent to 4.5 percent since 1960 and which, with mild inflation, was pouring extraordinary amounts of money into federal coffers. This "social surplus," the excess of revenues over expenditures, provided nearly four billion dollars a year for new public spending. The flow of money was so great the Governor Earl Long of Louisiana whimsically suggested massive spending for two highway systems, one reserved for drunks. Johnson's economic advisers assured him that the unprecedented surpluses would continue indefinitely. Pointing to the great success of the 1964 tax cut, which seemed to demonstrate their ability to put their theories into practice, the "new" economists claimed that, through Keynesian "demand management," they had discovered the secret of constant noninflationary growth. In short, the continuing surplus created by "demand management" meant that poverty could be abolished without undue sacrifice from the rest of the population. There would be a "maximum of reform with a minimum of social disruption."

While the economists were guiding the fiscal ship of state, their fellow experts, the sociologists, devised programs to provide the poor with nutritional aid, health and schooling benefits, job training, and even dignity and respect. The programs were institutionalized as part of Johnson's Economic Opportunity Act of 1964. The act appropriated nearly a billion dollars for projects such as the Head Start program to assist disadvantaged preschoolers, the Job Corps for high school dropouts, a domestic Peace Corps— Volunteers in Service to America (VISTA)—a Neighborhood Youth Corps, and a Community Action Program designed for the "maximum feasible participation" by the poor it was meant to aid.

Flushed by his legislative successes, LBJ headed into the 1964 presidential campaign by asking for even broader social measures as part of what he called "The Great Society." Like Kennedy's New Frontier, the Great Society was a presidential answer to the quest for national and thus in many cases individual purpose in an increasingly secular age. It was to be the fulfillment of the American creed of equal opportunity—a grand mobilization of expertise, this time to fight poverty and disease, as depression, fascism, and communism had been fought previously. In LBJ's own inspiring words: "This nation . . . has man's first chance to create a Great Society: a society of success without squalor, beauty without barrenness, of genius without the wretchedness of poverty. We can open the doors of learning. We can open the doors of opportunity and closed community—not just to the privileged few, but, thank God, we can open doors to everyone." Rhetoric (glorious though it was) aside, Johnson's proposals for a Great Society hinged on passing a twenty-five-year backlog of liberal Democratic legislation on health, education, racial discrimination, and conservation that had been sitting on the rear burner every since the New Deal flame was snuffed out by the Republican/Dixiecrat coalition in 1937.

The Great Society program, which vested vast new powers in the federal government, promised to rearrange the relationship between Washington and the rest of the nation. For American liberals the growth of federal power meant the chance to complete the racial reforms begun by Reconstruction and the economic reforms begun by the New Deal without a fundamental restructuring of American society. But for many others, those who "understood the American creed, not as a common set of national values, but as a justification for their particular set of local values," the Great Society proved to be deeply unsettling. Their fears, however, were never fully aired, nor was Johnson given the chance to build a national consensus for the Great Society, because Barry Goldwater, his opponent in 1964, gave LBJ the enormous advantage of running as a social reformer while still seeming to be the less radical of the two.

Johnson's Republican opposition came from a group of youth activists deeply opposed to American policies in Vietnam and bitterly hostile to what they called the "Establishment," symbolized by Nelson Rockefeller. Their movement was directed by Stephen Shadeg, who had been heavily influenced by the thought and tactics of Chairman Mao. Their candidate, described by conservative William Buckley as one of "the few genuine radicals in American life," was Barry Morris Goldwater, junior senator from Arizona.

The Goldwater movement was built on the strength of the old Taftite right, the "veterans of the thirty years' war with the New Deal." Like Taft, Goldwater would say, "Yes, I fear Washington, more than I fear Moscow." But most of all Goldwater feared what he saw as Moscow's influence in Washington, so that as a first-term senator he was one of the diehards who opposed the censure of McCarthy after almost the entire Senate had turned against the demagogue from Wisconsin. The old right had been repeatedly defeated, in its struggle to control the Republican Party, by what it called the Eastern establishment, otherwise known as the "two-bit New Dealers" or "me-too Republicans." But in 1964 the Goldwater movement defeated the Rockefeller Republicans by mobilizing two new political elements: nouveau riche anti-union oilmen and aerospace men of the Southwest, and ideologically charged conservative youth.

Like their left-wing counterparts, these young conservatives disdained the soft society of welfarism with all its compromises and government paternalism. They complained of a "sickness in our society and the lack of a common purpose" that might "restore inner meaning to every man's life in a time too often rushed, too often obsessed with petty needs and material greeds." Contemptuous of businessmen who placed profit before free market ethics, they dreamed of a world made whole by the heroic deeds of rugged individuals untrammeled by the heavy hand of the state. Their allies, the Texas oilmen and aerospace entrepreneurs, however, were beneficiaries of vast government subsidies such as the oil-depletion allowance. But both were united in their hostility to the Rockfeller wing of the Republican Party. And both subscribed to the notion that only a laissez-faire economy could create the disciplined individuals with the character and fortitude necessary to sustain democracy. Politics for the activists was not so much a matter of pursuing material interests as a national screen on which to project their deepest cultural fears. They were part of a mood, a mood of deluxe puritanism, as much as an ideology, and in the words of Richard Whalen, "Barry Goldwater was the favorite son of their state of mind."

But even with his activists and oilmen, Goldwater, like Taft before him, might have lost the nomination if it hadn't been for the first nationwide stirrings of a white backlash against the civil rights movement. Interest in Goldwater was flagging when Alabama's Governor George Wallace, a flaming segregationist, made a surprising showing in liberal Wisconsin's Democratic primary. The Wallace showing revived interest in Goldwater, who was seen as the Republican most opposed to federal intervention on behalf of Afro-Americans. When Goldwater was nominated, Wallace's candidacy collapsed, suggesting a considerable overlap in the two men's donors and constituencies. Tall, trim, and handsome, the altogether affable Goldwater was not personally a bigot. A member of the NAACP, Goldwater was the kind of terribly sincere fellow everyone like to have for a neighbor or fraternity brother. He came to popular attention by spearheading congressional criticism of Walter Reuther and by his outspoken calls for a holy crusade against communism in general and Castro in particular. But as Goldwater told reporter Joseph Alsop: "You know, I haven't really got a first-class brain." And it showed. His combination of bland and outrageous statements alienated all but the right wing of the Republican Party from his candidacy. He could in the same speech assert that "where fraternities are not allowed, Communism flourishes" and then, warming to his message, suggest that nuclear weapons be used against Cuba, China, and North Vietnam if they refused to accede to American demands. Goldwater was unafraid of voicing unpopular views. He called from the abolition of the TVA, an end to the graduated income tax, and the elimination of Social Security, while campaigning forth-rightly for the elimination of the union shop. "My aim," he said, "is not to pass laws but to repeal them." Here, in the words of Phyllis Schlafly, was "a choice and not an echo."

There was really no need for Johnson to criticize Goldwater's campaign for being too radical. Goldwater did it for him, proclaiming on national TV that "extremism in the defense of liberty is no vice." When the Goldwaterites adopted the slogan "In your hearts you know he's right," Democrats responded with "In your guts you know he's nuts." Johnson replied to Goldwater's "no substitute for victory" rhetoric on Vietnam with a proclamation of restraint. "We are not," LBJ told the American people, "about to send American boys nine or ten thousand miles from home to do what Asian boys ought to be doing for themselves." It is a virtual replay of the Truman-MacArthur struggle, with the same outcome.

With the successful focusing of the campaign on Goldwater's artless "shoot from the lip" pronouncements—"The child has no right to an education; in most cases he will get along very well without it"—Johnson's own measures at home and abroad went undebated. It was a curious consequence of the 1964 campaign that the fundamental issues raised by both Johnson's social innovations and Goldwater's ideological thrust went almost unnoticed, producing a curiously empty campaign which ironically denied Johnson the opportunity to build support for the Great Society. The consensus that emerged instead was that Barry Goldwater was unfit for office. The reaction to Goldwater was so broadly negative that the party which once denounced "economic royalists" now found Wall Street and big business flocking to its banner. Johnson attracted the nation's corporate elite in creating what Oscar Gass has called a Grossblock, a coalition of upper-middle-class professionals and lower-middle-class blue-collar workers, big business and labor, Catholics and Protestants, blacks and whites outside the Deep South, in a national replication of the Texas Democratic Party's "one big tent."

LBJ swept to victory with 61 percent of the vote, only 5 points short of doubling Goldwater's total. The Democrats gained 2 seats in the Senate and 37 in the House, creating enormous Democratic majorities.

LBJ's victory was so overwhelming that commentators openly

speculated about the impending death of both conservatism and the Republican Party. We are left, said one observer, with a "one and a half party system." But an analysis of local voting patterns revealed something very different. On a host of social issues, ranging from prayer in the public schools to calls for cutting federal expenditures and reducing welfare spending, the electorate was far closer to Goldwater than to Johnson. Goldwater the candidate was repudiated, but on a local level conservatism was intact and even thriving. In California, for instance, areas which went strongly for LBJ also voted to repeal the state's anti-discriminatory fair housing laws by a better than two-to-one margin. Similarly, in Maryland, areas which had supported George Wallace when he made his strong showing in the Democratic primary there went overwhelmingly for LBJ in the general election. These Maryland voters were in favor of the civil rights bill even as they feared black militancy.

Goldwater's defeat was of such proportion that ironically it served to break the hold conservative Democrats held over their own party. So many Northern liberals triumphed in congressional races against Republicans "dragged down by Barry" that for the first time the Democrats had clear majorities in both houses without having to rely on their Dixiecrat allies. On the other hand, Goldwater, by piggybacking his right-to-work rhetoric on George Wallace's states' rights racism, had carried the Deep South, breaking the Democrats' century-long hold over that region. And while the Goldwater campaign rhetoric was most noted for its fire-eating foreign policy, it was Goldwater's appeal to the white backlash against black militancy that had garnered most of his votes North and South.

Lyndon Johnson was keenly aware that the American political system's balance of powers had been designed for stalemate. As a young congressman, he had seen FDR, at the height of his power, humbled when he tried to pack the Supreme Court. Johnson realized that unless he moved quickly to take advantage of his landslide victory, the naturally parochial tendencies of the Congress would block his Great Society initiatives. Johnson moved rapidly to circumvent the established interests in Congress. Instead of asking congressmen for legislative proposals, he organized task forces composed of administration aides and social reform academics to draw up legislation which would then be presented to the sachems as a fait accompli. Or as LBJ put it to his aides, "I want to see a whole bunch of coonskins on the wall."

The programs Johnson deemed most important were Medicare to protect the elderly from catastrophic losses and aid to elementary education to upgrade the schooling for both black and white poor. Legislation for Medicare and aid to elementary education had been proposed by Democrats every since the mid-1940s but had always met fierce opposition from the American Medical Association and proponents of states' rights. Johnson knew that if he won on these two issues, "the momentum," as historian Jim Heath has put it, "would carry over, making it relatively easy to enact the rest of his legislative program." As before, the powerful AMA put up a tenacious fight against any form of federally guaranteed health insurance for the elderly, portraying it as a step on the road to socialized medicine. But Johnson, aided by the wily Wilbur Mills, of the House Ways and Means Committee, not only got Medicare passed; in a little-noticed maneuver, Medicaid, health care for the indigent, was tacked on. LBJ flew to Independence, Missouri, to sign the bill in front of a smiling Harry S. Truman. On January 12, 1965, only five days after the Medicare legislation was approved, LBJ sent the politically explosive aid to elementary education bill to the Congress. Part and parcel of the War on Poverty, the bill was opposed by Protestant fundamentalists who wanted to deny federal money to the Catholic schools and by segregationists who saw Washington's money as the beginning of federal control over local schools. Here Johnson, aided by Senator Wayne Morse, achieved what the senator called a "back-door victory," by overtly ignoring racial and religious questions in order to target money regionally on the basis of population below the poverty level in a given area.

With Medicare and aid to education passed, Johnson moved quickly to complete what critics called his "revolution from above." If the word "revolution" was overblown, the critics were right to see that LBJ made unprecedented use of the federal budget. "No previous budget had ever been so contrived to do something for every major economic interest in the nation." But LBJ offered something for almost all his supporters: tax cuts for big business; billions of dollars for Appalachian social and economic development; the first major additions to our national

parks and the first comprehensive air and water pollution standards for environmentalists; truth in packaging legislation for
consumers; federal aid for mass transit for city dwellers; a subsidy
boost for farmers; a National Arts and Humanities Foundation
for academics; and, in LBJ's own words, "the goddamnedest
toughest voting rights act" and Model Cities, low-cost housing,
job-training programs, and slum clearance for blacks. At the end
of this spate of legislation, the Democratic leadership on the Hill
spoke jubilantly of the "fabulous 89th" Congress as "the Congress
of fulfillment," "the Congress of accomplished hopes," "the Congress of realized dreams."

In the words of liberal policy analyst Sar Levitan, a great deal
of LBJ's agenda involved "unabashedly class legislation. . . . desig-
nating a special group in the population as eligible to receive the
benefits of American law." Class legislation was nothing new in
American politics—federal insurance for overseas corporate investments and the mortgage tax deduction for homeowners are
examples. What was different about the Great Society was that it
extended such special benefits to those who were least well off.
Johnson's left-wing critics complained that in order to aid the
poor, his legislation provided a windfall for a multitude of contractors and middlemen who ultimately were the greatest beneficiaries. There is a good deal of truth to this charge. The doctors
who fought Medicare so bitterly were to number among its prime
beneficiaries. Building contractors often became wealthy through
Model Cities renewal efforts. This said, however, it is unlikely that
any of the legislation directed at alleviating poverty could have
passed a Congress composed of men representing American business and middle-class interests unless they too were cut in on
federal largess.

Johnson, the adventurous conservative, was denounced as a
"Red" by fiscal conservatives and simply a pork-barrel New Dealer
by leftists, but both charges were wide of the mark. The New Deal
was designed to aid widows, orphans, and the indigent; in short, it
represented help for those worst off without addressing the underlying issues of social fairness. The Great Society, without being
socialist, tried to partially redefine the structure of opportunity in
America. Its aim was not simply to provide handouts to the poor;
rather, it attempted to make the competitive race of life a bit
fairer. The Great Society had a dramatic effect in relieving pov-

erty. From 1964 to 1968 more than 14 million Americans moved out of poverty as the proportion of the impoverished was halved from 22 to 11 percent of the nation. Just as FDR's New Deal had incorporated working-class immigrants and organized them into the mainstream of American life, LBJ's Great Society tried to do the same for blacks and the poverty-stricken.

The Great Society

Lyndon B. Johnson

Suddenly elevated to the presidency on November 22, 1963, Lyndon Baines Johnson sought to use his tremendous powers to impose his personal stamp on national politics and to secure his place in history's pantheon. From the start, he repeatedly assured the American people that "we have the power to shape the civilization that we want." He desired to fulfill the promises of the New Deal, and much more. Johnson stressed that the Great Society "asks not only how much, but how good; not only how to create wealth, but how to use it. It proposes as the first test for a nation: the quality of its people." In May 1964, he spelled out his tenets of "qualitative liberalism" in an address at the University of Michigan reprinted below.

Congress granted most of his far-reaching legislative requests in the next two years, but then the intensifying war in Vietnam undermined the liberal climate of opinion and caused cuts in domestic spending. The Great Society could not survive. Ironically, the President who aimed to promote harmony by concentrating on domestic reform became thoroughly preoccupied with foreign affairs and greatly increased social tension and conflict by promising more than he could deliver. As an index of change, one might consider how the current president would define the Great Society and how his priorities would differ from Johnson's.

. . . For a century we labored to settle and to subdue a continent. For half a century we called upon unbounded invention and untiring industry to create an order of plenty for all of our people.

From *Public Papers of the Presidents of the United States: Lyndon B. Johnson* (Washington, D.C., 1965), I (1963–64), 704–7.

The challenge of the next half century is whether we have the wisdom to use that wealth to enrich and elevate our national life, and to advance the quality of our American civilization.

Your imagination, your initiative, and your indignation will determine whether we build a society where progress is the servant of our needs, or a society where old values and new visions are buried under unbridled growth. For in your time we have the opportunity to move not only toward the rich society and the powerful society, but upward to the Great Society.

The Great Society rests on abundance and liberty for all. It demands an end to poverty and racial injustice, to which we are totally committed in our time. But that is just the beginning.

The Great Society is a place where every child can find knowledge to enrich his mind and to enlarge his talents. It is a place where leisure is a welcome chance to build and reflect, not a feared cause of boredom and restlessness. It is a place where the city of man serves not only the needs of the body and the demands of commerce but the desire for beauty and the hunger for community.

It is a place where man can renew contact with nature. It is a place which honors creation for its own sake and for what it adds to the understanding of the race. It is a place where men are more concerned with the quality of their goals than the quantity of their goods.

But most of all, the Great Society is not a safe harbor, a resting place, a final objective, a finished work. It is a challenge constantly renewed, beckoning us toward a destiny where the meaning of our lives matches the marvelous products of our labor.

Aristotle said: "Men come together in cities in order to live, but they remain together in order to live the good life." It is harder and harder to live the good life in American cities today.

The catalogue of ills is long: there is the decay of the centers and the despoiling of the suburbs. There is not enough housing for our people or transportation for our traffic. Open land is vanishing and old landmarks are violated.

Worst of all expansion is eroding the precious and time-honored values of community with neighbors and communion with nature. The loss of these values breeds loneliness and boredom and indifference.

Our society will never be great until our cities are great. Today the frontier of imagination and innovation is inside those cities and not beyond their borders.

A second place where we begin to build the Great Society is in our countryside. We have always prided ourselves on being not only America the strong and America the free, but America the beautiful. Today that beauty is in danger. The water we drink, the food we eat, the very air that we breathe, are threatened with pollution. Our parks are overcrowded, our seashores over-burdened. Green fields and dense forests are disappearing.

A third place to build the Great Society is in the classrooms of America. There your children's lives will be shaped. Our society will not be great until every young mind is set free to scan the farthest reaches of thought and imagination. We are still far from that goal.

In many places, classrooms are overcrowded and curricula are outdated. Most of our qualified teachers are underpaid, and many of our paid teachers are unqualified. So we must give every child a place to sit and a teacher to learn from. Poverty must not be a bar to learning, and learning must offer an escape from poverty.

But more classrooms and more teachers are not enough. We must seek an educational system which grows in excellence as it grows in size. This means better training for our teachers. It means preparing youth to enjoy their hours of leisure as well as their hours of labor. It means exploring new techniques of teaching, to find new ways to stimulate the love of learning and the capacity for creation.

For better or for worse, your generation has been appointed by history to deal with those problems and to lead America toward a new age. You have the chance never before afforded to any people in any age. You can help build a society where the demands of morality, and the needs of the spirit, can be realized in the life of the nation.

So, will you join in the battle to give every citizen the full equality which God enjoins and the law requires, whatever his belief, or race, or the color of his skin?

Will you join in the battle to give every citizen an escape from the crushing weight of poverty?

Will you join in the battle to make it possible for all nations to live in enduring peace—as neighbors and not as mortal enemies?

Will you join in the battle to build the Great Society, to prove that our material progress is only the foundation on which we will build a richer life of mind and spirit?

There are those timid souls who say this battle cannot be won; that we are condemned to a soulless wealth. I do not agree. We have the power to shape the civilization that we want. But we need your will, your labor, your hearts, if we are to build that kind of society.

So let us from this moment begin our work so that in the future men will look back and say: It was then, after a long and weary way, that man turned the exploits of his genius to the full enrichment of his life.

Part Four

THE BLACK STRUGGLE

No domestic development has been more important to postwar American society than the struggle for racial equality. During the three quarters of a century after the end of Reconstruction, little occurred to improve the status of Afro-Americans. The vast majority lived in the South, were denied the right to vote, suffered the overt and covert consequences of segregation, experienced dire poverty, and were subject—at virtually every moment—to the threat of physical intimidation and violence. Through most of that time, black Americans strove to build the best schools, churches, and homes they could for their children and themselves. Yet in an environment shaped and defined by white supremacy, the possibilities of substantial change were minimal.

The modern civil rights struggle received a major impetus from the New Deal and World War II. Hundreds of thousands of blacks left the rural south to take new jobs that were opening up in the north, the west, and urban areas of the south. The number of blacks in labor unions doubled, some economic improvements occurred, and in the north especially there was the opportunity for political participation. On the other hand, both the New Deal and the war witnessed callous indifference toward racial sensibilities, the perpetuation of Jim Crow, and vicious forms of racism. Black soldiers were not allowed to fight beside white soldiers, black blood supplies were segregated from white blood supplies, and black soldiers in southern training camps were subject to the brutality of southern white racism. Together, the New Deal and Second World War brought some progress, but in a context of continued and pervasive discrimination. The combination spurred black anger and frustration, helping to galvanize a new mood of protest.

In the face of evergrowing black militancy, liberal Democrats and Republicans began to pay more attention to the issue of civil rights. Through much of the postwar era the major theme of race relations in America was the gap between promises of change and the reality of continued oppression. When blacks protested, whites responded with words of concern and promises of change. There then would follow years of inaction until black protest initiated the cycle once more. By the 1960s, it had become evident that only when blacks forced white institutions into action could any substantive change be anticipated.

There are two general interpretations of the developments in race relations since World War II. One emphasizes the importance of external and impersonal factors such as migration, economic progress, a shift in government policies, and the emergence of an environment more conducive toward racial justice. The second interpretation focuses more on the collective demand of black Americans themselves for change, stressing the critical role of black protest in bringing about whatever progress has taken place. The first interpretation accentuates the role of objective and external forces; the second highlights the role of individual and collective activism. Both sources of change are clearly important, and, in most cases, only when the two complement each other does significant progress occur.

The following selections provide the basis for an assessment of the black struggle during the postwar period. Harvard Sitkoff analyzes the consequences of some of the structural changes in the economy, social values and intellectual attitudes, the law and national politics. Vincent Harding offers both a personal and historical judgment of Martin Luther King, Jr.'s role in the movement. King himself shows the powerful impact of religion in the black struggle in his "Letter from a Birmingham Jail," while Stokely Carmichael brings a first-person perspective to the emergence of black power. Clayborne Carson assesses the significance of black power ten years after its emergence.

Many questions emerge from these readings: Has the black struggle really brought significant change in race relations? Was black power a repudiation of, or an extension of the civil rights movement? Could America have progressed further and faster than it did, or were the conflicts of the 1960s necessary before significant change could take place? Racial equality remains one of the primary issues on America's national agenda, and these as well as other questions, are crucial to understanding how we have gotten to where we are, and where we need to go.

The Preconditions for Racial Change

Harvard Sitkoff

Although McCarthyism and the ideology of consensus did much to mute black discontent in the first postwar decade, the black quest for justice and equality steadily grew more determined and insistent following the 1954 landmark decision of the Supreme Court in Brown v. Board of Education of Topeka. *In short order, thousands of black families withstood harassment, economic intimidation, and violence to desegregate their local schools; the mass of blacks in Montgomery, Alabama, boycotted city buses for 381 days to topple Jim Crow; and, in 1960, black college students in Greensboro, North Carolina, "sat in" at a white lunch counter and set off a wave of similar challenges to the Southern caste system. But the ruling that "separate educational facilities are inherently unequal," according to Harvard Sitkoff, did not start the modern black freedom struggle. This movement, he contends, stemmed from the basic socioeconomic changes in American society set in motion by the New Deal and, especially, World War II. These structural developments set the stage for black activism and made possible far-reaching racial changes in national policies and legislation.*

Of the interrelated causes of progress in race relations since the start of the Great Depression, none was more important than the changes in the American economy. No facet of the race problem

Excerpted and revised from Harvard Sitkoff, "Race Relations: Progress and Prospects," in James T. Patterson, ed. *Paths to the Present* (Minneapolis: Burgess Publishing Co., 1975). Reprinted by Permission of the Author.

was untouched by the elephantine growth of the Gross National Product, which rose from $206 billion in 1940 to $500 billion in 1960, and then in the 1960s increased by an additional 60 percent. By 1970, the economy topped the trillion dollar mark. This spectacular rate of economic growth produced some 25 million new jobs in the quarter of a century after World War II and raised real wage earnings by at least 50 percent. It made possible the increasing income of blacks; their entry into industries and labor unions previously closed to them; gains for blacks in occupational status; and created a shortage of workers that necessitated a slackening of restrictive promotion policies and the introduction of scores of government and private industry special job training programs for Afro-Americans. It also meant that the economic progress of blacks did not have to come at the expense of whites, thus undermining the most powerful source of white resistance to the advancement of blacks.

The effect of economic changes on race relations was particularly marked in the South. The rapid industrialization of the South since 1940 ended the dominance of the cotton culture. With its demise went the need for a vast underclass of unskilled, subjugated laborers. Power shifted from rural areas to the cities, and from tradition-oriented landed families to the new officers and professional workers in absentee-owned corporations. The latter had neither the historical allegiances nor the nonrational attachment to racial mores to risk economic growth for the sake of tradition. The old system of race relations had no place in the new economic order. Time and again in the 1950s and 1960s, the industrial and business elite took the lead in accommodating the South to the changes sought by the civil rights movement.

The existence of an "affluent society" boosted the fortunes of the civil rights movement itself in countless ways. Most obviously, it enabled millions of dollars in contributions from wealthy liberals and philanthropic organizations to pour into the coffers of the NAACP, Urban League, Southern Christian Leadership Conference, and countless other civil rights groups. Without those funds it is difficult to comprehend how the movement could have accomplished those tasks so essential to its success: legislative lobbying and court litigation; nationwide speaking tours and the daily mailings of press releases all over the country; the organization of mass marches, demonstrations, and rallies; constant, rapid communication and traveling over long distances; and the convocation of innumerable public conferences and private strategy sessions.

Prosperity also increased the leisure time of many Americans and enabled them to react immediately to the changing times. The sons and daughters of the newly affluent increasingly went to college. By 1970, five times as many students were in college as in 1940. What they learned helped lead to pronounced changes in white attitudes toward racial discrimination and segregation. Other whites learned from the TV sets in their homes. By the time Lyndon Johnson signed the Voting Rights Act of 1965, some 95 percent of all American families owned at least one television. The race problem entered their living rooms. Tens of millions nightly watched the drama of the Negro Revolution. The growing majority of Americans favoring racial equality and justice had those sentiments reinforced by TV shots of snarling police dogs attacking black demonstrators, rowdy white hoods molesting young blacks patiently waiting to be served at a lunch counter, and hate-filled white faces in a frenzy because of the effrontery of little black children entering a previously all-white school.

Blacks viewed the same scenes on their TV sets, and the rage these scenes engendered helped transform isolated battles into a national campaign. Concurrently, the conspicuous display of white affluence on TV vividly awakened blacks to a new sense of their relative deprivation. That, too, aroused black anger. And now something could be done about it. The growing black middle and working classes put their money and bodies on the line. In addition, because the consumer economy depended on consumer purchasing, black demands had to be taken seriously. By 1970, black buying power topped $25 billion, a large enough sum to make the threat of boycotts an effective weapon for social change. Afro-American economic advances also made blacks less patient in demanding alterations in their social status. They desired all the decencies and dignity they believed their full paycheck promised. Lastly, nationwide prosperity contributed to more blacks entering college, which stimulated higher expectations and a heightened confidence that American society need not be static.

Most importantly, changes in the economy radically affected black migration. Cotton mechanization pushed blacks off the farms, and the lure of jobs pulled them to the cities. In 1930, three-quarters of the Afro-Americans lived in or near the rural black belt. By 1973, over half the blacks lived outside the South, and nationally, nearly 80 percent resided in urban areas. Indeed, in the two decades prior to 1970, the black population in metropolitan areas rose by more than seven million—a number greater than the total immigration by any single nationality group in American history. Such a mass migration, in conjunction with prosperity, fundamentally altered the whole configuration of the race problem. First, the issue of race became national in scope. No longer did it affect only one region, and no longer could it be left in the hands of Southern whites. Second, it modified the objective conditions of life for blacks and changed their perception of what was right and how to get it. For the first time in American history the great mass of blacks were freed from the confines of a rigid caste structure. Now subject to new formative experiences, blacks developed new norms and beliefs. In the relative anonymity and freedom of the North and the big city, aggression could be turned against one's oppressor rather than against one's self; more educational and employment opportunities could be secured; and political power could be mobilized. Similarly, as expectations of racial equality increased with the size of black migration from the rural South, so the religious faith that had for so long sustained Afro-Americans working on plantations declined. The promise of a better world in the next one could not suffice. The urban black would not wait for his rewards until the afterlife.

Because blacks could vote in the North, they stopped believing they would have to wait. Enfranchisement promised all in this life that religion did in the next. The heavenly city, to put it mildly, was not achieved; but vital legislative and legal accomplishments did flow from the growing black vote. Without the presence of black political power in the North, the demonstrations in the South would not have led to the civil rights laws and presidential actions necessary to realize the objectives of those protesting against Jim Crow in Montgomery, Greensboro, Birmingham, Jackson, and Selma. Although the claim of black publicists that the concentration of Northern black votes in the industrial cities made the Afro-American electorate a "balance of power" in national politics was never wholly accepted by either major party, the desire of every president from Franklin Roosevelt to Lyndon Johnson to win and hold the black vote became a factor in determining public policy. And as the Democratic party became less dependent upon Southern electoral votes, and less able to garner them, it had to champion civil rights more in order to win the populous states of the North and Midwest where blacks were increasingly becoming an indispensable component of the liberal coalition.

The prominence of the United States as a world power further pushed politicians into making race relations a matter of national concern. During World War II millions of Americans became aware for the first time of the danger of racism to national security. The costs of racism went even higher during the Cold War. The Soviet Union continuously undercut American appeals to the nations of Africa and Asia by publicizing American ill-treatment of blacks. As the competition between the United States and international Communism intensified, foreign-policy makers came to recognize racism as the American's own worst enemy. President Harry Truman justified his asking Congress for civil rights legislation squarely on the world-wide implications of American race relations. Rarely in the next twenty years did a plea for civil rights before the Supreme Court, on the floor of Congress, and emanating from the White House, fail to emphasize that point. In short, fear forced the nation to hasten the redefining of the black status. The more involved in world affairs the United States became, the more imperative grew the task of setting its racial affairs in order.

The rapid growth of nationalistic independence movements among the world's colored peoples had special significance for Afro-Americans. In 1960 alone, sixteen African nations emerged from under white colonial rule. Each proclamation of independence in part shamed blacks in the United States to intensify their struggle for equality and justice, and in part caused a surge of racial pride in Afro-Americans, an affirmation of blackness. The experience of African independence proved . the feasibility of change and the vulnerability of white supremacy, while at the same time aiding Afro-Americans to see themselves as members of a world majority rather than as just a hopelessly outnumbered American minority.

The decline in intellectual respectability of ideas used to justify segregation and discrimination similarly provided Afro-Americans with new weapons and shields. The excesses of Nazism and the decline of Western imperialism combined with internal developments in the academic disciplines of anthropology, biology, history, psychology, and sociology to discredit notions of inherent racial differences or predispositions. First in the 1930s, then with accelerating rapidity during World War II and every year thereafter, books and essays attacking racial injustice and inequality rolled off the presses. As early as 1944, Gunnar Myrdal in his monumental *An American Dilemma* termed the pronounced change in scholarship about race "the most important of all social trends in the field of interracial relations." This conclusion overstated the power of the word, but undoubtedly the mountain of new data, theory, and exposition at least helped to erode the pseudo-scientific rationalizations once popularly accepted as the basis for white supremacy.

In such an atmosphere, young blacks could mature without "the mark of oppression." Blacks could safely abandon the "nigger" role. To the extent that textbooks, sermons, declarations by governmental officials, advertising, and movies and TV affirmed the need to transform relationships between the races and to support black demands for full citizenship, blacks could confidently and openly rebel against the inequities they viewed as the sources of their oppression. They could publicly express the rage their parents had been forced to internalize; they could battle for what they deemed their birthright rather than wage war against themselves. Thus, in conjunction with the migration to cities, these new cultural processes helped to produce the "New Negro" hailed by essayists ever since the Montgomery bus boycott in 1956 inaugurated a more aggressive stage in the Afro-American's quest for equality.

In sum, changes in the American economy after 1940 set in motion a host of developments which made possible a transformation in race relations. The increasing income and number of jobs available to blacks and whites, and black migration and social mobility, coalesced with converging trends in politics, foreign affairs, and the mass media to endow those intent on improving race relations with both the resources and consciousness necessary to challenge the status quo. Objective conditions that had little to do with race in a primary sense thus created a context in which organizations and leaders could press successfully for racial changes. This is not to suggest that individuals do not matter in history or that the civil rights movement did not make an indispensable contribution to progress in race relations. It is, however, to emphasize the preconditions for such an endeavor to prevail. Desire and will are not enough. Significant and long-lasting alterations in society flow neither from the barrel of a gun nor from individual conversions. Mass marches, demonstrations, and rhetoric alone cannot modify entrenched behavior and values. Fundamental social change is accomplished only when individuals seize the moment to mobilize the latent power inherent in an institutional structure in flux.

Beginning in the 1930s, blacks, no longer facing a monolithic white power structure solidly arrayed against them, demanded with numbers and a unity that had never existed before the total elimination of racial inequality in American life. For three decades, the tactics and goals of the movement steadily grew more militant as the organization, protests, and power of blacks jumped exponentially. Each small triumph held out the promise of a greater one, heightening expectations and causing blacks to become ever more anxious about the pace of progress.

The first stage centered on securing the enforcement of the Fourteenth and Fifteenth Amendments. Supported mainly by white liberals and upper-middle-class blacks, the civil rights movement in the 1930s and 1940s relied on publicity, agitation, litigation in the courts, and lobbying in the halls of political power to gain the full inclusion of blacks in American life. Advances came in the legal and economic status of blacks, and in the minor social, political, and cultural concessions afforded Afro-Americans in the North, but the all-oppressive system of Jim Crow in the South remained virtually intact.

First in the court system, then in executive actions, and finally in Congress, this unceasing and mounting pressure from the civil rights movement prodded the government consistently in the direction of *real* racial equality. In the 1930s, the black movement failed to secure its two major legislative goals—anti-poll tax and anti-lynching laws—but it did manage to get Franklin D. Roosevelt and other members of his official family to speak on behalf of racial justice, to increase the numbers of blacks in government, to establish a Civil Rights Section in the Justice Department, and to ensure blacks a share of the relief and recovery assistance.

The gains during the New Deal, however, functioned primarily

as a prelude to the take-off of the civil rights movement during
World War II. The ideological character of the war and the government's need for the loyalty and manpower of all Americans
stimulated blacks to expect a better deal from the government;
this led to a militancy never before seen in black communities.
Membership in the NAACP multiplied nearly ten times; the Congress of Racial Equality, organized in 1942, experimented with
various forms of nonviolent direct action confrontations to challenge segregation; and A. Philip Randolph attempted to build his
March-on-Washington Committee into an all-black mass protest
movement. In 1941, his threat of a march on Washington, combined with the growth of the black vote and the exigencies of a
foreign threat to American security, forced Roosevelt to issue Executive Order 8802 (the first such order dealing with race since
Reconstruction), establishing the first President's Committee on
Fair Employment Practices (FEPC). And, with increasing firmness, liberal politicians pressed for civil rights legislation and emphasized that the practices of white supremacy brought into disrepute America's stated war aims. Minimal gains to be sure, but the
expectations they aroused set the stage for the greater advances in
the postwar period. By 1945, Afro-Americans had benefited
enough from the expansion in jobs and income, service in the
armed forces and the massive migration to Northern cities to
know better what they now wanted; and they had developed
enough political influence, white alliances, and organizational
skills to know how to go about getting their civil rights.

Equally vital, the Supreme Court began to dismantle the sepa-
rate-but-equal doctrine in 1938. That year, the high court ruled
that Missouri could not exclude a Negro from its state university
law school when its only alternative was a scholarship to an out-
of-state institution. Other Supreme Court decisions prior to
World War II whittled away at discrimination in interstate travel,
in employment, in judicial and police practices, and in the exclusion of blacks from jury service. During the war, the Court outlawed the white primary, holding that the nominating process of
a political party constituted "state action." In other decisions
handed down during the Truman presidency, the Supreme
Court moved vigorously against all forms of segregation in interstate commerce, decided that states and the federal government
cannot enforce restrictive racial covenants on housing, and so

emphasized the importance of "intangible factors" in quality education that the demise of legally segregated schooling for students at all levels became a near certainty.

Meanwhile, the Truman administration emerged as an ally of the cause of civil rights. Responding to the growth of the black vote, the need to blunt the Soviet Union's exploitation of the race issue, and the firmly organized campaign for the advancement of blacks, Harry Truman acted where Roosevelt had feared to. In late 1946, the President appointed a Committee on Civil Rights to recommend specific measures to safeguard the civil rights of minorities. This was the first such committee in American history, and its 1947 report, *To Secure These Rights,* eloquently pointed out all the inequities of life in Jim Crow America and spelled out the moral, economic, and international reasons for government action. It called for the end of segregation and discrimination in public education, employment, housing, the armed forces, public accommodations, and interstate transportation. Other commissions appointed by Truman stressed the need for racial equality in the armed services and the field of education. Early in 1948, Truman sent the first presidential message on civil rights to Congress. Congress failed to pass any of the measures he proposed, but Truman later issued executive orders ending segregation in the military and barring discrimination in federal employment and in work done under government contract. In addition, his Justice Department prepared *amicus curiae* briefs to gain favorable court decisions in civil rights cases, and Truman's rhetoric in behalf of racial justice helped legitimize goals of the civil rights movement. However small the meaningful accomplishment remained, the identification of the Supreme Court and the Presidency with the cause of racial equality further aroused the expectations of blacks that they would soon share in the American Dream.

No single event did more to quicken black hopes than the coup de grâce to segregated education delivered by a unanimous Supreme Court on May 17, 1954. The *Brown* ruling that separate educational facilities "are inherently unequal" struck at the very heart of white supremacy in the South. A year later, the Court called for compliance "with all deliberate speed," mandating the lower federal courts to require from local school boards "a prompt and reasonable start toward full compliance." The end of legally mandated segregation in education started a chain reaction which led the Supreme Court ever further down the road toward the total elimination of all racial distinctions in the law. For all practical purposes, the legal quest for equality had succeeded: the emphasis on legalism had accomplished its goals. Constitutionally, blacks had become first-class citizens.

But in the decade after the *Brown* decision, the promise of change far outran the reality of it. While individual blacks of talent desegregated most professions, the recessions of the Fifties caused black unemployment to soar and the gap between black and white family income to widen. And despite the rulings of the Supreme Court and the noble gestures and speeches of politicians, massive resistance to desegregation throughout the South proved the rule. This was the context for the second stage of the civil rights movement. When the nation's attempt to forestall integration and racial equality collided with both the Afro-Americans' leaping expectations and their dissatisfaction with the speed of change, blacks took to the streets in a wave of nonviolent, direct-action protests against every aspect of racism still humiliating them.

So Much History, So Much Future: Martin Luther King, Jr., and the Second Coming of America

Vincent Harding

Catapulted into national prominence by the Montgomery bus boycott of 1955–56, Martin Luther King, Jr., became the foremost symbol and spokesman for the direct action phase of the civil rights struggle that produced the Civil Rights Act of 1964 and the Voter Registration Act of 1965. With extraordinary eloquence and charisma, King communicated the essence of the black demand for freedom to white America, even as he inspired and mobilized black Americans to join that struggle. King's articulation of nonviolence as a philosophical principle, and his reliance on the Christian doctrine of unconditional love as the starting point for his leadership, helped to make acceptable to millions of white Americans a program of change that, by previous standards of action, seemed revolutionary. At the same time, King was always in danger of not proceeding far enough or fast enough to satisfy his black supporters.

In this article, Vincent Harding offers a personal, as well as historical, assessment of King's journey as he sought both to respond to those who prodded him to take a more radical path, and to address the realities of white political power. With sensitivity and passion, Harding helps us to gain an inner sense of King's own struggle, and a greater awareness of what King's life meant to the values and direction of American society.

I met Martin King in 1958, twenty years ago this month, and for the ten years of his life that we knew each other he was for me, to me, a brother, comrade, neighbor, and friend. From 1961 to the time of his death he regularly encouraged me to carry out the role I had chosen for myself as one who was both an engaged participant in the movement, and at the same time a committed historian and critical analyst of its development, as one who worked at the vortex of the struggle and yet remained outside of the official structures of the main civil rights organizations. . . . I come then as Martin's friend, his brother, as one who is crazy enough still to find myself talking to him on occasion, sometimes shouting his name—along with Malcolm's, along with Fannie Lou's, along with Clarence Jordan's and Tom Merton's and Ruby Doris Smith's. (Many of these names you don't know, and if you are to get an education at this university—or any other—you must demand to know them.)

The second thing I need to indicate is probably already implicit in my first comment. In 1961, three years after first having met King, I came south from Chicago with Rosemarie Harding, my wife and comrade, to work full-time in the freedom struggle. I do not hesitate to proclaim that I am biased towards that struggle and its participants. Indeed, at the same time I seek to understand and record its past, I am totally committed to work actively towards the creation of its next, still unclear stages of development. And I expect always to maintain that partisan bias in favor of a new, more humane American society, in favor of freedom for all the men, women, and children who seek new beginnings, new opportunities to break the shackles of the many external and internal oppressive realities that still bind so many of us down to lives that are less than our best, most human selves. . . . Within that context, it is clear that we shall understand the role Martin King played in the movement only as we understand that he was at once created by the movement and a creator of some of its major thrusts. He made much history, but in doing so he was aided, limited, and defined by the struggle that was mounting all around him, making him.

This dialectic, the dynamic, ecstatic, often agonized interplay between Martin and the movement may be illustrated in many ways, at many points, but we shall choose five developments to illustrate briefly the relationship between the man and the movement and to comment on its nature and its strengths and weaknesses. Those reference points are Montgomery, Alabama, in 1955–1956; Albany, Georgia, in 1961–1962; Birmingham, Alabama, and Washington, D.C.., in 1963; Mississippi and Chicago in 1966, and the fateful, desperate road from Riverside Church, New York, on April 4, 1967, to Memphis, Tennessee, on April 4, 1968.

Let us begin at Montgomery, where black folks took the U.S. Supreme Court more seriously than the court took itself, firmly grasped the *Brown* decision, intuitively recognized its many broader implications, and began immediately to press it far beyond the limited arena of the segregated school systems. Even before he arrived in Montgomery as the new pastor of the prestigious, black middle-class dominated Dexter Avenue Baptist Church, Martin King had entered the dialectic. He was a child of one of those comfortable Atlanta black bourgeoisie, church-dominating families; but nothing could insulate him against the reality of his people's existence in the South, in America. Nothing could blind him to the fact that ever since World War II a new phase of our freedom struggle had been mounted against rugged, often savage opposition, and he knew that what we were doing, largely through the courts at first, and through early, dangerous attempts at voter registration, was somehow tied to the anti-colonial struggles being waged across the world.

Then, just a bit more than a year after he had been in Montgomery, not long after he had completed his doctoral dissertation for Boston University, while thoughts of a relatively easy life as part-pastor and part-academic danced in his head, a strong, gentle woman named Rosa Parks refused to do the usual, agonized black dance on a segregated Montgomery bus. As a result, she was arrested, and a new time was opened in the struggle . . . the new time was building on the efforts and the people of the time before, and King was initially pressed into the role by a small group of genuine local leaders who had proven themselves in the past, and in a real sense he was later anointed by the larger masses of the Montgomery black people to be the public representative of their struggle. Even then no one fully realized that the new time had really begun to come, that it was possible now to make more history than they had ever made before in Montgomery, Alabama.

Before examining that particular [moment], it will probably be helpful to remind ourselves that at the outset of the Montgomery struggle the black folk of the city established their boycott of the segregated buses for very simple goals. They did not initially demand an end to bus segregation. Indeed, as late as April 1956, four months after the beginning of the boycott, King was articulating three objectives which assured continued segregation. The three goals were:

1. More courteous treatment of black passengers.
2. Seating on a first-come, first-served basis, but with blacks continuing the current practice of filling up from the rear of the bus forward, while whites filled in from the front towards the back.
3. Hiring of black bus drivers on predominantly black lines.

That was all. That was all they asked at first, and they did not march, sit-in, or fill up the jails—they just refused to ride the buses. That was all. It seems so simple now, but it was a great step then, and it was the local context in which King began.

In the weekly mass meetings that developed as a series of increasingly politicized, religious revival sessions, King set out to put forward his evolving philosophy of Christian nonviolence. At first, it was defined primarily as a refusal to react violently to the violence of whites, as a willingness to return love for hatred, and a conviction that their action was not only constitutional but within the will of God—therefore also within the onward, righteous flow of history. So, at the first mass meeting on December 5, 1955, in his exhortation to the fearful, courageous, wondering, determined people, King said, "We are not wrong in what we are doing. If we are wrong, the Supreme Court of this nation is wrong. If we are wrong, the Constitution of the United States is wrong. If we are wrong, God Almighty is wrong. If we are wrong, Jesus of Nazareth was merely a Utopian dreamer who never came down to earth." Then he closed with one of his typically rousing and inspiring perorations: "When the history books are written in the future, somebody will have to say, 'There lived a race of people, a black people, fleecy locks and black complexion, but a people who had the marvelous courage to stand up for their rights and thereby they injected a new meaning into the being of history and of civilization.' And we are going to do that."

From that auspicious beginning, one of King's major roles was interpreter, inspirer, the prophet who saw the significance, the larger meaning of what was happening in the immediate movement. He learned that role, grew into it, made important errors in it, but it was his. . . .

So the young pastor, moving into his twenty-seventh year, had found a black community ready to take certain initial risks on behalf of a limited vision of its rights and a new determination to establish its dignity. Beginning where they were, he took the people's courage and lifted it to the highest possible level, called upon them to see themselves as far more than black men and women of Montgomery Alabama, striving for decent treatment on a bus. Instead he pressed them forward, urging them to claim their roles as actors in a great cosmic drama, one in which they were at once in unity with the best teachings of American democracy, with the winds of universal social change, and at the same time walking faithfully within the unchanging will of God. . . . So, by the time the boycott had successfully ended in December 1956, by the time blacks were free to sit wherever they chose on the city buses, the possibility of an entire community of black men and women in the South taking large risks on the basis of conscience, justice, and a belief in the will of God had begun to be established. Those men and women and children of Montgomery, with their leader-spokesman, had made it possible for others to go beyond them and make even more history, create an even greater future.

Yet, once the Montgomery bus boycott had ended, King was without the base of direct mass action that he needed for the fullest, continuing development of his own role. . . . On the last day of November 1959, Martin King announced his decision to move to Atlanta by February 1, 1960. Then he said, "The time has come for a bold, broad advance of the Southern campaign for equality . . . a full scale assault will be made upon discrimination and segregation in all forms. We must train our youth and adult leaders in the techniques of social change through nonviolent resistance. We must employ new methods of struggle involving the masses of the people."

Clearly, King was speaking to himself, to the moving black community, and to the white and nonwhite world all around. Then, only two months after the announcement, on the very day of the planned move, almost as if by orchestrated agreement, an explosive response to King's vision came from the very "youth" he had hoped to train. They were not waiting for that training, and when the student sit-in movement erupted, beginning in February 1960, in Greensboro, North Carolina, it drove immediately towards the center of King's life, transforming it in ways that he had likely not quite anticipated. That was, of course, appropriate. For these neatly dressed, amazingly disciplined black young men and women, who with a few white allies began the new phase of the movement, were not only the products of the on-going school desegregation struggles of the South, they were really the children of Martin Luther King. In spite of many mixed feelings about him, they saw him as hero and model. But as is so often the case in such situations, they also went beyond him, creating what he could not create on his own, establishing the basis for the South-wide movement of massive, direct nonviolent confrontation with the segregated public facilities of the section which King had just announced. . . . They truly believed that through the power of their organized, disciplined, confrontative, nonviolent struggle, they were to be the builders of "the beloved community" in America, the harbingers of the new society Martin King had so continually evoked. Black and white together, they believed and they struggled, taking into their own flesh and spirit many of the hardest blows of white hatred and fear. . . .

But because we often create more history than we realize, because we often give birth to children that we do not understand and cannot control, it was not until the development of the Albany movement that Martin King was really able to catch up with the newest, rapid, explosive expansion of his people's struggle. What happened in this southwestern Georgia community from the fall of 1961 through the summer of 1962 was critical to the development of his role in the movement. Having moved from Montgomery to Atlanta in 1959, having developed no similar nonviolent mass action base in Atlanta, but sensing the new moment of history and its needs, King now became a kind of roving leader, responding to calls from the local movements that were springing up in hundreds of communities all over the South. . . . When in December 1961, the Albany movement invited King to come and help them, new patterns in his role began to be clear.

One of his major functions was admittedly to help inspire the local populace to greater efforts, for by now King had begun to be idolized by large sections of the black community, a development fraught with great pitfalls, of course, both for the idol and his idolizers. Nevertheless, King was their national leader, the acknowledged symbol of their struggle. And he was a great exhorter in every sense of the word. In addition, his presence was now considered a guarantee of national and even international media attention. Moreover, because Martin had begun since Montgomery to establish certain ambivalent contacts and significant influence with "liberal" white forces, especially in the religious, educational, and labor union communities, he began to be seen as the one person who could mobilize the "people of good will" (as he called them) from across the nation to come help in the struggle of local southern communities. Even more important in the minds of some persons was the fact that King seemed to have access to the Kennedy White House and its great potential power. Of course, it also came to be understood that Martin would lead marches and go to jail, and that his own organization, SCLC, with its rapidly growing staff, would provide experienced aid to those who might be new in the ways of nonviolent struggle. Albany actually was the first real testing ground for this developing role of King, the visiting leader/symbol, and SCLC, the black church-based organization, in the new phase of the southern movement.

In many ways, as one might have expected, the first experiment was an ambivalent one. In Albany, King was able with the local movement leaders to test what was essentially a new strategy, one forced upon them by the powerful thrust of the freedom movement. Rather than focusing on a single issue, such as bus desegregation, they decided to make multiple demands for changes toward racial and economic justice in their city. The internal force of the people's rush towards justice, their sense that the new time was indeed upon them, their growing understanding of the wider significance of their movement and the stubborn recalcitrance and evasiveness of the white leadership—all these pushed the black freedom fighters out of the churches, out of the train and bus stations, out of the dime stores, out into the streets.

In this motion, King was a crucial element, constantly in dynamic interaction with the force of its thrust. Through his words, his actions, and the very fact of his presence, Martin served as a great inspiration to the movement of the local black community,

especially in the early weeks of their activity. Hundreds of persons
for the first time in southern freedom movement history volun-
teered for acts of direct action civil disobedience right out on the
streets—which meant certain jailing in some of the most notorious and dangerous jails of Georgia. Out from the church mass
meetings they marched, singing "We Shall Overcome," "Ain't
Gonna Let Nobody Turn Me 'Round," and "This Little Light of
Mine." They went to jail, singing, "I'm gonna let it shine." They
sang and prayed in jail, "Paul and Silas locked in jail had nobody
to go their bail, keep your eye on the prize, hold on." In the dirty
jails where the memories of blood from older times were still
present, they were threatened for singing and praying, and they
kept on singing and praying. . . . "Over my head I see freedom in
the air. There must be a God somewhere." Indeed out of the
Albany jails came one of the most dynamic cultural forces of the
southern movement, the SNCC freedom singers, carrying the
songs of the movement across the nation and over the world,
songs which were bought at a great price "Woke up this morning
with my mind stayed on Freedom." . . .

But there were major problems as well. The Albany movement
had not really jelled as an organization before they called on
King. Thus, there were both understandable confusions in its
goals and in his role. On the one hand, their sense of the need for
nonviolent struggle was constantly being strained by the rush of
their own motion and the violence they were meeting. On the
other hand there was a temptation to see King, to encourage him
to see himself, as a savior—too often a peripatetic savior, one who
had to leave town at various points to keep speaking and fund-
raising engagements elsewhere. This created real difficulties, especially for a leader who was not essentially a day-to-day strategist
in the first place. In addition, there were understandable hard
feelings among the SNCC forces—who were often brilliant, brave,
and sometimes foolhardy strategists. These young people were
often resentful when, after their initial, lonely, and often dangerous weeks of local organizing, Martin King would arrive on the
scene, trailing a coterie of supporters and a crowd of media persons behind him, and the hard, dangerous spade-work of these
young freedom soldiers would tend largely to be forgotten in the
aura of *Martin Luther King.* Moreover, King's leadership style,
which was also SCLC's style, derived largely from the semiauto-

cratic world of the black Baptist church, and it simply grated against the spirits of the young people from SNCC. For they were working out their own forms of sometimes anarchistic-appearing participatory democracy. . . .

Nevertheless, two final words must be spoken about Albany. First it is to King's credit that he recognized many of the problems that were built into his own new role and tried to deal with some of them, but the role of a roving leader in the midst of a mass movement spread over such a massive area, often under the glare of television cameras, was fraught with deep and intrinsic difficulties. These were especially dangerous when added to the tendency to sycophancy and adulation that was building in some of the people around him, and the tendency to psychic murder that was built into the media of mass television. Second, in spite of the mistakes of King, SCLC, SNCC, the NAACP, CORE, and the Albany movement itself, Albany and its black and white people were changed and have been changed in profound, significant ways. There is no way that the black community will ever be pushed back to 1961; there is no way that white Albany will ever be the same again. But the question blacks now ask, as we must all ask, as Martin asked, is, where do we go from here?

In 1963, for King and SCLC, the geographic answer to that question was Birmingham, Alabama. But as we all knew, Birmingham, like Mississippi, was much more than a physical place. It had a bloody reputation, it was a frightening name. It was pronounced by some as "Bombingham" because of the violence whites had consistently brought against any black movements towards justice and equal rights there. And every black person in this country likely knew someone who had been run out of, beaten or killed in Birmingham, Alabama. But the Reverend Fred Shuttlesworth had not been run out, though he had been beaten more than once and almost killed, at one point with national television cameras running. It was largely at Shuttlesworth's insistence that King and SCLC came to Birmingham in the spring of 1963. . . .

By the time that King himself began to lead demonstrations—a week after they began—he was faced with the reality that a very volatile situation was at hand, the most difficult he had ever faced. Birmingham was "bigger and badder" than either Albany or Montgomery, and whites were not the only bad dudes in that town. So certain powerful contradictions began to surface. On the one hand, the "Commandments" handed out to demonstrators began, "Meditate daily on the teachings and life of Jesus," and included such additional admonitions as "walk and talk in the manner of love for God is love. . . . Refrain from violence of fist, tongue or heart." But at the same time, Jim Bevel and other staff members were confiscating a good number of knives and other weapons from some of the brothers who had come prepared for other ways of walking and talking. Obviously, then, the tensions were there, felt more sharply, drawn more clearly than ever before. . . .

These young people of Birmingham and others like them had a powerful effect on Martin King, on the shaping of his role, on the history he was making. He saw the great forces of energy and power, black power, stored up within them, and he knew where it could lead. He realized that now they were at least potentially the children of Malcolm X as well, and he was not unmoved by that recognition. He saw them take on the dogs and the firehoses with courageous anger, and he knew that anger was not easily controlled.

So his rationale for nonviolence began to expand to account for such young men and women in Birmingham and everywhere, began to account for Malcolm and the Nation of Islam and other, even more radical and revolutionary voices abroad in the land. Now it was not simply a weapon of love. As he explained it to an increasingly perplexed white world, nonviolence was also a defense against black retaliatory violence. More explicitly than ever before, King was forced to face the stormy potential of the black young people around him, and what they meant for his own sense of the future. When forcibly given a time to rest and think in the Birmingham jail, these children, spawned out of his own body, were clearly on his mind as he wrote his famous letter. Speaking of the American blacks he said,

> Consciously and unconsciously, [the Negro] has been swept in by what the Germans call the Zeitgeist, and with his black brothers of Africa, and his brown and yellow brothers of Asia, South America, and the Caribbean, he is moving with a sense of cosmic urgency toward the promised land of racial justice. Recognizing this vital urge that has engulfed the Negro community, one should readily

understand public demonstrations. The Negro has many pent-up resentments and latent frustrations. He has to get them out. So let him march some times; let him have his prayer pilgrimages to the city hall; understand why he must have sit-ins and freedom rides. If his repressed emotions do not come out in these nonviolent ways, they will come out in ominous expressions of violence. This is not a threat; it is a fact of history.

From that point onward, King increasingly found himself caught between the rising rage, nationalistic fervor, and questioning of nonviolence in the black community, and the fear of the white community that would seek to hold down all those black energies, to break them up, at worst to destroy them. So while Birmingham represented the largest number of blacks ever engaged in massive direct civil disobedient action up to then, and while the agreement worked out with the city was considered a victory of sorts, King's role was clearly undergoing transition again. Forces were now at work that had long been kept in check; . . .

In a sense, Montgomery was a long, long time ago. Seen from the late spring of 1963, the bus boycott was now a time of quiet, gentle protest compared with the massive action sweeping across the South, challenging the old regime, elciting some of its most brutal responses. This new massive direction-action pressed King more fully into another role—that of chief movement emissary to the White House. John Kennedy, who had said in January 1963, that civil rights action was not among his highest priorities, was forced to change his priorities by the whirlwind of the black movement. So White House conferences with King and others, by phone and in person, became almost *de rigueur*. But some persons soon learned—King later than some, earlier than others—that conferences with presidents may do more to divert the force of a movement than to fuel and inspire it, especially if that is one of the intentions of the president. . . . As a result, King became, partly unwarily, a tool for defusing a powerful current in a critical struggle for the future of the movement.

This is what I mean: for more than two years before Birmingham, Martin and others had talked about the development of a trained, disciplined nonviolent army that would become the spearhead for a national movement of powerful, disruptive non-violent civil disobedience, from coast to coast. . . .

During the Birmingham demonstrations the group pressing for the development of such a nonviolent army proposed that its first action be aimed at Washington, D.C., to shut down the activities of the city until adequate civil rights legislation of many kinds was passed. Without going into the details of the transformation, it is enough to say that King allowed himself to be convinced by other more moderate black and white leaders of the civil rights coalition that such a move would be exceedingly unwise. They were convinced and were probably right that it would lose friends and anger many "neutrals" in the white community. It would certainly lose the president's supposed support for civil rights legislation specifically and racial justice generally. So, instead of a disciplined, nonviolent force—largely from the southern testing grounds—descending on Washington for an extended campaign of disruptive divil disobedience, the summer of 1963 produced the one-day, unthreatening March on Washington for Jobs and Freedom. As a result, King passed up an opportunity possibly to transform his role in the struggle, to transform the struggle itself, losing perhaps more than we can ever know. And it was not until the fiery, bloody summers of 1964–1967 had passed that he was eventually forced by the movement of his people and the larger forces of history back to the idea of an organized, national nonviolent revolutionary force. By then it would be too late—at least for *that* time. . . .

The issues which had been simering, rolling the waters of the movement for a long time—sometimes pressed audaciously to the surface in the recent speeches of Adam Clayton Powell, Jr., the issues of power, the issues of racial pride, solidarity, and nationalism that had poured out anew in the North after the assassination of Malcolm X, El Hajj Malik El Shabazz; the issue of black control over the organizations of our struggle; the issue of the role of whites in the struggle; the issue of the need for black "liberation" as opposed to "integration," raised to a new level by the introduction of Frantz Fanon's *Wretched of the Earth* into the reading experience of many of the SNCC members; the concomitant rising discussion of black "revolution" as opposed to finding a place in the American status quo; the issue of the relationship between the black middle class and the masses of poor blacks, South and North; the issue of the need for the development of black leadership; the issue of sexual relations between white women and black men—all these exciting, frightening, dangerously explosive matters and many more leaped out in a compressed code from the lips of Willie Ricks of SNCC and they found their national identity in Stokely Carmichael, twenty-four-year-old veteran of the freedom rides, of the Black Panther party in Lowndes County, Alabama, of Greenwood, Mississippi. (Always remember that Stokely at his best was no dilettante. But, like the rest of us, he was not always at his best.) *Black Power! Black Power!* Black Power had officially begun its time: June 1966, on the road from Memphis to Jackson, cities of our music and our martyrs. . . .

At many points in the fall and winter of 1966–1967, after another summer of urban rebellions, as the fierce debate over Black Power raged, as he recognized the essential failure of his heroic/quixotic foray into Chicago, as the war in Vietnam continued to expand, as white anger mounted and black criticism of his positions grew more strident, King seemed at times like a great, courageous, but deeply perplexed captain, trying desperately to control a ship that was being rocked by mutinies from within and raging storms from without.

Yet, the truth of that perilous time was even more difficult. For by then there was no longer any one entity—even symbolically speaking—which could be called the Black Freedom movement and which Martin could really lead. Indeed, the very internal power of the movement that he had done so much to create and focus, that had shaped and molded him, had now broken out in many new directions, reviving, inspiring a plethora of older black—and white—traditions. . . .

It was impossible for King—or any other single individual—to understand, much less command all the tendencies now set loose in the black communities of the land. (Of course, he knew that he was being falsely identified as an "Uncle Tom" by many northern black rhetoreticians of revolution who had never once risked their lives as King had done so many times in the cause of his people's freedom.) At the same time, Martin was trying to understand where the real, critical centers of power lay in American society, trying to understand how he could tackle the powerful forces that supported war, racism, poverty, and the internal subversion of the freedom movement's many parts.

No easy task. Still King seemed convinced that he would be unfaithful to the history he had already made with others, untrue to his forebears and his children in the struggle for justice, unless he followed what appeared to be the logic of the movement. For him, that logic, that history, that sense of integrity pressed him toward a more radical challenge than he had ever mounted before, one that would leave him more naked to his enemies than ever before. . . .

First, King decided to try to respond fully to the unspeakable agony, the terrible crime of Vietnam, defying all his critics and many of his friends, from the White House to members of his own organization and his own family. On April 4, 1967, at Riverside Church in New York City, the struggling leader-searcher addressed a major meeting sponsored by Clergy and Laymen Concerned About Vietnam. Near the beginning of his vibrant presentation, King admitted that he had not spoken clearly and early enough, but vowed that he would never make that mistake again. Justifying the connection he saw among the struggles for equal rights and economic justice in America and the demand for an end to American military involvement in Vietnam, King placed them all within the context of his commission as a minister of Jesus Christ and a Nobel Peace Prize laureate. Unflinchingly, he identified America as the essential aggressor in the war and called his nation "the greatest purveyor of violence in the world." . . .

Soon he turned from Riverside Church to forge the second prong of his militant challenge to white American power. In the summer of 1967, after two of the decade's most deadly urban uprisings—in Newark and Detroit—had stunned the nation, after a national Black Power convention had done much to stamp that variously defined slogan in the minds of black folk everywhere, King announced his plans for a major attack on America's internal structures of inequality and injustice. . . .

It was a version of the nonviolent army again, now surfacing at a far more volatile, confused, and dangerous moment in the nation's history and in King's own career. . . . By the end of 1967, King and his staff had again decided to focus this potentially revolutionary challenge in Washington, D.C., fully aware of the ugly, angry, and unreceptive mood at work in the White House and elsewhere.

At his radical best, King was determined to press the logic of his position, the movement of his people's history. Having attacked the nation's antiliberationist overseas actions, he now intended to move on the heart of the government, demanding a response to the suffering of its own semicolonized peoples. (Nor was King paving a way of welcome for his move by saying late in 1967: "I am not sad that black Americans are rebelling; this was not only inevitable but eminently desirable. Without this magnificent ferment among Negroes, the old evasions and procrastinations would have continued indefinitely." He was not paving a way, but he was indicating his own way, his own movement in the vortex of "this magnificent ferment.")

Martin was trying to be on time, trying to be faithful, trying to go forward, to create whatever openings toward the future that he could. Jamming his life against the advice of many of his black and white movement supporters, defying the angry warnings of Lyndon Johnson, King searched for his new role, for the new role of his people. In an America that seemed at times on the edge of armed racial warfare, an America increasingly torn over the Vietnam war, an America unresponsive to the deepest needs of its own people, especially its poor—in the midst of this history King was desperately searching for the connections with his past, for the openings to his and our future.

By December 1967, Martin had at least temporarily taken his new powerful and dangerous position. In a series of broadcasts for Canadian public radio, he said, "Negroes . . . must not only formulate a program; they must fashion new tactics which do not count on government goodwill." Instead he said the new tactics must be those which are forceful enough "*to compel unwilling authorities to yield to the mandates of justice.*" But here at the end, at the beginning of the end, in his last major published document, King was not talking about blacks alone. The movement had grown; there was no way to "overcome" without taking on much more than we have ever taken on before. Thus he said,

The dispossessed of this nation—the poor, both white and Negro— live in a cruelly unjust society. *They must organize a revolution against that injustice,* not against the lives of the persons who are their fellow citizens, but against the structures through which the society is refusing to take means which have been called for, and which are at hand, to lift the load of poverty.

Martin King was talking about a nonviolent revolution in America, to transform the entire society on behalf of its poorest people, for the sake of us all. Martin King was moving towards an experiment with truth and power, and he was calling for three thousand persons to join him for three months of intensive training to begin that revolution at the seat of America's political power, Washington, D.C. Martin King was shaping a new role for himself, leader of a nonviolent revolutionary army/movement, one which he also saw connecting with the oppressed peoples of other nations. . . .

Perhaps Martin King had seen and felt more than he was able to accomplish. Perhaps he could not ever be ready for this new role. Perhaps in the violent climate of America, it was impossible to be ready for such a campaign of revolutionary, nonviolent civil disobedience without an organization that was fully prepared for all the dangers, all the opportunities, and all the long, hard, preparatory work. SCLC was not that organization. Nevertheless, ready or not, King appeared to be trying to get ready—facing toward Washington, D.C.

But first there were garbage collectors to help in Memphis, and there were powerful forces at every level of American society who were determined that Martin Luther King would never be ready for the kind of revolution he had now announced. As a result, Martin never made it to Washington, never found out if he was ready or not. . . .

This man who grew from a spokesperson for his people's search for simple dignity in a medium-sized southern city to become a giant symbol of the search for justice across the globe—this man, with all his weaknesses, all his flaws, all his blindspots and all of his creative, courageous greatness, made all the history he could make. Perhaps of even more importance to us here and now, we are able to see that he helped force open the way to the possibility of a new vision, a second coming of America, an America in which justice, compassion, and humanity prevail. . . .

King helped create the possibility that all of us might break beyond our own individual and group interests and catch a vision of a new America, create a vision of a new common good in a new future which will serve us all. He saw that our needs were economic *and* spiritual, political *and* moral, social *and* personal, and as the end, the beginning approached, he was groping his way towards a new integration—one that had very little to do with the legalities of *Brown* v. *The Board of Education.*

But in the midst of this struggle, this groping, this searching, King learned some things, and the message he left was the message he had learned, the message he had been given by the earlier generations of our freedom-striving people: Freedom is a constant struggle. The message he left was that a new America cannot be created without an even more difficult, radical, and dangerous struggle than we have known up to now. The message he left is that black people can no longer make any separate peace with America, that our needs are the needs of other millions of Americans, that the entire society must be challenged with the force of revolutionary change in all its political, economic, social, and psychic structures.

Letter from a Birmingham Jail

Martin Luther King, Jr.

In the spring of 1963, the Southern Christian Leadership Conference and Martin Luther King, Jr., joined Reverend Fred Shuttlesworth's Birmingham movement to demand the desegregation of what was known as the most racist and segregated city in America. The opposition was strident and brutal, with Bull Connor's police using fire hoses and billy clubs to repel the black demonstrators. Even when SCLC mobilized the young people of Birmingham to lead the marches downtown, police terrorized the children, siccing police dogs on them. The pictures from those demonstrations helped galvanize Americans everywhere in support of civil rights legislation, and eventually forced the Kennedy administration to take a more activist stance in support of civil rights.

In the midst of these demonstrations, King was arrested. While in jail, he responded in this letter to a statement of "moderate" white ministers in Birmingham who had asked that the demonstrations be curtailed, and who seemed to blame the victims of violence as much if not more than the perpetrators. Here, King eloquently preaches his own sermon to those ministers, calling into question a position that would use "moderation" as a means of reinforcing oppression. King's sermon is similar to an Old Testament "Jeremiad" where the prophets of Israel insisted on declaring the truth about their people.

My dear fellow clergymen:

While confined here in the Birmingham city jail, I came across your recent statement calling my present activities "unwise and

From *Why We Can't Wait* © 1963, 1964 Martin Luther King, Jr. Reprinted by permission of Harper & Row Publishers, Inc.

untimely." Seldom do I pause to answer criticism of my work and ideas. . . . But since I feel that you are men of genuine good will and that your criticisms are sincerely set forth, I want to try to answer your statement in what I hope will be patient and reasonable terms. . . .

I think I should indicate why I am here in Birmingham, since you have been influenced by the view which argues against "outsiders coming in." . . . I am here because I have organizational ties here. . . . But more basically, I am in Birmingham because injustice is here. . . .

Moreover, I am cognizant of the interrelatedness of all communities and states. I cannot sit idly by in Atlanta and not be concerned about what happens in Birmingham. Injustice anywhere is a threat to justice everywhere. We are caught in an inescapable network of mutuality, tied in a single garment of destiny.

Whatever affects one directly, affects all indirectly. Never again can we afford to live with the narrow, provincial "outside agitator" idea. Anyone who lives inside the United States can never be considered an outsider anywhere within its bounds.

You deplore the demonstrations taking place in Birmingham. But your statement, I am sorry to say, fails to express a similar concern for the conditions that brought about the demonstrations.

I am sure that none of you would want to rest content with the superficial kind of social analysis that deals merely with effects and does not grapple with underlying causes. It is unfortunate that demonstrations are taking place in Birmingham, but it is even more unfortunate that the city's white power structure left the Negro community with no alternative.

In any nonviolent campaign there are four basic steps: collection of the facts to determine whether injustices exist; negotiation; self-purification; and direct action. We have gone through all these steps in Birmingham.

There can be no gainsaying the fact that racial injustice engulfs this community. Birmingham is probably the most thoroughly segregated city in the United States. Its ugly record of brutality is widely know. Negroes have experienced grossly unjust treatment in the courts. There have been more unsolved bombing of Negro homes and churches in Birmingham than in any other city in the nation. These are the hard, brutal facts of the case. . . .

On the basis of these conditions, Negro leaders sought to negotiate with the city fathers. But the latter consistently refused to
engage in good-faith negotiation. Then, last September, came the
opportunity to talk with leaders of Birmingham's economic community. In the course of the negotiations, certain promises were
made by the merchants—for example, to remove the stores' humiliating racial signs.

On the basis of these promises, the Revered Fred Shuttlesworth
and the leaders of the Alabama Christian Movement for Human
Rights agreed to a moratorium on all demonstrations. As the
weeks and months went by, we realized that we were the victims
of a broken promise. A few signs, briefly removed, returned; the
others remained.

As in so many past experiences, our hopes had been blasted,
and the shadow of deep disappointment settled upon us. We had
no alternative except to prepare for direct action, whereby we
would present our very bodies as a means of laying our case
before the conscience of the local and the national community.

Mindful of the difficulties involved, we decided to undertake
the process of self-purification. We began a series of workshops
on nonviolence, and we repeatedly asked ourselves: "Are you able
to accept blows without retaliation?" "Are you able to endure the
ordeal of jail?" . . .

You may well ask, "Why direct action? Why sit-ins, marches,
and so forth? Isn't negotiation a better path?" You are quite right
in calling for negotiation. Indeed, this is the very purpose of
direct action. Nonviolent direct action seeks to create such a crisis
and foster such a tension that a community which has constantly
refused to negotiate is forced to confront the issue. It seeks so to
dramatize the issue that it can no longer be ignored.

My citing the creation of tension as part of the work of the
nonviolent resister may sound rather shocking. But I must confess
that I am not afraid of the word "tension." I have earnestly opposed violent tension, but there is a type of constructive, nonviolent tension which is necessary for growth.

Just as Socrates felt that is was necessary to create a tension in
the mind so that individuals could rise from the bondage of myths
and half-truths to the unfettered realm of creative analysis and
objective appraisal, so must we see the need for nonviolent gad-
flies to create the kind of tension in society that will help men rise

from the dark depths of prejudice and racism to the majestic heights of understanding and brotherhood.

The purpose of our direct-action program is to create a situation so crisis-packed that it will inevitably open the door to negotiation. I therefore concur with you in your call for negotiation. Too long has our beloved Southland been bogged down in a tragic effort to live in monologue rather than dialogue.

One of the basic points in your statement is that the action that I and my associates have taken in Birmingham is untimely. Some have asked: "Why didn't you give the new city administration time to act?" The only answer that I can give to this query is that the new Birmingham administration must be prodded about as much as the outgoing one, before it will act. . . .

We have not made a single gain in civil rights without determined legal and nonviolent pressure. . . . Lamentably, it is an historical fact that privileged groups seldom give up their privileges voluntarily. Individuals may see the moral light and voluntarily give up their unjust posture; but, as Reinhold Niebuhr has reminded us, groups tend to be more immoral than individuals.

We know through painful experience that freedom is never voluntarily given by the oppressor. It must be demanded by the oppressed. Frankly, I have yet to engage in a direct-action campaign that was "well timed" in view of those who have not suffered unduly from the disease of segregation.

For years now I have heard the word "Wait!" It rings in the ear of every Negro with piercing familiarity. This "Wait!" has almost always meant "Never." We must come to see, with one of our distinguished jurists, that "justice too long delayed is justice denied."

We have waited for more than 340 years for our constitutional and God-given rights. The nations of Asia and Africa are moving with jetlike speed toward gaining political independence, but we still creep at horse-and-buggy pace toward gaining a cup of coffee at a lunch counter. Perhaps it is easy for those who have never felt the stinging darts of segregation to say, "Wait."

But when you have seen vicious mobs lynch your mothers and fathers at will and drown your sisters and brothers at whim;

when you have seen hate-filled policemen curse, kick and even kill your black brothers and sisters;

when you see the vast majority of your twenty million Negro

brothers smothering in an airtight cage of poverty in the midst of an affluent society;

when you suddenly find your tongue twisted and your speech stammering as you seek to explain to your six-year-old daughter why she can't go to the public amusement park that has just been advertised on television, and see tears welling up in her eyes when she is told that Funtown is closed to colored children, and see ominous clouds of inferiority beginning to form in her little mental sky, and see her beginning to distort her personality by developing an unconscious bitterness toward white people;

when you have to concoct an answer for a five-year-old son who is asking, "Daddy, why do white people treat colored people so mean?";

when you take a cross-country drive and find it necessary to sleep night after night in the uncomfortable corners of your automobile because no motel will accept you;

when you are humiliated day in and day out by nagging signs reading "white" and "colored";

when your first names becomes "nigger," your middle names becomes "boy" (however old you are) and your last name becomes "John," and your wife and mother are never given the respected title "Mrs.";

when you are harried by day and haunted by night by the fact that you are a Negro, living-constantly at tiptoe stance, never quite knowing what to expect next, and are plagued with inner fears and outer resentments;

when you are forever fighting a degenerating sense of "nobodiness"—then you will understand why we find it difficult to wait.

There comes a time when the cup of endurance runs over, and men are no longer willing to be plunged into the abyss of despair. I hope, sirs, you can understand our legitimate and unavoidable impatience.

You express a great deal of anxiety over our willingness to break laws. This is certainly a legitimate concern. Since we so diligently urge people to obey the Supreme Court's decision of 1954 outlawing segregation in the public schools, at first glance it may seem rather paradoxical for us consciously to break laws.

One may well ask: "How can you advocate breaking some laws and obeying others?" The answer lies in the fact that there are two types of laws: just and unjust. I would be the first to advocate obeying just laws. One has not only a legal but a moral responsibility to obey just laws. Conversely, one has a moral responsibility to disobey unjust laws. I would agree with St. Augustine that "an unjust law is no law at all."

Now, what is the difference between the two? How does one determine whether a law is just or unjust? A just law is a man-made code that squares with the moral law or the law of God. An unjust law is a code that is out of harmony with the moral law.

To put it in the terms of St. Thomas Aquinas: An unjust law is a human law that is not rooted in eternal law and natural law. Any law that uplifts human personality is just. Any law that degrades human personality is unjust.

All segregation statutes are unjust because segregation distorts the soul and damages the personality. It gives the segregator a false sense of superiority and the segregated a false sense of inferiority. . . .

Let us consider a more concrete example of just and unjust laws. An unjust law is a code that a numerical or power majority group compels a minority group to obey but does not making binding on itself. This is *difference* made legal. By the same token, a just law is a code that a majority compels a minority to follow and that it is willing to follow itself. This is *sameness* made legal.

Let me give another explanation. A law is unjust if it is inflicted on a minority that, as a result of being deiend the right to vote, had no part in enacting or devising the law. Who can say that the legislature of Alabama which set up that state's segregation laws was democratically elected?

Throughout Alabama all sorts of devious methods are used to prevent Negroes from becoming registered voters, and there are some counties in which, even though Negroes constitute a majority of the population, not a single Negro is registered. Can any law enacted under such circumstances be considered democratically structured?

Sometimes a law is just on its face and unjust in its application. For instance, I have been arrested on a charge of parading without a permit. Now, there is nothing wrong in having an ordinance which requires a permit for a parade. But such an ordinance becomes unjust when it is used to maintain segregation and to deny citizens the First-Amendment privilege of peaceful assembly and protest.

I hope you are able to see the distinction I am trying to point out. In no sense do I advocate evading or defying the law, as would the rabid segregationist. That would lead to anarchy.

One who breaks an unjust law must do so openly, lovingly and with a willingness to accept the penalty. I submit that an individual who breaks a law that conscience tells him is unjust, and who willingly accepts the penalty of imprisonment in order to arouse the conscience of the community over its injustice, is in reality expressing the highest respect for law.

Of course, there is nothing new about this kind of civil disobedience. It was evidenced sublimely in the refusal of Shadrach, Meshach, and Abednego to obey the laws of Nebuchadnezzar, on the ground that a higher moral law was at stake. It was practiced superbly by the early Christians, who were willing to face hungry lions and the excruciating pain of chopping blocks rather than submit to certain unjust laws of the Roman Empire.

To a degree, academic freedom is a reality today because Socrates practiced civil disobedience. In our own nation, the Boston Tea Party represented a massive act of civil disobedience.

We should never forget that everything Adolf Hitler did in Germany was "legal" and everything the Hungarian freedom fighters did in Hungary was "illegal." It was "illegal" to aid and comfort a Jew in Hitler's Germany. Even so, I am sure that, had I lived in Germany at the time, I would have aided and comforted my Jewish brothers. If today I lived in a Communist country where certain principles dear to the Christian faith are suppressed, I would openly advocate disobeying that country's anti-religious laws.

I must make two honest confessions to you, my Christian and Jewish brothers. First, I must confess that over the past few years I have been gravely disappointed with the white moderate. I have almost reached the regrettable conclusion that the Negro's great stumbling block in his stride toward freedom is not the White Citizen's Councilor or the Ku Klux Klanner, but the white moderate, who is more devoted to "order" than to justice; who prefers a negative peace which is the absence of tension to a positive peace which is the presence of justice; who constantly says, "I agree with you in the goal you seek, but I cannot agree with your methods of direct action"; who paternalistically believes he can set the timetable for another man's freedom; who lives by a mythical concept of time and who constantly advises the Negro to wait for a "more convenient season."

Shallow understanding from people of good will is more frustrating than absolute misunderstanding from people of ill will. Lukewarm acceptance is much more bewildering than outright rejection.

I had hoped that the white moderate would understand that law and order exist for the purpose of establishing justice and that when they fail in this purpose they become the dangerously structured dams that block the flow of social progress.

I had hoped that the white moderate would understand that the present tension in the South is a necessary phase of the transition from an obnoxious negative peace, in which the Negro passively accepted his unjust plight, to a substantive and positive peace, in which all men will respect the dignity and worth of human personality.

Actually, we who engage in nonviolent direct action are not the creators of tension. We merely bring to the surface the hidden tension that is already alive. We bring it out in the open, where it can be seen and dealt with. Like a boil that can never be cured so long as it is covered up but must be opened with all its ugliness to the natural medicines of air and light, injustice must be exposed, with all the tension its exposure creates, to the light of human conscience and the air of national opinion, before it can be cured.

In your statement you assert that our actions, even though peaceful, must be condemned because they precipitate violence. But is this a logical assertion? Isn't this like condemning a robbed man because his possession of money precipitated the evil act of robbery? . . .

We must come to see that, as the federal courts have consistently affirmed, it is wrong to urge an individual to cease his efforts to gain his basic constitutional rights because the quest may precipitate violence. Society must protect the robbed and punish the robber.

I had also hoped that the white moderate would reject the myth concerning time in relation to the struggle for freedom. . . . Actually, time itself is neutral: it can be used either destructively or constructively. More and more I feel that people of ill will have used time much more effectively than have the people of good will. We will have to repent in this generation not merely for the hateful words and actions of the bad people, but for the appalling silence of the good people.

Human progress never rolls in on wheels of inevitability: it comes through the tireless efforts of men willing to be co-workers with God, and without this hard work, time itself becomes an ally of the forces of stagnation. We must use time creatively, in the knowledge that the time is always ripe to do right.

Now is the time to make real the promise of democracy and transform our pending national elegy into a creative psalm of brotherhood. Now is the time to lift our national policy from the quicksand or racial injustice to the solid rock of human dignity.

You speak of our activity in Birmingham as extreme. At first I was rather disappointed that fellow clergymen would see my non-violent efforts as those of an extremist. I began thinking about the fact that I stand in the middle of two opposing forces in the Negro community.

One is a force of complacency, made up in part of Negroes who, as a result of long years of oppression, are so drained of self-respect and a sense of "somebodiness" that they have adjusted to segregation; and in part of a few middle-class Negroes who, because of a degree of academic and economic security and because in some ways they profit by segregation, have become insensitive to the problems of the masses.

The other force is one of bitterness and hatred, and it comes perilously close to advocating violence. It is expressed in the various black nationalist groups that are springing up across the nation, the largest and best-known being Elijah Muhammad's Muslim movement. Nourished by the Negro's frustration over the continued existence of racial discrimination, this movement is made up of people who have lost faith in America, who have absolutely repudiated Christianity, and who have concluded that the white man is an incorrigible "devil."

I have tried to stand between these two forces, saying that we need emulate neither the "do-nothingism" of the complacent nor the hatred and despair of the black nationalist. For there is the more excellent way of love and nonviolent protest. I am grateful to God that, through the influence of the Negro church, the way of nonviolence became an integral part of our struggle.

If this philosophy had not emerged, by now many streets of the

South would, I am convinced, be flowing with blood. And I am further convinced that if our white brothers dismiss as "rabble-rousers" and "outside agitators" those of us who employ nonviolent direct action, and if they refuse to support our nonviolent efforts, millions of Negroes will, out of frustration and despair, seek solace and security in black-nationalist ideologies—a development that would inevitably lead to a frightening racial nightmare.

Oppressed people cannot remain oppressed forever. The yearning for freedom eventually manifests itself, and that is what has happened to the American Negro. Something within has reminded him of his birthright of freedom, and something without has reminded him that it can be gained. Consciously or unconsciously, he has been caught up by the Zeitgeist, and with his black brothers of Africa and his brown and yellow brothers of Asia, South America and the Caribbean, the United States Negro is moving with a sense of great urgency toward the promised land of racial justice.

If one recognizes this vital urge that has engulfed the Negro community, one should readily understand why public demonstrations are taking place. The Negro has many pent-up resentments and latent frustrations, and he must release them. So let him march; let him make prayer pilgrimages to the city hall; let him go on freedom rides—and try to understand why he must do so.

If his repressed emotions are not released in nonviolent ways, they will seek expression through violence; this is not a threat but a fact of history. So I have not said to my people, "Get rid of your discontent." Rather, I have tried to say that this normal and healthy discontent can be channeled into the creative outlet of nonviolent direct action. And now this approach is being termed extremist.

But though I was initially disappointed at being categorized as an extremist, as I continued to think about the matter I gradually gained a measure of satisfaction from the label.

Was not Jesus an extremist for love: "Love your enemies, bless them that curse you, do good to them that hate you, and pray for them which despitefully use you, and persecute you."

Was not Amos an extremist for justice: "Let justice roll down like waters and righteousness like an ever-flowing stream." . . .

And John Bunyan: "I will stay in jail to the end of my days before I make a butchery of my conscience."

And Abraham Lincoln: "This nation cannot survive half slave

and half free." And Thomas Jefferson: "We hold these truths to be self-evident, that all men are created equal. . . . "

So the question is not whether we will be extremists, but what kind of extremists we will be. Will we be extremists for hate or for love? Will we be extremists for the preservation of injustice or for the extension of justice? . . . Perhaps the South, the nation, and the world are in dire need of creative extremists.

I had hoped that the white moderate would see this need. Perhaps I was too optimistic; perhaps I expected too much. I suppose I should have realized that few members of the oppressor race can understand the deep groans and passionate yearnings of the oppressed race, and still fewer have the vision to see that injustice must be rooted out by strong, persistent, and determined action.

I am thankful, however, that some of our white brothers in the South have grasped the meaning of this social revolution and committed themselves to it. They are still all too few in quantity, but they are big in quality. Some—such as Ralph McGill, Lillian Smith, Harry Golden, James McBride Dabbs, Ann Braden, and Sarah Patton Boyle—have written about our struggle in eloquent and prophetic terms.

Others have marched with us down nameless streets of the South. They have languished in filthy, roach-infested jails, suffering the abuse and brutality of policemen who view them as "dirty nigger-lovers." Unlike so many of their moderate brothers and sisters, they have recognized the urgency of the moment and sensed the need for powerful "action" antidotes to combat the disease of segregation.

Let me take note of my other major disappointment. I have been so greatly disappointed with the white church and its leadership.

Of course, there are some notable exceptions. I am not unmindful of the fact that each of you has taken some significant stands on this issue. I commend you, Reverend Stallings, for your Christian stand on this past Sunday, in welcoming Negroes to your worship service on a nonsegregated basis. I commend the Catholic leaders of this state for integrating Spring Hill College several years ago.

But despite these notable exceptions, I must honestly reiterate that I have been disappointed with the church. I do not say this as one of those negative critics who can always find something wrong with the church. I say this as a minister of the gospel, who loves the church; who was nurtured in its bosom; who has been sustained by its spiritual blessings and who will remain true to it as long as the cord of life shall lengthen.

When I was suddenly catapulted into the leadership of the bus protest in Montgomery, Alabama, a few years ago, I felt we would be supported by the white church. I felt that the white ministers, priests and rabbis of the South would be among our strongest allies. Instead, some have been outright opponents, refusing to understand the freedom movement and misrepresenting its leaders; all too many others have been more cautious than courageous and have remained silent behind the anesthetizing security of stained-glass windows.

In spite of my shattered dreams, I came to Birmingham with the hope that the white religious leadership of this community would see the justice of our cause and, with deep moral concern, would serve as the channel through which our just grievances could reach the power structure. I had hoped that each of you would understand. But again I have been disappointed.

I have heard numerous southern religious leaders admonish their worshipers to comply with a desegregation decision because it is the law, but I have longed to hear white ministers declare: "Follow this decree because integration is morally right and because the Negro is your brother."

In the midst of blatant injustices inflicted upon the Negro, I have watched white churchmen stand on the sideline and mouth pious irrelevancies and sanctimonious trivialities. In the midst of a mighty struggle to rid our nation of racial and economic injustice, I have heard many ministers say: "Those are social issues, with which the gospel has no real concern." And I have watched many churches commit themselves to a completely otherworldly religion which makes a strange, un-Biblical distinction between body and soul; between the sacred and the secular. . . .

I hope the church as a whole will meet the challenge of this decisive hour. But even if the church does not come to the aid of justice, I have no despair about the future. I have no fear about the outcome of our struggle in Birmingham, even if our motives are at present misunderstood. We will reach the goal of freedom in Birmingham and all over the nation, because the goal of America is freedom.

Abused and scorned though we may be, our destiny is tied up with America's destiny. Before the pilgrims landed at Plymouth, we were here. For more than two centuries our forebears labored in this country, without wages; they made cotton king; they built the homes of their masters while suffering gross injustice and shameful humiliation—and yet out of a bottomless vitality they continued to thrive and develop.

If the inexpressible cruelties of slavery could not stop us, the opposition we now face will surely fail. We will win our freedom because the sacred heritage of our nation and the eternal will of God are embodied in our echoing demands.

Before closing I feel impelled to mention one other point in your statement that has troubled me profoundly. You warmly commended the Birmingham police force for keeping "order" and "preventing violence."

I doubt that you would have so warmly commended the police force if you had seen its dogs sinking their teeth into unarmed, nonviolent Negroes. I doubt that you would so quickly commend the policemen if you were to observe their ugly and inhumane treatment of Negroes here in the city jail; if you were to watch them push and curse old Negro women and young Negro girls; if you were to see them slap and kick old Negro men and young boys; if you were to observe them, as they did on two occasions, refuse to give us food because we wanted to sing our grace together. I cannot join you in your praise of the Birmingham police department.

It is true that the police have exercised a degree of discipline in handling the demonstrators. In this sense they have conducted themselves rather "nonviolently" in public. But for what purpose? To preserve the evil system of segregation.

Over the past few years I have consistently preached that nonviolence demands that the means we use must be as pure as the ends we seek. I have tried to make clear that it is wrong to use immoral means to attain moral ends. But now I must affirm that it is just as wrong, or perhaps even more so, to use moral means to preserve immoral ends. . . . As T. S. Eliot has said, "The last temptation is the greatest treason: To do the right deed for the wrong reason."

I wish you had commended the Negro sit-inners and demonstrators of Birmingham for their sublime courage, their willingness to suffer, and their amazing discipline in the midst of great provocation. One day the South will recognize its real heroes. They will be the James Merediths, with the noble sense of purpose that enables them to face jeering and hostile mobs, and with the agonizing loneliness that characterizes the life of the pioneer. They will be old, oppressed, battered Negro women, symbolized in a seventy-two-year-old woman in Montgomery, Alabama, who rose up with a sense of dignity and with her people decided not to ride segregated buses, and who responded with ungrammatical profundity to one who inquired about her weariness: "My feets is tired, but my soul is at rest."

They will be the young high school and college students, the young ministers of the gospel and a host of their elders, courageously and nonviolently sitting in at lunch counters and willingly going to jail for conscience' sake. One day the South will know that when these disinherited children of God sat down at lunch counters, they were in reality standing up for what is best in the American dream and for the most sacred values in our Judeo-Christian heritage, thereby bringing our nation back to those great wells of democracy which were dug deep by the founding fathers in their formulation of the Constitution and the Declaration of Independence.

Never before have I written so long a letter. I'm afraid it is much too long to take your precious time. I can assure you that it would have been much shorter if I had been writing from a comfortable desk, but what else can one do when he is alone in a narrow jail cell, other than write long letters, think long thoughts and pray long prayers? . . .

Yours for the cause of peace and brotherhood,

Martin Luther King, Jr.

Black Power

Stokely Carmichael

Paralleling the rage expressed by Northern blacks in the urban riots, many of the activists in the struggle for racial equality in the South began demanding Black Power in 1966. First used as a slogan by the newly elected head of the Southern Nonviolent Coordinating Committee, Stokely Carmichael, in the Meredith March Against Fear, the Black Power phase of the movement developed out of frustration over the limited pace and scope of racial change and out of bitterness toward unceasing, brutal white opposition to the most minimal black advances. More a slogan than a program, it was an angry reaction against nonviolence as a tactic and integration as a goal. By 1966, the growing white backlash had made King's goal of an integrated society seem even more an impossible dream. Why not, therefore, battle for self-determination rather than pursue an illusionary desegregation? Most of the Southern freedom fighters, moreover, had turned the other cheek too often, with too little to show for it. Why not assert the right of self-defense, or endorse retaliatory violence, or even advocate violence as a legitimate tactic wherever feasible? Virtually every black organization soon adopted some variant of Black Power, each giving it its own congenial connotation. Whatever Black Power meant, it had surely captured the imagination of black America. No other topic was more discussed and debated in the next several years. In the following excerpt from a speech given at the University of California, Berkeley, Carmichael postulates an early explanation and definition of Black Power.

. . . Now we are engaged in a psychological struggle in this country and that struggle is whether or not black people have the right

From a speech by Stokely Carmichael, University of California, Berkeley, November 19, 1966.

to use the words they want to use without white people giving their sanction to it. We maintain, whether they like it or not, we gon' use the word "black power" and let them address themselves to that. We are not gonna wait for white people to sanction black power. We're tired of waiting. Every time black people move in this country, they're forced to defend their position before they move. It's time that the people who're supposed to be defending their position do that. That's white people. They ought to start defending themselves, as to why they have oppressed and exploited us.

It is clear that when this country started to move in terms of slavery, the reason for a man being picked as a slave was one reason: because of the color of his skin. If one was black, one was automatically inferior, inhuman, and therefore fit for slavery. So that the question of whether or not we are individually suppressed is nonsensical and is a downright lie. We are oppressed as a group because we are black, not because we are lazy, not because we're apathetic, not because we're stupid, not because we smell, not because we eat watermelon and have good rhythm. We are oppressed because we are black and in order to get out of that oppression, one must feel the group power that one has. Not the individual power which this country then sets the criteria under which a man may come into it. That is what is called in this country as integration. You do what I tell you to do, and then we'll let you sit at the table with us. And then we are saying that we have to be opposed to that. We must now set a criteria, and that if there's going to be any integration it's going to be a two-way thing. If you believe in integration, you can come live in Watts. You can send your children to the ghetto schools. Let's talk about that. If you believe in integration, then we're going to start adopting us some white people to live in our neighborhood. So it is clear that the question is not one of integration or segregation. Integration is a man's ability to want to move in there by himself. If someone wants to live in a white neighborhood and he is black, that is his choice. It should be his right. It is not because white people will allow him. So vice-versa, if a black man wants to live in the slums, that should be his right. Black people will let him, that is the difference. . . .

The political parties in this country do not meet the needs of the people on a day-to-day basis. The question is, how can we build new political institutions that will become the political expressions of people on a day-to-day basis. The question is, how can you build political institutions that will begin to meet the needs of Oakland, California; and the needs of Oakland, California is not 1,000 policemen with submachine guns. They don't need that. They need that least of all. The question is, how can we build institutions where those people can begin to function on a day-to-day basis, where they can get decent jobs, where they can get decent housing, and where they can begin to participate in the policy and major decisions that affect their lives. That's what they need. Not Gestapo troops. Because this is not 1942. And if you play like Nazis, we're playing back with you this time around. Get hip to that. . . .

We've been saying that we cannot have white people working in the black community and we've based it on psychological grounds. The fact is that all black people often question whether or not they are equal to whites because everytime they start to do something white people are around showing them how to do it. If we are going to eliminate that for the generations that come after us, then black people must be seen in positions of power doing and articulating for themselves. . . .

It is impossible for white and black people to talk about building a relationship based on humanity when the country is the way it is, when the institutions are clearly against us. We have taken all the myths of this country and we've found them to be nothing but downright lies. This country told us that if we worked hard we would succeed, and if that were true we would own this country lock, stock and barrel. It is we who have picked the cotton for nothing; it is we who are the maids in the kitchens of liberal white people; it is we who are the janitors, the porters, the elevator men; it is we who sweep up your college floors; yes, it is we who are the hardest working and the lowest paid. And that it is nonsensical for people to start talking about human relationships until they're willing to build new institutions. Black people are economically insecure. White liberals are economically secure. Can you begin an economic coalition? Are the liberals willing to share their salaries with the economically insecure black people who they so much love? Then if you're not, are you willing to start building new institutions that will provide economic security for black people? That's the question we want to deal with. . . .

We have to raise questions about whether or not we need new

types of political institutions in this country and we in SNCC maintain that we need them now. We need new political institutions in this country. And any time Lyndon Baines Johnson can head a party which has in it Bobby Kennedy, Wayne Morse, Eastland, Wallace and all those other supposedly liberal cats, there's something wrong with the party. They're moving politically, not morally. And if that party refuses to seat black people from Mississippi and goes ahead and seats racists like Eastland and his clique, then it is clear to me that they're moving politically and that one cannot begin to talk morality to people like that. We must begin to think politically and see if we can have the power to impose and keep the moral values that we hold high. We must question the values of this society. And I maintain that black people are the best people to do that because we have been excluded from that society and the question is, we ought to think whether or not we want to become a part of that society. That's what we want. And that is precisely what, it seems to me, the Student Nonviolent Coordinating Committee is doing. We are raising questions about this country. I do not want to be a part of the American pride. The American pride means raping South Africa, beating Vietnam, beating South America, raping the Philippines, raping every country you've been in. I don't want any of your blood money. I don't want it . . . don't want to be part of that system. And the question is, how do we raise those questions. . . . How do we raise them as activists?

We have grown up and we are the generation that has found this country to be a world power, that has found this country to be the wealthiest country in the world. We must question how she got her wealth. That's what we're questioning. And whether or not we want this country to continue being the wealthiest country in the world at the price of raping everybody across the world. That's what we must begin to question. And because black people are saying we do not now want to become a part of you, we are called reverse racists. Ain't that a gas?

We are never going to get caught up with questions about power. This country knows what power is and knows it very well. And knows what black power is because it's deprived black people of it for 400 years. So it knows what black power is. But the question is, why do white people in this country associate black power with violence? Because of their own inability to deal with blackness. If we had said Negro power, nobody would get scared. Everybody would support it. And if we said power for colored people, everybody would be for that. But it is the word "black," it is the word "black" that bothers people in this country, and that's their problem, not mine. . . .

So that in conclusion, we want to say that first, it is clear to me that we have to wage a psychological battle on the right for black people to define their own terms, define themselves as they see fit and organize themselves as they see fit. Now, the question is, how is the white community going to begin to allow for that organizing, because once they start to do that, they will also allow for the organizing that they want to do inside their communities. It doesn't make any difference. Because we're going to organize our way anyway. We're going to do it. The question is, how we're going to facilitate those matters. Whether it's going to be done with a thousand policemen with sub-machine guns or whether or not it's going to be done in the context where it's allowed to be done by white people warding off those policemen. That is the question. . . .

And then, in a larger sense, there is the question of black people. We are on the move for our liberation. We have been tired of trying to prove things to white people. We are tired of trying to explain to white people that we're not going to hurt them. We are concerned with getting the things we want, the things that we have to have to be able to function. The question is, can white people allow for that in this country? The question is, will white people overcome their racism and allow for that to happen in this country? If that does not happen, brothers and sisters, we have no choice, but to say very clearly, move on over, or we're going to move on over you.

Black Power after Ten Years

Clayborne Carson

However many things it meant to blacks, "to most whites," as Carmichael observed, Black Power meant that "the Mau Mau are coming to the suburbs at night." It became synonomous with "Burn, Baby, Burn" and "offing the pigs." To that extent, Black Power helped to polarize the races, sanction the cult of violence, fuel the white backlash, and destroy the civil rights movement. Yet it also generated valuable changes. It galvanized many whom the movement had never mobilized. It spawned a vast array of new community organizations. It spurred self-reliance. It focused attention on the needs of the lower classes. It forced the nation to contemplate the plight of powerlessness.

Fundamentally, Black Power made blacks proud to be black, a psychological precondition for equality. It revolutionized the black perspective, proving invaluable in aiding blacks to discard the disabling self-hatred inculcated by white culture. The following retrospective view by a former activist and present historian at Stanford University analyzes some of the positive and negative consequences of Black Power.

In a single decade, an era of Afro-American politics came and went. A legacy remains, but its full meaning is still to be determined, even by blacks who came of age during the 1960s and were transformed by the events of those years. Now we must search our memories to recall the effect on our lives of the evolution from nonviolent desegregation sit-ins to massive marches and

From *The Nation*, August 14, 1976. Reprinted by permission.

rallies to convulsive urban rebellions—the evolution from Martin Luther King to Malcolm X to Stokely Carmichael to Eldridge Cleaver. The 1963 march on Washington is separated from us by thirteen years and three Presidents and the rise and fall of a succession of movements, leaders and dreams.

Just a decade ago, in the midst of the march through Mississippi undertaken after James Meredith was wounded by a shotgun blast, a new form of racial militancy suddenly gained national attention. The cry for "Black Power" arose as a conscious attempt by the young black activists in the Student Non-Violent Coordinating Committee (SNCC) to alter the direction of black politics. Willie Ricks, an Alabama-born SNCC worker who gained his political education in the streets of Chattanooga, Albany and Montgomery and in isolated black-belt regions of Georgia and Alabama, was chosen in June 1966 to test the readiness of blacks for a new militant vocabulary. Nightly venturing away from the main body of marchers, Ricks launched a new phase of Afro-American history in small black Mississippi towns that time seemed to have ignored. He returned each night with reports of enthusiastic receptions for the rhetoric of Black Power.

A year earlier, in similar communities of Lowndes County, Alabama, Ricks and other SNCC workers had organized the Lowndes County Freedom Organization. In that poor, predominantly black county between Selma and Montgomery, SNCC organizers took an important and original political departure simply by doing what they thought necessary. Since their supporters were black and not welcomed by the Democratic Party, they built an independent all-black party. Since blacks in the Deep South understood white power and resented their own powerlessness, they used the slogan, "Black Power for Black People." And since the panther is black and powerful, they called the new party the Black Panther Party. Stokely Carmichael's work as an organizer in Lowndes County became the basis for his successful bid for the chairmanship of SNCC a few weeks before the Mississippi march and by June 1966, the SNCC militants were ready to assert their claim to national black leadership.

Carmichael, who had directed the 1964 voter registration campaign in Mississippi's 2nd Congressional District, when hundreds of Northern whites came South to help, soon concluded that it was time to break loose from the constraints imposed by SNCC's white liberal supporters. Thus, when the march reached Green-wood, the site of his 1964 headquarters, Carmichael told the nation's press that there was a new black response to the question, "What do you want?" Black Power.

Carmichael—handsome, articulate, always consciouse of the effect of his words on his listeners—was quickly identified as the principal spokesman for Black Power. In most reports, he was described as the firebrand who had sparked the new militancy, when in fact he was the mirror of a new mood among blacks. Carmichael, like nearly all important black leaders since the antebellum period, gained a following among blacks not as a prophet of the future but as an interpreter of the past. As was true of Malcolm X, Carmichael was able to surpass other black leaders because he cut through the verbiage of the white oppressors' language to utter the truths that lay dormant in the experiences of oppressed blacks. Most blacks recognized that their leaders could do little to shape the future, but they were willing to give their support to those who understood their lives. Carmichael became an oracle for the Black Power movement, because he was singularly skillful at expressing conclusions, drawn from years of organizing among Southern blacks, in terms that could be understood by urban blacks and whites who were closer than poor black sharecroppers to the mainstream of American politics. He not only expressed the desire of rural Southern blacks to gain control over local institutions but also the desire of urban blacks, like himself, to reject the white-controlled institutions in which they were enmeshed. . . .

The celebrated black militants of the past decade gained almost overnight a fame they did not deserve, and gradually they fell into an obscurity they could not have expected. There is little to suggest that they learned enough from their experiences to build a movement capable of achieving fundamental changes in American society; at present, few militant black leaders possess even the illusion of revolutionary potential. Ricks and Carmichael were among those blacks who came to identify with Africa during the late 1960s, but their political views are now separated both from the Marxist programs of most African revolutionary movements and from the pragmatism and opportunism that dominate contemporary Afro-American politics. They have been unable to transform the black discontent expressed by the Black Power slogan into mass support for their present goal of building a power base in a unified Africa.

Other militant spokesmen have similarly found themselves exiled, imprisoned, or simply ignored. Bobby Seale of the Black Panther Party has long since left that moribund organization. Huey Newton, the other co-founder of the party, is now in Cuban exile. Eldridge Cleaver, whose obscenities once helped shape the image of the party, has become a repentant fugitive who expresses support for the American political system and wishes to be allowed to make his singular contribution to men's fashion design. Imamu Amiri Baraka (formerly LeRoi Jones), the poetic ideologue of black separatism, has more recently concluded that Marx was right as well as white and found that his audience has decreased as dialectics replaced theatrical diatribes. James Forman, whose "Black Manifesto," as delivered to white religious organizations, revealed a prevalent confusion of militant tactics and rhetoric with revolutionary strategy, seems now a burned-out firebrand. . . .

The significant changes that did occur during the past decade merely illustrate the paradoxes of the period. The limited nature of those gains has made many blacks more skeptical about the possibility of fundamentally improving their positions in U.S. life through collective action. Racial pride has risen, but it has neither created an effective national black political movement nor measurably increased racial unity. The attempt by blacks to prove themselves "blacker than thou" has proved quite as divisive as earlier efforts to gain acceptance from whites. Blacks who rejected the term Negro did not abandon the term "niggah."

An increase in the number of black politicians holding public office has been accompanied by a decrease in the proportion of blacks who bother to vote and by an increase in factionalism as blacks compete for leadership. Indeed, black political power has grown largely as a result of the inability of blacks to escape from deteriorating conditions in segregated communities. Mass activism among poor and working-class blacks provided the push for the gains of the 1960s, but the poorest segment of the black population has profited least from those gains. Black leaders who claim to speak for "the people" have diverted the black struggle from the effort to wrest economic concessions directly

from the white establishment to the problematic strategy of in-
terposing between the black masses and the white elite a buffer
of black businessmen and bureaucrats who equate their own success with that of the race. Although the overall failure of blacks
to advance economically in recent years can be attributed to the
economic downturn affecting the larger society, it is significant
that the black middle class has expanded during this period—
from 1965 to 1974—the percentage of blacks making more than
$15,000 a year increased by more than 100 percent (to 19 per-
cent of the total black population). Growth of black college enrollment, white-collar employment and entrepreneurship has
gone hand in hand with continued high unemployment. The
rising black bourgeoisie urges self-reliance on the black poor and
working classes, while it as a class has gradually abandoned the
relative independence of self-employment for jobs as hired
hands of government and big business. Black students have
learned to market their blackness as well as to find it. If affirma-
tive-action programs suddenly were to alter their criteria in
order to provide greater opportunities for those who are poor
rather than simply for those who are black, the loudest cries of
protest would doubtless come from middle-class blacks, many of
whom claim that class analysis does not apply to them.

The demand for Black Power was basically a response to the
recognition that blacks were effectively powerless, but the demand
was often tied to the naive notion that power could be achieved by
unifying a black populace whose common concerns and objective
bases for unity were being rapidly eroded by the advances in the
struggle for civil rights. To go on repeating some variant of the
assertion that, no matter how rich or educated, a black man is still
a "nigger," is to obscure the fact that the battle against racism has
widened rather than narrowed the class divisions among blacks.
Those who ignore this trend not only condemn Afro-American
politics to a future of stagnation but also contribute to the erosion
of the racial trust and empathy that made past gains possible.

Despite the remarkable upsurge in political mobilization and
militancy that occurred among blacks during the 1960s, real
power has remained outside their communities. Civil rights laws
were achieved because protests took place when the national political climate was sympathetic to their goals. This climate enabled
the champions of civil rights to prod powerful forces into action

and, to some extent, restrained the Southern repression that could have destroyed the movement in the South. The most perceptive of the black leaders of the 1960s were able to view their own activism in its proper perspective: as a catalyst in the process of social change, but not as a determinant.

A source of the 1960s militancy was Afro-American awareness of the rise of independent Third World leaders who seemed to have broken free of the constraints imposed by the Western political and economic order. There is irony, however, in the fact that, while young black radicals in this country were making their initial contacts with Third World leaders, they were losing the leverage that had been provided by the attempt of the United States to win support in the nonwhite world. During the early 1960s the State Department was directly involved in attempts to end domestic segregation policies that generated negative publicity abroad and to prevent embarrassing incidents involving African diplomats on visits here. By the mid-1960s, however, as the war in Vietnam escalated, it became evident that the future of Africa and Asia would not be decided primarily through propaganda battles but through the use of military and economic power, and American leaders became less concerned about the effect of domestic racial conflicts on the hearts and minds of Africans and Asians. Thus, the indirect relationship between the domestic and foreign policies of the United States during the early 1960s had greater impact on the fortunes of Afro-Americans than did the haphazard efforts of black radicals later in the 1960s to establish direct ties with distant revolutionary movements.

The belief that Afro-Americans were a colonized group analogous to subject peoples elsewhere in the world was widely accepted by the black radical intelligentsia of the late 1960s, but the colonial analogy obscured as much as it clarified. While many blacks identified with the African demand for nationhood, some Third World revolutionary writers were noting that the direction of change in the newly independent African and Asian nations was toward military domination, economic exploitation by native elites, and the continued disruption of internal affairs by the covert and overt agents of Western capitalism. Robert Allen, author of *Black Awakening in Capitalist America*, was among the few blacks in this country who understood by the late 1960s that the crucial lesson to be learned from the recent experiences of Third World nations was that colonization was no longer the principal issue. Allen argued that black nationalism in the United States was being manipulated and co-opted by the white establishment in order to achieve the kind of neo-colonial domination it had already gained in many Third World nations. However, he was no more able than most African and Asian leaders to offer a viable program to end economic exploitation, and the absence of such a program led to cynicism and disillusionment.

Within the United States, blacks gained their equivalent of political independence—that is, nominal control of a few areas where blacks were in the majority—but, as had been the case for African nations, it was a hollow prize. Large corporations were able to retain the benefits of a black market and labor force, while avoiding the problems that arose from the fact that many blacks were not needed by the economic system. Whites were somewhat upset by the growth of black electoral power, but they were also relieved of a burden of guilt and responsibility. As "blackness" became a much desired commodity (there were many rewards for those who could mimic the distinctive forms of black lowerclass behavior) there were some expressions of dismay among whites. But the communications media quickly appropriated the exotic behavior of the black masses as another faddish diversion to attract mass audiences to their clients. As in Africa during the early 1960s, apparent agreement regarding the desirability of black control masked internal divisions that were deep and exploitable. . . .

At present, after an exceptional period of militancy, black leadership is most effectively exercised by those who have traditionally exercised it: black professionals, businessmen, clergymen and elected officials. The Congressional Black Caucus has emerged as the most significant national black political institution, but it has offered neither consistent nor farsighted leadership. The black legislators recognize, perhaps more clearly than most of their constituents, that the period when the issue of racial status took precedence over all others is coming to an end and that the crucial concerns of the future will be economic. Yet they have developed no plans that avoid the drawbacks of previous liberal social welfare programs. Such programs have succeeded only in supplying temporary jobs outside the manufacturing sector and some more permanent jobs for those who study, evaluate, advise and speak for the poor and needy.

For better or worse, the future of Afro-American society will involve a gradual and inexorable movement from the periphery closer to the center of the world economic system. It is this movement that made possible the emergence of viable black social movements during the 1960s, and the same trend will define the character and potential of future black movements. Doubtless, some blacks will remain outside the mainstream of change, but they will also be at the margins of the main currents of Afro-American life. The common experiences that once permeated black racial consciousness are rapidly being displaced as blacks assume new and varied roles in the modern industrial world. Racial unity has become increasingly difficult to achieve as Afro-American society becomes less distinguishable from the pervading mass culture surrounding it. New opportunities exist, however, to develop collective movements among blacks who recognize that important aspirations have remained submerged in order to maintain the illusion that all blacks share the same interests. The persistence of the outworn rhetoric of the past has obscured the continued widening of class divisions among blacks. The present course of Afro-American politics must be reassessed, not only to confront future realities but also to allow all segments of the black populace a share in the valuable legacy from earlier struggles: an awareness of the potential power of people who come to realize their common destiny.

Part Five

THE CHALLENGE TO SEXISM

Together with issues of race and class, the division of society into "masculine" and "feminine" spheres has been one of the major organizing themes of American society. To this day, whether one is born male or female has more to do with shaping one's life possibilities than almost any other factor. It determines the clothes we wear, the emotions we are taught to cultivate, the jobs we are told we should aspire to, the power we exercise—even our sense of who we are and what we are about. Through most of American history, cultural norms prescribed that women should be the tenders of the hearth, keepers of the home, rearers of children, and the moral, spiritual members of the family. Men, by contrast, were to be assertive, dominant, in control, the major source of power, influence, and income. Even though frequently these norms were not implemented in reality, they remained powerful forces in the culture. Particularly for white women of the middle and upper class, the norms defined as off-limits any active involvement in the world outside the home. Those women who worked prior to 1940 were primarily single, young, and poor. It was virtually unheard of for a married, middle-class white woman to have a job or pursue a career. For her to do so would be repudiation of her natural role, and a negative reflection of her husband's ability to provide for her. In a culture which defined success for a woman as marriage and homemaking, any deviation from that role marked failure.

As in the case of Afro-Americans, World War II generated significant change. Millions of women took jobs, and under the press of a wartime crisis, old definitions of women's "proper" place were set aside, at least for the moment. On the other hand, discrimination continued. Women were paid less than men, they were barred from executive positions, and despite wartime needs, day care centers were not provided in adequate numbers.

After the war, many of the advances that had occurred were reversed. What Betty Friedan called the "Feminine Mystique" became once again a pervasive cultural force, urging women to return to the home and to aspire to suburban domesticity. On the other hand, employment figures for women continued to increase, with more and more middle-class women taking jobs simply in order to make it possible for a family to aspire to a better life. By the late 1960s, a revitalized feminism became a powerful force in the society, exposing the contradiction between traditional definitions of women's place and the new frequency with which women were assuming roles outside the home. Questioning most of the traditional definitions of masculinity and femininity, the women's liberation movement became one of the most significant forces of social change in the 1960s and 1970s.

In the case of the challenge to sexism, as in the black struggle, there are some who focus attention on external and impersonal sources of change, and others who emphasize the role of activists in bringing about social progress. In the following selections, William Chafe writes about some of the aggregate trends in the society that established the framework within which a revitalized feminism developed. Sara Evans discusses the origins of the women's liberation movement in the civil rights struggles of the early 1960s, showing how the experience of fighting for racial equality generated a new commitment to fight for sex equality as well. Robin Morgan gives a first-person account of changes that have taken place in her own life and in the lives of her friends as a consequence of the women's liberation movement.

Among the questions of most interest with regard to the challenge to sexism is why it took until the middle of the 1960s for a women's liberation movement to develop; why more women did not become active feminists during and after World War II; whether the family is dependent upon traditional roles for men and women; and what the implications for the society will be of greater equality for women and men. Perhaps the largest issue is how and whether sex equality can be achieved given the values and the institutions of contemporary American society.

Social Change and the American Woman, 1940–1970

William H. Chafe

In the later years of the 1970s, feminism encountered intense resistance from the anti-ERA movement and the right-to-life groups opposing abortion. More generally, a new conservatism gained force. Many believed that progress had gone too far and that it was time to call a halt to change. Nevertheless, the feminist movement had already succeeded in increasing opportunities for women, in heightening their self-awareness, and in helping to reshape American thinking about such fundamentals as social equality, the family and sexuality.

More difficult to ascertain than the gains of the women's movement, however, were its causes and origins. In the following analysis of the relationship between social change and the contemporary feminist movement, William Chafe focuses on the consequences of increasing female participation in the labor force. He is particularly concerned with the complicated interaction of objective conditions, such as employment patterns and income, and people's perceptions of those conditions, their attitudes and values. His account should provoke a deeper understanding of the sources and nature of women's liberation.

Although historians have largely neglected the role of women in America's past, few groups in the population merit closer study as a barometer of how American society operates. Not only do

Excerpted from William H. Chafe, "The Paradox of Progress: Social Change Since 1930," in James T. Patterson, ed. *Paths to the Present* (Minneapolis: Burgess Publishing Co., 1975). Reprinted by permission of the author.

women comprise a majority of the population, but gender—to-gether with race and class—serves as one of the principal reference points around which American society is organized. The sociologist Peter Berger has observed that "identity is socially bestowed, socially sanctioned and socially transformed," and gender has been one of the enduring foundations on which social identity has rested. It has provided the basis for dividing up the labor of life ("breadwinning" versus "homemaking"), it has been central to the delineation of roles and authority in the family, and it has served as the source for two powerful cultural stereotypes—"masculine" and "feminine." Any change in the nature of male and female roles thus automatically affects the home, the economy, the school, and perhaps above all, the definition of who we are as human beings. . . .

The eruption of World War II made a significant dent in this pattern. The national emergency caused new industries to develop and new jobs to open up, providing an opportunity for women, like other excluded groups, to improve their economic position. . . . Hardly a job existed which women did not perform.

The statistics of female employment suggest the dimensions of the change. Between 1941 and 1945, 6.5 million women took jobs, increasing the size of the female labor force by 57 percent. At the end of 1940 approximately 25 percent of all women were gainfully employed; four years later the figure had soared to 36 percent—an increase greater than that of the previous forty years combined. Perhaps most important from a social point of view, the largest number of new workers were married and middle-aged. Prior to 1940 young and single women had made up the vast majority of the female labor force. During the war, in contrast, 75 percent of the new workers were married, and within four years the number of wives in the labor force had doubled. Although some of the new labor recruits were newlyweds who might have been expected to work in any event, the majority listed themselves as former housewives and many, including 60 percent of those hired by the War Department, had children of school and preschool age. By the time victory was achieved, it was just as likely that a wife over forty would be employed as a single woman under twenty-five. The urgency of defeating the Axis powers had swept away, temporarily at least, one of America's entrenched customs.

If women took jobs in unprecedented numbers, however, there was little evidence of a parallel shift in attitudes toward equality between the sexes. Women were consistently excluded from top policy-making committees concerned with running the war, and from higher-level management and executive positions. In addition, the war had only a minimal effect on the traditional disparity between men's and women's wages. Although the War Manpower Commission announced a firm policy of equal pay for equal work, enforcement was spotty, and employers continued to pay women less than men simply by changing the description of the job from "heavy" to "light."

The staying power of traditional values received vigorous confirmation in the postwar years. Despite effusive expressions of gratitude for women's contribution to the war effort, many Americans believed that women should return to their rightful place in the home as soon as the war had ended. In one of the most popular treatises of the postwar years, Ferdinand Lundberg and Marynia Farnham argued that female employment was a feminist conspiracy to seduce women into betraying their biological destiny. The independent woman, they claimed, was a "contradiction in terms." Women were born to be soft, nurturant, and dependent on men; motherhood represented the true goal of female life. Sounding the same theme, Agnes Meyer wrote in the *Atlantic* that though women had many careers, "they have only one vocation—motherhood." The task of modern women, she concluded, was to "boldly announce that no job is more exacting, more necessary, or more rewarding than that of housewife and mother." Most Americans seemed to agree. A series of public opinion polls taken in the postwar years showed that a large majority of people continued to subscribe to the idea of a sharp division of labor between the sexes, with husbands making the "big" decisions and wives caring for the home.

In fact, the situation was more complicated than either public opinion polls or magazine rhetoric seemed to indicate. It was one thing to focus renewed attention on traditional values, and quite another to eradicate the impact of four years of experience. As observers noted at the time, women had discovered something new about themselves in the course of the war, and many were unwilling to give up that discovery just because the war had ended. Although most of the women workers viewed their employment as temporary when the war began, a Women's Bureau survey disclosed that by war's end, 75 percent wished to remain in the labor force.

To a surprising extent, these women succeeded in their desire to remain in the job market. Although the number of women workers declined temporarily in the period immediately after the war, female employment figures showed a sharp upturn beginning in 1947, and by 1950 had once again reached wartime peaks. By 1960 the number of women workers was growing at a rate four times faster than that of men, and 40 percent of all women over sixteen were in the labor force compared to 25 percent in 1940. More important, the women who spearheaded the change were from the same groups that had first gone to work in the war. By 1970, 45 percent of the nation's wives were employed (compared to 11.5 percent in 1930 and 15 percent in 1940), and the 1970 figure included 51 percent of all mothers with children aged six to seventeen. In addition, the economic background of the women workers had shifted significantly. During the 1930s employment of married women had been limited almost exclusively to families with poverty level incomes. By 1970, in contrast, 60 percent of all families with an income of more than $10,000 had wives who worked. In short, the whole pattern of female employment had been reversed. Through legitimizing employment for the average wife and making it a matter of patriotic necessity, the war had initiated a dramatic alteration in the behavior of women and had permanently changed the day-to-day content of their lives.

But if the "objective" conditions of female employment changed so much, why did attitudes toward equality not follow suit? Why, if so many wives and mothers were holding jobs, was there so little protest about continued low pay and discrimination? Why, above all, did the woman's movement not revive in the forties or fifties instead of developing only in the late sixties? Such questions have no easy answers, but to the extent that an explanation is possible, it has to do with the context of the times. The prospect for value changes in any period depends on the frame of reference of the participants, their awareness of the possibility or need for action, and the dominant influences at work in shaping the society. When the appropriate conditions are present, change can be explosive. When they are not present, change can take on the character of an underground fire—important in the long run but for the moment beneath the surface. The latter description fits the situation of women in the forties and fifties and a consideration of the context in which their employment increased during these years is crucial to an understanding of the relationship between behavior and attitudes.

To begin with, most women in the forties and fifties lacked the frame of reference from which to challenge prevailing attitudes on sex roles. Although many women worked, the assumptions about male and female spheres of responsibility were so deeply ingrained that to question them amounted to heresy. If social values are to be changed, there must be a critical mass of protestors who can provide an alternative ideology and mobilize opposition toward traditional points of view. In the postwar period, that protest group did not exist. Feminists at the time simply had no popular support and were generally viewed as a group of cranky women who constituted a "lunatic fringe."

In such a situation, it was not surprising that most women workers exhibited little feminist consciousness. Most had taken jobs because of the benefits associated with employment, not out of a desire to compete with men or prove their equality. When a pattern of discrimination is so pervasive that it is viewed as part of the rules of the game, few individuals will have the wherewithal to protest. It takes time and an appropriate set of social conditions before a basis for ideological protest can develop. With their experience in World War II, women had gone through the first stage of a monumental change. But it would be unrealistic to think that they could move immediately into a posture of feminist rebellion without a series of intervening stages. New perceptions had to evolve; new ideas had to gain currency. And both depended to some extent on the dominant influences at work in the immediate environment.

The second reason for the persistence of traditional attitudes was that women's employment expanded under conditions which emphasized women's role as "helpmates." The continued entry of women into the labor force was directly related to skyrocketing inflation and the pent-up desire of millions of families to achieve a higher living standard. In many instances, husbands and wives could not build new homes, buy new appliances, or purchase new cars on one income alone, and the impulse not to be left behind in the race for affluence offered a convenient rationale for women to remain in the labor force. Men who might oppose in theory the idea of married women holding jobs were willing to have their own wives go to work to help the family achieve its middle-class aspirations. But under such circumstances, the wife who held a job was playing a supportive role, not striking out on her own as an "independent" woman. The distinction was crucial. If women had been taking jobs because of a desire to prove their equality with men, their employment would probably have encountered bitter resistance. In contrast, the fact that they were thought to be only "helping out" made it possible for their efforts to receive social sanction as a fulfillment of their traditional family role.

To say that attitudes did not change, however, did not mean that behavior was without important long-range effects. Indeed, the growing employment of women offers an excellent example of the way in which changes in behavior can pave the way for subsequent changes in attitudes. As more and more wives joined the labor force after 1940, the sexual segregation of roles and responsibilities within the family slowly gave way to greater sharing. Sociological surveys showed that wherever wives held jobs, husbands performed more household tasks, especially in the areas of child care, cleaning, and shopping. In addition, power relationships between men and women underwent some change. Women who worked exercised considerably more influence on "major" economic decisions than wives who did not work. In no instance did the changes result in total equality, nor were they ideologically inspired; but sociologists unanimously concluded that women's employment played a key role in modifying the traditional distribution of tasks and authority within the family.

Similarly, the presence of an employed mother exercised a substantial impact on the socialization patterns of children. Young boys and girls who were raised in households where both parents worked grew up with the expectation that women—as well as men—would play active roles in the outside world. A number of surveys of children in elementary and junior high school showed that daughters of working mothers planned to work themselves after marriage, and the same studies suggested that young girls were more likely to name their mother as the person they most admired if she worked than if she did not work. At the same time, it appeared that these daughters developed a revised idea of what it meant to be born female. On a series of personality tests, daughters of working mothers scored lower on scales of traditional femininity and agreed that both men and women should enjoy a variety of work, household, and recreational experiences. Thus if behavioral change did not itself produce a challenge to traditional attitudes, it set in motion a process which prepared a foundation for such a challenge.

All that was required to complete the process was the development of an appropriate context, and in the early 1960s that context began to emerge. After eight years of consolidation and consensus in national politics during the Eisenhower administration, a new mood of criticism and reform started to surface in the nation. Sparked by the demands of black Americans for full equality, public leaders focused new attention on a whole variety of problems which had been festering for years. Poverty, racial injustice, and sex discrimination had a lengthy history in America, but awareness of them crystallized in a climate which emphasized the need for activism to eradicate the nation's ills. Once the process of protest had begun, it generated a momentum of its own, spreading to groups which previously had been quiescent.

Again, the experience of women dramatized the process of change. Just as World War II had served as a catalyst to behavioral change among women, the ferment of the sixties served as a catalyst to ideological change. The first major sign of the impending drive for women's liberation appeared with the publication in 1963 of Betty Friedan's best-selling *The Feminine Mystique*. Writing with eloquence and passion, Friedan traced the origins of women's oppression to a social system which persistently denied women the opportunity to develop their talents as individual human beings. "The core of the problem of women today," she wrote, "is not sexual but a problem of identity—a stunting or evasion of growth. . . ." Friedan pointed out that while men had abundant opportunities to test their mettle, women saw their entire lives circumscribed by the condition of their birth and were told repeatedly "that they could desire no greater destiny than to glory in their own femininity." If a woman had aspirations for a career, she was urged instead to find a full measure of satisfaction in the role of housewife and mother. Magazines insisted that there was no other route to happiness; consumer industries glorified her life as homemaker; and psychologists warned her that if she

left her position in the home, the whole society would be endangered. The result was that she was imprisoned in a "comfortable concentration camp," prevented from discovering who she
really *was* by a society which told her only what she *could be*.
Although Friedan's assessment contained little that had not been
said before by other feminists, her book spoke to millions of
women in a fresh way, driving home the message that what had
previously been perceived as only a personal problem was in fact a
woman problem, shared by others and rooted in a set of social
attitudes that required change if a better life was to be achieved.

A second—and equally important—influence feeding the
woman's movement came from the burgeoning drive for civil
rights. Although it was true that blacks and women had strikingly
different problems, they suffered from modes of oppression
which in some ways were similar. For women as well as blacks, the
denial of equality occurred through the assignment of separate
and unequal roles. Both were taught to "keep their place," and
were excluded from social and economic opportunities on the
grounds that assertive behavior was deviant. The principal theme
of the civil rights movement was the immorality of treating any
human being as less equal than another on the basis of a physical
characteristic, and that theme spoke as much to the condition of
women as to that of blacks. In its tactics, its message, and its moral
fervor, the civil rights movement provided inspiration and an organizational model for the activities of women.

Just as significant, the civil rights movement exposed many
women to the direct experience of sex discrimination. Younger
activists in particular found that they frequently were treated as
servants whose chief function was to be sex partners for male
leaders. ("The place of women in the movement," Stokely Carmichael said, "is prone.") Instead of having an equal voice in policy
making, women were relegated to tasks such as making coffee or
sweeping floors. Faced with such discrimination, some female activists concluded that they had to free *themselves* before they could
work effectively for the freedom of others. The same women
became the principal leaders of the younger, more radical segment of women's liberation, taking the organizing skills and ideological fervor which they had learned in the fight for blacks and
applying them to the struggle for women.

Perhaps the most important precondition for the revival of

feminism, however, was the amount of change which had already occurred in women's lives. As long as the overwhelming majority of women remained in the home, there was no frame of reference from which to question the status quo. Woman's "place" was a fact as well as an idea. With the changes which began in World War II, on the other hand, reality ceased to conform to attitudes. The march of events had already delivered a fatal blow to conventional ideas on woman's place, thereby creating a condition which made feminist arguments both timely and relevant. The experience of *some* change gave millions of women the perspective which allowed them to hear the feminist call for more change. Thus if the women who took jobs during the forties did not themselves mount an ideological assault on the status quo, they prepared a foundation which enabled the subsequent generation to take up the battle for a change in attitudes and ideas.

Women's Consciousness and the Southern Black Movement

Sara Evans

"There is no overt anti-feminism in our society in 1964," observed sociologist Alice Rossi, "not because sex equality has been achieved, but because there is practically no feminist spark left among American women." The tinder existed, as Chafe describes in the preceding selection, but an acute awareness of oppression, a fiery consciousness did not. The combustion, however, would soon be provided by the young female participants in the civil rights and New Left movements. These daughters of the middle class ignited a radical critique of sexism and a mass mobilization of American women. In the voter registration campaigns of the South and in the community organizing efforts in Northern ghettos, the female volunteers found the inner strength and self-respect, the new vistas of possibility, and the political skills to pursue their own quest for equality. There they also experienced having their work minimized, even disregarded, by the men they had considered their colleagues. This shattering ordeal spun them out of the male-dominated movements and into a new one for women's liberation. Personal Politics *(1979), by Sara Evans, and the following selection provocatively analyze these collective biographical roots of the revitalized challenge to sexism.*

Twice in the history of the United States the struggle for racial equality has been midwife to a feminist movement. In the abolition movement of the 1830s and 1840s and again in the civil-rights revolt of the 1960s, women experiencing the contradictory

Reprinted by permission of the author.

expectations and stresses of changing roles began to move from individual discontents to a social movement in their own behalf. Working for racial justice, they developed both political skills and a belief in human rights which could justify their own claim to equality. . . .

Following the first wave of sit-ins in 1960, the Southern Christian Leadership Conference (SCLC), at the insistence of its assistant director, Ella Baker, called a conference at Shaw University in Raleigh, N.C., on Easter weekend. There black youth founded their own organization, the Student Nonviolent Coordinating Committee (SNCC) to provide a support network for direct action. SNCC set the style and tone of grass-roots organizing in the rural South and led the movement into the black belt. The spirit of adventure and commitment which animated the organization added new vitality to a deeply rooted struggle for racial equality.

In addition to this crucial role within the black movement, SNCC also created the social space within which women began to develop a new sense of their own potential. A critical vanguard of young women accumulated the tools for movement building: a language to describe oppression and justify revolt, experience in the strategy and tactics of organizing, and a beginning sense of themselves collectively as objects of discrimination.

Relative deprivation is an overused and overly clinical term to describe the pain, the anger, and the ambiguity of their experience.

Nevertheless, it was precisely the clash between the heightened sense of self-worth which the movement offered to its participants and the replication of traditional sex roles within it that gave birth to a new feminism. Treated as housewives, sex objects, nurturers, and political auxiliaries, and finally threatened with banishment from the movement, young white Southern women responded with the first articulation of the modern challenge to the sexual status quo. . . .

The movement's vision translated into daily realities of hard work and responsibility which admitted few sexual limitations. Young white women's sense of purpose was reinforced by the knowledge that the work they did and the responsibilities they assumed were central to the movement. In the beginning, black and white alike agreed that whites should work primarily in the white community. They had an appropriate role in urban direct-action movements where the goal was integration, but their principal job was generating support for civil rights within the white population. The handful of white women involved in the early '60s either worked in the SNCC office—gathering news, writing pamphlets, facilitating communications—or organized campus support through such agencies as the YWCA.

In direct-action demonstrations, many women discovered untapped reservoirs of courage. Cathy Cade attended Spelman College as an exchange student in the spring of 1962. She had been there only two days when she joined Howard Zinn in a sit-in in the black section of the Georgia Legislature. Never before had she so much as joined a picket line. Years later she testified: "To this day I am amazed. I just did it." Though she understood the risks involved, she does not remember being afraid. Rather she was exhilarated, for with one stroke she undid much of the fear of blacks that she had developed as a high school student in Tennessee.

Others, like Mimi Feingold, jumped eagerly at the chance to join the freedom rides but then found the experience more harrowing than they had expected. Her group had a bomb scare in Montgomery and knew that the last freedom bus in Alabama had been blown up. They never left the bus from Atlanta to Jackson, Mississippi. The arrest in Jackson was anti-climactic. Then there was a month in jail where she could hear women screaming as they were subjected to humiliating vaginal "searches."

When SNCC moved into voter registration projects in the Deep South, the experiences of white women acquired a new dimension. The years of enduring the brutality of intransigent racism finally convinced SNCC to invite several hundred white students into Mississippi for the 1964 "freedom summer." For the first time, large numbers of white women would be allowed into "the field," to work in the rural South.

They had previously been excluded because white women in rural communities were highly visible; their presence, violating both racial and sexual taboos, often provoked repression. According to Mary King, "the start of violence in a community was often tied to the point at which white women appeared to be in the civil-rights movement." However, the presence of whites also brought the attention of the national media, and, in the face of the apparent impotence of the federal law enforcement apparatus, the media became the chief weapon of the movement against violence and brutality. Thus, with considerable ambivalence, SNCC began to include whites—both men and women—in certain voter registration projects.

The freedom summer brought hundreds of Northern white women into the Southern movement. They taught in freedom schools, ran libraries, canvassed for voter registration, and endured constant harassment from the local whites. Many reached well beyond their previously assumed limits: "I was overwhelmed at the idea of setting up a library all by myself," wrote one woman. "Then can you imagine how I felt when at Oxford, while I was learning how to drop on the ground to protect my face, my ears, and my breasts, I was asked to *coordinate* the libraries in the entire project's community centers? I wanted to cry 'HELP' in a number of ways."

And while they tested themselves and questioned their own courage, they also experienced poverty, oppression and discrimination in raw form. As one volunteer wrote:

> For the first time in my life, I am seeing what it is like to be poor, oppressed, and hated. And what I see here does not apply only to Gulfport or to Mississippi or even to the South. . . . This summer is only the briefest beginning of this experience."

Some women virtually ran the projects they were in. And they learned to live with an intensity of fear that they had never known before. By October 1964, there had been 15 murders, 4 woundings, 37 churches bombed or burned, and over 1,000 arrests in Mississippi. Every project set up elaborate security precautions— regular communication by two-way radio, rules against going out at night or walking downtown in interracial groups. One woman summed up the experience of hundreds when she explained, "I learned a lot of respect for myself for having gone through all that."

As white women tested themselves in the movement, they were constantly inspired by the examples of black women who shattered cultural images of appropriate "female" behavior. "For the first time," according to one white Southerner, "I had role models I could respect."

Within the movement many of the legendary figures were black women around whom circulated stories of exemplary courage and audacity. Rarely did women expect or receive any special protection in demonstrations or jails. Frequently, direct-action teams were equally divided between women and men, on the theory that the presence of women in sit-in demonstrations might lessen the violent reaction. In 1960, slender Diane Nash had been transformed overnight from a Fisk University beauty queen to a principal leader of the direct-action movement in Nashville, Tennessee. . . .

Perhaps even more important than the daring of younger activists was the towering strength of older black women. There is no doubt that women were key to organizing the black community. In 1962, SNCC staff member Charles Sherrod wrote the office that in every southwest Georgia county "there is always a 'mama.' She is usually a militant woman in the community, out-spoken, understanding, and willing to catch hell, having already caught her share."

Stories of such women abound. For providing housing, food, and active support to SNCC workers, their homes were fired upon and bombed. Fannie Lou Hamer, the Sunflower County sharecropper who forfeited her livelihood to emerge as one of the most courageous and eloquent leaders of the Mississippi Freedom Democratic Party, was only the most famous. "Mama Dolly" in Lee County, Georgia, was a seventy-year-old, grey-haired lady "who can pick more cotton, slop more pigs, plow more ground, chop more wood, and do a hundred more things better than the best farmer in the area." For many white volunteers, they were also "mamas" in the sense of being mother-figures, new models of the meaning of womanhood.

Yet new models bumped up against old ones; self-assertion generated anxiety; new expectations existed alongside traditional ones; ideas about freedom and equality bent under assumptions about women as mere houseworkers and sexual objects. These contradictory forces finally generated a feminist response from those who could not deny the reality of their new-found strength.

Black and white women took on important administrative roles in the Atlanta SNCC office, but they also performed virtually all typing and clerical work. Very few women assumed the public roles of national leadership. In 1964, black women held a half-serious, half-joking sit-in to protest these conditions. By 1965, the situation had changed enough that a quarrel over who would take notes at staff meetings was settled by buying a tape recorder.

In the field, there was a tendency to assume that housework around the freedom house would be performed by women. As early as 1963, Joni Rabinowitz, a white volunteer in the southwest Georgia Project, submitted a stinging series of reports on the "woman's role."

"Monday, 15 April: . . . The attitude around here toward keeping the house neat (as well as the general attitude toward the inferiority and 'proper place' of women) is disgusting and also terribly depressing. I never saw a cooperative enterprize (sic) that was less cooperative."

There were also ambiguities in the position of women who had been in the movement for many years and were perceived by others as important leaders. While women increasingly became a central force in SNCC between 1960 and 1965, white women were always in a somewhat anomalous position. New recruits saw Casey Hayden and Mary King as very powerful. Hayden had been an activist since the late '50s. Her involvement in the YWCA and the Christian Faith and Life Community at the University of Texas led her to join the demonstrations which erupted in Austin in 1959. From that time on she worked full-time against segregation, sometimes through the Y, sometimes through the National Student Association or Students for a Democratic Society, but always most closely with SNCC. Mary King, daughter of a Southern Methodist minister, had visited SNCC on a trip sponsored by the Y at Ohio Wesleyan University in 1962 and soon returned to work full-time.

They and others who had joined the young movement when it included only a handful of whites knew the inner circles of SNCC through years of shared work and risk. They had an easy familiarity with the top leadership which bespoke considerable influence. Yet Hayden and King could virtually run a freedom registration program and at the same time remain outside the basic political decision-making process.

Mary King described herself and Hayden as being in "positions of relative powerlessness." They were powerful because they worked very hard. According to King, "If you were a hard worker and you were good, at least before 1965 . . . you could definitely have an influence on policy."

222 THE CHALLENGE TO SEXISM

The key phrase is "at least before 1965," for by 1965 the positions of white women in SNCC, especially Southern women whose goals had been shaped by the vision of the "beloved community," was in steep decline. Ultimately, a growing spirit of black nationalism, fed by the tensions of large numbers of whites, especially women, entering the movement, forced these women out of SNCC and precipitated the articulation of a new feminism.

White women's presence inevitably heightened the sexual tension which runs as a constant current through racist culture. Southern women understood that in the struggle against racial discrimination they were at war with their culture. They reacted to the label "Southern lady" as though it were an obscene epithet, for they had emerged from a society that used the symbol of "Southern white womanhood" to justify an insidious pattern of racial discrimination and brutal repression. They had, of necessity, to forge a new sense of self, a new definition of femininity apart from the one they had inherited. Gradually they came to understand the struggle against racism as "a key to pulling down all the . . . fascist notions and mythologies and institutions in the South," including "notions about white women and repression."

Thus, for Southern women this tension was a key to their incipient feminism, but it also became a disruptive force within the civil-rights movement itself. The entrance of white women in large numbers into the movement could hardly have been anything but explosive. Interracial sex was the most potent social taboo in the South. And the struggle against racism brought together young, naive, sometimes insensitive, rebellious, and idealistic white women with young, angry black men, some of whom had hardly been allowed to speak to white women before. They sat-in together. If they really believed in equality, why shouldn't they sleep together?

In many such relationships there was much warmth and caring. Several marriages resulted. One young woman described how "a whole lot of things got shared around sexuality—like black men with white women—it wasn't just sex, it was also sharing ideas and fears, and emotional support . . . My sexuality for myself was confirmed by black men for the first time ever in my life, see . . . and I needed that very badly . . . It's a positive advantage to be a big woman in the black community."

On the other hand, there remained a dehumanizing quality in

many relationships. According to one woman, it "had a lot to do with the fact that people thought they might die." They lived their lives at an incredible pace and could not be very loving toward anybody. "So [people] would go to a staff meeting and . . . sleep with whoever was there."

Sexual relationships did not become a serious problem, however, until interracial sex became a widespread phenomenon in local communities in the summer of 1964. The same summer that opened new horizons to hundreds of women simultaneously induced serious strains within the movement itself. Accounts of what happened vary according to the perspectives of the observer.

Some paint a picture of hordes of "loose" white women coming to the South and spreading corruption wherever they went. One male black leader recounted that "where I was project director we put white women out of the project within the first three weeks because they tried to screw themselves across the city." He agreed that black neighborhood youth tended to be sexually aggressive. "I mean you are trained to be aggressive in this country, but you are also not expected to get a positive response."

Others saw the initiative coming almost entirely from males. According to historian Staughton Lynd, director of the Freedom Schools, "Every black SNCC worker with perhaps a few exceptions counted it a notch on his gun to have slept with a white woman—as many as possible. And I think that was just very traumatic for the women who encountered that, who hadn't thought that was what going South was about." A white woman who worked in Virginia for several years explained, "It's much harder to say 'No' to the advances of a black guy because of the strong possibility of that being taken as racist."

Clearly the boundary between sexual freedom and sexual exploitation was a thin one. Many women consciously avoided all romantic involvements in intuitive recognition of that fact. Yet the presence of hundreds of young whites from middle- and upper-middle-income families in a movement primarily of poor, rural blacks exacerbated latent racial and sexual tensions beyond the breaking point. The first angry response came not from the surrounding white community (which continually assumed sexual excesses far beyond the reality) but from young black women in the movement.

A black woman pointed out that white women would "do all the shit work and do it in a feminine kind of way while [black women] . . . were out in the streets battling with the cops. So it did something to what [our] femininity was about. We became amazons, less than and more than women at the same time." Another black woman added, "If white women had a problem in SNCC, it was not just a male/woman problem . . . it was also a black woman/ white woman problem. It was a race problem rather than a woman's problem." And a white woman, asked whether she experienced any hostility from black women, responded, "Oh tons and tons! I was very, very afraid of black women, very afraid." Though she admired them and was continually awed by their courage and strength, her sexual relationships with black men placed a barrier between herself and black women.

Soon after the 1964 summer project, black women in SNCC sharply confronted male leadership. They charged that they could not develop relationships with black men because the men did not have to be responsible to them as long as they could turn to involvement with white women.

Black women's anger and demands constituted one part of an intricate maze of tensions and struggles that were in the process of transforming the civil-rights movement. SNCC had grown from a small band of sixteen to a swollen staff of 180, of whom 50% were white. The earlier dream of a beloved community was dead. The vision of freedom lay crushed under the weight of intransigent racism, disillusion with electoral politics and nonviolence, and differences of race, class, and culture within the movement itself. Within the rising spirit of black nationalism, the anger of black women toward white women was only one element. . . .

For Southern white women who had devoted several years of their lives to the vision of a beloved community, the rejection of nonviolence and movement toward a more ideological, centralized, and black nationalist movement was bitterly disillusioning. Mary King recalled, "It was very sad to see something that was so creative and so dynamic and so strong [disintegrating] . . . . I was terribly disappointed for a long time. . . . I was most affected by the way that black women turned against me. That hurt more than the guys. But it had been there, you know. You could see it coming."

In the fall of 1965, Mary King and Casey Hayden spent several days of long discussions in the mountains of Virginia. Both of them were on their way out of the movement, though they were not fully conscious of that fact. Finally they decided to write a "kind of memo" addressed to "a number of other women in the peace and freedom movements." In it they argued that women, like blacks, "seem to be caught in a common-law caste system that operates, sometimes subtly, forcing them to work around or outside hierarchical structures of power which may exclude them. Women seem to be placed in the same position of assumed subordination in personal situations too. It is a caste system which, at its worst, uses and exploits women."

Hayden and King set the precedent of contrasting the movement's egalitarian ideas with the replication of sex roles within it. They noted the ways in which women's position in society determined women's roles in the movement—like cleaning houses, doing secretarial work, and refraining from active or public leadership. At the same time, they observed, "having learned from the movement to think radically about the personal worth and abilities of people whose role in society had gone unchallenged before, a lot of women in the movement have begun trying to apply those lessons to their own relationships with men. Each of us probably has her own story of the various results."

They spoke of the pain of trying to put aside "deeply learned fears, needs, and self-perceptions . . . and . . . to replace them with concepts of people and freedom learned from the movement and organizing." In this process many people in the movement had questioned basic institutions, such as marriage and child-rearing. Indeed, such issues had been discussed over and over again, but seriously only among women. The usual male response was laughter, and women were left feeling silly. Hayden and King lamented the "lack of community for discussion: Nobody is writing, or organizing, or talking publicly about women, in any way that reflects the problems that various women in the movement came across." Yet despite their feelings of invisibility, their words also demonstrated the ability to take the considerable risks involved in sharp criticisms. Through the movement they had developed too much self-confidence and self-respect to accept passively subordinate roles.

The memo was addressed principally to black women—long time friends and comrades-in-nonviolent-arms—in the hope that, "perhaps we can start to talk with each other more openly than in the past and create a community of support for each other so we can deal with ourselves and others with integrity and can therefore keep working." In some ways, it was a parting attempt to halt the metamorphosis in the civil-rights movement from nonviolence to nationalism, from beloved community to black power. It expressed Hayden and King's pain and isolation as white women in the movement. The black women who received it were on a different historic trajectory. They would fight some of the same battles as women, but in a different context and in their own way.

This "kind of memo" represented a flowering of women's consciousness that articulated contradictions felt most acutely by middle-class white women. While black women had been gaining strength and power within the movement, white women's position—at the nexus of sexual and racial conflicts—had become increasingly precarious. Their feminist response, then, was precipitated by loss in the immediate situation, but it was a sense of loss against the even deeper background of new strength and self-worth which the movement had allowed them to develop. Like their foremothers in the nineteenth century, they confronted this dilemma with the tools which the movement had given them: a language to name and describe oppression; a deep belief in freedom, equality and community soon to be translated into "sisterhood"; a willingness to question and challenge any social institution which failed to meet human needs; and the ability to organize.

It is not surprising that the issues were defined and confronted first by Southern women whose consciousness developed in a context which inextricably and paradoxically linked the fate of women and black people. These spiritual daughters of Sarah and Angelina Grimke kept their expectations low in November, 1965. "Objectively," Hayden and King wrote, "the chances seem nil that we could start a movement based on anything as distant to general American thought as a sex-caste system." But change was in the air and youth was on the march.

In the North there were hundreds of women who had shared in the Southern experience for a week, a month, a year, and thousands more who participated vicariously or worked to extend the struggle for freedom and equality into Northern communities. These women were ready to hear what their Southern sisters had to say. The debate within Students for a Democratic Society (SDS) which started in response to Hayden and King's ideas led, two years later, to the founding of the women's liberation movement.

Thus, the fullest expression of conscious feminism within the civil-rights movement ricocheted off the fury of black power and landed with explosive force in the Northern, white new left. One month after Hayden and King mailed out their memo, women who had read it staged an angry walkout of a national SDS conference in Champaign-Urbana, Illinois. The only man to defend their action was a black man from SNCC.

Rights of Passage

Robin Morgan

The relationship of women's liberation to the civil rights movement can also be viewed through their analogous stages of protest. Both began with educational campaigns designed to overcome inequities assumed to be largely the result of ignorance or inadvertence. Then, when separate individuals realized that their plight was not unique but actually common to a very large group, they sought a political solution to rectify their powerlessness. Finally, the two movements engaged in a cultural and psychological assault against racism *and* sexism *and the institutions that perpetuate them.*

Because those complex amalgams of attitudes and convictions are the creation of thousands of years of thought and reinforced patterns of behavior so deeply imprinted that they are assumed to be "natural" or "instinctive," their eradication is surely the most difficult aspect of liberation. For individuals, it is often the most painful of passages. Robin Morgan—radical feminist, wife, poet, mother, and director of the New York Women's Law Center—in this excerpt from an autobiographical essay which appeared in Ms. *in 1975 describes her personal odyssey in the women's movement. Students should consider the revolutionary meaning of Morgan's conclusions, and the ways in which the demise of sexism can free both sexes to develop and contribute to their full potential.*

I wanted to write a sort of "personal retrospective" on the Women's Movement: where we've been, where we are, where we

From Robin Morgan, "Rights of Passage," *Ms. Magazine*, November 1975. Reprinted by permission of the publisher.

might be going—all this in a classically theoretical style, preferably obscure, yea, unintelligible, so that people would be unable to understand what in hell I was saying and would label me, therefore, A Brilliant Thinker. But the risk-taking, subjective voice of poetry is more honestly my style, and so, to look at the Women's Movement, I go to the mirror—and gaze at myself. Everywoman? Surely a staggering egotism, that! I hardly believe "Le Mouvement, c'est moi." I *do* still believe, though, that the personal is political, and vice versa (the *politics* of sex, the *politics* of housework, the *politics* of motherhood), and that this insight into the necessary integration of exterior realities and interior imperatives is one of the themes of consciousness that makes the Women's Movement unique, less abstract, and more functionally *possible* than previous movements for social change.

So I must dare to begin with myself, my own experience.

Ten years ago I was a woman who believed in the reality of the vaginal orgasm (and had become adept at faking spiffy ones). I felt legitimized by a successful crown roast and was the fastest hand in the east at emptying ashtrays. I never condemned pornography for fear of seeming unsophisticated and prudish. My teenage rebellion against my mother had atrophied into a permanent standoff. Despite hours of priming myself to reflect the acceptable beauty standards, I was convinced that my body was lumpy, my face was possessed of a caterpillar's bone structure, and my hair was resolutely unyielding to *any* flattering style. And ten years ago my poems quietly began muttering something about my personal pain as a woman—unconnected, of course, to anyone else, since I saw this merely as my own inadequacy, my own battle. . . .

That was the period when I still could fake a convincing orgasm, still wouldn't be caught dead confronting an issue like pornography (for fear, this time, of being "a bad-vibes, uptight, unhip chick"). I could now afford to reject my mother for a new, radical-chic reason: the generation gap. I learned to pretend contempt for monogamy as both my husband and I careened (secretly grieving for each other) through the fake "sexual revolution" of the sixties. Meanwhile, correctly Maoist beancurd and class-conscious rice and beans filled our menus—and I *still* put in hours priming myself to reflect the acceptable "beauty" standards, those of a tough-broad street fighter: uniform jeans, combat boots, long hair, and sunglasses worn even at night (which didn't help one see better when running from rioting cops). And my poems lurched forth guiltily, unevenly, while I developed a chronic case of Leningitis and mostly churned out those "political" essays—although Donne and Dickinson, Kafka, Woolf, and James were still read in secret at our home (dangerous intellectual tendencies), and television was surreptitiously watched (decadent bourgeois privileges).

For years my essays implored, in escalating tones, the "brothers" of the "revolution" to let us women in, to take more-than-lip-service notice of what the women's caucuses were saying, especially since "they" (women) constitute more than half the human species. Then, at a certain point, I began to stop addressing such men as "brothers," and began (O language, thou subtle Richter scale of attitudinal earthquakes!) to use the word "we" when speaking of women. And there was no turning back.

The ensuing years can seem to me a blur of joy, misery, and daily surprise: my first consciousness-raising group and all the "daughter" groups I was in; the guerrilla theater, the marches, meetings, demonstrations, picketings, sit-ins, conferences, workshops, plenaries; the newspaper projects, the child-care collectives, the first anti-rape squads, the earliest seminars (some women now prefer the word "ovulars"—how lovely!) on women's health, women's legal rights, women's sexuality. And all the while, the profound "interior" changes: the transformation of my work—content, language, *and* form—released by this consciousness; the tears and shouts and laughter and despair and growth wrought in the struggle with my husband; the birth of our child (a radicalizing experience, to say the least); the detailed examinations of life experiences, of power, honesty, commitment, bravely explored through so many vulnerable hours with other women— the discovery of a shared suffering and of a shared determination to become whole.

During those years we felt a desparate urgency, arising partly from the barrage of brain-boggling "clicks" our consciousness encountered about our condition as females in a partriarchal world; but also, I must confess, arising from the leftover influence of the male movements, which were given to abstract rhetoric but "ejaculatory tactics." That is, if the revolution as they defined it didn't occur within the next week, month, five years at the minimum—

then the hell with it. We wouldn't be alive, anyway, to see it, so we must die for it (this comfortably settled the necessity for any long-range *planning*).

Today, my just-as-ever-urgent anger is tempered by a patience born of the recognition that the *process*, the *form of change itself, is everything:* the means and the goal justifying *each other.*

There are no easy victories, no pat answers—and anyone who purveys such solutions alarms me now. But when I look back from my still-militantly rocking chair, or sit at my ultimate weapon, the typewriter, I see the transformations spiraling upward so rapidly and so astonishingly that my heart swells with gratitude to have been a part of such changes.

We were an "American phenomenon," they said—an outgrowth of the neurosis and stridency of spoiled American women. ("They" were the patriarchal left, right, and middle, the media, most men, and some women.) They overlooked certain little facts: that women had been oppressed longer than any other group, this subjugation having stood as the model for all subsequent forms of oppression; that women were a *majority* of the world's population; that specific commonalities of biology, attitude, and certainly treatment potentially united us across all the patriarchally imposed barriers of race, age, class, sexual preference, superficial politics, and lifestyles. Now, as I write, this potential is vibrating throughout the globe—among Women's Movements in Senegal and Tanzania, Japan and Australia, China and South America, and all across Europe, New Zealand, Algeria, Canada, Israel, Egypt, and the Indian subcontinent.

We were "a white, middle-class, youth movement," they said. And even as some of us wrung our hands with guilt hand lotion, we knew otherwise. Because there were from the beginning women involved who were of every class and race and age, even if the media did focus on a conveniently stereotyped "feminist image." . . .

They said we were "anti-housewife," though many of us *were* housewives, and it was not us, but society itself, as structured by men, which had contempt for life-sustenance tasks. Today, too many housewives are in open participation in the Women's Movement to be ignored—and many are talking of a housewives' union. (Not to speak of the phenomenon of "runaway wives," as the news media calls them in articles which puzzle over the "motivation" of women who simply have picked up one dirty sock too many from the living-room floor.)

They said we were "a lesbian plot," and the carefully implanted and fostered bigotry of many heterosexual feminists rose eagerly, destructively, to deny that, thereby driving many lesbian women out of the Movement, back into the arms of their gay "brothers," who promptly shoved mimeograph machines at them. What a choice. But the process did continue, and so the pendulum swung into its tactically tragic but expectable position, a reply-in-kind from some lesbian-feminists who created the politics of "dyke separatism," the refusal to work with or sometimes even speak to women who could not prove lesbian credentials. This was sometimes accompanied by the proclamation that lesbians were the only true feminists, or were the feminist "vanguard," and the accusation that all heterosexual women were forever "sold out" to men (leaving lesbian mothers, by the way, in a no-woman's-land). In some parts of the country it was called "the lesbian-straight split"—or even the "lesbian-feminist split"—with a terrifying antagonism on both sides. Yet most serious feminists continued to work together, across sexual-preference labeling, and the process endured (through many, many tears), and we survived. . . .

They said we were "anti-motherhood"—and in the growing pains of certain periods, some of us were. There were times when I was made to feel guilty for having wanted and borne a child—let alone a male one, forgodsake. There were other times when we "collectivized" around children, and I found myself miffed at the temporary loss of that relationship unique to the specific mother and specific child. So much of the transition is understandable now. Since the patriarchy commanded women to be mothers (the thesis), we had to rebel with our own polarity and declare motherhood a reactionary cabal (antithesis). Today, a *new* synthesis is emerging: the concept of mother-right, the affirmation of childbearing and/or child-rearing when it is a woman's *choice*. And while that synthesis itself will in turn become a new thesis (a dialectic, a process, a development), it is refreshing at last to be able to come out of my mother-closet and yell to the world that I love my dear wonderful delicious child—and am not one damned whit less the radical feminist for that.

None of the above-mentioned issues, or even "splits," among us as women is simple. None is "solved." Struggle, experimentation, and examination of each of these differences (and new ones yet to come will continue, must continue, for years.) And we can expect these divisions to be exploited as *diversions* by those who would love to see us fail. But that no longer scares or depresses me, despite the enormity of the job ahead. The only thing that does frighten me is the superficial treatment of any such issue, the simplifying of complexities out of intellectual laziness, fear of the unknown, or rigidified thinking. Yet despite the temptation to fall into such traps of "non-thought," the growth does continue and the motion cannot be stopped. There is no turning back.

I call myself a radical feminist, and that means specific things to me. The etymology of the word "radical" refers to "one who goes to the root." I believe that sexism is the root oppression, the one which, until and unless we *up*root it, will continue to put forth the branches of racism, war, class hatred, ageism, competition, ecological disaster, and economic exploitation. This means, to me, that all the so-called revolutions to date have been *coups d'etat* between men, in a halfhearted attempt to prune the branches but leave the root embedded—for the sake of preserving their own male privileges. Yet this also means that I'm not out for us as women to settle for a "piece of the pie," equality in an unjust society, or for mere "top-down" change which can be corrupted into leaving the basic system unaltered. I think our feminist revolution gains momentum from a "ripple effect"—from each individual woman gaining self-respect and yes, power, over her own body and soul first, then within her family, on her block, in her town, state, and so on out from the center, overlapping with similar changes other women are experiencing, the circles rippling more widely and inclusively as they go. This is a revolution in consciousness, rising expectations, and the actions which reflect that organic process.

In the past decade I have seen just such methods give birth to hundreds of alternate feminist institutions, created and sustained by women's energy—all concrete moves toward self-determination and power. . . .

Whenever I hear certain men sonorously announce that the Women's Movement is dead (a prediction they have been promoting hopefully since 1968), I am moved to an awkwardly unmili-

tant hilarity. I know, of course, that they mean we seem less sensational: "Where are all those bra-burnings?" (none of which ever
took place anyway, to my knowledge). Such death-knell articula-
tions are not only (deliberately?) unaware of multiform alternate
institutions that are mushrooming, but unconscious of the more
profound and threatening-to-the-status-quo political *attitudes*
which underlie that surface. It is, for example, a grave error to
see feminists as "retrenching" when the reality is that we have
been maturing beyond those aforementioned "ejaculatory tactics"
into a long-term, committed attitude toward *winning*. We are dig-
ging in, since we know that patriarchy won't be unbuilt in a day,
and the revolution we are making is one on *every* front: economic,
social, political, cultural, personal, public, sexual, biological, and
yes, even metaphysical.

The early ultra-egalitarianism and guilt-ridden "downward mobility" motifs of certain radical feminist groups, for instance, have
modulated into a realization that women deserve to have credit
for what we accomplish, whether that be the author's name signed
to her article (after centuries of being "Anonymous"), or the right
to be paid a living wage for her work at a feminist business (instead of falling prey to a new volunteerism—this one "for the
revolution's sake"). The early antipathy toward any and all structure has given way to a recognition that we must evolve totally
new ways of organizing ourselves, something else than chaotic
spontaneity or masculinist hierarchy. The early excesses of collective tyranny have shifted into an understanding that there is a
difference between individualism and individuality—and that the
latter is precious and to be cherished. The emphases on women's
studies reflect the welcome end of anti-intellectual trends (again
picked up from male movements—a "line" created by privileged
men who already had their college educations along with their
charisma points in SDS or the counter-culture). We are daring to
demand and explore the delights of hard intellectual work, both
as personal challenge and as shared necessity. All the jargon ex-
horting us to "seize power" won't help if we "seize" the labs, for
instance, and stand ignorantly gaping at the test tubes. We are
daring to research our own cleverly buried herstorical past, even
to develop new radical teaching methods as joint odysseys between teachers and students, without deification—or degradation—of either. . . .

And where, my dear reader may well ask, does this Pollyanna writer see the dangers, the failures, the losses? Or is she so blind, the woman in the mirror, that she thinks we've really come a long way, baby? Hardly.

These arms have held the vomitous shudderings of a sister-prostitute undergoing forced jail-withdrawal from her heroin addiction. These eyes have wept over the suicide of a sister-poet. These shoulders have tightened at the vilifications of men—on the street, in the media, on the lecture platform. These fists have clenched at the reality of backlash against us: the well-financed "friends of the fetus" mobilizing again to retake what small ground we have gained in the area of abortion; the rise in rape statistics (not only because more women are daring to *report* rapes, but also because more rapes are *occurring*); the ghastly mutilation-murders of women rumored to be witches (in the Catskill and Appalachian regions during the past two years) as an ominous message to all women who challenge patriarchal definitions. This stomach has knotted at the anonymous phone calls, the unsigned death threats, the real bombs planted in real auditoriums before a poetry reading or speech, the real bullet fired from a real pistol at the real podium behind which I was standing. (Those who have real power over our lives recognize the threat we pose—even when we ourselves do not.)

And yes, these fingers have knotted *their* versions of "correct lines"—strangling my own neck and the necks of other sisters.

I have watched some of the best minds of *my feminist* generation go mad with impatience and despair. So many other "oldie" radical feminists lost, having themselves lost the vision in all its intricacy, having let themselves be driven into irrelevance: the analytical pioneer whose "premature" brilliance isolated her into solipsism and finally self-signed-in commitment for "mental treatment"; the theorist whose nihilistic fear of "womanly" emotion led her into an obfuscated style and a "negative charisma"—an obsessive "I accuse" acridity corrosive to herself and other women; the fine minds lost to alcohol, or to "personal solutions," or to inertia, or to the comforting central-committeeist neat blueprint of outmoded politics, or to the equally reassuring glaze of "humanism," a word often misused as a bludgeon to convince women that we must put our suffering back at the bottom of the priority list. Some of these women never actually worked on a tangible feminist project—

storefront legal counseling or a nursery or a self-help clinic—or if
they did so at one time they have long ago stopped, lost touch with
women outside their own "feminist café society" circles. Such alienation from the world of women's genuine daily needs seems to
have provoked in some of my sister "oldies" a bizarre new definition of "radical feminist"; that is, one who relentlessly assails any
political effectiveness on the part of other feminists, while frequently choosing to do so in terms of personalities and with slash-
ing cruelty. After so many centuries of spending all our compassion on men, could we not spare a little for each other?

I've watched the bloody internecine warfare between groups,
between individuals. All that fantastic energy going to fight each
other instead of our oppression! (It is, after all, safer to attack
"just women.") So much false excitement, self-righteousness and
judgmental posturing! Gossip, accusations, counter-accusations,
smears—all leapt to, spread, and sometimes believed without the
impediments of such things as facts. I've come to think that we
need a feminist code of ethics, that we need to create a new
women's morality, an antidote of honor against this contagion by
male supremacist values. . . .

I would say to those few dear "oldies" who are burned out or
embittered: you have forgotten that women are not fools, not
sheep. We know about the dangers of commercialism and token-
ism from the male right, and the dangers of manipulation and
cooptation from the male left (the boys' establishment and the
boys' movement). We are, frankly, bored by correct lines and
vanguards and failurism and particularly by that chronic disease—guilt. Those of us who choose to struggle with men we
love, well, we demand respect and support for that, and an end to
psychological torture. Those of us who choose to relate solely to
other women demand respect and support for *that,* and an end to
the legal persecution and attitudinal bigotry that condemns freedom of sexual choice. Those of us who choose to have or choose
not to have children demand support and respect for *that.* We
know that the emerging women's art and women's spirituality are
lifeblood for our survival—resilient cultures have kept oppressed
groups alive even when economic analyses and revolutionary
strategy have fizzled.

We know that serious, lasting change does not come about
overnight, or simply, or without enormous pain and diligent examination and tireless, undramatic, everyday-a-bit-more-one-

step-at-a-time work. We know that such change seems to move in cycles (thesis, antithesis, and synthesis—which itself in turn becomes a new thesis . . .), and we also know that those cycles are not merely going around in circles. They are, rather, an *upward spiral*, so that each time we reevaluate a position or place we've been before we do so from a new perspective. We are *in process*, continually evolving, and we will no longer be made to feel inferior or ineffectual for knowing and being what we are at any given moment.

This process has changed my life. Today, my sexuality unfolds in ever more complex, beautiful, and self-satisfying layers. Today, I can affirm my mother and identify with her beyond all my intricate ambivalence. I can confront ersatz "sexual liberation" and its pornographic manifestos for what they are—degrading sexist propaganda. And I can confess my pride at an ongoing committed relationship with the husband I love and have always loved and whose transformation by feminism I have watched over and struggled with and marveled at. This process has given me the tools, as well, to affirm the woman I love, to help raise the child I love in new and freer ways. I have now curled round another spiral, and can admit that I *like* good food and enjoy cooking it (when that's not assumed to be my reason for existing). I have found my own appearance at last. No more "uniforms," but clothes that are comfortable, simple, pleasant, and *me;* hair that I cut or let grow as *I* choose, unconforming to fashion as dictated by *Vogue* or its inverse image, *Rolling Stone.* And this process, most of all, has given me the tools of self-respect as a woman artist, so that I am reclaiming my own shameless singing poet's voice beyond the untenable choices of "ivory tower, uninvolved" fake art or that grim "socialist-realist" polemical pseudo-art.

This ecstatic reclamation of my own art (and my brazen affirmation, indeed of *all* art) is inseparable from what I have lovingly named "metaphysical feminism"—the refusal to simplify or polarize, the insatiable demand for a passionate, intelligent, complex, visionary, and *continuing* process which dares to include in its patterns everything from the scientific transformation which stars express as they nova, to the metaphorical use of that expression in a poem; a process which dares to celebrate contradiction and diversity, dares to see each field-daisy as miraculous, each pebble as profound, each sentient being as holy.

And also, more humbly, this process, this Women's Movement,

has given me the chance to travel through it, to witness the splendor of women's faces all over America blossoming with hope, to hear women's voices rising in an at-first fragile, then stronger chorus of anger and determination. Pocatello, Idaho, and Escanaba, Michigan, and Lawrence, Kansas, and Sarasota, Florida, and Sacramento, California, and Portales, New Mexico, and Northampton, Massachusetts—and how many others? It has exhausted me, this Women's Movement, and sometimes made me cranky and guilty and gossipy and manipulative and self-pitying and self-righteous and sour. It has exasperated me, frustrated me, and driven me gloriously crazy.

But it is in my blood, and I love it, do you hear? I know in my bones that women's consciousness and our desire for freedom and the power to forge a humane world society will survive even the mistakes the Women's Movement makes—as if feminism were a card-carrying nitsy little sect and not what it *is*, a profoundly radical and perpetually enlarging vision of what can save this planet. . . . There are millions of us now, and the vision is expanding its process to include us all.

I trust that process with my life. I have learned to love that Women's Movement, that face in the mirror, wearing its new, wry, patient smile; those eyes that have rained grief but can still see clearly; that body with its unashamed sags and stretch marks; that mind, with all its failings and its cowardices and its courage and its inexhaustible will to try again.

I want to say to that woman: we've only just begun, and there's no stopping us. I want to tell her that she is maturing and stretching and daring and yes, succeeding, in ways undreamt until now. She will survive the naysayers, male *and* female, and she will coalesce in all her wondrously various forms and diverse lifestyles, ages, races, classes, and internationalities into one harmonious blessing on this agonized world. She is so very beautiful, and I love her. The face in the mirror is myself.

And the face in the mirror is you.

Part Six

VIETNAM

The war in Vietnam represents one of the most difficult military and foreign policy experiences in American history. Each step of American involvement seemed merely a modification of past practice, an increment to existing policy, and therefore nothing that required a declaration of war or a full scale reassessment of underlying policies. Through such a process American participation in Vietnam grew from 800 troops in 1960 to 15,000 in 1963 to more than 500,000 in 1968. A civil war between the Vietnamese became an American war; the United States was perceived by most people in the world as a colonialist aggressor; and the American people themselves divided into warring factions over support or opposition to the war.

Ironically, the United States became involved in Vietnam less because of any interest in Southeast Asia itself than in order to achieve other foreign policy goals. Franklin Roosevelt had decided during World War II that colonialism should end in Southeast Asia. But after the war American officials reversed that stance. To mollify France's unhappiness over the rebuilding of Germany, the U.S. countenanced French policy in Southeast Asia. By 1948, the U.S. was providing crucial economic and political sustenance for the French occupation of Indochina.

When the French lost their own Vietnam war in 1954 and the Geneva conference divided Vietnam into two regions, the United States stepped in to provide support for the pro-western government of President Diem. This seemed a moderate enough action at the time, particularly given the fact that President Eisenhower had earlier refused a French request to use atomic weapons against the Vietnamese. But that moderate involvement in support of Diem provided the basis for ever increasing commitments of American money and manpower. When John F. Kennedy became president, Vietnam became a testing point of the battle against communism—again, not so much because of its own intrinsic importance as because of events elsewhere. After the debacle at the Bay of Pigs in April 1961, and Kennedy's confrontation with Khrushchev at Vienna in June 1961, the young American president wanted to find some place where he could take a stand and convey to the Russians his determination to hold firm against communism. Vietnam became such a place, and during the Kennedy years the United States significantly expanded the flow of foreign aid and military equipment to South Vietnam, increased the number of American troops engaged in the conflict to over 15,000, and launched a major effort at counterinsurgency. At the same time, however, the U.S. remained publicly committed to political reform in Vietnam and to the proposition that it was impossible for the United States itself to fight a war that the Vietnamese did not wish to wage.

It was Lyndon Johnson's misfortune to preside over the most massive and disastrous expansion of the war. Deeply committed to maintaining a strong military presence, fearful of abandoning Kennedy's policy, and anxious to put forward an image of strength and power, Johnson never asked the hard questions as to why we were in Vietnam, where our policy would lead, or what would happen as a consequence. As one coup d'état after another brought successive military regimes to power in South Vietnam, Johnson kept pouring more American troops and money into the country, attempting to provide, through external military support, a degree of stability that clearly was not present among the South Vietnamese themselves. The long range results are now history. The Vietnamese countryside was destroyed, millions of lives were lost, search and destroy missions became the hallmark of a senseless effort to accumulate military victories measured by body counts of Vietnamese dead, and the nation entered a downward spiral of divisiveness and mistrust.

There are various ways of interpreting American involvement in Vietnam. Some see the war as simply a logical extension of a Cold War mentality, in which any civil war or nationalist struggle was perceived as part of a communist conspiracy that must be stopped. According to that interpretation, U.S. involvement grew directly from a distorted definition of world events in which all subtleties of internal and cultural politics were lost. A second interpretation views Vietnam as the one exception to a generally successful foreign policy in the postwar world. The Vietnam experience was not the product of erroneous Cold War attitudes, but rather an unrelated mistake in which the United States became too deeply involved before it could make a correct assessment of the situation. A third interpretation is that the war represented a wise policy which went awry. According to this view, U.S. commitment to political reform in South Vietnam was intelligent, and only when America attempted to use military power in place of political persuasion did a good policy turn bad. Finally, there is the view that the policy was wise all along and was prevented from being successful only because the military was hindered by political decisions at home. According to General William Westmoreland, the war was won militarily; it was lost politically.

Whichever interpretation one accepts, there can be little question that the war was a traumatic event for America and the world. The following selections explore some of the explanations for the war, as well as the consequences it brought. John Garry Clifford places the war within the long-term framework of American foreign policy. Lyndon Johnson cogently states the reasons why Americans must fight and win. Leslie Gelb, a State Department official, analyzes the major explanations of the causes of the war and offers his own view of how and why the United States became involved so deeply. Richard Hammer describes the consequences of American policy for the Vietnamese people as well as for United States soldiers and those at home. His description of My Lai speaks as powerfully as anything to the horror of what occurred as a result of Vietnam. And John Kerry, a representative of Vietnam Veterans Against the War, just as poignantly testifies about what he had observed and learned in the war.

Some critical questions remain. Was there ever a way that United States involvement could have led to a democratic government in Vietnam? How much racism was involved in U.S. policy? Did an episode such as My Lai represent the natural consequence of a "search and destroy" mentality, or was it a complete aberration? Finally, there is the question of how much American policy in Vietnam represented a fatal flaw in the idea that America has a moral right to tell the rest of the world how to behave.

Vietnam in Historical Perspective

John Garry Clifford

American involvement in Vietnam resulted from a series of assumptions about America's place in the world. John Garry Clifford, a diplomatic historian from the University of Connecticut, has written extensively about postwar American foreign policy. Here, he shows how the war in Vietnam reflected American ideas about the Cold War. Clifford concludes that the Vietnam experience challenged the basic tenets of American policy-makers, forcing a reassessment of how we proceed to achieve our goals. Clifford's essay accurately describes the immediate consequences of the Vietnam war. During the 1970's, Congress limited presidential power to make war without congressional approval, and circumscribed the freedom of action of the CIA. Nevertheless, students may ask whether Clifford's conclusions still hold in the 1980s.

Although it is too early to determine, the Vietnam war may well prove to have been both the logical culmination of American foreign policy since 1945 and a turning point comparable to that of World War II. Certainly on a perceptual level, in the way Americans viewed the world, the war set in motion changes that became obvious by 1970. On an institutional level, in the way government agencies connected with foreign policy defined their goals and procedures, the evidence of change by the early 1970s was less

Excerpted from John Garry Clifford, "Change and Continuity in American Foreign Policy Since 1930," in James T. Patterson, ed. *Paths to the Present* (Minneapolis: Burgess Publishing Co., 1975). Reprinted by permission of the author.

marked. One thing became certain: the options available to American diplomatists were more varied than at any other time since the fall of France in 1940.

Vietnam, which Senator John F. Kennedy described in 1956 as the "cornerstone of the Free World in Southeast Asia, the Keystone to the arch, the finger in the dike," was the logical, if erroneous, culmination of Cold War perceptions. The "lessons" of the past were constantly invoked. "If we don't stop the Reds in South Vietnam," said Lyndon Johnson, "tomorrow they will be in Hawaii, and next week they will be in San Francisco." Former Undersecretary of the Air Force, Townsend Hoopes, described the thinking of Dean Rusk: "In his always articulate, sometimes eloquent, formulations, Asia seemed to be Europe, China was either Stalinist Russia or Hitler Germany, and SEATO was either NATO or the Grand Alliance of World War II." If these analogies seemed somewhat strained, intended more for public persuasion than for internal conviction, the leaders in Washington all subscribed to the belief—unquestioned since Pearl Harbor—that aggression must be deterred. Vietnam became a test of America's will. "I don't need to remind you of what happened in the Civil War," Johnson told a press conference in 1967. "People were here in the White House begging Lincoln to concede and to work out a deal with the Confederacy when word came of his victories. . . . I think you know what Roosevelt went through and President Wilson in World War I. . . . We are going to have this criticism. We are going to have this difference. . . . No one likes war. All people love peace. But you can't have freedom without defending it. . . . We are going to do whatever it is necessary to do to see that the aggressor does not succeed."

But who was the aggressor in Vietnam? The Soviet Union? As the "quagmire" deepened, observers noted that Soviet supplies indeed helped the "enemy," but that Moscow was not masterminding a world-wide Communist conspiracy. The Sino-Soviet split became so evident by the mid-1960s that even the most militant Cold Warriors had to take notice. Perhaps the "enemy" was China, and Dean Rusk conjured up the frightening image of a billion Chinese armed with hydrogen bombs. But even after President Nixon's trips to Moscow and Peking in 1972, the war continued. The suggestion persisted that it was a *civil* war, an internal conflict between two versions of Vietnamese nationality, but this reality did not gibe with Cold War perceptions. Not enough was known in Washington about the fundamental differences in Asian societies, and belief in the Domino Theory came easily, along with visions of armed Communist hordes. Bureaucrats did not want to change their perceptions. James C. Thomson, a White House consultant during the early 1960s, recalls a conversation in March of 1964 with an Assistant Secretary of State. "But in some ways, of course, it *is* a civil war," Thomson said. "Don't play word games with me!" the official snapped.

Bureaucratic style contributed significantly to the tragedy. Part of it derived from technological superiority, which in turn gave rise to a "can do" philosophy. At one extreme, in Walter La-Feber's phrase, was "General Curtis LeMay's notion that Communism could best be handled from a height of 50,000 feet." At a more sophisticated level was the conviction that no matter how resilient the enemy proved, the United States could work its will through "smart" bombs, search and destroy tactics, electronic barriers, superior air power, or sheer economic momentum. A crazy sense of bloodlessness began to emerge. "Every quantitative measurement we have shows we're winning this war," McNamara stated in 1962. Statistics proliferated—infiltration rates, weapons-loss ratios, aircraft sorties rates, expended ammunition tonnages, allied troop contributions, enemy "body counts," friendly casualties. Bureaucratic jargon ("free fire zones," "surgical" air strikes, "threshold of pain," "slow squeeze") obscured the reality of flesh being mangled, villages devastated, ecology ruined. Describing the gradual pressure imposed by the "Rolling Thunder" bombing campaign, one State Department official said: "Our orchestration should be mainly violins, but with periodic touches of brass."

This armchair atmosphere could not be dispelled by battle reports or occasional trips to Saigon. A process of self-hypnosis seemed at work. David Halberstam has told the story of Daniel Ellsberg's return from a tour of duty in Vietnam and his attempts to tell presidential adviser Walt Rostow how badly the war was going. "No, you don't understand," said Rostow. "Victory is very near. I'll show you the charts. The charts are very good." "I don't want to see any charts," Ellsberg replied. "But, Dan, the charts are very good," Rostow insisted. Similarly, James Thomson has described his shock on returning to Harvard after several years in the State Department. He suddenly realized that "the young men, the flesh and blood I taught and saw on these university streets, were potentially some of the numbers on the charts of those far-away planners. In a curious sense, Cambridge is closer to this war than Washington."

The imperviousness of official Washington from external dissent contributed to the debacle. The smugness that came with access to classified information was partly responsible. The experts knew the facts, the critics did not. Internal dissenters were rarer and somehow safer to government leaders. President Johnson used to greet Bill Moyers rather affectionately: "Well, here comes Mr. Stop-the-Bombing." And when the war protest became especially shrill in 1966 and 1967, Johnson, who had followed the experts into the morass, displayed his furious temper. Dissenters, he said, were "nervous Nellies," "chickenshit." "I'm the only President you have," he would say. "Why don't you get on the team?" When hawks like Bundy and McNamara began to waver, Johnson sarcastically called the former "George McBundy" and unceremoniously nominated the latter to head the World Bank. This presidential temperament reinforced the natural bureaucratic tendency to remain silent so as not to lose one's effectiveness. Townsend Hoopes has described Vic-President Hubert Humphrey's abortive dissent in 1965: "His views were received at the White House with particular coldness, and he was banished from the inner councils for some months thereafter, until he decided to 'get back on the team.' " Not until the Tet offensive of early 1968 did effective criticism penetrate the Oval Office, and then it took someone of the stature of Dean Acheson to shake Lyndon Johnson. "With all due respect, Mr. President," said the mustachioed Dean of Middletown, "the Joint Chiefs of Staff don't know what they are talking about." When the Senior Advisory Group on Vietnam corroborated Acheson's estimates a few weeks later, the President's plaintive reaction underlined the extent to which policy had been made in a vacuum. "What did you tell them that you didn't tell me?" he asked his staff. "You must have given them a different briefing."

Momentum was another reason for escalation. The men in Washington may have thought they controlled events, but in actuality the genii of war were beyond control. For all their sophisticated technology, for all their favorable statistics, for all their "can do" spirit, American leaders never understood the extent to which decisions closed options previously available, making other decisions almost inevitable. Moreover, policy decisions often resulted from compromise, as in the case of the Kennedy administration sending military advisers to South Vietnam in 1961, notwithstanding the Taylor-Rostow report which recommended 8,000 troops. These compromises represented the usual adjustment of differences between the various agencies involved: the Saigon embassy, CIA, the State Department, the White House Staff, and the Joint Chiefs. Once advisers were committed, however, pressure rose for increasing their numbers.

Similarly, in the winter of 1964–65, certain "dovish" planners in the State Department who were strongly opposed to bombing the North urged instead that ground forces be sent to the South. They thought such a move would increase bargaining leverage against the North and be a prod for negotiations. At the same time, military men determined not to fight another "land war" in Asia were calling for the air-strike option. Still other civilians seeking peace wanted to bomb Hanoi into early peace talks. Within eight months all factions were disappointed: there was a costly and ineffective air campaign against the North, a mushrooming ground commitment in the South, and negotiations farther away than before. Each step also added greater weight to the military's demands. As soon as the Army's mission had changed from advising to saving Saigon, it was inevitable that the Joint Chiefs should press for escalation. Each service had its special panaceas, and under a tacit agreement the Joint Chiefs usually spoke in unison. McNamara then scaled down their demands. The result: escalation. Even after Nixon began withdrawing ground forces in 1969, military pressure to "protect" these troops resulted in decisions to invade Cambodian sanctuaries, to mine the harbors of Haiphong and Hanoi, and to resume aerial bombardment of the North at ever-increasing rates.

Vietnam brought about an "agonizing reappraisal" in American foreign policy far more searching than anything John Foster Dulles had envisaged in the 1950s. Dissent in American wars was not a new phenomenon. New England Federalists had opposed the War of 1812, abolitionists had protested the Mexican War, and Mugwumps and anti-imperialists had been vocal in 1898. Generally these dissenters were relatively small in number, well educated, respectable (usually upper class WASP), and quite orthodox in the way they protested—pamphlets, petitions, rallies, letter writing campaigns, efforts in behalf of anti-war candidates. The Vietnam war protest was different. The movement had enough diversity to include such heterogeneous spokesmen as Norman Mailer, Muhammed Ali, Abby Hoffman, John Kenneth Galbraith, George Kennan, Jane Fonda, Joan Baez, Jeannette Rankin, Martin Luther King, Robert Kennedy, Timothy Leary, Dick Gregory, and Noam Chomsky. Protest went from genteel teach-ins, to Senator Eugene McCarthy's brash campaign for the Democratic nomination in 1968, to marches on Washington, moratoria, and violent attempts by revolutionary groups to bring the war "home" to America. Protest literature ranged from the witty to the obscene.

People opposed the war for different reasons. Some still clung to the Cold War arguments for containment, but denied that the doctrine applied to Asia, or particularly to Vietnam. Others saw the war as killing reform at home, diverting attention from desperate conditions in the cities and in race relations. A less articulate group protested the deaths of American soldiers in Asian jungles, but seemed willing to permit American aircraft to drop billions of tons of bombs on yellow peoples. Others blamed President Johnson. "We've got a wild man in the White House," said Senator McCarthy. "A desperate man who was likely to get us into war with China," warned Senator Albert Gore of Tennessee.

More and more, protest occurred because of a moral revulsion to the war. Reaction to napalm bombing and "defoliation," horror at the destruction of the city of Hue in order to "save" it, incredulity at the My Lai massacre and the shootings of students at Kent State and Jackson State in 1970—all these events called into question the ethical standards of American policy. Confused about the identity of the aggressor in Vietnam—the Viet Cong? Hanoi? China?—more and more Americans came to agree with Walt Kelly's possum, Pogo: "We have met the enemy and they are us."

By the late 1960s this moral revulsion, fueled by the obvious *practical* failure of the American effort, had prompted a reassessment of long-held assumptions. One State Department official complained in 1966: "There is a considerable sort of feeling of unhappiness here that elements in the population that used to be thought of as our 'natural constituency' are not doing yeoman service for the Department now. We do have a constituency of sorts—the Foreign Policy Association, the Council on Foreign Relations, and all the other groups like that. These people have helped us all along for years, with the United Nations, the Marshall Plan, NATO, Korea, and all the others. But they are not helping us with the American public on the Vietnam issue. When they come to town to be briefed on Vietnam, they do not leave with marching orders, as they used to." When Dean Acheson told President Johnson that the generals did not know what they were talking about, he was also serving notice that the foreign policy consensus in existence since World War II had shattered. Another symbolic confrontation occurred in the spring of 1970 following the Cambodia invasion, when a group of prominent academicians, headed by Richard Neustadt, visited Henry Kissinger and recanted their support for executive predominance in foreign policy. These defections did not mean that Nixon could not count on continued support from the "silent majority," that Congress suddenly cut off military appropriations, or that the Navy decided to convert its aircraft carriers into hospital ships. What did emerge was an eventual repudiation of the Vietnam war by a majority of the so-called "foreign policy public." "What the hell is an Establishment for, if it's not to support the President," Kissinger complained. The reaction was especially strong among academicians. The political scientist Bruce Russett wrote: "Vietnam has been to social scientists what Alamogordo was to the physicists. Few of those who have observed it can easily return to their comfortable presumptions about America's duty, or right, to fight in distant lands." . . .

Historians cannot predict the future. To suggest, however, that changes in American assumptions about the world began in the 1960s and that Watergate and Vietnam accelerated these changes, is not presumptuous. The "lower profile" of American involvement abroad, as proclaimed by the Nixon Doctrine, will result in "lower" perceptions about American power and responsibilities. The intellectual capital that financed the Marshall Plan, NATO, and Korea was expended in Southeast Asia in the 1960s. The Nixon-Kissinger policies of détente toward the Soviet Union and the People's Republic of China have in themselves altered Cold War patterns. Do these changes signal a return to the isolationism of the 1930s, as defenders of the Vietnam war sometimes suggested? In the sense that domestic needs will not automatically take second place to foreign policy, or that Congress will not rubber-stamp executive initiatives, these changes do reflect some of the concerns of the Stimson-Hoover era. Nevertheless, the huge foreign policy bureaucracy spawned by World War II and the Cold War will remain, and it will take time for new perceptions to become embedded. Public opinion, decidedly noninterventionist in Asia because of the failure of the ground war in Vietnam, may well permit intervention by means of naval and aerial bombardment in future crises. The renewal of war between Israel and the Arab states in the fall of 1973, combined with the Arab embargo of oil, raised the prospect of American intervention in the Middle East, and with it the possibility of a Soviet-American confrontation. Like all previous empires in decline, the United States will retreat reluctantly.

Nevertheless, Vietnam and Watergate have left an ambivalence which allows room for cautious optimism. As the political scientist Robert W. Tucker has observed, Pearl Harbor and the Berlin Blockade will not be automatic reference points for the coming generation of "foreign policy elites." Rather, memories of My Lai and the Cuban Missile Crisis will be much sharper. "Never again," a slogan which the Army brought out of the Korean War, ought to remain a convenient watchword. The waning of anti-Communism as a political issue, as well as the need to combat industrial pollution, to conserve energy, to revitalize public transportation, and to obtain public health insurance, should tend to "lower" profiles and "cool" American foreign policy. Gradually, one may predict, the traditional American mission of erecting a "city on the hill" and solving domestic problems will take precedence over building "democratic" governments in remote areas of the world.

John Quincy Adams said it well more than 150 years earlier:

> Wherever the standard of freedom and Independence has been or shall be unfurled, there will her [America's] heart, her benediction and her prayers be. But she goes not abroad in search of monsters to destroy.... She well knows that by once enlisting under other banners than her own, were they even the banners of foreign independence, she would involve herself beyond the power of extrication.... The fundamental maxims of her policy would change from *liberty* to *force*.

Why We Are In Vietnam

Lyndon B. Johnson

In April 1965 Lyndon Johnson gave an address at Johns Hopkins University that garnered headlines and plaudits because the president offered incentives he hoped would bring North Vietnam to the bargaining table. Indeed, for much of the next three years Johnson would talk about negotiations while continuing to escalate the war. In retrospect, what now appears most striking about this speech, excerpted here, are the explanations given the American public about the nature of the conflict, the reasons for the U.S. involvement, and the American objectives in Vietnam. Privately, Johnson complained that "the only thing I know to do is more of the same and do it more efficiently and effectively." Did he have other alternatives? Why did he reject them?

Tonight Americans and Asians are dying for a world where each people may choose its own path to change.

This is the principle for which our ancestors fought in the valleys of Pennsylvania. It is the principle for which our sons fight tonight in the jungles of Vietnam.

Vietnam is far away from this quiet campus. We have no territory there, nor do we seek any. The war is dirty and brutal and difficult. And some 400 young men, born into an America that is bursting with opportunity and promise, have ended their lives on Vietnam's steaming soil.

Why must we take this painful road?

From Lyndon Baines Johnson, "Peace Without Conquest," Address at Johns Hopkins University, April 6, 1965, Department of State Bulletin, April 26, 1965.

Why must this Nation hazard its ease, and its interest, and its power for the sake of a people so far away?

We fight because we must fight if we are to live in a world where every country can shape its own destiny. And only in such a world will our own freedom be finally secure.

This kind of world will never be built by bombs or bullets. Yet the infirmities of man are such that force must often precede reason, and the waste of war, the works of peace.

We wish that this were not so. But we must deal with the world as it is, if it is ever to be as we wish.

The world as it is in Asia is not a serene or peaceful place.

The first reality is that North Vietnam has attacked the independent nation of South Vietnam. Its object is total conquest.

Of course, some of the people of South Vietnam are participating in attack on their own government. But trained men and supplies, orders and arms, flow in a constant stream from north to south.

This support is the heartbeat of the war.

And it is a war of unparalleled brutality. Simple farmers are the targets of assassination and kidnapping. Women and children are strangled in the night because their men are loyal to their government. And helpless villages are ravaged by sneak attacks. Large-scale raids are conducted on towns, and terror strikes in the heart of cities.

The confused nature of this conflict cannot mask the fact that it is the new face of an old enemy.

Over this war—and all Asia—is another reality: the deepening shadow of Communist China. The rulers in Hanoi are urged on by Peking. This is a regime which has destroyed freedom in Tibet, which has attacked India, and has been condemned by the United Nations for aggression in Korea. It is a nation which is helping the forces of violence in almost every continent. The contest in Vietnam is part of a wider pattern of aggressive purposes.

Why are these realities our concern? Why are we in South Vietnam?

We are there because we have a promise to keep. Since 1954 every American President has offered support to the people of South Vietnam. We have helped to build, and we have helped to defend. Thus, over many years, we have made a national pledge to help South Vietnam defend its independence.

And I intend to keep that promise.

To dishonor that pledge, to abandon this small and brave nation to its enemies, and to the terror that must follow, would be an unforgivable wrong.

We are also there to strengthen world order. Around the globe, from Berlin to Thailand, are people whose well-being rests, in part, on the belief that they can count on us if they are attacked. To leave Vietnam to its fate would shake the confidence of all these people in the value of an American commitment and in the value of America's word. The result would be increased unrest and instability, and even wider war.

We are also there because there are great stakes in the balance. Let no one think for a moment that retreat from Vietnam would bring an end to conflict. The battle would be renewed in one country and then another. The central lesson of our time is that the appetite of aggression is never satisfied. To withdraw from one battlefield means only to prepare for the next. We must say in southeast Asia—as we did in Europe—in the words of the Bible: "Hitherto shalt thou come, but no further."

There are those who say that all our effort there will be futile—that China's power is such that it is bound to dominate all southeast Asia. But there is no end to that argument until all of the nations of Asia are swallowed up.

There are those who wonder why we have a responsibility there. Well, we have it there for the same reason that we have a responsibility for the defense of Europe. World War II was fought in both Europe and Asia, and when it ended we found ourselves with continued responsibility for the defense of freedom.

Our objective is the independence of South Vietnam, and its freedom from attack. We want nothing for ourselves—only that the people of South Vietnam be allowed to guide their own country in their own way.

We will do everything necessary to reach that objective. And we will do only what is absolutely necessary.

In recent months attacks on South Vietnam were stepped up. Thus, it became necessary for us to increase our response and to make attacks by air. This is not a change of purpose. It is a change in what we believe that purpose requires.

We do this in order to slow down aggression.

We do this to increase the confidence of the brave people of

South Vietnam who have bravely borne this brutal battle for so many years with so many casualties.

And we do this to convince the leaders of North Vietnam—and all who seek to share their conquest—of a very simple fact:

We will not be defeated.

We will not grow tired.

We will not withdraw, either openly or under the cloak of a meaningless agreement.

We know that air attacks alone will not accomplish all of these purposes. But it is our best and prayerful judgment that they are a necessary part of the surest road to peace.

We hope that peace will come swiftly. But that is in the hands of others besides ourselves. And we must be prepared for a long continued conflict. It will require patience as well as bravery, the will to endure as well as the will to resist.

I wish it were possible to convince others with words of what we now find it necessary to say with guns and planes: Armed hostility is futile. Our resources are equal to any challenge. Because we fight for values and we fight for principles, rather than territory or colonies, our patience and our determination are unending.

Once this is clear, then it should also be clear that the only path for reasonable men is the path of peaceful settlement.

Such peace demands an independent South Vietnam—securely guaranteed and able to shape its own relationships to all others—free from outside interference—tied to no alliance—a military base for no other country.

These are the essentials of any final settlement.

We will never be second in the search for such a peaceful settlement in Vietnam.

There may be many ways to this kind of peace: in discussion or negotiation with the governments concerned; in large groups or in small ones; in the reaffirmation of old agreements or their strengthening with new ones.

We have stated this position over and over again, fifty times and more, to friend and foe alike. And we remain ready, with this purpose, for unconditional discussions.

And until that bright and necessary day of peace we will try to keep conflict from spreading. We have no desire to see thousands die in battle—Asians or Americans. We have no desire to devastate that which the people of North Vietnam have built with toil and sacrifice. We will use our power with restraint and with all the wisdom that we can command.

But we will use it.

This war, like most wars, is filled with terrible irony. For what do the people of North Vietnam want? They want what their neighbors also desire: food for their hunger; health for their bodies; a chance to learn; progress for their country; and an end to the bondage of material misery. And they would find all these things far more readily in peaceful association with others than in the endless course of battle. . . .

We often say how impressive power is. But I do not find it impressive at all. The guns and the bombs, the rockets and the warships, are all symbols of human failure. They are necessary symbols. They protect what we cherish. But they are witness to human folly.

A dam built across a great river is impressive.

In the countryside where I was born, and where I live, I have seen the night illuminated, and the kitchens warmed, and the homes heated, where once the cheerless night and the ceaseless cold held sway. And all this happened because electricity came to our area along the humming wires of the REA [Rural Electrification Administrative]. Electrification of the countryside—yes, that, too, is impressive.

A rich harvest in a hungry land is impressive.

The sight of healthy children in a classroom is impressive.

These—not mighty arms—are the achievements which the American Nation believes to be impressive.

And, if we are steadfast, the time may come when all other nations will also find it so.

Every night before I turn out the lights to sleep I ask myself this question: Have I done everything that I can do to unite this country? Have I done everything I can to help unite the world, to try to bring peace and hope to all the peoples of the world? Have I done enough?

Ask yourselves that question in your homes—and in this hall tonight. Have we, each of us, all done all we could? Have we done enough?

We may well be living in the time foretold many years ago when it was said: "I call heaven and earth to record this day against you, that I have set before you life and death, blessing and

cursing: therefore choose life, that both thou and thy seed may
live."

This generation of the world must choose: destroy or build, kill
or aid, hate or understand.

We can do all these things on a scale never dreamed of before.

Well, we will choose life. In so doing we will prevail over the
enemies within man, and over the natural enemies of all mankind. . . .

Causes of the War

Leslie Gelb

Those who know most about the decision-making process in American foreign policy frequently can say least about it. Officials at the State Department and the Pentagon see a myriad of classified information everyday. While lacking the independence and detachment of external observers, they have a unique vantage point on how and why particular policies are pursued. Leslie Gelb, a State Department official during the Vietnam war years, reflects this "insider's" familiarity with all the currents and cross currents of advice shaping American foreign policy decisions on Vietnam. In this selection from testimony given before Congress, Gelb assesses the relative influence of the various forces acting upon the presidential decision-making process. Although Gelb does not cite chapter and verse of secret memoranda supporting various positions on the war, his is one of the most informed studies of how and why the United States became so deeply involved in Vietnam. His conclusion that pervasive anti-communist attitudes provide the key to our involvement in Southeast Asia supports the argument that the Vietnam war, far from being a deviation from postwar foreign policy, was in fact a logical extension of the Cold War.

Wars are supposed to tell us about ourselves. Are we a wise and just nation? Or are we foolish and aggressive? Merciless or humane? Well led or misled? Vital or decadent? Hopeful or hope-

From Leslie H. Gelb statement to Hearings before the Committee on Foreign Relations, United States Senate, 82 Congress, 2nd Session, May 1972.

less? Nations in war and after war, win or lose, try to scratch away at the paste or glue or traditions or values that held their societies together and see of what they are made. It is arguable whether a society should indulge in such self-scrutiny. Societies are, as Edmund Burke wrote, "delicate, intricate wholes" that are more easily damaged than improved when subjected to the glare of Grand Inquisitors.

But in the case of our society and the war in Vietnam, too many people are seeking answers and are entitled to them, and many are only too eager to fill in the blanks. The families and friends of those who were killed and wounded will want to know whether it was worth it after all? Intellectuals will want to know "why Vietnam"? Men seeking and holding political office will demand to know who was responsible? The answers to these questions will themselves become political facts and forces, shaping the United States' role in the world and our lives at home for years to come.

CAUSES OF THE WAR: THE RANGE OF EXPLANATIONS

Central to this inquiry is the issue of causes of U.S. involvement in Vietnam. I have found eight discernible explanations advanced in the Vietnam literature. Different authors combine these explanations in various ways, but I will keep them separate for the purpose of analysis. I will, then, sketch my own position.

The Arrogance of Power

This view holds that a driving force in American involvement in Vietnam was the fact that we were a nation of enormous power and like comparable nations in history, we would seek to use this power at every opportunity. To have power is to want to employ it, is to be corrupted by it. The arrogance derives from the belief that to have power, is to be able to do anything. Power invokes right and justifies itself. Vietnam was there, a challenge to this power and an opportunity for its exercise, and no task was beyond accomplishment.

There can be no doubt about this strain in the behavior of other great powers and in the American character. But this is not a universal law. Great powers, and especially the United States have demonstrated self-restraint. The arrogance of power, I think, had more to do with our persisting in the war than with our initial involvement. It always was difficult for our leaders back in Washington and for operatives in the field to believe that American resources and ingenuity could not devise some way to overcome the adversary.

Bureaucratic Politics

There are two, not mutually exclusive, approaches within this view. One has it that national security bureaucrats (the professionals who make up the military services, civilian Defense, AID, State and the CIA) are afflicted with the curse of machismo, the need to assert and prove manhood and toughness. Career advancement and acceptability within the bureaucracy depended on showing that you were not afraid to propose the use of force. The other approach has it that bureaucrats purposefully misled their superiors about the situation in Vietnam and carefully constructed policy alternatives so as to circumscribe their superiors, thus forcing further involvement in Vietnam.

The machismo phenomenon is not unknown in the bureaucracy. It was difficult, if not damaging, to careers to appear conciliatory or "soft." Similarly, the constriction of options is a well-known bureaucratic device. But, I think, these approaches unduly emphasize the degree to which the President and his immediate advisers were trapped by the bureaucrats. The President was always in a position to ask for new options or to exclude certain others. The role of the bureaucracy was much more central to shaping the programs or the means used to fight the war than the key decisions to make the commitments in the first place.

Domestic Politics

This view is quite complicated, and authors argue their case on serveral different levels. The variants are if you were responsible for losing Vietnam to communism, you would: (a) lose the next election and lose the White House in particular; (b) jeopardize your domestic legislative program, your influence in general, by having to defend yourself constantly against political attack; (c) invite the return of a McCarthyite right-wing reaction; and (d) risk undermining domestic support for a continuing U.S. role abroad, in turn, risking dangerous probes by Russia and China.

There can be no doubt, despite the lack of supporting evidence in the Pentagon Papers, about the importance of domestic political considerations in both the initial commitment to and the subsequent increase in our Vietnam involvement. Officials are reluctant, for obvious reasons, to put these considerations down in writing, and scholars therefore learn too little about them. It should also be noted that domestic political factors played a key part in shaping the manner in which the war was fought—no reserve call-ups, certain limitations on bombing targeting, paying for the war, and the like.

Imperialism

This explanation is a variant of the domestic politics explanation. Proponents of this view argue that special interest groups maneuvered the United States into the war. Their goal was to capture export markets and natural resources at public expense for private economic gain.

The evidence put forward to support this "devil theory" has not been persuasive. Certain groups do gain economically from wars, but their power to drive our political system into war tends to be exaggerated and over-dramatized.

Men Making Hard Choices Pragmatically

This is the view that our leaders over the years were not men who were inspired by any particular ideology, but were pragmatists weighing the evidence and looking at each problem on its merits. According to this perspective, our leaders knew they were facing tough choices, and their decisions always were close ones. But having decided 51 to 49 to go ahead, they tried to sell and implement their policies one hundred percent.

This view cannot be dismissed out-of-hand. Most of our leaders, and especially our Presidents, occupied centrist political positions. But Vietnam is a case, I believe, where practical politicians allowed an anti-communist world view to get the best of them.

Balance of Power Politics

Intimately related to the pragmatic explanations is the conception which often accompanies pragmatism—the desire to maintain some perceived balance-of-power among nations. The principal considerations in pursuing this goal were: seeing that "the illegal use of force" is not allowed to succeed, honoring commitments, and keeping credibility with allies and potential adversaries. The underlying judgment was that failure to stop aggression in one place would tempt others to aggress in ever more dangerous places.

These represent the words and arguments most commonly and persuasively used in the executive branch, the Congress, and elsewhere. They seemed commonsensical and prudential. Most Americans were prepared to stretch their meaning to Vietnam. No doubt many believed these arguments on their own merits, but in most cases, I think, the broader tenet of anti-communism made them convincing.

The Slippery Slope

Tied to the pragmatic approach, the conception of balance of power, and the arrogance of power, is the explanation which holds that United States involvement in Vietnam is the story of the slippery slope. According to this view, Vietnam was not always critical to U.S. national security; it became so over the years as each succeeding administration piled commitment on commitment. Each administration sort of slid further into the Vietnam quagmire, not really understanding the depth of the problems in Vietnam and convinced that it could win. The catchwords of this view are optimism and inadvertence.

While this explanation undoubtedly fits certain individuals and certain periods of time, it is, by itself, a fundamental distortion of the Vietnam experience. From the Korean War, stated American objectives for Vietnam were continuously high and absolute. U.S. involvement, not U.S. objectives, increased over time. Moreover, to scrutinize the range of official public statements and the private memos as revealed in the Pentagon Papers makes it difficult to argue that our leaders were deceived by the enormity of the Vietnam task before them. It was not necessary for our leaders to believe they were going to win. It was sufficient for them to believe that they could not afford to lose Vietnam to communism.

Anti-Communism

The analysts who offer this explanation hold that anti-communism was the central and all-pervasive fact of U.S. foreign policy from at least 1947 until the end of the sixties. After World War II, an ideology whose very existence seemed to threaten basic American values had combined with the national force of first Russia and then China. This combination of ideology and power brought our leaders to see the world in "we-they" terms and to insist that peace was indivisible. Going well beyond balance of power considerations, every piece of territory became critical, and every besieged nation, a potential domino. Communism came to be seen as an infection to be quarantined rather than a force to be judiciously and appropriately balanced. Vietnam, in particular, became the cockpit of confrontation between the "Free World" and Totalitarianism; it was where the action was for 20 years.

In my opinion, simple anti-communism was the principal reason for United States involvement in Vietnam. It is not the whole story, but it is the biggest part.

As of this point in my own research, I advance three propositions to explain why, how, and with what expectations the United States became involved in the Vietnam war.

First, U.S. involvement in Vietnam is not mainly or mostly a story of step by step, inadvertent descent into unforeseen quicksand. It is primarily a story of why U.S. leaders considered that it was vital not to lose Vietnam by force to Communism. Our leaders believed Vietnam to be vital not for itself, but for what they thought its "loss" would mean internationally and domestically. Previous involvement made further involvement more unavoidable, and, to this extent, commitments were inherited. But judgments of Vietnam's "vitalness"—beginning with the Korean War—were sufficient in themselves to set the course for escalation.

Second, our Presidents were never actually seeking a military victory in Vietnam. They were doing only what they thought was minimally necessary at each stage to keep Indochina, and later South Vietnam, out of Communist hands. This forced our Presidents to be brakemen, to do less than those who were urging military victory and to reject proposals for disengagement. It also meant that our Presidents wanted a negotiated settlement without fully realizing (though realizing more than their critics) that a civil war cannot be ended by political compromise.

Third, our Presidents and most of their lieutenants were not deluded by optimistic reports of progress and did not proceed on the basis of wishful thinking about winning a military victory in South Vietnam. They recognized that the steps they were taking were not adequate to win the war and that unless Hanoi relented, they would have to do more and more. Their strategy was to persevere in hope that their will to continue—if not the practical effects of their actions—would cause the Communists to relent.

One Morning in the War

Richard Hammer

More than any other single group in the population, journalists were responsible for bringing to public attention the shortcomings and contradictions of American policy in Vietnam. As early as 1963, David Halberstam, The New York Times *correspondent in Vietnam, pointed out that conventional military tactics had no place in a guerrilla war, and that a civil struggle between competing Vietnamese political factions could not be resolved by external military intervention. The contradiction between journalistic accounts of the war and official reports sent to the Pentagon and the White House continued throughout the years of American involvement in Southeast Asia.*

During the last half of the 1960s, television and newspaper reporters played a major role in turning American public opinion against the war as people saw American soldiers igniting Vietnamese thatched huts and heard an Army major say that "we had to destroy the village in order to save it." It was a journalist who first made public the atrocities committed at My Lai. In the following selection, Richard Hammer describes in searing detail one "search and destroy" mission of the war. To some, the My Laï episode represented a total abberation, with a single company going insane for one day. To others, the episode typified—in extreme form—a practice that was all too frequent. Almost everyone agrees that the My Lai tragedy dramatized the impossibility of attempting to use external military force to fight a civil war where one could not tell who was a friend and who was an enemy.

Excerpted from Richard Hammer, *One Morning in the War* (New York: Coward, McCann & Geohegan, 2nd ed., 1970). Reprinted by permission of Coward, McCann, and Geohegan, Inc. Copyright © 1970 by Richard Hammer.

In these early days of combat, the men began to solidify their previously formed and now lasting impressions of their officers and sergeants. Medina, for one, seemed totally impervious to danger. In fact, he seemed almost to be searching for it, to test the courage of his men and of himself. At the same time, he seemed totally dedicated to the welfare of his own men, concerned about them, grieving when one of them was wounded, concerned that they be fed well, have shelter and ammunition. It was, one of the men remembers, "like he was some kind of hen taking care of her brood, if you know what I mean. If we was out in the field, one platoon going one way and another going a different way and there was some shots, then Medina'd be on the field phone right away, wanting to know what the shooting was about, if anybody was hurt, if reinforcements were needed, that kind of thing. He had to know everything that was happening everywhere in the company."

But if Medina was concerned about his own men, those who served under him noticed that he seemed utterly oblivious to the Vietnamese. On occasions when the company entered a hamlet and all was peaceful, Medina seemed bored, anxious to get moving after he had posed a few questions to the village chiefs through his interpreter, and there would be a look of weary impatience when his soldiers passed out cigarettes and canned fruit to the villagers. "I mean," one of his soldiers says, "he didn't ever talk about the gooks. He didn't call them any names, just didn't seem to care one way or another about them. . . . Except, of course, when some guy got hit, then Medina'd get real angry and talk about how we'd get ours back at them. . . ."

Calley was something different. About the best that anyone had to say for him was the summation by one corporal in his platoon: "He wasn't the best officer in the world, but then he wasn't the worst one, either."

There were others, however, who weren't quite so sure of that. . . . "It was like he was all wound up tight, just waiting to bust loose. And when he busted, everyone around him was going to be hit by the pieces. . . . Like he was a little guy, see, all puffed up, trying to make himself bigger and taller than anybody else. I guess maybe you can only do that for so long and then look out, man."

There were a number of men who pointed to an episode early

in February when they were looking for some concrete evidence to back their then-vague feelings about Calley. According to James Bergthold, for one, one afternoon Calley deliberately murdered a Vietnamese civilian without any provocation. The platoon was on a routine patrol when Bergthold brought in a Vietnamese civilian, about sixty years old, whom he had just discovered in a paddy. "I brought the guy in," he said. "He was standing in a field all by himself. I brought him in, and the lieutenant asked him questions and then threw him in a well and shot him in the head. He never said why he did it." . . .

More and more as these daily patrols went on without end, the men in Task Force Barker grew to hate the dirty war they were part of, a war where everything and nothing was the enemy and fair game, where trouble could come from anyone or anything. And they began to take casualties now and again, here and there. Moving down a trail one afternoon somewhere in their district (no one is sure exactly where, as most of the men were never really sure where they were except that they were somewhere in Vietnam), a mine suddenly exploded. Three men went down, one of them dead. Just off the trail, hidden in the brush, was a fifteen year old girl, her hand still on the detonator of the mine. Simultaneously, four or five soldiers fired. The girl fell over the detonator, riddled with bullets, dead.

Another hamlet. Some of the men see a young Vietnamese girl. They grab her and pull her inside the nearest hootch. There are screams and cries from inside and then silence. Soon the men come walking out, satisfied.

The people have gathered in the center of another hamlet, smiling and greeting the Americans, milling around them while cigarettes, gum, canned fruits are passed out. A couple of the men wander casually about the settlement. They go into one hootch and emerge carrying a number of trinkets, relics and family heirlooms and start to rejoin the rest of the platoon. An old man breaks away from the group and trots after them. He bows his head, folds his hands and with a humble, obsequious smile murmurs words in Vietnamese to them and points with anguish at the souvenirs they are carrying away. It was his hootch and he would like his possessions returned. He grows tiresome and one of the soldiers turns and without a thought shoots him.

Day after day the dirty incidents of this kind, in this kind of war, mount. . . .

There was no way to tell when a fire fight might break out. The morning would start as usual, with a routine search-and-destroy mission scheduled. But sometime during the day, the VC would be waiting, the blood would be spilled on the land. Day after day it was the same thing. There was no relief. It was days out on patrol, many nights bivouacked in some field or in some hamlet, the men sleeping only from fatigue, the sentries constantly on the alert. Then it would be back to the fire base, back to LZ Dottie, back to the bunkers with no amusements, no nights off for a drink or a girl. Just the grinding fear and hate and frustration of war.

Then word came that the opportunity to strike back at the enemy in what might well be a major engagement had arrived.

At dusk that evening, Medina gathered his company together at the fire base to brief them on the operation for the next day. "I told them," he says, "that the intelligence reports indicated that the 48th VC Battalion was in the village and the intelligence reports indicated that there would be no women and children in the village, that they would have gone to market." . . .

Others, however, remember the briefing in a different way. Richard Pendleton says, "He told us there were Viet Cong in the village and we should kill them before they kill us."

It was just about seven in the morning when the first shells began to rain on Xom Lang that March 16th. Those who were still at home—most of the people in the sub-hamlet, for it was still early and many of them were just beginning breakfast—quickly sought shelter in their family bunkers. Almost every house had its bunker dug into the ground nearby. The VC when they had arrived had forced the people to build them, and from friends in other hamlets they had heard enough tales to know that in case of a bombardment, a bunker was one of the few hopes of survival. So each family dug its own.

The shells continued to thud into the ground and explode, destroying houses and gouging deep craters for about twenty minutes. The artillery barrage marched up and down the hamlet and the area around it, preparing the landing zone for the troop-carrying helicopters. Overhead, helicopter gunships hovered without any opposition, pounding the hamlet and the ground around it with rockets and machine gun fire. . . .

Captain Ernest Medina was in the lead chopper, watching the artillery and the gunships level Xom Lang. He "could see the smoke and flash of artillery" as the settlement was ripped apart. Then his helicopter settled into a paddy about a hundred and fifty meters west. Immediately the door gunners strafed the surrounding countryside with machine gun fire in case there happened to be VC waiting among the growing rice and brush.

As far as Medina could tell there was no return fire. "My instant impression," he says, "was that I didn't hear the familiar crackle of rifle bullets zinging over my head."

Accompanied by his radio operator and other company aides, Medina clambered down from the helicopter and rushed across the paddy to the edge of a small graveyard just at the edge of Xom Lang. Still there was no return fire, and all around him the other choppers were settling to the ground and the men of Company C were pouring through the doors, firing toward the houses as they emerged. It seemed to have occurred to no one at that moment that the lack of return fire might mean that this was not the hamlet where the VC was centered, that this was not "Pinkville." . . .

"When the attack started," Sergeant Charles West recalls, "it couldn't have been stopped by anyone. We were mad and we had been told that the enemy was there and we were going in there to give them a fight for what they had done to our dead buddies."

Approaching Xom Lang, "we went in shooting," West says. "We'd shoot into the hootches and there were people running around. There were big craters in the village from the bombing. When I got there I saw some of the people, some of the women and kids all torn up."

"I was just coming to the first row of houses, with five or six other guys," says another member of the platoon, "when we heard this noise behind us. Everybody was scared and on edge, and keyed up, too, to kill, and somebody turned quick and snapped off a shot. We all turned and shot. And there was this big old water buffalo, I guess that's what it was, standing in the middle of this field behind us. Everybody was shooting at it and you could see little puffs jumping out where the bullets hit. It was like something in slow motion, and finally that cow just slumped down and collapsed." His face contorted by the remembrance, he adds, "Now it seems kind of funny, but it didn't then. And once the shooting started, I guess it affected everyone. From then on it was like nobody could stop. Everyone was just shooting at everything and anything, like the ammo wouldn't ever give out."

The contagion of slaughter was spreading throughout the platoon.

Combat photographer Ronald Haeberle and Army Correspondent Jay Roberts had requested permission to accompany a combat mission in order to get both pictures and a story of American soldiers in action. They had been assigned to Charley Company and to Calley's platoon. Leaving their helicopter with about ten or fifteen other soldiers, they came upon a cow being slaughtered, and then the picture turned sickenly grisly. "Off to the right," Haeberle said, "a woman's form, a head appeared from some brush. All the other GI's started firing at her, aiming at her, firing at her over and over again."

The bullets riddled the woman's body. She slumped against a well pump in the middle of the rice paddy, her head caught between two of its poles. She was obviously already dead, but the infection, the hysteria was now ascendant. The men were oblivious to everything but slaughter. "They just kept shooting at her. You could see the bones flying in the air, chip by chip."

There were the sounds: the shots running into and over each other from inside the hamlet; it sounded as though everyone had his rifle on automatic, no one bothering to save ammunition by switching to single shot. And not drowned by the sharp bark of the rifles and duller thuds of grenades were screams; they sounded like women and children, but how can anyone tell in that kind of moment from a distance who is screaming?

Four or five Americans were outside the hamlet, moving along its perimeter. The job of their platoon was to seal it off and so prevent the VC inside from fleeing from Calley's men, to catch them in a pincer and slaughter them. Vernardo Simpson and these other soldiers were probing the bushes on the outskirts, delicately, searching for mines and booby traps. As they neared the first group of houses, a man dressed in black pajamas—the dress convinced Simpson that he must be a VC even though black

pajamas were traditional peasant dress—suddenly appeared from
nowhere, from some bushes and began running toward the hamlet. A woman and child popped up from the same underbrush
and started "running away from us toward some huts."

"Dong lai! Dong lai!" The Americans shouted after the Vietnamese. But they kept on running. Lieutenant Brooks, the leader
of this second platoon, gave the orders to shoot. If these people
did not stop on command, then they must necessarily be VC.
"This is what I did," Simpson says. "I shot them, the lady and the
little boy. He was about two years old."

A woman and a child? Why?

"I was reluctant, but I was following a direct order. If I didn't
do this I could stand court martial for not following a direct
order."

Before the day was over, Simpson says, he would have killed at
least ten Vietnamese in Xom Lang.

With the number killed there, his total was about the average
for each soldier.

When the shelling stopped, Pham Phon crept from the bunker
near his hootch. About fifty meters away, he saw a small group of
American soldiers. Poking his head back into the bunker, he told
his wife and three children—two sons aged nine and four, and a
seven year old daughter—to come up and walk slowly toward the
Americans.

Like almost all Vietnamese in the hamlets around the country,
Phon and his family had learned from the three previous American vists and from the tales told by refugees who had come to
Xom Lang to seek shelter after their hamlets had been turned
into battlegrounds and from tales carried by others from far
away, just how to act when American troops arrived.

It was imperative not to run, either toward the Americans or
away from them. If you ran, the Americans would think that you
were VC, running away from them or running toward them with
a grenade, and they would shoot.

It was imperative not to stay inside the house or the bunker. If
you did, then the Americans would think you were VC hiding in
ambush, and they would shoot or throw grenades into the house
or bunker.

It was imperative to walk slowly toward the Americans, with
hands in plain view, or to gather in small groups in some central

spot and wait for the Americans to arrive—but never to gather in
large groups, for then the Americans would think the group was
VC waiting to fire. It was absolutely imperative to show only ser-
vility so that the Americans would know that you were not VC
and had only peaceful intent.

So Phon and his family walked slowly toward the soldiers. The
three children smiled and shouted, "Hello! Hello! Okay! Okay!"

Only this time, unlike the three previous American visitations,
there were no answering grins, no gifts of candy and rations. The
Americans pointed their rifles at the family and sternly ordered
them to walk to the canal about a hundred meters away.

Inside the hamlet, the men of the first platoon were racing from
house to house. They planted dynamite and explosive to the brick
ones and blew them into dust. They set fires with their lighters to
the thatched roofs and to the hootches, watched them flare into a
ritual bonfire and then raced on to the next hootch. Some soldiers
were pulling people from bunkers and out of the houses and
herding them into groups. Some of the Vietnamese tried to run
and were immediately shot. Others didn't seem to know what was
happening, didn't understand what the Americans were doing or
why. But most of them behaved as they had learned they must
behave. Meekly they followed any order given.

Some of the groups were marched away in the direction of the
canal, and those who straggled behind, could not keep up, were
promptly shot.

There were soldiers standing outside the hootches, watching
them burn, and as Vietnamese suddenly emerged from the pyres,
would shoot them.

And through everything, through the sound of gunfire and
through the crackling of flames, through the smoke that had
begun to cover everything like a pall, came high pitched screams
of pain and terror, bewildered cries, pleading cries. All were
ignored.

Michael Bernhardt remembers coming into the hamlet and seeing his fellow soldiers "doing a whole lot of shooting up. But none
of it was incoming. I'd been around enough to tell that. I figured
we were advancing on the village with fire power."

Inside the hamlet, Bernhardt "saw these guys doing strange

things. They were doing it in three ways. They were setting fire to
the hootches and huts and waiting for the people to come out and
then shooting them. They were going into the hootches and
shooting them up. They were gathering people in groups and
shooting them."

The raging fever in the other members of his platoon stunned
and shocked Bernhardt. He watched one soldier shooting at
everything he saw, blazing away indiscriminately and laughing
hysterically as he kept pulling the trigger, kept his finger on the
trigger until all the bullets in a clip were gone, then throwing
away the clip and reloading and starting again. And laughing all
the time. "He just couldn't stop. He thought it was funny, funny,
funny." . . .

For Private Herbert Carter it was too much, a nightmare from
which there seemed no awakening. "People began coming out of
their hootches and the guys shot them and burned the hootches—
or burned the hootches and then shot the people when they came
out. Sometimes they would round up a bunch and shoot them
together. It went on like that for what seemed like all day. Some
of the guys seemed to be having a lot of fun. They were wise-
cracking and yelling, 'Chalk that one up for me.' "

When he could stand the sight no longer, Carter turned and
stumbled out of the hamlet. He sat down under a tree and shot
himself in the foot.

He was Charley Company's only casualty that morning.

When the first shells hurled their way into Xom Lang, Nguyen
Thi Nien and her family took shelter in their bunker adjacent to
their house. In the bunker with her were her eighty-year-old
father-in-law, her sister and her sister's seven-year-old daughter,
her own husband and their three children. They cowered in the
bunker for a considerable length of time. Finally they heard
steady rifle fire around them and American voices yelling: "VC di
ra! VC di ra!"—VC, get out! VC, get out!

The family crawled slowly and carefully out of the bunker,
making every effort to display no hostility. But once they were out
they noticed that the Americans were still some distance away.
Taking her youngest child, still a baby, in one arm and holding
her second youngest by the hand, Nguyen Thi Nien started away,
toward the rice paddies. She did not run, but walked on steadily.
Her husband and the oldest child started to follow her. But her

sister and her sister's daughter hung back, then started in another direction. And her father-in-law turned and started back to the house.

"I am too old," she remembers him calling after her. "I cannot keep up. You get out and I will stay here to keep the house."

There was almost no argument. "We told him," Nguyen Thi Nien says, "all right, you are too old. So you stay here and if the GI's arrive you ask them not to shoot you and not to burn the house."

The old man called that that was exactly what he intended to do. He would stand guard over the family house. But then Nguyen Thi Nien's husband decided that he could not leave his father alone in the house. He turned, sending the oldest child after his wife and the other children, and went back to his father. They stood outside the house for a brief moment arguing. The son trying to convince the old man to get out of the house and go with them to the paddies before the Americans arrived. The Americans were approaching and they could hear the clatter of shots, they could see the flames licking around other houses, and the smoke.

But the old man remained adamant. He was too old, he kept insisting. He could not make it to the paddy. He refused to leave, turning from his son and starting into the house.

The Americans were almost on them; the firing was all around them now. Nien realized that he could wait no longer. If he were to escape the approaching Americans—he realized by then that this was not a friendly visit, that the Americans were hostile this time and were shooting at everything—he would have to flee immediately.

About four hundred meters away, he saw his wife and three children just ducking into the rice paddies, safe. He started after them. Ahead of him, just a few feet, was an old woman, a nearby neighbor. "But suddenly," he says, "five GI's were in front of me, about a hundred meters or so from me. The GI's saw us and started to shoot and the lady was killed. I was hit and so I lay down. Then I saw blood coming from my stomach and so I took a handkerchief and put it over my wound. I lay on the ground there for a little while and then I tried to get back to my house, to my old father and my sister-in-law and her child who must still be there. I could not walk very well and so I was crawling. On the

way back to my house I saw five children and one father lying
dead on the ground. When I reached my house, I saw it was on
fire. Through the fire I could see the bodies of my old father, my
sister-in-law and her child inside the house. Then I lost consciousness and I do not know anything more of what happened." . . .

"I was just coming into the middle of that ville," remembers
one soldier, refusing to look around or to meet his questioner's
eyes as he talks, "and I saw this guy. He was one of my best
friends in the company. But honest to Christ, at first I didn't
even recognize him. He was kneeling on the ground, this absolutely incredible . . . I don't know what you'd call it, a smile or a
snarl or something, but anyway, his whole face was distorted. He
was covered with smoke, his face streaked with it, and it looked
like there was blood on him, too. You couldn't tell, but there was
blood everywhere. Anyway, he was kneeling there holding this
grenade launcher, and he was launching grenades at the
hootches. A couple of times he launched grenades at groups of
people. The grenades would explode, you know, KAPLOW, and
then you'd see pieces of bodies flying around. Some of the
groups were just piles of bodies. But I remember there was this
one group a little distance away. Maybe there was ten people,
most of them women and little kids, huddled all together and
you could see they were really scared, they just couldn't seem to
move. Anyway, he turns around toward them and lets fly with a
grenade. It landed right in the middle of them. You could hear
the screams and then the sound and then see the pieces of
bodies scatter out, and the whole area just suddenly turned red
like somebody had turned on a faucet."

Did you do anything to try to stop him?

"You got rocks or something? All you had to do was take one
look at him, at his face and you knew the best thing was to leave
him alone. I think if I had even said a word to him at all, he
would have turned and killed me and not thought a damn thing
about it." . . .

Jay Roberts and Ronald Haeberle moved about the havoc taking pictures. They came upon one group of Americans surrounding a small group of women, children and a teen-age girl. She was
perhaps twelve or thirteen and was wearing the traditional peasant black pajamas. One of the Americans grabbed her by the
shoulders while another began to try to strip the pajamas off her,
pulling at the top of the blouse to undo it.

"Let's see what she's made of," one of the soldiers laughed.

Another moved close to her, laughing and pointing at her. "VC, boom-boom," he said. He was telling her in the GI patois that she was a whore for the VC, and indicating that if she did it for them why not for the Americans.

A third soldier examined her carefully and then turned to the others. "Jesus," he said, "I'm horny."

All around there were burning buildings and bodies and the sounds of firing and screams. But the Americans seemed totally oblivious to anything but the girl. They had almost stripped her when her mother rushed over and tried to help her escape. She clutched at the American soldiers, scratched them, clawed at their faces, screaming invectives at them. They pushed her off. One soldier slapped her across the face; another hit her in the stomach with his fist; a third kicked her in the behind, knocking her sprawling to the ground.

But the mother's actions had given the girl a chance to escape a little. She took shelter behind some of the other women in the group and tried to button the top of her blouse. Haeberle stepped in, knelt and took a picture of the scene.

Roberts remembers that at that moment, "when they noticed Ron, they left off and turned away as if everything was normal. Then a soldier asked, 'Well, what'll we do with 'em?'

" 'Kill 'em,' another answered.

"I heard an M-60 go off, a light machine gun, and when we turned all of them and the kids with them were dead." . . .

Another soldier says he saw a teen-age girl running across a rice paddy, trying to hide from an American who was chasing her. As he watched, he saw this American soldier aim with his rifle and shoot. The girl gave a cry and fell down. The soldier went after her and vanished into the paddy. A few minutes later there was another shot from the area and then the soldier walked back from the field into the hamlet. . . .

A small boy, three or four, suddenly appears from nowhere on the trail in front of a group of Americans. He is wounded in the arm. Michael Terry sees "the boy clutching his wounded arm with his other hand while the blood trickled between his fingers. He was staring around himself in shock and disbelief at what he saw. He just stood there with big eyes staring around like he didn't understand what was happening. Then the captain's radio operator put a burst of 16 into him."

When Paul Meadlo came into Xom Lang, Lieutenant Calley set him and some of the other men to work gathering the people together in groups in a central location. "There was about forty, forty-five people that we gathered in the center of the village," Meadlo told an interviewer. "And we placed them in there, and it was like a little island, right there in the center of the village."

The soldiers forced the people in the group to squat on the ground. "Lieutenant Calley came over and said, 'You know what to do with them, don't you?' And I said, 'Yes.' So I took it for granted he just wanted us to watch them. And he left and came back about ten or fifteen minutes later, and said, 'How come you ain't killed them yet?' And I told him that I didn't think he wanted us to kill them, that you just wanted us to guard them. He said, 'No, I want them dead.' "

At first Meadlo was surprised by the order—not shocked or horrified, but surprised. "But three, four guys heard it and then he stepped back about ten, fifteen feet, and he started shooting them. And he told me to start shooting. I poured about four clips into the group."

A clip is seventeen rounds. Meadlo fired sixty-eight rounds into this group of people. "I fired them on automatic," he said, "so you can't . . . you just spray the area on them and so you can't know how many you killed 'cause they were going fast. So I might have killed ten or fifteen of them."

One slaughter was over, but there was more to come, and the thirst for blood had become so contagious that no one thought anything about what he was doing. "We started to gather them up, more people, " Meadlo says, "and we had about seven or eight people that we was gonna put into a hootch and we dropped a hand grenade in there with them."

Then Meadlo and several other soldiers took a group of civilians—almost exclusively women and children, some of the children still too young to walk—toward one of the two canals on the outskirts of Xom Lang. "They had about seventy, seventy-five people all gathered up. So we threw ours in with them and Lieutenant Calley told me, he said, 'Meadlo, we got another job to do.' And so he walked over to the people and started pushing them off and started shooting."

Taking his cue from Calley, Meadlo and then the other members of this squad "started pushing them off and we started shooting them. So altogether we just pushed them all off and just started using automatics on them. And somebody told us to switch off to single shot so that we could save ammo. So we switched off to single shot and shot a few more rounds."

In the heat and the passion of that morning, it is almost impossible to know who is telling the real truth about any of the events or any of the people, or if there is even any real truth. And perhaps it is less than the major quest in the story of what happened and why it happened that morning in March to discover and decide just who killed whom, where and when. Many hundreds of people, most of them children, women and old men, were slaughtered at Xom Lang and Binh Dong. A mass hysteria swept over a large number of American soldiers who became executioners, indiscriminate butchers. And in the horror of it all, is there really sense and meaning in saying that one did such and such and this one did this and that? In a senseless slaughter, the attempt to fix blame for specific killings on specific people is an attempt to find sense and logic where it does not and cannot exist. The responsibility for what happened at Xom Lang lies not just with the man or the men who pulled the triggers and threw the grenades. The responsibility goes further and higher.

As darkness fell that night over Xom Lang, over Son My, over all of Vietnam, it was morning half a world away, in Washington, D.C. If the repercussions of what had happened that morning in this one corner of Vietnam had not yet reached the American capital, repercussions of Vietnam itself, of all that had led up to that morning in the war, had reached the center of government of the United States.

Senator Eugene McCarthy and his young idealists, the advocates of the "New Politics," were celebrating the victory earlier in the week over Lyndon Johnson in the New Hampshire Democratic primary. Eugene McCarthy, until then not a well-known national politician, had upset the incumbent President, the leader of his own party. The issue which he had raised to win that victory was that of the war in Vietnam.

In the caucus room of the United States Senate, Robert Francis Kennedy was about to declare that he was a candidate for his party's presidential nomination, that he, too, would take on the

President, his brother's Vice President. And the quarrel which had led to this break was the war in Vietnam, what the United States under Lyndon Johnson had done to Vietnam and what it had done to itself.

In the White House, the President was in an anguished personal struggle. As a result of the war in Vietnam, the people had turned against him, had lost confidence in his ability to lead the nation. Less than four years after he had won the greatest political victory in American history as a candidate of peace, even the voters of his own party had rejected him, now identified as the candidate of war. Within two weeks, he would make his fateful decision. He would stop the bombing of North Vietnam. He would seek a beginning of peace negotiations. And he would not seek re-nomination or re-election as President of the United States. He, too, had been destroyed by the war in Vietnam.

But on that March 16, 1968, Xom Lang and Binh Dong and My Hoi, My Lai and Son My and Pinkville were names that these political leaders had never heard. They were names that most of the military in Vietnam had never heard.

There had been a minor engagement there that day. On the next day and in the days to follow, it would be hailed as a victory.

But the target of the day, the Viet Cong soldiers, had been untouched. From their camp at My Khe sub-hamlet they had heard, early in the morning, the sound of planes and guns to the west; they had heard the sounds moving across the village as the day progressed. And before the Americans came near to My Khe—My Lai (1) or Pinkville—the VC had faded from the scene, moving silently out of the hamlet and north to the sanctuary of Batangan. They would be back.

Vietnam Veterans Against the War

John Kerry

*By the early 1970s the antiwar movement assumed massive proportions
and became a major force in American political affairs. To the ranks of
university students and professors, of peace and church groups who initially protested against the war, came Americans from all walks of life,
including Vietnam veterans. In his testimony to the Senate Committee on
Foreign Relations in April 1971, exerpted here, John Kerry, a representative of the Vietnam Veterans Against the War, highlighted many of the
antiwar movement's major criticisms of the American effort in Vietnam.
He expressed revulsion at the war's brutal horrors, denied that the United
States was advancing the cause of freedom, disputed the official explanation of the nature of the conflict, decried the corrupt and dictatorial
government in Saigon, and charged American officials with deceiving the
public and deserting those they sent off to war. Kerry's eloquent indictment
received nationwide coverage in the media. In 1984 the voters of Massachusetts elected him to the United States Senate.*

I would like to talk on behalf of all those veterans and say that
several months ago in Detroit we had an investigation at which
over 150 honorably discharged, and many very highly decorated,
veterans testified to war crimes committed in Southeast Asia.
These were not isolated incidents but crimes committed on a day-
to-day basis with the full awareness of officers at all levels of
command.

From Vietnam Veterans Against the War Statement by John Kerry to the
Senate Committee of Foreign Relations, April 23, 1971.

It is impossible to describe to you exactly what did happen in Detroit—the emotions in the room and the feelings of the men who were reliving their experiences in Vietnam. They relived the absolute horror of what this country, in a sense, made them do.

They told stories that at times they had personally raped, cut off ears, cut off heads, taped wires from portable telephones to human genitals and turned up the power, cut off limbs, blown up bodies, randomly shot at civilians, razed villages in fashion reminiscent of Genghis Khan, shot cattle and dogs for fun, poisoned food stocks, and generally ravaged the countryside of South Vietnam in addition to the normal ravage of war and the normal and very particular ravaging which is done by the applied bombing power of this country.

We call this investigation the Winter Soldier Investigation. The term Winter Soldier is a play on words of Thomas Paine's in 1776 when he spoke of the Sunshine Patriots and summer time soldiers who deserted at Valley Forge because the going was rough.

We who have come here to Washington have come here because we feel we have to be winter soldiers now. We could come back to this country, we could be quiet, we could hold our silence, we could not tell what went on in Vietnam, but we feel because of what threatens this country, not the reds, but the crimes which we are commiting that threaten it, that we have to speak out. . . .

In our opinion and from our experience, there is nothing in South Vietnam which could happen that realistically threatens the United States of America. And to attempt to justify the loss of one American life in Vietnam, Cambodia or Laos by linking such loss to the preservation of freedom, which those misfits supposedly abuse, is to us the height of criminal hypocrisy, and it is that kind of hyprocrisy which we feel has torn this country apart.

We found that not only was it a civil war, an effort by a people who had for years been seeking their liberation from any colonial influence whatsoever, but also we found that the Vietnamese whom we had enthusiastically molded after our own image were hard put to take up the fight against the threat we were supposedly saving them from.

We found most people didn't even know the difference between communism and democracy. They only wanted to work in rice paddies without helicopters strafing them and bombs with napalm burning their villages and tearing their country apart.

They wanted everything to do with the war, particularly with this foreign presence of the United States of America, to leave them alone in peace, and they practiced the art of survival by siding with whichever military force was present at a particular time, be it Viet Cong, North Vietnamese or American.

We found also that all too often American men were dying in those rice paddies for want of support from their allies. We saw first hand how monies from American taxes were used for a corrupt dictatorial regime. We saw that many people in this country had a one-sided idea of who was kept free by our flag, and blacks provided the highest percentage of casualties. We saw Vietnam ravaged equally by American bombs and search and destroy missions, as well as by Viet Cong terrorism and yet we listened while this country tried to blame all of the havoc on the Viet Cong.

We rationalized destroying villages in order to save them. We saw America lose her sense of morality as she accepted very coolly a My Lai and refused to give up the image of American soldiers who hand out chocolate bars and chewing gum.

We learned the meaning of free fire zones, shooting anything that moves, and we watched while America placed a cheapness on the lives of orientals.

We watched the United States falsification of body counts, in fact the glorification of body counts. We listened while month after month we were told the back of the enemy was about to break. We fought using weapons against "oriental human beings." We fought using weapons against those people which I do not believe this country would dream of using were we fighting in the European theater. We watched while men charged up hills because a general said that hill has to be taken, and after losing one platoon or two platoons they marched away to leave the hill for reoccupation by the North Vietnamese. We watched pride allow the most unimportant battles to be blown into extravaganzas, because we couldn't lose, and we couldn't retreat, and because it didn't matter how many American bodies were lost to prove that point, and so there were Hamburger Hills and Khe Sanhs and Hill 81s and Fire Base 6s, and so many others.

Now we are told that the men who fought there must watch quietly while American lives are lost so that we can exercise the incredible arrogance of Vietnamizing the Vietnamese.

Each day to facilitate the process by which the United States washes her hands of Vietnam someone has to give up his life so that the United States doesn't have to admit something that the entire world already knows, so that we can't say that we have made a mistake. Someone has to die so that President Nixon won't be, and these are his words, "the first President to lose a war."

We are asking Americans to think about that because how do you ask a man to be the last man to die in Vietnam? How do you ask a man to be the last man to die for a mistake? . . . We are here in Washington also to say that the problem of this war is not just a question of war and diplomacy. It is part and parcel of everything that we are trying as human beings to communicate to people in this country—the question of racism which is rampant in the military, and so many other questions such as the use of weapons; the hypocrisy in our taking umbrage at the Geneva Conventions and using that as justification for a continuation of this war when we are more guilty than any other body of violations of those Geneva Conventions: in the use of free fire zones, harassment interdiction fire, search and destroy missions, the bombings, the torture of prisoners, the killing of prisoners, all accepted policy by many units in South Vietnam. That is what we are trying to say. It is part and parcel of everything.

An American Indian friend of mine who lives in the Indian Nation of Alcatraz put it to me very succinctly. He told me how as a boy on an Indian reservation he had watched television and he used to cheer the cowboys when they came in and shot the Indians, and then suddenly one day he stopped in Vietnam and he said "my God, I am doing to these people the very same thing that was done to my people," and he stopped. And that is what we are trying to say, that we think this thing has to end.

We are here to ask, and we are here to ask vehemently, where are the leaders of our country. Where is the leadership? We're here to ask where are McNamara, Rostow, Bundy, Gilpatrick, and so many others. Where are they now that we, the men they sent off to war, have returned. These are commanders who have deserted their troops. And there is no more serious crime in the laws of war. The Army says they never leave their wounded. The marines say they never leave even their dead. These men have left all the casualties and retreated behind a pious shield of public rectitude. They've left the real stuff of their reputations bleaching behind them in the sun in this country. . . .

We wish that a merciful God could wipe away our own memories of that service as easily as this administration has wiped away their memories of us. But all that they have done and all that they can do by this denial is to make more clear than ever our own determination to undertake one last mission—to search out and destroy the last vestige of this barbaric war, to pacify our own hearts, to conquer the hate and the fear that have driven this country these last ten years and more. And more. And so when thirty years from now our brothers go down the street without a leg, without an arm, or a face, and small boys ask why, we will be able to say "Vietnam" and not mean a desert, not a filthy obscene memory, but mean instead the place where America finally turned and where soldiers like us helped it in the turning.

Part Seven

YEARS OF POLARIZATION

During the late 1960s American society was more profoundly divided than at any time since the Civil War. As the peaceful petitions of the nonviolent civil rights movement were replaced by black power slogans, white support for blacks plummeted. The emergence of feminism created profound divisions over traditional family roles and definitions of masculinity and femininity. The student movement began as a request for moderate changes, but with the growing crisis over Vietnam became a major challenge to the very structure of the university and government. As the protest over Vietnam grew, many cities and university campuses became domestic battlefields, with police barricades confronting student demonstrators.

The civil rights movement was crucial to the development of political activism on America's campuses. As white students and black students joined together in civil rights protests, they came face to face with the duplicity and brutality of law enforcement officials in the South. When, as frequently happened, the federal government failed to provide corrective assistance, demonstrators began to suspect that even those authorities they thought they could trust were part of the problem. What had begun as a specific protest against Southern racism gradually developed into a more critical challenge to established authority generally.

When Mario Savio and others came back to campus from summer civil rights demonstrations in Mississippi in 1964, they carried their newfound criticism to university life itself. After officials at the University of California at Berkeley attempted to control distribution of political materials on a campus plaza, the Berkeley free speech movement began. Significantly, the issues were not

specific, but involved protest against the "university machine" itself as a manifestation of corporate control of America. Students
protested the depersonalization of the multiversity with its com-
puterized systems, its huge classrooms, and its insensitivity to
issues of human community.

By 1967 and 1968, the spirit of Berkeley had spread across the
country, fueled by the fires of anti-war demonstrations. Universities were denounced for being instruments of the military-industrial complex. Students demanded the cancellation of university
contracts to conduct research on weapons development. Army and
Navy ROTC courses came under attack for providing a bond between the university and U.S. policy in Vietnam. When weapons
manufacturers came to campus to recruit, students protested their
presence, insisting that the university had no right to support the
war effort—even indirectly—by making its facilities available to
those who profited from the war.

Culture and politics became intermixed as long hair, marijuana, more casual attitudes toward sex, and rejection of middle-
class values became associated with the anti-war movement. When
students took over university buildings to protest the war, they
boasted of their communal lifestyle, their hostility to monogamy,
and their freedom to carve out a different lifestyle than that of
their parents or elders. The so-called generation gap involved not
only political disagreements, but also fundamental personal conflicts over how one would dress, what kind of language one would
use, and who one would sleep with. By the end of the 1960s the
moderate reformism of the Students for a Democratic Society in
1962 had given way to the militant and violent rhetoric of the
Weathermen. In the meantime, reaction against youthful protest
and the counterculture had spread. Commentators developed a
new phrase—"Middle America"—to describe those who rejected
totally the assault on middle-class values by young people of the
left.

The following selections highlight some of the tensions of that
era. The Port Huron statement of SDS in 1962 offers a vivid
contrast to the Weatherman SDS statement of the late 1960s, illus-
trating how the moderation of the early years was transformed
into a posture that justified the trashing of university buildings
and the use of terrorism. The selection by Jerry Avorn and others
on the Columbia "Revolution" of 1968 shows how, on one cam-

pus, protest over the war and racism evolved, and how university response to that protest helped to radicalize the majority of "moderate" students.

Allen J. Matusow's assessment of the counterculture portrays some of the parallel shifts taking place in lifestyle, music, art, and attitudes toward sex and drugs. Although the counterculture was in some senses different from political activism, it also represented a vehicle through which the young felt they could contribute toward changing the values of the society. Finally, the article on Joe Kelly describes vividly the clash between cultural perspectives and generations in the 1960s.

Some of the key questions that remain are why the earlier, more moderate protests of the 1960s met with such little success. Did the intransigence of those in power necessitate the shift toward a more radical position? How basic were the issues raised by political activists and supporters of the counterculture? Did they call into serious question the structures and values of the larger society? Was there a way in which young and old could have talked to each other with less hostility and intolerance? Finally, have we lost some of the valuable perspectives which that era brought, as well as its coercive divisiveness?

The Port Huron Statement

Students for a Democratic Society

To young Americans in the early 1960s, everything seemed possible. A youthful, activist President had come into office promising that "we can do better." Black students throughout the South had demonstrated through sit-ins and kneel-ins that people willing to act on their convictions could help to turn society around. Inspired by these examples and given hope by the new leadership in Washington, young white reformers came together to draw up a manifesto for social change. Those who formed Students for a Democratic Society (SDS) were deeply critical of the complacency and indifference of their society. They hoped to marshall the resources of technology, the university, corporations, and government to eliminate poverty and racism. Hence, their agenda of reform. What remains most impressive from the Port Huron Statement, however, is its moderation, its faith that change can take place within the system, its conviction that social democracy could be achieved quickly and effectively, without revolution. The Port Huron Statement speaks eloquently to the idealism of a generation of student activists. Just as eloquently, it testifies to their innocence.

INTRODUCTION: AGENDA FOR A GENERATION

We are people of this generation, bred in at least modest comfort, housed now in universities, looking uncomfortably to the world we inherit.

Excerpted from Tom Hayden et al., Port Huron Statement, mimeographed (n.p., Students for a Democratic Society, 1962)

When we were kids the United States was the wealthiest and strongest country in the world; the only one with the atom bomb, the least scarred by modern war, an initiator of the United Nations that we thought would distribute Western influence throughout the world. Freedom and equality for each individual, government of, by, and for the people—these American values we found good, principles by which we could live as men. Many of us began maturing in complacency.

As we grew, however, our comfort was penetrated by events too troubling to dismiss. First, the permeating and victimizing fact of human degradation, symbolized by the Southern struggle against racial bigotry, compelled most of us from silence to activism. Second, the enclosing fact of the Cold War, symbolized by the presence of the Bomb, brought awareness that we ourselves, and our friends, and millions of abstract "others" we knew more directly because of our common peril, might die at any time. We might deliberately ignore, or avoid, or fail to feel all other human problems, but not these two, for these were too immediate and crushing in their impact, too challenging in the demand that we as individuals take the responsibility for encounter and resolution.

While these and other problems either directly oppressed us or rankled our consciences and became our own subjective concerns, we began to see complicated and disturbing paradoxes in our surrounding America. The declaration "all men are created equal . . ." rang hollow before the facts of Negro life in the South and the big cities of the North. The proclaimed peaceful intentions of the United States contradicted its economic and military investments in the Cold War status quo. . . .

Our work is guided by the sense that we may be the last generation in the experiment with living. But we are a minority—the vast majority of our people regard the temporary equilibriums of our society and world as eternally-functional parts. In this is perhaps the outstanding paradox: we ourselves are imbued with urgency, yet the message of our society is that there is no viable alternative to the present. Beneath the reassuring tones of the politicians, beneath the common opinion that America will "muddle through," beneath the stagnation of those who have closed their minds to the future, is the pervading feeling that there simply are no alternatives, that our times have witnessed the exhaustion not only of Utopias, but of any new departures as well. . . .

Some would have us believe that Americans feel contentment

amidst prosperity—but might it not be better be called a glaze above deeply-felt anxieties about their role in the new world? And if these anxieties produce a developed indifference to human affairs, do they not as well produce a yearning to believe there *is* an alternative to the present, that something *can* be done to change circumstances in the school, the workplaces, the bureaucracies, the government? It is to this latter yearning, at once the spark and engine of change, that we direct our present appeal. The search for truly democratic alternatives to the present, and a commitment to social experimentation with them, is a worthy and fulfilling human enterprise, one which moves us and, we hope, others today. On such a basis do we offer this document of our convictions and analysis: as an effort in understanding and changing the conditions of humanity in the late twentieth century, an effort rooted in the ancient, still unfulfilled conception of man attaining determining influence over his circumstances of life. . . .

THE STUDENTS

If student movements for change are still rareties on the campus scene, what is commonplace there? The real campus, the familiar campus, is a place of private people, engaged in their notorious "inner emigration." It is a place of commitment to business-as-usual, getting ahead, playing it cool. It is a place of mass affirmation of the Twist, but mass reluctance toward the controversial public stance. Rules are accepted as "inevitable," bureaucracy as "just circumstances," irrelevance as "scholarship," selflessness as "martyrdom," politics as "just another way to make people, and an unprofitable one, too." . . .

Tragically, the university could serve as a significant source of social criticism and an initiator of new modes and molders of attitudes. But the actual intellectual effect of the college experience is hardly distinguishable from that of any other communications channel—say, a television set—passing on the stock truths of the day. Students leave college somewhat more "tolerant" than when they arrived, but basically unchallenged in their values and political orientations. With administrators ordering the institution, and faculty the curriculum, the student learns by his isolation to accept elite rule within the university, which prepares him to accept later forms of minority control. The real function of the educational system—as opposed to its more rhetorical function of "searching for truth"—is to impart the key information and styles that will help the student get by, modestly but comfortably, in the big society beyond.

THE SOCIETY BEYOND

Look beyond the campus, to America itself. That student life is more intellectual, and perhaps more comfortable, does not obscure the fact that the fundamental qualities of life on the campus reflect the habits of society at large. The fraternity president is seen at the junior manager levels; the sorority queen has gone to Grosse Pointe; the serious poet burns for a place, any place, to work; the once-serious and never-serious poets work at the advertising agencies. The desperation of people threatened by forces about which they know little and of which they can say less; the cheerful emptiness of people "giving up" all hope of changing things; the faceless ones polled by Gallup who listed "international affairs" fourteenth on their list of "problems" but who also expected thermonuclear war in the next few years; in these and other forms, Americans are in withdrawal from public life, from any collective effort at directing their own affairs.

The very isolation of the individual—from power and community and ability to aspire—means the rise of a democracy without publics. With the great mass of people structurally remote and psychologically hesitant with respect to democratic institutions, those institutions themselves attenuate and become, in the fashion of the vicious circle, progressively less accessible to those few who aspire to serious participation in social affairs. The vital democratic connection between community and leadership, between the mass and the several elites, has been so wrenched and perverted that disastrous policies go unchallenged time and again.

POLITICS WITHOUT PUBLICS

The American political system is not the democratic model of which its glorifiers speak. In actuality it frustrates democracy by confusing the individual citizen, paralyzing policy discussion, and consolidating the irresponsible power of military and business interests.

A most alarming fact is that few, if any, politicians are calling for changes in these conditions. Only a handful even are calling on the President to "live up to" platform pledges; no one is demanding structural changes, such as the shuttling of Southern Democrats out of the Democratic Party. Rather than protesting the state of politics, most politicians are reinforcing and aggravating that state. . . .

THE ECONOMY

We live amidst a national celebration of economic prosperity while poverty and deprivation remain an unbreakable way of life for millions in the "affluent society," including many of our own generation. We hear glib references to the "welfare state," "free enterprise," and "shareholder's democracy" while military defense is the main item of "public" spending and obvious oligopoly and other forms of minority rule defy real individual initiative or popular control. Work, too, is often unfulfilling and victimizing, accepted as a channel to status or plenty, if not a way to pay the bills, rarely as a means of understanding and controlling self and events. In work and leisure the individual is regulated as part of the system, a consuming unit, bombarded by hard-sell, soft-sell, lies and semi-true appeals to his basest drives. He is always told that he is a "free" man because of "free enterprise." . . .

The Military-Industrial Complex

The most spectacular and important creation of the authoritarian and oligopolistic structure of economic decision-making in America is the institution called "the military-industrial complex" by former President Eisenhower—the powerful congruence of interest and structure among military and business elites which affects so much of our development and destiny. Not only is ours the first generation to live with the possibility of world-wide cataclysm—it is the first to experience the actual social preparation for cataclysm, the general militarization of American society. . . .

Since our childhood these two trends—the rise of the military and the installation of a defense-based economy—have grown fan-

tastically. The Department of Defense, ironically the world's largest
single organization, is worth $160 billion, owns 32 million acres of
America and employs half the 7.5 million persons directly dependent on the military for subsistence, has an $11 billion payroll
which is larger than the net annual income of all American corporations. Defense spending in the Eisenhower era totaled $350 bil-
lions and President Kennedy entered office pledged to go even
beyond the present defense allocation of 60 cents from every public dollar spent. Except for a war-induced boom immediately after
"our side" bombed Hiroshima. American economic prosperity has
coincided with a growing dependence on military outlay—from
1911 to 1959 America's Gross National Product of $5.25 trillion
included $700 billion in goods and services purchased for the de-
fense effort, about one-seventh of the accumulated GNP. . . .

TOWARDS AMERICAN DEMOCRACY

Every effort to end the Cold War and expand the process of
world industrialization is an effort hostile to people and institutions whose interests lie in perpetuation of the East-West military
threat and the postponement of change in the "have not" nations
of the world. Every such effort, too, is bound to establish greater
democracy in America. The major goals of a domestic effort
would be:

1. America must abolish its political party stalemate.
2. Mechanisms of voluntary association must be created
   through which political information can be imparted and
   political participation encouraged.
3. Institutions and practices which stifle dissent should be
   abolished, and the promotion of peaceful dissent should
   be actively promoted.
4. Corporations must be made publicly responsible.
5. The allocation of resources must be based on social
   needs. A truly "public sector" must be established, and its
   nature debated and planned.
6. America should concentrate on its genuine social priorities: abolish squalor, terminate neglect, and establish
   an environment for people to live in with dignity and
   creativeness.

You Don't Need a Weatherman To Know Which Way the Wind Blows

(Submitted by Karin Ashley, Bill Ayers, Bernardine Dourn, John Jacobs, Jeff Jones, Gerry Long, Howie Machtinger, Jim Mellen, Terry Robbins, Mark Rudd and Steve Tappis)

Just seven years after the Port Huron Statement, SDS met again in national convention. In the intervening years the war in Vietnam had expanded dramatically, the integrationist petitions of the early civil rights movement had turned into demands for Black Power, and a movement for student autonomy had generated massive protests on university campuses. For at least some, the primary lesson of the sixties had been the impossibility of securing change peacefully. Teach-ins at universities had not changed the government's Vietnam policy; campaigns on behalf of anti-war candidates seemed an exercise in futility; for those who were most bitter and radicalized, revolution seemed the only answer. With young people as an advance party, these activists demanded that SDS support a world-wide revolution against capitalism and imperialism. The following selection from the Weatherman Manifesto—"you don't need a weatherman to tell which way the wind is blowing"—appears, in retrospect, a hopelessly doctrinaire plea. Just one year later, three of those who endorsed it blew themselves to pieces making bombs in Greenwich Village. Yet the statement also reflects just how corrosive the 1960s had been in destroying the idealism of seven years earlier.

INTERNATIONAL REVOLUTION

> *The contradiction between the revolutionary peoples of Asia, Africa and Latin America and the imperialists headed by the United States is the principal contradiction in the contemporary world. The development of this con-*

Excerpted from Karin Ashley et al. "You Don't Need A Weatherman To Know Which Way The Wind Blows," mimeographed statement, 1969.

tradiction is promoting the struggle of the people of the whole world against US imperialism and its lackeys.

> Lin Piao
> *Long Live the Victory of People's War!*

People ask, what is the nature of the revolution that we talk about? Who will it be made by, and for, and what are its goals and strategy,

The overriding consideration in answering these questions is that the main struggle going on in the world today is between US imperialism and the national liberation struggles against it. . . .

So the very first question people in this country must ask in considering the question of revolution is where they stand in relation to the United States as an oppressor nation, and where they stand in relation to the masses of people throughout the world whom US imperialism is oppressing. . . .

It is in this context that we must examine the revolutionary struggles in the United States. We are within the heartland of a world-wide monster, a country so rich from its world-wide plunder that even the crumbs doled out to the enslaved masses within its borders provide for material existence very much above the conditions of the masses of people of the world. The US empire, as world-wide system, channels wealth, based upon the labor and resources of the rest of the world, into the United States. The relative affluence existing in the United States is directly dependent upon the labor and natural resources of the Vietnamese, the Angolans, the Bolivians and the rest of the peoples of the Third World. All of the United Airlines Astrojets, all of the Holiday Inns, all of Hertz's automobiles, your television set, car and wardrobe already belong, to a large degree, to the people of the rest of the world. . . .

The goal is the destruction of US imperialism and the achievement of a classless world: world communism. Winning state power in the US will occur as a result of the military forces of the US overextending themselves around the world and being defeated piecemeal; struggle within the US will be a vital part of this process, but when the revolution triumphs in the US it will have been made by the people of the whole world. For socialism to be defined in national terms within so extreme and historical an oppressor nation as this is only imperialist national chauvinism on the part of the "movement."

In this context, why an emphasis on youth? Why should young people be willing to fight on the side of Third World peoples? . . .

As imperialism struggles to hold together this decaying, social fabric, it inevitably resorts to brute force and authoritarian ideology. People, especially young people, more and more find themselves in the iron grip of authoritarian institutions. Reaction against the pigs or teachers in the schools, welfare pigs or the army is generalizable and extends beyond the particular repressive institution to the society and the State as a whole. The legitimacy of the State is called into question for the first time in at least 20 years, and the anti-authoritarianism which characterizes the youth rebellion turns into rejection of the State, a refusal to be socialized into American society. Kids used to try to beat the system from inside the army or from inside the schools; now they desert from the army and burn down the schools.

The crisis in imperialism has brought about a breakdown in bourgeois social forms, culture and ideology. The family falls apart, kids leave home, women begin to break out of traditional "female" and "mother" roles. There develops a "generation gap" and a "youth problem." Our heroes are no longer struggling businessmen, and we also begin to reject the ideal career of the professional and look to Mao, Che, the Panthers, the Third World, for our models, for motion. We reject the elitist, technocratic bullshit that tells us only experts can rule, and look instead to leadership from the people's war of the Vietnamese. Chuck Berry, Elvis, the Temptations brought us closer to the "people's culture" of Black America. The racist response to the civil rights movement revealed the depth of racism in America, as well as the impossibility of real change through American institutions. And the war against Vietnam is not "the heroic war against the Nazis"; it's the big lie, with napalm, burning through everything we had heard this country stood for. Kids begin to ask questions: Where is the Free World? And who do the pigs protect at home?

THE RYM AND THE PIGS

A major focus in our neighborhood and citywide work is the pigs, because they tie together the various struggles around the state as the enemy, and thus point to the need for a movement oriented toward power to defeat it.

The pigs are the capitalist state, and as such define the limits of all political struggles; to the extent that a revolutionary struggle shows signs of success, they come in and mark the point it can't go beyond. . . . Our job is not to avoid the issue of the pigs as "diverting" from anti-imperialist struggle, but to emphasize that they are our real enemy if we fight that struggle to win.

The most important task for us toward making the revolution, and the work our collectives should engage in, is the creation of a mass revolutionary movement, without which a clandestine revolutionary party will be impossible. A revolutionary mass movement is different from the traditional revisionist mass base of "sympathizers." Rather it is akin to the Red Guard in China, based on the full participation and involvement of masses of people in the practice of making revolution; a movement with a full willingness to participate in the violent and illegal struggle. It is a movement diametrically opposed to the elitist idea that only leaders are smart enough or interested enough to accept full revolutionary conclusions. It is a movement built on the basis of faith in the masses of people.

The task of collectives is to create this kind of movement. (The party is not a substitute for it, and in fact is totally dependent on it.) This will be done at this stage principally among youth, through implementing the Revolutionary Youth Movement strategy discussed in this paper. It is practice at this, and not political "teachings" in the abstract, which will determine the relevance of the political collectives which are formed.

The strategy of the RYM for developing an active mass base, tying the city-wide fights to community and city-wide anti-pig movement, and for building a party eventually out of this motion, fits with the world strategy for winning the revolution, builds a movement oriented toward the power, and will become one division of the International Liberation Army, while its battlefields are added to the many Vietnams which will dismember and dispose of US imperialism. Long Live the Victory of People's War!

Up Against the Ivy Wall

Jerry Avorn, Robert Freedman, and Members of the
Staff of the Columbia Daily Spectator

No campus experienced greater upheaval than Columbia University in
1968. A Hollywood producer could hardly have created a scenario more
replete with typecast characters and issues. On one side stood a rigid,
conservative university president, tied through board membership to corpo-
rate America and through university contracts to government policy in
Vietnam, refusing consistently to make any concessions to student protes-
tors. On the other stood an assortment of radicals frustrated by the intran-
sigence of the university and committed to finding any available issue as a
basis for confrontation. Add to the picture a black student body intent
upon acting independently of white movements, and a faculty desperately
searching for some middle ground to avoid a campus tragedy.

The immediate issues were simple. Columbia sought to construct a uni-
versity gymnasium in a public park overlooking Harlem, with a separate
entrance at the back of the gym for community people who wished to use
the facility. A second issue involved the university's ties to the Defense
Department through research contracts that, at least indirectly, helped to
support the war. Compounding each of these was a failure of communica-
tion between students and administration. All these strands came together
in the spring of 1968. The following selection, written by the editors of the
student newspaper, highlights how a combination of university stubborn-
ness, student rebellion, and the overuse of police force resulted in the
radicalization of a significant portion of the university student body. The
Columbia story became a microcosm of what was to happen on other
campuses throughout the country, helping to create a widespread sense that
everything was coming apart, and that no institution—no matter how
venerated—was safe from radical challenge.

"What is the singular of 'swine'?" asked Warren Goodell, vice president for administration of Columbia University, as he walked into the offices of the *Columbia Daily Spectator.*

"It must be 'pig,' " one of the editors suggested. "Why?"

"They called me one yesterday," the vice president said with a nervous smile. "They marched over to my office, and one of them yelled, 'There's another one of these swine around here,' and they came looking for me. But I wasn't in."

The incident had occurred on March 27, 1968, during a demonstration in which over one hundred members of the Columbia chapter of Students for a Democratic Society marched into Low Memorial Library, the domed-and-columned edifice that houses the offices of Columbia's top administrators. Officially the demonstration had been called to protest Columbia's affiliation with the Institute for Defense Analyses, an organization that does military research for the federal government. But beyond this it had another goal: to flout an edict, issued at the start of the academic year by Columbia President Grayson Kirk, banning all protests inside University buildings. SDS claimed that the rule was an attempt at political repression and wanted to draw the administration into a confrontation over the regulation. Inside Low, chanting "IDA Must Go!", the mass of students burst into several offices, including that of one administrator who admitted he was against the war but said he had more pressing problems. The students presented him with a petition calling for Columbia's disaffiliation from IDA, signed by more than 1,500 students and faculty. They then coursed through the building for the next fifteen minutes, chanting anti-war slogans and distracting secretaries.

Now, as Goodell spoke of the event, he grew agitated. "Take over," he murmured, "the word has gone out from national SDS—take over the universities. . . . Those students have no respect for property," the vice president said. "You should have seen the things they were doing in Low yesterday—writing on the wall, everything. I have a Picasso hanging in my office, you know. Those kids probably won't even know it's a Picasso. If they touch my Picasso they're going to the state penitentiary! . . .

In the midst of a rapidly changing University climate, Grayson Kirk, sixty-four years old, imposing, President of Columbia University, meticulously clad in gray vest and suit, sat in his large Low Library office surrounded by his familiar mementos and objets d'art. He leaned forward in a leather chair and lit his pipe. It was five days before the uprising. His ample jowls swelling red as he puffed, Kirk explained to a small group of student editors why he had refused for eight months to make public the contents of a report he had commissioned on student life at Columbia. The report had been submitted in late August by a committee of students, faculty and administrators who had worked for nearly two years on the project. It contained an extensive set of proposals for student involvement in University decision-making, as well as rules governing student rights and protest. Kirk had finally released the report only after the student council threatened to make its copy public, and now declined to comment on any of the proposals it contained.

"For me to comment on the Student Life Report would foreclose discussion about it on campus," the President remarked with the stammer that mars much of his speech. "I would not want to say at this time in what spheres of University life the students should have a voice, because there hasn't been time to read the report carefully enough."

Discussion turned to the March 27 political demonstration inside Low Library and the disciplining of students that might follow. "The University is free to expel anyone for any reason it deems equitable," Kirk stated, "and that is as it should be. Of course, I have—under the Trustees—the final disciplinary authority." . . .

April 22, the day before it all began at Columbia, a student sent an open letter to President Kirk. It began with a quotation:

> *Our young people, in disturbing numbers, appear to reject all forms of authority, from whatever source derived, and they have taken refuge in a turbulent and inchoate nihilism whose sole objectives are destruction. I know of no time in our history when the gap between the generations has been wider or more potentially dangerous.*
>
> *Grayson Kirk, April 12, 1968*
> *Charlottesville, Va.*

DEAR GRAYSON,

Your charge of nihilism is indeed ominous; for if it were true, our nihilism would bring the whole civilized world, from Columbia to Rockefeller Center, crashing down upon all our heads.

Though it is not true, your charge does represent something: you call it the generation gap. I see it as a real conflict between those who run things now—you, Grayson Kirk—and those who feel oppressed by, and disgusted with, the society you rule—we, the young people.

You might want to know what is wrong with this society, since, after all, you live in a very tight self-created dream world. We can point to the war in Vietnam as an example of the unimaginable wars of aggression you are prepared to fight to maintain your control over your empire (now you've been beaten by the Vietnamese, so you call for a tactical retreat). We can point to your using us as cannon fodder to fight your war. We can point out your mansion window to the ghetto below you've helped to create through your racist University expansion policies, through your unfair labor practices, through your city government and your police. We can point to this University, your University, which train us to be lawyers and engineers, and managers for your IBM, your Socony Mobil, your IDA, your Con Edison (or else to be scholars and teachers in more universities like this one). We can point, in short, to our own meaningless studies, our identity crises, and our revulsion with being cogs in your corporate machines as a product of and reaction to a basically sick society. . . .

You are quite right in feeling that the situation is "potentially dangerous." For if we win, we will take control of your world, your corporation, your University and attempt to mold a world in which we and other people can live as human beings. Your power is directly threatened, since we will have to destroy that power before we take over. We begin by fighting you about your support of the war in Vietnam and American imperialism—IDA and the School of International Affairs. We will fight you about your control of black people in Morningside Heights, Harlem, and the campus itself. And we will fight you about the type of mis-education you are trying to channel us through. We will have to destroy at times, even violently, in order to end your power and your system—but that is a far cry from nihilism.

Grayson, I doubt if you will understand any of this, since your fantasies have shut out the world as it really is from your thinking. Vice President Truman says the society is basically sound; you say the war in Vietnam was a well-intentioned accident. We, the young people, who you so rightly fear, say that the society is sick and you and your capitalism are the sickness.

You call for order and respect for authority; we call for justice, freedom and socialism.

There is only one thing left to say. It may sound nihilistic to you, since it is the opening shot in a war of liberation. I'll use the words of LeRoi Jones, whom I'm sure you don't like a whole lot: "Up against the wall, motherfucker, this is a stick-up."

Yours for freedom,
Mark [Rudd]

. . . By the time of the IDA demonstration a new sub-group had come to dominate SDS. It became known as the "action faction," and advocated a new tactical approach—confrontation politics—to replace the dramatization-politicization style of the "praxis axis." The superficial dynamic of the tactic was simple: a physical confrontation—a sit-in, a blockade, the takeover of a building—is set up to discomfit the adversary who holds the power, in this case the University administration. He can respond by giving in to the substantive demands of the radicals or by crushing them with coercion of his own. If he is unusually perceptive, he may be able to trace a third course, resorting to neither capitulation nor repression, but making small concessions to "co-opt" the dissidents and seduce them to coöperate with the power structure. But, in the coming days, such political sophistication was to prove beyond the resources of the men who ran Columbia.

The tactical elegance of confrontation politics lay in the fact that the radicals had a good chance of winning whether the administration gave in to their substantive demands or overcame them by repression. The use of coercive force on the part of the adversary—whether it came in the form of the University discipline or police violence—could be a powerful force to "radicalize" liberal or moderate students. For the crucial part of the SDS view is that while escalated tactics are necessary to bring pressure for change on substantive issues, the "radicalization" of large segments of the population is far more important. As Rudd said later:

> Confrontation politics puts the enemy up against the wall and forces him to define himself. In addition, it puts the individual up against the wall. He has to make a choice. Radicalization of the individual means that he must commit himself to the struggle to

change society as well as share the radical view of what is wrong
with society.

Shortly after the March 27 demonstration in Low the administration formulated its response to the confrontation. . . . Six students were singled out—Rudd, four other members of the SDS
steering committee and the chairman of a campus draft-resistance
organization—and summoned to the office of a dean to discuss
their participation in the protest. . . . On April 22 the students—
who came to be known as the "IDA Six"—finally agreed to meet
with the dean but declined to discuss their participation in the
IDA demonstration. They were summarily placed on disciplinary
probation.

That evening SDS called an emergency general assembly meeting in a classroom in Fayerweather Hall. . . .

The "ideal" course for SDS to take was suggested in a rather
remarkable proposal presented by sophomore Steve Komm, who
several weeks before had lost to Rudd in the race for the chairmanship. His manifesto was entitled, "PROPOSAL FOR A SPRING OFFENSIVE
AGAINST COLUMBIA RACISM" and was marked in heavy letters, "For
internal circulation." It stated the problem in the following way:

> [The administration's action] comes at a time when SDS is vocif-
> erous but isolated from a mass student and faculty base of sup-
> port. . . . Moderation would give credence to and ratify the admin-
> istration's conduct regulations, which amount to a political castra-
> tion of SDS. Our reply to the administration's attack must be a
> political offensive against the University on the substantive issues
> which maximize the opportunities for student and faculty support.

Komm went on to outline immediate and longer-range tactics.
The former were fairly conventional for SDS. The demonstrators
would first stage a rally at the Sundial. Following the rally the
demonstration would flow inside Low Library where Rudd would
present President Kirk with a written demand for open hearings
for the "IDA Six" on Monday April 29.

The reminder of Komm's proposal—in which concrete plans
gave way to less "realistic" but strangely prophetic suggestions—
was offered lightly, even whimsically, with the understanding that

the actual plans for longer-range tactics would be developed at a steering committee meeting the next night. It read:

> CONTINGENCY A: Fistfights, police violence, similar excitement. Steering Comm. Tues. night plans large demo. Wed., perhaps with. campus ant-racism coalition [black students]. We all pull out quotations from M. L. King. Dorm canvassing late into night. If Wed. all right, see "Escalate," below (d). (Two scenarios: one, ever-bigger demonstrations effectively shutting down afternoon classes until they give in; two, Thurs. 500 or more people sit in [take over] Kirk's/Platt's office until demands granted; Fri. morning they call a sympathy strike.) . . .

As ex-chairman Ted Kaptchuk commented after the disturbances:

> All SDS tactics are based on the assumption that you use the sit-in, takeover and strike when you can. That much is taken for granted. We knew that day that we would try to get into Low to demonstrate, because that was the natural consequence of our politics. When someone gets busted for breaking a rule, like demonstrating inside a building, the thing to do is for everyone to break the rule *en masse;* it flows from our egalitarian ideology. After all, these assumptions are common to all SDS chapters' tactics. They are the unwritten standard radical student tactics. . . .

The sun broke through a gray cloud cover shortly before noon Tuesday, April 23, 1968. Nearly one thousand Columbia students and faculty milled on Low Plaza waiting for the featured event of the afternoon—a march into Low Library sponsored by Students for a Democratic Society.

Cicero Wilson, newly elected president of the Students' Afro-American Society, stepped onto the Sundial. In a sense, Wilson's presence at the SDS rally was as significant as his speech. SDS had never been able to unite with black militants on campus and, until now, the white radicals had been unable even to get a representative of the blacks to speak at an SDS function.

"This is Harlem Heights, not Morningside Heights," Wilson told the crowd that had now grown to five hundred. Waving his fists in the air, he attacked the University's plans to build a gymnasium in Morningside Park. "What would you do if somebody came and took your property? Took your property as they're doing over at Morningside with this gym?" Wilson asked. "Would you sit still? No, you'd use every means possible to get your property back—and this is what the black people are engaged in right now." . . .

After conferring again with his fellows, Rudd mounted the Sundial. . . . Rudd looked up toward Low and saw his runner signal that the huge front door was indeed locked. "The doors are locked at Low," Rudd yelled. "We won't get in the fucking office. Maybe—"

Suddenly, before Rudd could complete his sentence, Tom Hurwitz, a radical junior sporting a revolutionary red bandana around his forehead, leapt onto the Sundial and shouted, "Did we come here to talk or did we come here to go to Low?"

Raising his right arm to the sky, Hurwitz started toward Low. The six leftist leaders who had been disciplined the day before linked arms and pushed to the front of the crowd that was following Hurwitz across the plaza. As the demonstrators strode swiftly up the steps to Low, chanting "IDA Must Go! IDA Must Go!" several administrators frantically tried to stop the surging crowd. . . .

Rudd jumped on top of a trash can just outside the security entrance and asked for quiet so he could address the crowd. Jeff Sokolow, a sophomore member of SDS, tugged at Rudd and said, "Tell 'em we could have gotten in, but someone would have gotten hurt." Rudd told the crowd just that and then once again outlined the alternatives open to them. In the middle of Rudd's speech, however, someone in the front of the crowd shouted, "To the gym, to the gym site!" and nearly three hundred of the demonstrators streamed away from Low toward a gate at Amsterdam Avenue and 117th Street. The students moved off the campus led by Cicero Wilson and several other SAS members.

By 12:30 P.M., just one-half hour after the protest had begun at the Sundial, students had pulled down nearly forty feet of fence at the gym site. As protesters continued to rush down the hill toward the open gate fifteen more policemen converged on the demonstrators and started pulling people away from the fallen fence.

Several scuffles broke out between students and police. An officer from the 24th Precinct grabbed Fred Wilson, a white student, and tried to arrest him. A large circle of students gathered around the pair as they struggled. The crowd began shouting, "Let him go, let him go! Take all of us!" and pushed in around the policeman and his prisoner. The officer slipped in the loose dirt and fell to the ground, dragging Wilson down on top of him. The circle of demonstrators piled onto the policeman, kicking at his hands and body, trying to free Wilson.

Robbie Roth, a thin Columbia sophomore from Queens, suggested that the entire crowd regroup at the Sundial. "We're going to have to go back and get together," he said, "with the crowd building, we can still salvage it." The group filed out of the gym site, walking slowly back through the park toward the campus.

Rudd stepped onto the Sundial again. "We don't have an incoherent mob; it just looks that way. I'll tell you what we want to do. We want the people under discipline to get off of discipline. We want this guy who got busted today to get the charges dropped against him; to get unbusted—I guess that's how you say it. We want them to *stop* the fucking gym over there. So I think there's really one thing we have to do and we're all together here; we're all ready to go—now. We'll start by holding a hostage."

"Where are we going to get one?" one student asked.

"We're going to hold whoever we can," Rudd said, "in return for them letting go of the six people under discipline, letting go of IDA and letting go of the fucking gym. We can't get into Low Library. We can't hold the administrators in Low hostage because we can't get in that place and, also, it's too big a place. *But*—there is one part of this administration that's responsible for what's happened today—and that's the administration of Columbia College."

Someone in front of the Sundial boomed, "SEIZE HAMILTON!" and Rudd shouted, "Hamilton Hall is right over there. Let's go!" The crowd surged along the narrow path leading to the classroom building. Within minutes the lobby of the building was overflowing with four hundred students chanting thunderously. "IDA MUST GO! IDA MUST GO!"

"Now we've got the Man where we want him," Rudd told the crowd. "He can't leave unless he gives into some of our demands." A roar rose from the demonstrators.

"Now, let me tell Dean Coleman why we're here; We're here because of the University's bullshit with IDA. After we demand an end to affiliation in IDA, they keep doing research to kill people in Vietnam and in Harlem. That's one of the reasons why we're here. We're here because the University steals land from black people, because we want them to stop building that gym. We're here because the University busts people for political stuff, as it tried to bust six of us, including myself and five other leaders of SDS for leading a demonstration against IDA. We're not going to leave until that demand, no discipline for us, is met." After sustained applause, Rudd continued, "Another demand is that our brother who got busted today—he got some sort of assault charge—that brother is released, and all the other people who have been busted for demonstrating over there. So it's clear that we can't leave this place until most of our demands are met." ...

When it became apparent late Tuesday night that there would be no new developments at least until dawn, the Hamilton Hall demonstration turned from a sit-in to a sleep-in. As the tired speakers said their last words, the last of the tired demonstrators left the lobby for the upper floors of the building where they made temporary lodgings on corridor and classroom floors. Scattered on blankets, informal groups on each floor held bedtime parties with peanut butter and jelly sandwiches, beer, and guitars. The main classroom building of the all-male College had been transformed for one night into a coed hostel. But, though sexually integrated, the demonstration was becoming racially strained. The fragile alliance between SAS and SDS, born on the Sundial in the afternoon, was dying with the night. The blacks had segregated themselves on the third floor, leaving the remainder of the building to the whites. But the sleeping arrangements were only a sign. Though the integrated steering committee still hung together, a split over tactics was becoming more pronounced. ...

SDS had always been concerned with mass support. "Alienating the faculty would also be dangerous," Rudd warned, "because they could approve some of our demands." The blacks, however, were not at this point concerned with the psychological impact that barricading buildings would have on the rest of the University community. They did not share the ideology of the New Left and were not obsessed with visions of mass support from the white world. While the whites wanted to radicalize the rest of the campus and use the political pressure of popular support to win their demands, the blacks preferred to rely only on the more military advantage of holding buildings, regardless of whether the campus liked it or not.

When the three white delegates to the steering committee reached the first-floor room where the blacks had been meeting, they were told, "We want to make our stand here. It would be better if you left and took your own building." Although the whites had expected all night that the break would eventually come, many were nevertheless shaken by what amounted to an order. They were even more upset when the blacks told them that there were guns in the building. Rumors had been circulating all night, but now it seemed that many blacks were prepared to make a violent stand. The prospect scared the white radicals who were becoming brazen about taking buildings but remained timid about actual violence. The blacks tried to ease the bitterness by telling the white leaders that, by leaving the building, they could act as a diversion when the police came and possibly start a second front. . . .

In an attempt to keep the demoralized group together, Rudd proposed further action. "The blacks have chosen to make *their* stand," he said; "we should—not in support, but in attack of our common enemy, the administration—go and find our own building to make a stand in."

The large center doors to Hamilton Hall were opened and the whites filed out, dazed, into the dawn. Behind them the blacks hurriedly piled desks, chairs, file cabinets and anything else that could be used to block the doors. By 6 A.M. the white exodus was over, the building barricaded and locked. . . .

Out of the confusion, a band of about two hundred students shuffled slowly across a deserted College Walk and, as if drawn by a compulsion to repeat an earlier part of their scenario, they marched to the southeast security entrance of Low Library.

Three or four students at the front of the contingent charged the security door, trying unsuccessfully to force it with their shoulders. One student spotted a board lying on a nearby bench. It was picked up and positioned in front of the large plate glass window of the door. Twice, on the verge of launching the plank through the window, the students hesitated and dropped it. On the third attempt they brought the thick board back slowly and then, in one even motion, smashed the pane. The tinkling of the glass was the only sound to crack the clammy quiet of a gray sunrise. The crowd shuddered—some because of the temperature, others because of the act. The protest had crossed another line. . . .

The students toyed with office equipment, sipped Kirk's sherry and puffed his White Owl "President" cigars. There was the President's huge mahogany desk, his sofa, his telephones, his private bathroom, his $450,000 Rembrandt "Portrait of a Dutch Admiral," his sculptured ebony lion statuette. Everything was there just as Grayson Kirk had left it. . . .

More students from the groups at the Sundial and Hamilton had entered Low, and a plan of action became necessary. The meeting of almost two hundred students was shifted from the hallway to the center of the rotunda, a place normally reserved for formal receptions and lectures by distinguished speakers. Rudd stood before the crowd and in the well-established SDS tradition, outlined the alternative actions available to the demonstrators. Suggestions to leave Low or barricade the entire building were summarily dismissed. A proposed sit-in in the rotunda was rejected for tactical reasons, after Rudd pointed out that the administration could simply lock the huge iron gates that surround the rotunda and leave them sitting there forever. At this point a runner brought news that the New York City police had arrived on campus, were stationed in the basement of Low and would probably be ordered to clear the building. Rudd suggested that the group return to Kirk's office and barricade the doors. The plan was accepted, and the students reëntered the suite, moved into both Kirk's and Truman's private offices and placed desks, chairs and file cabinets against the three doors that lead to the hallway. They filled wastepaper baskets with water from the President's sink to be used as protection against tear gas, and they waited.

Meanwhile, as the demonstrators inside Low were deciding whether to occupy his office, Vice President Truman arrived on campus. Wearing a trench coat, his hat pulled down over his forehead, Truman paced worriedly back and forth on College Walk. The vice president, who normally smokes a pipe, chain-smoked cigarettes as he walked. Several students attempted to speak to him, but he brushed by them. . . .

At 6:50 A.M. Truman called Kirk to brief him and to ask him to come to the campus. Though Truman had argued against bringing in the police on Tuesday afternoon, with the breaking and entering into Low he changed his mind. Over the phone Kirk and Truman now agreed that it was time for the police to clear out Low.

At 7:15 A.M. a delegate from the administration was sent up to the President's office with an offer. He spoke to Rudd through the broken pane in Kirk's door and told him that if the students walked out now and turned in their identification cards they would face only University discipline and no criminal trespass charges. Rudd rejected the proposal, explaining later that it would have been foolish to accept the deal when they knew they had another way out—through the windows. . . .

Meanwhile, Truman was having trouble with the police officials. Kirk had arrived on campus, and the two were trying to arrange for the arrest of any students who remained in the President's office. As firm as they were in their decision that police should be used to clear out Low, they were also set against using the police in Hamilton, for fear of large-scale violence. . . .

The police, however, balked at this selectivity, Truman reported later, telling him that it would be impossible for them to clear out one building and not the other.[4] It was to be all or nothing, and the dangers that could arise in Hamilton Hall convinced the administrators to do nothing. That the police were not brought in proved critical. Had they been used to clear Low, the demonstration probably would have been contained, and the administration would have had to deal only with the blacks in Hamilton. . . .

Surrounded by statues of Buddha and bodhisattvas in the Faculty Room of Low Library, Kirk told reporters:

> The University is committed to maintaining order on the campus. We insist that there be respect for the rules and conditions that make University life possible. We have exercised great restraint in the use of police and security forces, because at almost all costs, we wish to avoid physical confrontation. We have constantly tried to communicate with those students who have seized the buildings, and as late as this morning, contact was made with all of the protesting groups, but with no success. We are prepared to talk with the protesting groups, but disciplinary action will have to be taken

against those students who flagrantly violated University rules. The students have had ample opportunity to leave the buildings and to engage in *lawful* protest if they so desire.

"We cannot give in on amnesty," Truman said. "This goes far beyond this University." Asked about the gym Kirk replied, "Contract obliges us to continue construction."

Professor Westin was disturbed by the hard-line approach he heard. "It was a disconcerting press conference," he said later, "because the President and vice president took a very strong position—a 'We have no alternative but to turn to law and order' type of presentation." At the close of the conference Westin turned to Vice President Goodell and asked whether it would be possible for Truman to meet with a group of faculty in Philosophy Hall. Westin wanted Truman to discuss the administration's policy with them and, as Westin later phrased it, "to share with us why he felt there was no possibility of give on these issues, and why he seemed to be heading toward such a climax." Goodell said he would try to arrange the meeting, and Westin left Low to gather together as many professors as possible.

When Truman arrived in Philosophy more than one hundred faculty members were there to hear him. He recapitulated the development of the crisis, adding at the end in an unsteady voice, "I just don't know how much longer this situation can go on." He maintained that the gym was not a real issue and that the University could not afford to stop construction because it would cost six million dollars to break the contracts. Westin told the vice president that as a lawyer, he could not believe that the contracts could not be severed for less. Truman insisted that this would be impossible.

"Is there anything the faculty can do?" Professor Rothman asked.

"Nothing," Truman answered.

After twenty minutes Truman cut off discussion, saying he was already late for another meeting in Low and that the faculty would have to excuse him. He left the group, probably without realizing that he had greatly alienated many former colleagues, some of whom later said that he had appeared "uncommunicative," "uncompromising," and unable to meet the crisis. Robert Belknap, a professor of Russian who was present during Truman's appearance, later said:

It was what he didn't say that bothered us. He hadn't said that negotiations were proceeding. He hadn't drawn up a statement saying what could or could not be done. He hadn't appointed a faculty group to advise him. . . . He lost his cool."

By Friday some of the strikers' demands seemed well on their way to realization. But victories on matters such as gym construction were not the developments in which the strike leaders took most satisfaction. More significant was the change that had come over the life-style of the students who occupied the buildings. This transformation of the quality of life and the existential involvement of the individual were the ends toward which all of the SDS ideology pointed. The radicals saw the routinized patterns of society as repressive, manipulative and dehumanizing. The "respectable" lives of businessmen, bureaucrats and professionals to which many of them had once aspired were seen as drab, confining, cardboard existences. Now, insulated from the norms and forms of American culture by several feet of office furniture and barricades, the students inside the "liberated" buildings were able to create social patterns of their own. The takeover of the buildings had begun as a political tactic designed to bring about the goal of social reconstruction. It quickly evolved into the realization, on a small scale, of that very goal. The process of personal liberation was founded in a common existential credential—all the students in the buildings had placed their careers at Columbia in some jeopardy by joining the protest; a common tactic—confrontation; a common enemy—the administration; and a common set of immediate goals—the six demands. In addition, in the day-to-day conduct of the demonstrations each student could feel that he was in direct touch with the sources of power and decision-making within the strike apparatus. This was accomplished through participatory democracy, a central element of SDS ideology as has been noted. Students could, within the strike context, *make the decisions that affected their lives.*

Shortly before noon Saturday hopes for a peaceful mediation of the crisis suffered another setback. Members of the board of Trustees, normally distant from campus affairs, were slowly being drawn into the crisis. On Friday morning, William Petersen, president of the Irving Trust Company, who serves as chairman of the Colum-

bia Trustees, made his first major attempt to bring peace to the
Morningside campus. He phoned the Mayor of New York City.
Lindsay aide Barry Gottehrer later described the conversation:

> Petersen wanted the Mayor to come up to Columbia and settle
> the situation. Lindsay was willing, but asked what leverage he
> would be given in mediating. Petersen said they would give him no
> leverage. He just asked the Mayor to come onto campus and walk
> around, talking to people, as he does in Harlem. He expected a
> miracle.

Lindsay never came, but Petersen continued his search for a solution. Friday evening the Trustees were called together for an
informal meeting downtown to discuss what was happening to
their University.

Chairman Petersen took it upon himself to issue a public statement Saturday morning stating his interpretation of the opinions
expressed by the quorum of Trustees present. The Petersen
statement was read to the Ad Hoc Faculty Group late Saturday
morning:

> The Trustees and the University met and conferred yesterday
> (Friday) regarding the situation on the Morningside Heights cam-
> pus. They expressed approval of the course which had been fol-
> lowed by the University administration. . . . In common with the
> administration the Trustees deplore the complete disruption of
> normal University operations and the illegal seizure and occupation
> of University buildings, perpetrated by a *small minority of students,
> aided and abetted by outsiders* who have injected themselves into the
> situation. . . .
> The Trustees have advised the President that they wholeheart-
> edly support the administration position that there shall be no am-
> nesty accorded to those who have engaged in this illegal conduct.
> Moreover, they not only support the President's stand, but *affirma-
> tively direct, that he shall maintain the ultimate disciplinary power* over the
> conduct of students of the University as required by the Charter
> and Statutes of the University.
> Insofar as the gymnasium is concerned, the Trustees feel that
> the attempt to depict the construction of the building as a matter
> involving a racial issue or discrimination is an attempt to create an
> *entirely false issue* by individuals who are either not conversant with,
> or who disregard, the facts. However, the Trustees have approved

the action taken by the administration *at the request of the Mayor* of New York City, on Thursday, April 25, to halt construction activities *temporarily*. This action represented an appropriate response, and *a courtesy to the chief executive of the City* at a time of tension. . . .

The Petersen statement was received with hostility in nearly every quarter of the campus and was seen as written proof that the Trustees were as out of touch with University life as everyone had imagined. Herbert Deane said later that the Petersen statement "almost blew us out of the water." The administration had announced on Thursday night that gym construction had been suspended, a partial concession to one of the Six Demands. Now on Saturday, when the gym had all but dropped out of the picture, the Trustees proclaimed that the gym was "an entirely false issue" and that construction had only been halted temporarily as a courtesy to the Mayor. Before the Petersen statement the administration had seemed ready to modify its stand on discipline by delegating some authority to the tripartite commission proposed by the Galanter committee. Now the Trustees ordered the President to "maintain the ultimate disciplinary power." . . .

If Mark Rudd had drafted the statement for the Trustees instead of Petersen it could not have made the situation more critical or the University look worse. . . . To the demonstrators a statement like Petersen's was tactically welcome, for in clearly defining the "enemy" position it further polarized the campus. And when sides were chosen few opted to be on the same team as Petersen.

The paradox of negotiations was now clear: the students had been listening to offers they would never consider; the faculty had been promising them things the administration would refuse to accept; and the administration had been making concessions which the Trustees now rejected out of hand. . . .

Inside Low Library the administrators were settling into routinized crisis operations. Kirk and Truman had inched as far as they would go in modifying their position. Faculty members who spoke to the two men over the weekend later said that it was clear then that the administration had no more to offer, especially regarding amnesty. Whatever timid departures they had begun to make from their old stand had been frozen by the Petersen statement, and they now stood rigid and immobile at a point somewhere between partial concession and no concession at all.

In the occupied buildings a similar sort of diplomatic rigor mortis prevailed among the strike leaders and negotiators, if not among their constituents. The strikers had not won their six demands. They had offered and would offer no compromise on any of those demands, especially amnesty. Over the weekend it became clear that the crisis was quickly heading for one of only two possible ends—amnesty or bust.

Rumors had been circulating all Monday night that the police would arrive within hours. But the same rumors had circulated Sunday night and throughout the rest of the occupation, and few students paid much attention to them. For hours busloads of police had been unloading at five precinct centers in different parts of Manhattan. Because the Columbia operation would be on such a massive scale the men had been drawn from precincts in all boroughs of the city—Manhattan, Brooklyn, Queens, Staten Island and the Bronx. Shortly after midnight the police began gathering on the periphery of the campus. Word of the mobilization was carried on radio news broadcasts, as breathless students ran among the occupied buildings to report that at the 100th Street precinct house police buses and paddy wagons were lined up for blocks along the street.

Since the middle of the occupation the black students in Hamilton had communicated with hardly anyone, except through an occasional press release. Their secrecy had reinforced the growing image of militancy hinted at by their official statements and the conclusions of observers. With the expected police attack, most people on campus expected a small-scale Armageddon. Now, with tension higher than it had been at any other time since the crisis began, the occupants of Hamilton were addressing a rally of Harlem residents from windows overlooking Amsterdam Avenue.

More than 150 demonstrators were marching peacefully on the sidewalk carrying crudely lettered anti-Columbia placards and chanting, "Columbia goes from jerk to jerk—Eisenhower to racist Kirk." As white students joined the demonstration and the rally grew, a window opened on the fourth floor of Hamilton and Cicero Wilson leaned out over the street to deliver his first public address since April 23.

"I'd like to thank you brothers for coming out here tonight," Wilson said. "We're here to stop the gym and to get amnesty for the black students in Hamilton Hall." Teddy Kaptchuk ap-

proached a reporter standing near him in the crowd and ner-
vously commented, "You know what he just said really doesn't
matter. They're still with us. It's just a tactical thing." But, despite
their protestations of unity, the white strike leaders had come to
realize that Hamilton was indeed a separate decision-making unit
whose actions in the next hours would be completely unpredict-
able. . . .

Near Low, professors and their teaching assistants pushed their
way through the dense crowd that continued to accumulate outside Kirk's offices. "Please don't stand here," they yelled, "it will
be very bad if you are standing here when the police come. Go
down to the Sundial where there is a rally taking place." Few
students moved—most wanted to see the action firsthand. One
young girl in tears, a teaching assistant in the English department,
began frantically tugging at the sleeves of people she recognized,
urging, "Please, go away from here. You will be badly hurt. Go to
the Sundial." . . .

All the occupied buildings were now being sealed off from the
inside. . . .

Tuesday, 2:10 A.M., April 30: a girl taking a drink of water in
Fayerweather noticed that the fountain trickled to a stop. The
water supply to the other occupied buildings was also shut off. At
Strike Central a student was speaking by phone with occupied
Low when the receiver went dead. Two minutes later the phones
in the *Spectator* office in Ferris Booth Hall were cut off. The bust
was beginning.

Mark Rudd left Strike Central with Lew Cole, Juan Gonzalez and
several other strike leaders. Almost running, he crossed the Sundial and headed for Low. As he arrived a student messenger
dashed to his side "They're—leaving—Hamilton—Mark," he
panted. Rudd sent another runner to Hamilton to get details.

The runner sent to Hamilton now returned. "The blacks are
letting themselves be taken out, Mark," the student said incredu-
lously. No shots rang out in the air over Hamilton. No angry
masses swarmed across Morningside Park from Harlem. . . .

In contrast with SDS the blacks had decided that there was
nothing to gain from a bloody arrest episode. . . .

A crowd of about 250 students and faculty was standing in

front of the security entrance to Low chanting, "No Violence!"
and "Cops Must Go!" They tried to sing Columbia's alma mater,
"Sans Souci," but after several false starts gave up because hardly
anybody remembered the words. The shouting changed to cries
of "STRIKE! STRIKE! STRIKE!" as a column of thirty-five Tactical
Patrol Force squared off directly in front of the crowd. . . .

While the captain talked Frederick Courtney, an instructor in
the Spanish department who was standing at the top of the steps,
remarked to students alongside him that he had left his motorcycle helmet and camera under a hedge by St. Paul's Chapel and
that he thought the helmet might be a good thing to have. He
stepped down and started walking across the grassy plot between
Low and the chapel. Suddenly six men leapt out of the hedges
and seized him. Courtney was knocked to the ground and, as the
demonstrators on the steps watched in amazement, he was
punched, kicked and blackjacked. The men were plainclothesmen; some were wearing dark slacks and blue nylon wind-
breakers, which resembled Columbia jackets, and had looked like
students in the dark. Courtney was dragged away, an officer holding each arm and leg.

As administration officials watched from a window above,
another column of TPF moved into position behind the first.

The TPF captain in charge announced to the crowd, "You are
obstructing police in the performance of their duty. Please move."
His order was met with more cries of "No Violence!" and "No
Cops!" A few athletes standing on a nearby ledge urged the police
to go in and smash the demonstrators, yelling Columbia's football
slogan, "Let's go, Lions!" Others yelled, "Beautiful!" and cheered
as they spotted more light blue police helmets. Again the captain
made his announcement: "You are blocking our progress here."
Again no one moved. The captain's jovial face hardened. Suddenly the police pulled out blackjacks and flashlights and charged,
ramming them into the nearest faces. Most students were merely
grabbed and thrown over the low hedges onto the brick pathways
out of the way of the police. Some were clubbed as they fell. The
front row of resisters was hurled back and to the sides and the
police now began plowing through the remaining five rows in a
similar manner, throwing people onto the grass or bricks. Dean
Platt, standing nearby to observe, was punched in the chest by a
badgeless plainclothesman. Screaming, the crowd split; some ran

north toward Avery and Fayerweather, others south to College Walk. "Is there a physician in the crowd?" someone yelled, helping a limping girl down the steps of Low Memorial Library, "we need a doctor." "Call Dr. Kirk!" an angry student shouted. The name was greeted with cries of "Butcher, Butcher!" One girl who had been in the security entrance rush now stood crying at the Sundial. "They knock you down but that's not enough, they don't let you up again. They just keep hitting. . . ." "They were pros," another student said, "those TPF guys don't even use clubs." Students returning from the confrontation reported, trembling, that girls were smashed against the stone walks when the police came in. "One guy, in uniform, grabbed me by the hair," said one student bleeding from a gash in his lips, "and said, okay, buddy, you're next. Then wham wham wham wham four times in the face." A Barnard girl who had been in the midst of the attack, nearly hysterical, kept screaming over and over, "Cops suck!" until she broke down into fits of sobbing. "This had to happen," quietly observed one student standing near her in the crowd, "it can't be a thinking process when you come to a stalemate." . . .

As each new crowd of prisoners was loaded into a van, the students lining the edge of College Walk cheered in support of the arrested strikers. Television lights blinked on, revealing about two hundred students, most of them from Math, many of them bleeding, holding their fingers aloft in the "V" symbol. The crowd, which included many students who until now had taken no sides in the demonstration responded by raising its hands in a "V" and chanting, "STRIKE! STRIKE!" and "KIRK MUST GO!" In the crowd of observers someone was listening to a professor on WKCR saying, "We had hoped for a breakthrough. . . ."

Melvin Morgulis, who had been filming the entire bust, went up to one of the police facing the College Walk crowd and earnestly began telling him that what was happening was a tragedy in American history. The policeman turned his back, but Melvin continued talking to him. The long-haired student went on, trying to communicate the misery he felt to another policeman on the line who just kept staring back at him with a blank, bored expression. Melvin began to break down. "Why won't you listen to me?" he cried, "Can't you see what you're doing to my buddies out there?" The rest of his words became unintelligible as he lapsed into tears, winding his movie camera convulsively.

As Melvin screamed at the policeman a tall student staggered toward the College Walk crowd from the area of the police vans. Blood dripped from his left eye and covered most of his face. He was controlled, but on the verge of delirium. "Anyone want to take a picture of me?" he asked calmly, dragging on a cigarette; "Are you going to stay in a University like this? Look what the men who run this University have done to me." Another student approached an officer standing on College Walk. He asked him whether he felt the slightest bit of guilt for what was going on behind him. "I'm a compartmentalized man," the lieutenant answered, smiling. "I do what I'm told, and I do it where I'm told."

As the arrested students were piled into police vans on College Walk, they began chanting and shouting furiously. Choruses of "We Shall Overcome" and "Up against the wall, motherfuckers!" resounded from the metallic innards of the paddy wagons. One group of prisoners began banging rhythmically on the inside of their van, and soon the occupants of each wagon took up the new protest.

The crowd of observers on the south side of College Walk had been chanting anti-cop slogans for some time when they noticed hundreds of police marching in drill formation and regrouping on Low Plaza. Through a series of right- and left-faces and advances the policemen, mostly TPF, maneuvered to within several yards of the crowd and ordered them to move back. The group retreated grudgingly and continued to taunt the police. A group of athletes stood on the Sundial chanting "TPF! TPF!" and shouting insults at the pro-demonstration students around them. A moment later, without warning, the line of uniformed officers and plainclothesmen charged into the crowd. The paddy wagons parked on College Walk swung around, their headlights spotlighting South Field and temporarily blinding the students staring up at the plaza. Flailing their clubs the police chased several hundred students onto the lawn, the glare of the bright lights at their backs as they charged. The athletes on the Sundial were overrun with the rest, their pro-police chants disregarded. The students who ran slowest in the stampede were struck with clubs, tripped or kicked. In the darker recesses of the field plainclothesmen stationed themselves near hedges and pummelled demonstrators who tried to run past them. The students who moved faster found, as they reached the south side of the campus, that all of the gates had been closed and locked. With the police sweeping across South Field, they had no place to go but inside the lobbies of the dormitories which were now filling up with the limping, the bruised and the frightened. One student running for Ferris Booth Hall was clubbed and kicked just outside the building. He lay bleeding near the door, jerking spasmodically, until he was carried away on a stretcher by volunteer medical aides.

For the next hour the police crisscrossed again and again over South Field and its environs, "clearing the campus" by chasing or clubbing the students they found. "It was the only way to disperse the crowd quickly," police spokesman Jacques Nevard explained later, "It is folly for people to stand around and watch when there is trouble. . . . Once you start using force, the chances of excessive force increase greatly."

As most police left Columbia with the coming of daylight a new armband appeared on campus. Students stood at the gates and on College Walk handing out strips of black crepe paper, signs of mourning for the death of a University. That morning *Spectator* carried a blank editorial surrounded by a black border. A new SDS flyer was hastily produced and distributed:

> At 2:30 this morning, Columbia University died. . . . WE WILL AVENGE THE 139 WOUNDED MEMBERS OF THE LIBERATION. . . . DOWN WITH THE UNIVERSITY, UP WITH THE STUDENTS, UP WITH THE COMMUNITY, LONG LIVE THE FORCES OF LIBERATION AT COLUMBIA. . . .

The black armbands were also a sign of outrage. Though the liberals had previously refused to identify themselves completely with the students in the buildings, they were now forced to take sides, and it was unlikely that they would move behind the forces of "legitimate violence." Most Columbia students and faculty had never come closer to mass violence than TV news broadcasts, and the new first-hand experience of police confrontation shook them—at least temporarily—out of middle-of-the-road politics. With many students and faculty members walking around campus wearing head bandages and slings as badges of brutalization, it was hard to remain placidly uncommitted.

The protest that had been born during the occupations grew enormously in scope and support as the newly activated liberals joined its ranks. The crisis developed into its next phase: a full-scale strike against the University. The same phenomenon had occurred at Berkeley in 1964, when a widespread student-faculty strike followed police clearance of a sit-in in Sproul Hall. Now at Columbia the pattern was being repeated. At 7:15 A.M. Mike Nichols, executive vice president of the Columbia University Student Council, stood on Low Plaza amid reporters and shouting students and announced that the student council would support a general strike against the administration. One year ago Nichols had appeared at a campus debate to condemn SDS and the New Left. Now he was joining forces with them against Kirk and Truman. Within hours hundreds of students joined the Strike Coordinating Committee in endorsing the strike.

Rise and Fall of a Counterculture

Allen J. Matusow

*In the eyes of many Americans, the counterculture of the late 1960s
represented a startling new development, threatening, in almost nihilistic
fashion, every tradition and norm inherited from the past. Yet as Allen
Matusow shows in this sharply written excerpt from* The Unraveling of
America, *many of the central themes of the counterculture went back to
intellectual and cultural developments of the forties and fifties. Beatnik
poets and novelists, black jazz musicians, and pioneer users of hallucinogenic drugs all helped to pave the way for the explosive rebellion of values
and behavior that occurred among middle and upper class young people
during the late sixties. Still, the confluence of cultural protests that took
place in these years went beyond anything that could have been anticipated
by a reader of Kerouac's* On The Road *in the fifties. At least some of the
children of America's "best" families were engaging in what their parents
could only see as bizarre and pathological activity—getting stoned on
drugs, grooving to atonal acid rock, challenging nearly every vestige of
"respectability" in social interaction, turning their backs on the Protestant
ethic that had made America what it was. Here, Allen Matusow gives us a
keen and precise look at the contours of that counterculture, even as he
exposes its fragility and contradictions.*

AMERICA discovered hippies at the world's first Human Be-In,
Golden Gate Park, San Francisco, January 14, 1967. The occasion
was something special, even in a Bay Area underground long

Excerpted from *The Unraveling of America: A History of Liberalism in the
1960s* by Allen J. Matusow. Copyright © 1984 by Allen J. Matusow.
Reprinted by permission of Harper and Row.

accustomed to spectacle. Political activists from Berkeley mingled with dropouts from Haight-Ashbury, ending their feud and initiating a "new epoch" in the history of man. "In unity we shall shower the country with waves of ecstasy and purification," sponsors of the Be-In prophesied. "Fear will be washed away; ignorance will be exposed to sunlight; profits and empire will lie drying on deserted beaches.". . .

Timothy Leary was there, dressed in white and wearing flowers in his hair. "Turn on to the scene, tune in to what is happening, and drop out—of high school, college, grad school, junior executive—and follow me, the hard way," said Leary, reciting his famous commercial for the synthetic hallucinogen LSD. . . . Music for the occasion was acid rock, performed by Quicksilver Messenger Service, Jefferson Airplane, and the Grateful Dead. Already an underground legend, the Dead had played Ken Kesey's notorious "acid tests," which had done so much to spread LSD and the psychedelic style throughout California a year or so before. Representing the new left was Jerry Rubin, released that very morning from jail, but not yet hip enough for this occasion. "Tune-In—Drop-Out—Take-Over." Rubin had said at a press conference prior to the event. But few at the Be-In were in a mood (or condition) to take over anything.

The real show was the crowd. "The costumes were a designer's dream," wrote music critic Ralph Gleason in the San Francisco *Chronicle,* "a wild polyglot mixture of Mod, Palladin, Ringling Brothers, Cochise, and Hells Angel's Formal." Bells tinkled, balloons floated, people on the grass played harmonicas, guitars, recorders, flutes. Beautiful girls handed out sticks of incense. A young man in a paisley parachute drifted from the sky, though no plane was in sight. An old man gave away his poems.

Newsweek was on hand to photograph the Be-In in gorgeous color and report that "it was a love feast, a psychedelic picnic, a hippie happening." Images of hip quickly began to seep into the public consciousness, provoking intense curiosity and endless analysis in the straight world. Most of the pop sociology deserved the rebuke of Bob Dylan's "Ballad of a Thin Man": "Something is happening here but you don't know what it is. Do you, Mr. Jones?" Yet understanding was imperative, for the hippie impulse that was spreading through a generation of the young challenged the traditional values of bourgeois culture, values still underpinning the liberal movement of the 1960s—reason, progress, order, achievement, social responsibility. Hippies mocked liberal politicians, scorned efforts to repair the social order, and repudiated bourgeois society. In so doing, they became cultural radicals opposed to established auhority. Among the movements arrayed against him toward the end of his tenure, none baffled Lyndon Johnson more than these hippies. Somehow, in the name of liberation, they rejected everything he stood for, including his strenuous efforts to liberate the poor and the black. Clearly, liberation meant something different to liberals like him from what it meant to radicals like them.

The history of hip began with the black hipsters of the 1930s. Black folk had always constituted something of a counterculture in America, representing, at least in the white imagination, pure id. Migrating into northern ghettos after World War I, young black men used their new freedom to improvise a new variation on black deviance—the hipster—who was not only hedonistic, sensual, and sexually uninhibited, but openly contemptuous of the white world that continued to exclude him. The language that hipsters invented on Harlem street corners was jive, an action language honed in verbal duels and inaccessible to most whites. Some jive words that became part of the permanent hip lexicon were *cat, solid, chick, Big Apple, square, tea, gas, dip, flip. Ofay,* the jive word for white, meant foe in pig Latin. The hipster costume was the zoot suit, designed, as hip garb always would be, to defy and outrage conventional taste. For kicks, the hipster smoked marijuana, which heightened his sense of immediacy and helped him soar above his mean surroundings. The only bigger kick was sex.

Vital to the hipster experience was the uninhibited black music called jazz. In 1922 a writer in the *Atlantic Monthly* described jazz as the result of "an unloosing of instincts that nature wisely has taught us to hold in check, but which, every now and then, for cryptic reasons, are allowed to break the bonds of civilization." Indeed, Louis Armstrong, playing his "hot," sensual, raunchy improvisations on trumpet, was the first hipster hero. As jazz changed, the hipster persona changed with it. In the early 1940s a group of rebel black jazzmen, hostile to the commercialization of the big bands, created bebop. Bebop relied on small groups and improvisation, as before, but the sound was cool, the rhythm variable, the volume low, and the technical virtuosity of its leading performers legend. The genius of bebop was Charlie "The Bird" Parker, who lived at "the level of total spontaneity," whether he was playing alto sax or getting kicks from booze, sex or heroin. By the mid-1940s, partly because of heroin, hot was out and cool was in. Hipster dress had become more conservative; noise and brash behavior, a breach of taste; detachment, a required pose. By then, too, the hipster had ceased to be a type restricted to blacks only. In New York and other big cities, some disaffiliates among the white young found the hipster persona so expressive of their own alienation that they adopted it as their own. Thus was born, in Norman Mailer's phrase, "the white Negro," living outside the law for sex, pot, jazz, kicks—in short, for Dionysian ecstasy. . . .

What the beats added to hip was the mystic quest. In the summer of 1948, living alone in East Harlem and grieving for his departed lover Neal Cassady, Allen Ginsberg had the defining experience of his life. As he lay in bed gazing at tenement roofs with a book of William Blake's *Songs of Innocence* before him, he heard the deep voice of the poet himself reciting the "Sunflower," and he knew it was the voice of God. "Looking out the widow, . . ." Ginsberg remembered, "suddenly it seemed that I saw into the depths of the universe, by looking simply into the ancient sky." Ginsberg had auditory experience of other poems that evening, and there were other visions in the days that followed, until, a week later, standing in the athletic field at Columbia, Ginsberg invoked the spirit and experienced the cosmos as monster. "The sky was not a blue hand anymore but like a hand of death coming down on me." It was years before Ginsberg would seek that void again, but in the meantime he did not forget those moments when the ego had overflowed the bounds of the self and illumination had been his. . . .

Jack Kerouac, the beat writer who shared so many of Ginsberg's adventures, also shared his mystic quest. Kerouac had gone to Columbia to play football but rebelled against the discipline, deciding instead to write novels and probe the cultural underground. Recalling the 1940s, he wrote, "Anyway, the hipsters, whose music was bop, they looked like criminals but they kept talking about the same things I liked, long outlines of personal experience and vision, nightlong confessions full of hope that became illicit and repressed by War. . . ."

Kerouac made his artistic breakthrough when he decided to write a semi-fictional account of his road experiences with Neal Cassady. Some people might have regarded Cassady as a bum. Reared on the streets of Denver by his wino father, in and out of jails mostly for stealing cars, Cassady possessed so much energy and lived so completely in the moment that the beat circle could not resist him. In April 1951 Kerouac fed a roll of teletype paper into a typewriter and let tales of Cassady flow spontaneously from his mind, in one paragraph 120 feet long. It took three weeks to write *On the Road,* six years to get it published.

On the Road portrayed Kerouac, Cassady, Ginsberg, and their hipster friends speeding across the continent in the late forties, consuming pot, jazz, and sex, envying the Negro his spontaneity, his soul, his cool. Cassady (Dean Moriarty in the book) was the natural man, the Dionysian ego, joyfully slaking his unquenchable thirst for food, sex, and life. but Kerouac saw Cassady as more than a glutton. He was "a holy con-man," "the HOLY GOOF," "Angel Dean," questing for "IT," the moment "when you know all and everything is decided forever,"—that moment in jazz, Dean explained, when the man making the music "rises to his fate and has to blow equal to it." In San Francisco, deserted by Cassady and delirious from hunger, Kerouac himself (Sal Paradise) had a mystic vision, reaching "the point of ecstasy that I always wanted to reach." Eventually, as Cassady became ensnared in complication, accusation, wounds of the body, he becomes, in Kerouac's view, "BEAT—the root, the soul of Beatific." A bestseller in 1957, *On the Road* became a literary inspiration for the restless young even then preparing to scale the walls of American suburbia in search of Dionysus.

In 1955 Kerouac, still an obscure writer, bummed his way across the country to visit Ginsberg in San Francisco. Kerouac was by then deep into Buddhism. Recognizing that the beat quest for satori had more in common with Oriental than Western religion, he vowed to end suffering and achieve nirvana by overcoming desire. In California he found that in turning East he was not alone. A pinch of Zen had by now been added to the witch's brew boiling over in North Beach. . . .

By the late 1950s, a fully developed beat subculture had emerged not only in North Beach but also in Venice West (near Los Angeles), New York's Greenwich Village, and a few other hip resorts in between. The beats possessed deviant tastes in language, literature, music, drugs, and religion. Profoundly alienated from dominant American values, practicing voluntary poverty and spade cool, they rejected materialism, competition, the work ethic, hygiene, sexual repression, monogamy, and the Faustian quest to subdue nature. There were, to be sure, never more than a few thousand full-time beats, but thanks to the scandalized media, images of beat penetrated and disconcerted the middle classes. Beats, like hula hoops, were a fad. Indeed, by the early 1960s the San Francisco poets had scattered, and cops and tourists had driven the rest of the beats from their old haunts in North Beach. A remnant survived, however, and found convenient shelter in another congenial San Francisco neighborhood. It was Haight-Ashbury, a racially integrated community, forty square blocks, bordering magnificent Golden Gate Park. There, beat old-timers kept alive the hip style and the Dionysian projects, until hippies moved in and appropriated both.

In the metamorphosis from beat to hippie, hallucinogenic drugs played an indispensable part. Indians had been using peyote and magic mushrooms for sacramental purposes since before the rise of the Aztec civilization. But in industrial civilizations, knowledge of mind-altering substances had virtually disappeared. . . .

The herald of the psychedelic revolution was the British author Aldous Huxley. Swallowing some mescaline in 1953, Huxley accidentally triggered a profound mystical experience, in which he watched "a slow dance of golden lights." discovered "Eternity in a flower" and even approached the "Pure Light of the Void," before fleeing in terror from "the burning brightness of unmitigated Reality." . . .

The man who purveyed Huxley's holy message to the millions was Timothy Leary. Possessor of a Ph.D. in psychology, Leary quit his job as director of the Kaiser Foundation Hospital in Oakland, California, in 1958, convinced that conventional psychiatry did not work. Accepting a post at Harvard to pursue his unorthodox ideas, Leary was on his way to a productive scientific career until, one day in Mexico, he discovered the magic mushrooms.

Leary had retreated to a villa on Cuernavaca in the summer of 1960 to write a paper that he hoped would win him points in the academic game. He had never smoked marijuana and knew nothing about mind-altering drugs. But, when a friend procured the mushrooms from a local Indian, Leary thought it might be fun to try some. On a hot afternoon sitting around a pool, Leary and a few companions choked down a bowl of filthy, foul-tasting *crudos*. The game for Leary ended right there. "Five hours after eating the mushrooms it was all changed," he wrote. "The revelation had come. The veil had been pulled back. The classic vision. The full-blown conversion experience. The prophetic call. The works. God had spoken."

Back at Harvard in the fall, Leary secured Huxley's help in designing a scientific experiment to investigate the behavioral effects of psilocybin (synthesized magic mushrooms). Soon Leary was turning on graduate students, ministers, convicts, and stray seekers showing up at his rented mansion in suburban Boston. In truth, Leary was using science to cloak his real purpose, which was to give away the keys to paradise. And he did grow in spiritual knowledge. He learned that drugs alone could not produce a state of blessedness, that they "had no specific effect on consciousness, except to expand it." God and the Devil resided together in the nervous system. Which of these was summoned depended on one's state of mind. Leary, therefore, emphasized the importance of proper "set and setting" (candles, incense, music, art, quiet) to help the seeker experience God.

In December 1960 Leary made the connection with the hip underground in the person of Allen Ginsberg. Having met him in New York, Ginsberg spent a week at Leary's home to enlist the professor in his own crusade for mind expansion. The two hit it off from the start. On Sunday, with dogs, children, and hangers-on scattered about, Leary gave Ginsberg and Peter Orlovsky the sacred mushrooms. The poets repaired to their room, stripped naked, and played Wagner on the record player. Lying in bed, Ginsberg began to succumb to hellish visions, until Leary came in, looked in his eyes, and pronounced him a great man. Ginsberg arose, and with Orlovsky padding behind, descended to the kitchen to proclaim himself the Messiah. We will go into the streets and call the people to peace and love, Leary reports him as saying. And we will get on the phone and hook up Burroughs, Kerouac, Mailer, Kennedy, and Khrushchev and "settle all this warfare bit." . . .

Not until late 1961 did Leary try LSD—"the most shattering

experience of my life." Taking him far beyond psilocybin, LSD enabled Leary to accomplish the projects of the counterculture—Dionysian ecstasies, mystic and bodily. He journeyed down the DNA ladder of evolution to the single cell at the beginning of life and then outward to the cosmic vibrations where he merged with pure energy, "the white light," nothingness. He also experienced the resurrection of the body. "Blow the mind and you are left with God and life—and life is sex," he said. Leary called LSD "a powerful aphrodisiac, probably the most powerful sexual releaser known to man. . . . The union was not just your body and her body but all of your racial and evolutionary entities with all of hers. It was mythic mating." *Playboy* asked Leary if it was true that women could have multiple orgasms under LSD. He replied with a straight face, "In a carefully prepared, loving LSD session, a woman can have several hundred orgasms.". . .

If Leary spread the psychedelic revolution, Ken Kesey created the psychedelic style, West Coast version. In 1959, three years before publication of his modern classic *One Flew Over the Cuckoo's Nest,* Kesey took LSD as a subject in a medical experiment, and for him, then and there, the doors of perception blew wide open. In 1964, with a group of disciples called the Merry Pranksters, he established a drug commune in rural La Honda, an hour's drive from San Francisco. One of the Pranksters was Neal Cassady. On acid, Kesey and friends experienced the illusion of self, the All-in-One, the energy field of which we are all an extension. They tried to break down psychic barriers, attain intersubjectivity or group mind, and achieve synchronization with the Cosmos. And they committed themselves to a life of Dionysian ecstasy.

The Pranksters were hip, but in a new way. They were not beaten disaffiliates, warring against technology land, cursing their fate that they had not been born black. In *The Electric Kool-Aid Acid Test,* a history of Kesey in the underground, Tom Wolfe described this new hip generation, these hippies, as products of postwar affluence. Their teen years were spent driving big cars through the California suburbs, believing, like the superheroes in their Marvel comics, that anything was possible. No spade cool for them, no Zen detachment, none of Leary's "set and setting." The Pranksters used LSD to propel themselves out of their skulls toward the outer edge of Western experience. Their style was the wacko style: lurid costumes, Day-Glo paint, crazy trips in Kesey's

1939 multicolored International Harvester school bus, complete with speakers, tapes, and microphones. It was lots of kicks, of course, but it was more than kicks. For Kesey was a religious prophet whose ultimate goal was to turn America, as Michael Bowen put it, into an "electric Tibet." . . .

The Dionysian impulse in the hippie counterculture was made up in equal measures of drugs, sex, and music—not jazz music but rock and roll. When hippies moved in, the black jazz bars on Haight Street moved out. Spade jazz was now as irrelevant to hip as spade soul. Rock had once been black music too, but was so thoroughly appropriated by whites that many hip kids never knew its origins. Rock originated in the 1940s as "rhythm and blues," an urban-based blues music played with electric instruments, pounding beat, and raunchy lyrics—music by blacks for blacks. In 1952 the legendary Cleveland disc jockey Alan Freed hosted the first rhythm and blues record show for a white audience, calling the music "rock and roll." The music caught on among teenagers tired of sexless, sentimental ballads, and soon white performers fused pop and country styles with rhythm and blues to create white rock and roll. That's what Elvis Presley sang when he emerged in 1956 to become the biggest star in pop history. From the beginning, rock and roll was protest music, protest against Tin Pan Alley, protest against parental taste, protest against instinctual repression. Music of the id, fifties rock and roll helped create a generation of cultural subversives who would in time heed the siren song of hip.

In 1958, when Elvis went into the Army, rock entered a period of decline. Meanwhile, the black sound that had inspired it was being assimilated anew by other talented musicians, this time in England, and it would return to America, bigger than before, with the Beatles. During their long years of apprenticeship, playing lower-class clubs in Liverpool and Hamburg, John Lennon, Paul McCartney, and George Harrison explored the roots of rock and roll, even as they slowly fashioned a style of their own. By 1963 that style had fully matured. No longer just another scruffy group of Teddy Boys playing electronic guitars, they had become well-tailored professionals with a distinctive hair style (Eton long), immense stage presence, the best song-writing team in pop history (Lennon and McCartney), a fluid sound, contagious vitality, and, above all, the irrepressible beat of rock and roll. The beat helped propel the Beatles to stardom in Britain in 1963 and created Beatlemania.

Within days of its release in the United States in January 1964, "I Want to Hold Your Hand" climbed to the top of the charts, to be followed quickly by "She Loves You" and "Please, Please Me." In February the Beatles themselves arrived for a tour that began with a sensational TV performance on the *Ed Sullivan Show* and continued before hysterical teen mobs in New York, Washington, and Miami. In April all five top singles in the United States were Beatles songs and the two top albums were Beatles albums. In July the first Beatles movie, *A Hard Day's Night,* amazed critics and delighted audiences with its wit and verve. Meanwhile that year Beatles merchandise—everything from dolls to dishcloths—was grossing over $50 million. Nothing comparable to Beatlemania had ever happened in the history of pop culture. . . .

The artist who first seized the power of rock and used it to change consciousness was Bob Dylan. Born Robert Zimmerman, Dylan tried on every style of teen alienation available during the fifties in Hibbing, Minnesota. Though he wanted to be a rock and roll star, he discovered on enrolling at the University of Minnesota in 1959 that folk music was the rage on campus. In 1961 Dylan arrived in Greenwich Village, the folk capital of America, determined to become the biggest folkie of them all. A little over a year later, he was. Audiences responded to his vulnerability, the nasal whine with which he delivered his songs, and lyrics so riveting they transformed the folk art. Immersing himself in the left-liberal-civil-rights ethos permeating the Village in the early 1960s, Dylan wrote folk songs as protest. He did not compose from the headlines, as other protest singers did. He used figurative language and elusive imagery to distill the political mood of his time and place. Gambling that a poet could become a star, he won big. Two weeks after Peter, Paul, and Mary recorded his song "Blowin' in the Wind," it sold more than 300,000 copies. Songs like "A Hard Rain's Gonna Fall" were hailed as true art. And his "Times They Are A-Changin'" became a generational anthem. It was no less appropriate for Dylan to sing at the 1963 March on Washington than for Martin Luther King to deliver a sermon there.

Meanwhile, the Beatles arrived and Dylan was listening. "Everybody else thought they were for the teenyboppers, that they were gonna pass right away," Dylan said. "But it was obvious to me that they had staying power. I knew they were pointing the direction of where music had to go." In July 1965 Dylan outraged the folk world by appearing at the Newport Folk Festival, no longer the ragged waif with acoustic guitar, but as a rock and roll singer, outfitted in black leather jacket and backed by an electric band. That summer his rock single, "Like a Rolling Stone," perhaps the greatest song he ever wrote, made it all the way to number one.

Dylan took rock and made it the medium for cultural statement—folk-rock, the critics quickly labeled it. As his music changed, so did the message. Moving with his generation, Dylan now abandoned liberal politics for cultural radicalism. The lyrics he sang in the mid-sixties were intensely personal and frequently obscure, but taken together, they formed a stunning mosaic of a corrupt and chaotic America. It is a fact of no small social consequence that in 1965 millions of radios and record players were daily pounding Dylan's message, subliminally or otherwise, into the skulls of a generation. There was, for example, "Highway 61," which depicted America as a junkyard road heading for war; "Maggie's Farm," a dropout's contemptuous farewell to the straight world; "Desolation Row," which portrayed an insane society, governed by insane men, teetering on the brink of apocalypse; "Ballad of a Thin Man," using homosexual imagery to describe an intellectual's confusion in a world bereft of reason; and "Gates of Eden," a mystical evocation of a realm beyond the senses, beyond ego, wherein resides the timeless Real. After Dylan, a host of other rock prophets arose to preach sex, love, peace, or revolution. After Dylan rock and roll became a music that both expressed the sixties counterculture and shaped it. . . .

By the time of the Monterey International Pop Festival, June 1967, the musical energies that had been gathering in San Francisco for two years could no longer be locally contained. Some of the hippie bands performing at the festival got their first national exposure there; others had already succumbed to the lure of fat recording contracts. By summer the San Francisco Sound was making the city the new rock mecca and its performers the newest rock superstars. The big song on the top forty stations that season was the Airplane's "White Rabbit," psychedelic variations on a theme from *Alice in Wonderland,* ending with the command to "feed a head, feed a head." That summer, too, thousands of teen-agers took literally Scott McKenzie's musical invitation, with its implicit promise of Dionysian revels, to come to "San Francisco (Be Sure to Wear Flowers in Your Hair)." Ralph Gleason, San Francisco's hip music critic, understood well the cultural signifi-cance of rock. "At no time in American history has youth pos-sessed the strength it possesses now," he wrote. "Trained by music and linked by music, it has the power for good to change the world." Significantly, he added, "That power for good carries the reverse, the power for evil."

By 1967 Haight-Ashbury had attained a population large enough to merit, at last, the designation "counterculture." . . .

Ginsberg's was the authentic voice of Haight-Ashbury. Ad-dicted to electronic amenities, hippies merely played at being In-dians, satisfied to wear Navaho jewelry and feathers. They com-muned with nature by picking Golden Gate Park bare of flowers; their notion of tribal harmony was to let everyone "do their own thing." As love had supposedly done for the Hopi, so it would do for them: it would conquer all. Armed with "flower power," hip-pies would overwhelm their enemies and live a life of ecstasy on the asphalt pavements of urban America. . . .

Emmett Grogan was perhaps Haight-Ashbury's most influential citizen. A veteran of gang wars in New York, a student of film in Italy, a draftee who was discharged from the Army in 1966 as a schizophrenic, Grogan found a home in the San Francisco Mime Troupe, which performed radical plays free on the streets. He also plunged into the city's drug culture. Grogan, however, was no ordi-nary head. During his first LSD session in 1965 it had come to him in a flash of illumination that property was theft. Joined by a few others from the Mime Troupe, Grogan began issuing anonymous mimeographed essays to provide the Haight with some politics. He called his essays "Digger Papers," after the seventeenth-century English radicals who appropriated common land and gave their surplus to the poor. The Digger Papers attacked hip capitalists like Thelin for hypocrisy, the hip *Oracle* for pansyness, and the psyche-delic transcendentalism of Swami Bhaktivedanta as "absolute bull-shit." But action counted with Grogan more than words, because action was theater, and theater could alter consciousness by alter-ing frame of reference. In October 1966 the Diggers announced that every day at 4 P.M., at the panhandle on Ashbury Street, they would distribute free food to anyone who wanted it. And very day for the next year, serving food they begged and food they stole, the Diggers kept their promise. . . .

By the summer of 1967 the Haight's bizarre cast of characters was performing for a national audience. This was the summer when *Time* described the neighborhood as "the vibrant epicenter of the hippie movement," hippies estimated their full-time population nationwide at 300,000, imitation Haight-Ashburys bloomed throughout urban America, acid rock dominated the music charts, prestigious museums exhibited psychedelic posters, and doing one's own thing became the national cliche. Once school ended, San Francisco expected one to two hundred thousand kids to flood the city for the Summer of Love. But the real story that summer, unreported by the media, was that few of the thousands who did come stayed very long, Haight-Ashbury was already dying.

Its demise, so similar to the demise of hippie ghettos elsewhere, resulted from official repression, black hostility, and media hype. In San Francisco where city fathers panicked at the prospect of runaway hordes descending upon them, police began routinely roughing up hippies, health officials harassed their communes, and narcotics agents infiltrated the neighborhood. Meanwhile, black hoods from the nearby Fillmore district cruised the streets, threatening rape and violence. Blacks did not like LSD, white kids pretending to be poor, or the fact that Haight-Ashbury was, in the words of a leftover beatnik, "the first segregated Bohemia I've ever seen." Longtime residents began staying home after dark. Finally, the beguiling images of Haight-Ashbury marketed by the media attracted not only an invasion of gawking tourists, but a floating population of the unstable, the psychotic, and the criminal. By the end of the year, *reported* crime in Haight-Ashbury included 17 murders, 100 rapes, and nearly 3,000 burglaries. . . .

As the decade closed, it became clear that drugs, sex, and rock and roll lacked intrinsic moral content. The acid prophets had warned from the beginning that LSD did not inevitably produce the God experience. God and the Devil resided together in the nervous system, Leary had said. LSD could evoke either, depending on set and setting. The streets of Haight-Ashbury, even in the best days, had been littered with kids who deranged their senses on drugs—only to experience spiritual stupor. A fair number ended their trips in hospital emergency rooms, possessed of one or another demon. Satanic cults were not unknown in the Haight. One of them, the Process, apparently influenced Charles Manson, a hippie who lived in the neighborhood in 1967 and recruited confused young girls and a few men into his "family." Manson was an "acid fascist" who somehow found in the lyrics of the Beatles license to commit ritual murder. As violence in the counterculture mounted, LSD became chiefly a means to pierce the false rationality of the hated bourgeois world. The always tenuous link between drugs and love was broken. . . .

Rock and roll was the principal art of the counterculture because of its demonstrable power to liberate the instincts. At the Woodstock Music Festival, held one weekend in August 1969 at Bethel, New York, Eros ran wild. An incredible 400,000 people gathered on a farm to hear the greatest line-up of rock talent ever assembled in one place. Overcoming conditions that could conventionally be described only as disastrous, the crowd created a loving community based on drugs, sex, and rock music. But four months later at the Altamont Raceway near San Francisco, rock revealed an equal affinity for death.

The occasion was a free concert conceived by the Rolling Stones as a fitting climax to their first American tour in three years and the documentary film that was recording it. Altamont was a calamity. Because of a last-minute cancellation elsewhere, concert promoters had only one day to ready the site for a crush of 300,000 kids. Sanitary facilities were inadequate; the sound system, terrible; the setting, cheerless. Lots of bad dope, including inferior acid spiked with speed, circulated through the crowd. Harried medics had to fly in an emergency supply of Thorazine to treat the epidemic of bad trips and were kept busy administering first aid to victims of the random violence. The violence originated with the Hell's Angels. On the advice of the Grateful Dead, the Stones had hired the Angles to guard the stage for $500 worth of beer. Armed with loaded pool cues sawed off to the length of billy clubs, high on bad dope washed down with Red Mountain vin rose, Angles indiscriminately clubbed people for offenses real or imagined. . . .

At nightfall, after keeping the crowd waiting in the cold for more than an hour, the Rolling Stones came on stage. Many critics regarded the Stones as the greatest rock and roll band in the world. Ever since their emergence, they had carefully cultivated an outlaw image—lewd, sneering, surly—to differentiate themselves from their fellow Britons, the Beatles. Their most recent music, including, notably. "Street Fighting Man" and "Sympathy for the Devil," reflected the growing violence of the culture of which they were superstars. Now at Altamont there was Mick Jagger, reveling in his image as rock's prince of evil, prancing on stage while the Angels flailed away with their pool cues below. It was too much even for him. Jagger stopped the music more than once to plead for order; but when the Angels ignored him, he had no choice except to sing on. Midway through "Sympathy for the Devil," only a few feet from the stage, an Angel knifed a black man named Meredith Hunter to death.

For a variety of reasons, after 1970 the counterculture faded. Economic recession signaled that affluence could no longer be assumed and induced a certain caution among the young. The Vietnam War, which did so much to discredit authority, rapidly deescalated. And its own revels brought the hippie movement into disrepute. Carried to the edge of sanity by their Dionysian revels, many of the once hip retreated, some to rural communes in New Mexico or Vermont, most all the way back to the straight world. . . .

Joe Kelly Has Reached His Boiling Point

Richard Rogin

Inevitably, the social protests of the 1960s provoked a counter-response. By the end of the decade a group, dubbed by the media as "middle-Americans," had rallied to the defense of the flag, traditional authority, and good manners. One definition of "middle-Americans" was primarily economic. Earning between $5,000 and $15,000 a year, they made up 55 percent of the population. The majority were blue-collar workers, lower-echelon bureaucrats, school teachers, and white-collar employees. As they saw the federal government pour money into impoverished areas, they developed a sense of neglect and resentment, believing that they were being ignored while vocal protestors received all the attention. Just as important, however, was a sense of crisis in cultural values, a belief that the rules were being changed in midstream. As Newsweek's *Karl Fleming observed, middle Americans felt "threatened by a terrifying array of enemies: hippies, Black Panthers, drugs, the sexually liberated, those who questioned the sanctity of marriage and the morality of work." Anti-war protests galvanized these "middle Americans" into action. From their perspective, it was blasphemy to wear the American flag on the seat of one's pants, burn one's draft card, or shout obscenities at authorities. In the following selection, Richard Rogin provides a first-hand account of how millions of Americans reacted to demonstrators who challenged their most deeply cherished values. In the process, he illuminates just how profound the polarization of the 1960s was.*

"When you were still up on Broadway you could hear the ruckus, the hollering. The peace demonstrators trying to outshout the construction workers. The construction workers hollering, 'U.S.A., all the way' and 'We're Number One.' And the peace demonstrators screaming up there that the war was unjust and everything else, right by the Treasury Building on Broad Street there.

"There was just a lot of hollering and screaming going back and forth until whoever the individual was—oh, he was no spring chicken, he was forty, forty-five years old—that spit on the flag. I was maybe four or five rows back in with the construction workers. I saw him make a gesture, you know, a forward motion. That was it. That was the spark that ignited the flame. It came out in the roar of the crowd. 'He spit on the flag! He spit on the flag!' And of course the construction worker got up there on top of the monument and he gave him a good whack and off came the guy's glasses and I guess he followed his glasses off the pedestal there.

"And then there just seemed to be a rush, a mob scene. The chant then was, 'Get the flags up on the steps where they belong. It's a government building.' And they can say what they want about the New York Police Department, they coulda had the National Guard there with fixed bayonets and they would not have held the construction workers back then.

"When we first went up on the steps and the flags went up there, the whole group started singing 'God Bless America' and it damn near put a lump in your throat. It was really something. I could never say I was sorry I was there. You just had a very proud feeling. If I live to be a hundred, I don't think I'll ever see anything quite like that again."

Joe Kelly's big chin and right hand tremble as he is caught in the deep, remembered passions of that noontime on Friday, May 8. He is thirty-one years old, a brawny 6 feet 4 inches, 210 pounds, blue eyes and receding red hair under his yellow plastic construction helmet decorated with U.S. flag decals and "FOR GOD AND COUNTRY."

It is now late afternoon, nearly two weeks later, and we are sitting in a gray wooden construction shanty on the sprawling World Trade Center site in lower Manhattan where he works. Joe is a well-liked, skillful mechanic in an intricate and demanding trade, elevator construction—installing the elevators and the heavy complex machinery to make the cars run.

On that violent day, soon after he came down for his half-hour lunch break from the forty-second floor of the soaring red steel skeleton of Tower A—another high, seemingly timeless, world which will rise 110 stories overlooking New York and the industrial hinterlands of New Jersey, where men walk almost casually on springy planks laid over open steel now seventy flights up—Joe Kelly reached his "boiling point." He found he could not "sit back" any longer, and he became a demonstrator for the first time in his life. Though "not much of a shouter," and a strong believer that violence solves nothing, he also shouted and threw his first punch in more than ten years.

During that long menacing midday several hundred construction workers, accused by reporters of using metal tools as weapons, were joined by office workers on a rampage through lower Manhattan. They beat up and injured seventy antiwar protesters and bystanders, including four policemen. With cries of "Kill the Commie bastards," "Lindsay's a Red," and "Love it or leave it," they surged up to City Hall. There they forced the flag, which had been lowered to half-staff in mourning for the four dead Kent State students, to be raised again. Then, provoked by peace banners, they stormed through Pace College across the street. It was a day that left New York shaken.

His face taut with fury, Mayor John V. Lindsay went on television to call the workers' attacks "tough and organized" though the unions promptly denied any influence. But he lashed out even more strongly at the outnumbered police whom many witnesses had accused of inadequate preparations and of standing by tolerantly during the assaults on the peaceful rally. Only six arrests were reported. He charged the police with failing as "the barrier between [the public] and wanton violence."

Others called the workers bullies or Nazi brownshirts. "We have no control over what they want to call us," says Joe Kelly. "But I think that the large majority of people, going as high as 85 to 90 percent, are more than happy. Not so much for the violence but for the stand that we took. And now they're standing up. the construction worker is only an image that's being used. The hard-hat is being used to represent all of the silent majority."

It was the wild start of two weeks of almost daily noon-hour, flag-waving, bellicose, damn-Lindsay (the most common signs called him a Communist or a faggot) and praise-Nixon counter-

marches through downtown New York, which Joe Kelly enthusiastically joined. Some of his fellow workers even happily lost an
hour's pay for marching too long after lunch. Despite the fact that
many of the men returned late following Friday's slugfest, none
were docked. "I was going to dock one man who came back an
hour and a half late," says Frank Pike, general elevator construction foreman, "but he said, 'I saw these kids spit on the flag. What
could I do?' How could I dock the man?"

The union word had come down: "Demonstrate all you want
but be careful, no violence." Others say that the union tried to
stop the men from all informal demonstrations. In any event,
there was no more major violence; thousands of helmeted police
patrolled the streets.

The construction workers loaded their unfinished skyscrapers
with huge U.S. flags and their hardhats became a national symbol
of fervent support for the Nixon Administration and its Indochina war policy. President Nixon was even presented with a
hardhat at a White House ceremony. The climax came on May 20
when an estimated one hundred thousand construction workers
and longshoremen sang and chanted from City Hall to Battery
Park in a massive display of jingoistic sentiment probably unparalleled during the uncertain years of the Vietnam conflict.

That day Joe Kelly was given the honor of carrying the gold-
fringed American flag with the gold eagle, its wings outspread,
on the top of the pole, leading a contingent of hundreds of his
fellow workers from Local No. 1, International Union of Elevator Constructors. With his yellow helmet on, he marched, resolutely serious-faced, rarely showing a thin smile, ignoring the
pretty secretaries leaning over the police barriers. He displayed
the training he received when he was an M.P. with an Army
honor guard stationed in Heidelberg, West Germany. Around
him Broadway boomed with the chants: "We're Number One,"
"U.S.A., all the way," "Good-by Lindsay, we hate to see you go."
The marchers sang "God Bless America" and "You're a Grand
Old Flag." "Yankee Doodle" and "Over There" blared forth.
The workers cheered and whistled through the applause from
spectators and the shower of ticker tape and computer cards
from high office windows.

They marched to the green lawns of Battery Park, with the
breeze coming off the upper bay cooling a hot blue day. Joe

Kelly's friends came up to him and shook his hand, saying: "Beautiful." "Like a champ, Joe." Joe clenched and unclenched the fingers of his right hand, which had held the flagpole for two hours. "I feel fine," he said. "This is terrific. It'll wake a few people up. This will happen not only down here but in the rest of New York and across the country now." The first thing to happen, though, was that Frank Pike docked himself and all the elevator constructors an hour's pay for parading instead of working. A few men never made it back to the job that afternoon.

Within the next few weeks in belligerent defense of Nixon's Southeast Asia policies, nearly twenty thousand construction workers paraded (and pummeled antiwar spectators) in St. Louis, and several hundred workers scuffled with students holding a peace rally at Arizona State University in Tempe.

Joe Kelly is proud, confident, and outspoken in the old American style. He is almost mystically proud of his flag, his country, the Establishment, and eager to end the Indochina war by striking more aggressively, though the deaths of young soldiers and innocent civilians sadden him. He is determined to be on guard against Communism and to crush it wherever it threatens his nation. Joe is convinced that a subversive conspiracy of teachers, influenced by foreign powers, is brainwashing the students to Communist beliefs. Distressed by the hippie lifestyle of so many youths, he is also furious at student radicals who burn and shut down schools which his taxes pay for and which most of his fellow workers cherish because they never had a chance to go to them. He is a stalwart charter member of Richard Nixon's silent majority, a devout Roman Catholic and fiercely loyal to his President, whose office he regards with almost holy respect.

"The Pope to the Catholic Church is the same as the President to the American people," he says. "He's the one who decides. He's infallible when he speaks of religion as far as the Catholic Church goes. I'm not saying Nixon is infallible. But he's Commander in Chief of the Armed Forces. He's in charge."

Vietnam: "I just hope that these people give Nixon the play to go in there in Cambodia and knock the living hell out of their supply lines. If this is what it takes to stop the loss of American lives, well, let's go the hell in there and get it over with."

My Lai massacre: "I don't believe anybody in the United States, nice and cozy, has a right to judge them [the accused] until every-thing comes out in the trial."

Kent State: "They [the National Guardsmen] must have felt their lives were threatened; that's why they shot."

Inflation: "I have faith in Nixon. I think he'll curb inflation, given the chance."

High taxes: "If this is what it takes to run this country, I don't mind paying them. You couldn't live anyplace else like you do here."

The flag: "I think of all the people that died for that flag. And somebody's gonna spit on it, it's like spitting on their grave. So they better not spit on it in front of me. You think you could get it better someplace else—well, then, don't hang around, go there."

Unemployment: "I don't know where they're getting these fig-ures from [up to a five-year high for all jobs and 11.9 percent in construction] because here in New York you got a [construction] boom going on."

Joe Kelly has what used to be faithfully accepted as the old-fashioned, authentic American credentials: he is hard-working, conscientious, obedient and trusting in authority, an adherent of law and order, patriotic, sentimental, gentle and affectionate with his loved ones, angry and determined to right wrongs as he sees them, moderately compassionate, a believer in the virtues of his way of life.

To the antiwar protesters and others grieving and critical over America's present course in Indochina and what they perceive as unfeeling repressive policies at home, he probably appears as an anachronism. To them, he is Joe Kelly, yesterday's comic-book hero, a relic from the somehow simpler, self-righteous days of the old world wars when, with a grin and a wave and a song, Americans marched off to solve the world's problems. "The Jack Armstrong of Tower A," one of his fellow workers called him approvingly.

Joe Kelly and millions of Americans like him would not share the gloomy conclusion of John W. Gardner, a Republican and chairman of the National Urban Coalition, that the country is disintegrating. They see a country in momentary disarray, under stress, but they retain a sturdy optimism. They know but do not suffer the dark fear that a complex and subtle civil war is wasting the land with hate and with overt and invisible violence: white against black, conservatives against liberals, workers against stu-

dents, old against young, fathers against sons. Even the old hawks
of organized labor now face opposition within their own ranks
over the Indochina war.

America heaves against the old grain. The kids are on the loose
trying to shake off the crusty habits of the country the way a
snake sheds its skin. The antis feel depressed by their own Government, if not worse, and sense mendacity everywhere.

The kids, Joe Kelly thinks, ought to feel lucky to be in America
where they have the legitimate right to dissent and stage peaceful
demonstrations. If they did the equivalent of burning draft cards
or desecrating the flag in Russia or China, they would, he says, be
shot down in the street.

"These kids," he says, "they can do as they feel like. I mean
burn, loot, steal, do anything they feel like in the name of social
reform. But can the average Joe Blow citizen go out and do this?"
A crime is a crime, he says, even if it's for social reform, and he
argues that there is a double standard of justice for students,
especially in New York.

What about the kids' mockery of the Puritan ethic? "If they
don't want to educate themselves or go out and work hard for a
living and make a few dollars, spend a few dollars, and save a few
dollars for a rainy day, that's their prerogative. But in general,
again, this has been bred into them somewhere. This is not the
American way."

Joe Kelly never thought the picture presented by his hardwork-
ing life would need any defense. There is his pretty blonde wife,
Karen; two strawberry-blonde daughters, Robin Lynn, four, and
Kerry Ann, one and a half, and now a newborn son, James Patrick. "I had two cheerleaders," he says, "now I got a ballplayer."
There is also a collie named Missy and a newly bought brick-and-
shingle, two-story, $40,000 house on an irregular 50 by 100 foot
lot, tastefully furnished, with a modern kitchen ("All you can get
for two arms"), and a freshly sodded lawn on one of those breezy
Staten Island streets with the gulls overhead, children pedaling
red tricycles, the hum of an electric mower, and a man hosing
down a gleaming red Dodge Challenger, all the residents of the
neighborhood blue-collar whites, doing well.

Joe Kelly and his neighbors, the steamfitter, the bus driver, the
policeman, the TV color processor, have worked too hard to get to
that street to give it all up. They have had too many peace protests,

too many moratoriums, too many harsh laments and shouted obscenities against their country, too many rock-throwings and strikes and fires on campuses where they want their children to make it, too many bombings and too many Vietcong flags waving down the streets of their city, too many long-haired youths and naked boys and girls, too many drugs, too much un-Americanism, not to feel angry and resentful.

Joe Kelly sits on his plastic-covered orange couch in front of his new Motorola Quasar color TV console and seethes as he watches the six o'clock news day after day. What really galls him, he says, is what he considers small groups of radical students closing down schools. "In California," he says, "they burned a bank to the ground. You just watch and boil. Who do these university presidents, responsible people, think they have an obligation to? The students are burning something every day. They're taking over something in the chancellor's office every day."

And then that Friday morning, Joe Kelly mounted his turquoise Triumph 500-cc. motorcycle, rode down to the ferry slip, read *The Daily News* and had a coffee as the ferry crossed to Manhattan, then rode his motorcycle again to his job. When he walked into the shanty on the building site, he heard that a shoving incident the previous day between peace demonstrators and construction workers elsewhere in the downtown area had triggered the men from a number of skyscrapers to action. For the workers, "it was the straw that broke the camel's back," he recalls. Spontaneously, Joe says, perhaps a quarter of the World Trade Center's 212 elevator constructors decided to go down the seven blocks and "see what this peace demonstration was all about."

"My partner, Tommy, he climbed up on top of the light stanchion down on Wall Street and planted the flag up there, right in front of the Treasury Building, to a great round of applause. The flags were up on the top steps. The construction workers and the Wall Street workers, they had the steps of the Treasury Building filled and the demonstrators were now down in the street.

"And they started to chant in unison '—, no, we won't go,' and they just kept it up. And all of a sudden, just the same as the movement had started up onto the steps, the movement started back down off the steps. This chant that they kept up, it just raised the anger to a degree that it just seemed that everybody would just want to get down there and disperse them. When I say, 'disperse,' I don't mean physically take these kids and manhandle them, but just to break them up, break up the group and break up this chant because it just seemed so un-American.

"I guess the average construction worker is what you would call a flag-waver. You can call me a flag-waver any day of the week. I think that's something to be proud of, to be a flag-waver, to be proud of your country. And these kids just kept it up and kept it up.

"As the movement started down off the steps, again there was a certain amount of them [protesters] that wanted to stand their ground, and they're dealing with men that work with iron and steel every day of the week and do manual labor every day of the week, and they just made a mistake. They just never heard about that discretion business. I will say this: there was as many of these anti-war demonstrators whacked by Wall Street and Broadway office workers as there were by construction workers. The feeling seemed to be that the white-collar-and-tie-man, he was actually getting in there and taking as much play on this thing as the construction worker was.

"This was something. Listen. I'm thirty-one years old. I'd never witnessed anything like this is my life before, and it kinda caught me in awe that you had to stop and see what was going on around you. It was almost unbelievable. This was the financial district of New York City, probably the financial district of the world, and here was this mass clash of opposite factions, right on Wall Street and Broad, and you could hardly move, there were so many people talking part in this aside from the five hundred construction workers. It was just something that you had to stand back and blink your eyes and actually look a second and third time, and you couldn't believe that this was actually taking place in that particular area.

"There was one kid came after me, I don't know why. He just came flying out of the crowd. I don't claim to be a violent person. I couldn't possibly remember the last time I ever struck anybody. It had to be at least ten years ago, maybe twelve years ago. And for some reason this guy picked out somebody and it just happened to be me. He came running at me with arms flailing and I gave him a whack and back he went. He went down, I know that, and I just figured he wouldn't be back for more."

. . . Joe attends noon Mass on Sundays and he also coaches basketball and baseball teams in a boy's league in Blessed Sacrament parish. (After the Army, he spent three years as a weekend counselor at an orphanage on Staten Island.) His reading consists of *The Daily News*, the *Advance*, the sports section of *The New York Post* and *Popular Mechanics* magazine. The Kellys go out to the movies perhaps every six weeks and may stop in afterward for "a couple of drinks in a nice, quiet, respectable place." Once a week his wife leaves him at home when she goes to play bingo. There is usually a Christmas party for the men on the job, and Otis [Elevator Co.] throws a picnic in the summer. Recently, the elevator constructors and their wives had a $20-a-couple dinner dance at the Commuter's Cafe on Cortlandt Street, across from the Trade Center site. . . .

On television, Joe enjoys Johnny Cash and Jackie Gleason and sometimes Dean Martin. He likes to be in bed by 11 P.M. Before he was married, Joe played basketball four nights a week in a community-center league. With family responsibilities, his heavy work schedule, and his relative slowness of foot today, he has cut it out completely. "I go down once in a while to watch and eat my heart out," he says.

Joe gets his extravocational workouts now around the house, putting in sod, helping to grade the backyard for a large aboveground plastic swimming pool for the children, planting two blue spruces and yews and rhododendrons in the front.

The Kellys haven't been able to take any vacations, though Joe has had two weeks off yearly and will get three weeks under the new contract starting this summer (there was either a strike, or they were saving for the house, or the children were too small). Perhaps twice a summer they drive down to the New Jersey shore around Belmar in their 1967 English Ford station wagon and go swimming.

Why does he work so hard? "A lot of people ask me that," he says. "I wanted the house. Right? I wanted something nice for the wife and the kids, someplace where the kids could grow up and have their own backyard. They wouldn't have to be running out in the street. And now I have the house and I want it fixed up nice. And maybe when it is fixed up nice, I'll relax a bit." Meanwhile, he is at the "boiling point."

"My belief is, physical violence doesn't solve a damn thing. One party has to sway the other party to his belief and then the argument is settled. I honestly don't believe that there will be any more physical violence in New York City. I think that one Friday and it's over with. I don't like to see anybody get bounced. I saw some of those kids go down and I didn't think they were gonna get up. I certainly don't agree with them. I would much rather prefer grabbing them by the head of the hair and taking a scissors and cutting their hair off, something that was much less violent but you still would have gotten your message across.

"Up at City Hall it became obvious that they had better get that flag back up to the top of the mast. Within a few minutes the flag went back up and everybody seemed nice and happy and again they started singing, 'God Bless America' and the national anthem and again it made you feel good. Not that I like seeing those four kids out in wherever it was, Kent, get killed. I don't like to see anybody get beat up, never mind lose their life.

"I don't think Mayor Lindsay has the right to put that flag at half-staff. That flag represents this country, so the leading representative of the country, who is President Nixon to me, is the only one that has the power or the right to raise or lower a flag."

Joe Kelly says he never even asked what his father's politics were, believing it to be a man's private affair. How did he arrive as a militant member of the no-longer-silent majority? What brought him to believe that Communism was undermining America from within?

"Two people stand out in my mind," Joe says, "why I'm taking part. Joe McCarthy often said, beware of this school system; they're going to infiltrate, brainwash the kids. And Khrushchev in 1960 banging on the UN table. He said they wouldn't have to take over this country physically, they'd do it from within." Though he was only a youngster during McCarthy's heyday, Kelly says: "It's something I've read somewhere along the line." He feels that the students are only dupes in the hands of subversive teachers who, Joe hints, are under the control of foreign powers. In some way, the bad teachers have to be weeded out, he says.

Joe Kelly first voted in 1960, when he chose John F. Kennedy over Nixon for President because he was impressed with Kennedy's performance in the TV debates. Though he still reveres President Kennedy, he wouldn't vote that way again. By 1964 he had swung to the right and voted for Goldwater over Johnson. In the 1965 and 1969 New York mayoral races, he voted the Conservative party line for William F. Buckley, Jr., and John Marchi. He cast his ballot for Nixon for President in 1968.

It was the Goldwater campaign that crystallized Joe's feeling about the war in Vietnam. "I think that it all goes back again, like history repeating itself, to Hitler," he says. "When Hitler kept marching into these countries and, instead of just fighting Hitler's country, you were fighting all these countries after a while. You just can't let Communism take over everything around you because when they got everything around you, they're gonna come after you."

Three men who command his admiration now are John Wayne, Vice-President Agnew, and Chicago Mayor Richard Daley. In fact, Joe wishes New York could borrow Daley for six months to give the city a stiff dose of law and order. He has complete disdain for Mayor Lindsay. He believes Lindsay has turned New York into "welfare city" and is trying to be the champion of welfare recipients and the young antiwar generation in a bid for the Presidency. "Do what you want in Lindsay's city—" he says caustically, "burn the schools. He's got to raise the budget this year to pay for what they burned down."

Of the recent influx of minority workers into his once closely bound union, he says: "They're here to stay, entitled to. But if they're going to work with us, if we go up on the iron and risk our lives walking it, by God, they have to go along with us. There've been several instances in the city where they've refused because they didn't have to."

As for a black family living on his street, he is adamantly against it, feeling that panic-selling would drive down the value of his property. "I had to bust my backside for five years to get that down payment for that house," he says. "I am not interested in seeing all that go down the drain."

It is on this precious ground—his home and his family—that he takes a defiant, mildly worried stand. He would like his daughters to go to college or nursing school and his son to get as much schooling as possible, to become a doctor or a lawyer—"something where he can use his head to make a living, not his back like his old man does."

While his wife hopes and prays that her daughters will never wear their hair straight and long like the hippies and that her children's minds will be protected in parochial schools despite the danger of lay teachers, Joe Kelly tells a story about a neighbor's friend's son, a boy of sixteen.

"This boy," he says, "came home from school one day and told his father he was a bum, that he was part of the Establishment. And this fellow was a World War II veteran, decorated several times and wounded twice. And he just turned around and he gave the kid a good whack and I guess he broke his jaw or broke his nose and the father was in a turmoil. This is his own flesh and blood talking to him.

"I cannot imagine having my kids come home and tell me I'm a bum because I believe in the Establishment—and there is nobody that believes in the Establishment more than I do. The more I see of this stuff, the closer I try to become to my kids. I believe that my way is correct, the Establishment way, law and order first, and this is what I'm gonna do my damndest to breed into them so that they don't get some other off-the-wall ideas."

Joe says that if his children ever called him a bum because he believes in the flag, they'd better leave his house. "I would do everything to control myself not to hit them. I mean, this is what I brought into the world. But it's awful hard. I certainly can see that man flying off the handle and whacking the kid. Oh, yeah, he certainly did regret it. But his big question is, Where did his kid get this trend of thinking?"

Joe Kelly doesn't believe that melees such as the memorable one at noon on May 8 are any solution. So his answer, he says reflectively, is to arm himself with education, engage in dialogue.

"When they throw a point at you," he says, "be able to talk to them on their theories on socialism, Communism. This is the best way—to talk them out of the stuff instead of just saying it's un-American or using your fists."

Ironically, Mayor Lindsay has said much the same thing: "Perhaps their [the construction workers'] demonstrations, in the end, will help us break through to a new dialogue in which we not only talk, but listen."

Part Eight

POLITICS OF
THE 1970s AND 1980s

The 1970s represented the end of an era. Throughout the thirty years after World War II American politics had functioned on the premise that nothing was impossible if America wished to achieve it. We would be guardians of freedom, send a man to the moon, conquer social injustice, eliminate poverty, develop impressive technology—in short, control the universe. That sense of confidence and of power had been a hallmark of all political factions in the country, even young radicals who thought that by their own endeavors they could change the world. In the 1970s, however, a new sense of limits struck home. The United States had suffered its first loss in war. Richard Nixon became the first president forced to resign in disgrace, in large part because he himself had no sense of limits as to how far he could abuse presidential power. The oil producing countries of OPEC quickly made Americans conscious of their dependence on the rest of the world during the oil boycott of 1973–74, and the sporadic shortages thereafter. When Iranian revolutionaries held American diplomats hostage for more than a year, the sense of being subject to powers beyond one's control became a reality reinforced by every newscast. The American tendency toward what the Greeks call *hubris*—the arrogant confidence that one can do anything—had come face to face with the realities of human frailty, mortality, and interdependency.

If tragedy is the working out of a fatal flaw that eventually destroys one's hopes, the Nixon administration represents perhaps the purest example of American political tragedy. Nixon's own political life covered the entire span of the postwar period. First elected to Congress in 1946, he came to power through his active participation in the anti-communist campaign of the postwar era, and particularly his investigation of Alger Hiss. As Vice-President under Dwight Eisenhower, Nixon led the attack on liberals, accusing Democratic presidential-nominee Adlai Stevenson of being soft on communism. It seemed to many that Nixon's career was over after he lost the presidential election to John Kennedy in 1960 and then two years later was defeated for the governorship of California. But Nixon's most fundamental characteristic was his tenacity. One of a series of "new" Nixons emerged in the middle 1960s, and in 1968, a supposedly more mature, relaxed, and flexible Nixon offered himself to the American people with a plan to end the war in Vietnam, and to "bring us together again."

Nixon's presidency was a series of contradictions. On the one hand, he scored major triumphs in foreign policy. As only an inveterate anti-communist could do, Nixon opened the door to China, reversing three decades of anti-Chinese policy in a period of weeks. Nixon also pressed hard for a relaxation of tensions with the Soviet Union, seeking to build a world order where Europe, China, the Soviet Union, and the United States could operate in a relative balance of power. He made major strides toward stability in the Middle East, using Presidential Advisor and Secretary of State Henry Kissinger to promote exchanges between Arab countries and Israel that might provide a basis for lasting peace in that area.

But these major achievements in foreign policy were dwarfed by Nixon's abuse of power domestically, and his almost inherent refusal to speak candidly of his goals. He promised to end the war in Vietnam, then expanded the war by the massive secret bombing of Cambodia. He pledged to run an open administration, then placed wiretaps on reporters and administration officials. The underlying problem was one of duplicity and pettiness. In order to disguise the illegal bombing of Cambodia, orders were given that military reports should be falsified. When former Pentagon official Daniel Ellsberg released the Pentagon Papers, an internal study of how the Vietnam war had come about, Nixon sought to discredit Ellsberg by having a secret unit of investigators—called the "plumbers"—break into Ellsberg's psychiatrist's office to get harmful information about him. Angry at anti-war demonstrators and those Democrats who supported them, the President encouraged a series of efforts, official and unofficial, to dig up information that would injure his opponents. The operation came to a head during the 1972 re-election campaign, when CREEP, the Committee to Re-elect the President, sponsored break-ins and wiretaps as well as false letters and rumors to subvert the Democratic opposition. When some of CREEP'S "plumbers," attempting to break in at the Democratic National Headquarters at the Watergate building, were caught, the entire web began to unravel.

The story of Watergate, like the story of Vietnam, embodies the ultimate destruction that occurs when tactics and weapons are used that go too far and stretch limits of tolerance beyond their capacity. Americans did not want to believe that My Lai had occured, that their president had lied about the bombing of Cambodia, or that the White House had been involved in the kind of "dirty tricks" that subverted basic American freedoms and violated the law of the land. But as newspaper and congressional investigations eventually demonstrated, there was no end to the Nixon administration's abuse of trust. America's basic faith in her political system was called into question. The country had been betrayed.

Jimmy Carter spoke directly to that sense of betrayal when in 1976 he told the American people that they deserved a government as good as they were, one based upon faith, honesty, integrity, dignity, and respect for traditional American values. Gerald Ford, Nixon's vice president, had done a superb job of healing the immediate wounds left by Watergate, but Carter offered an almost religious salve designed to reverse the damage. Running on the platform of an outsider who would bring a fresh perspective to Washington, Carter seemed to represent the simplicity and decency that would restore the faith of Americans in their political process.

The problem was that Carter knew very little about getting along in Washington. Oftentimes insensitive toward Congress, he entered into a permanent deadlock with the major institutions of the society. Although he accomplished some positive goals in foreign policy, particularly with the Camp David accords in the Middle East, he was never able to deliver on his pledge of turning the government around. While he diagnosed and articulated the crisis of confidence that existed in the American political process in the post-Nixon years, he was unable to mobilize support for constructive solutions to that crisis. The intractable problems of energy and Iran accurately reflected the sense of powerlessness that seemed to paralyze his administration.

The election of Ronald Reagan represented still another effort to recover what had been lost, this time by going back to a rhetoric and program that reminded the United States of its former power and moral leadership. Reagan possessed the genius to make people believe in simple verities. America should be strong. Communism represented a false God and the Soviet Union an "evil empire." Free enterprise worked. And every individual should be responsible for him or her self. With remarkable skill, the new president pushed through legislation to cut taxes, prune social welfare benefits, dramatically increase military expenditures, and restore conservative values. Reagan's success coincided with the rapid growth of the New Right, a congeries of single issue groups that focused on returning the country to the bedrock values of family discipline, evangelical Christianity, and patriotism. Whether galvanized by the Equal Rights Amendment, abortion, school busing, homosexuality, or prayer in the schools, such New Right groups added a different dimension to the American political scene. For many, Ronald Reagan was a true hero. And when he scored a decisive triumph in his re-election bid in 1984, the conservative ascendancy seemed to have reached its zenith.

Yet both in 1980 and 1984, Reagan had been elected by less than 30 percent of those Americans eligible to vote. Almost half of the electorate had failed to go to the polls, dramatizing the alienation and sense of distance that millions felt toward the political process. Many of those same people who had not voted became the primary victims of Reagan's social policies, as food stamps were cut, housing subsidies reduced, and health care benefits trimmed. Even as Reagan talked about restoring America's greatness, larger and larger segments of the population seemed to have no stake whatsoever in the government that ruled them.

The following selections chronicle this story of America in the 1970s and 1980s. Jonathan Schell explores the intricacies of Watergate, giving us some flavor of the bizarre quality of the Nixon White House. Jimmy Carter's 1978 energy speech poignantly presents his ability to articulate the "malaise of the American spirit" even as it reveals his failure to come forward with effective answers, while Ronald Reagan's "The Second American Revolution" effectively conveys the buoyancy and sense of direction he brought to American politics. Alan Crawford's description of the

"New Right" provides one backdrop against which to assess these changes in American politics.

Some of the questions that remain are whether it is possible for a democracy to function when half of its people fail to vote (as opposed to voting rates of over 80 percent in most western European democracies), how successful the American political system was in dealing with the poison of Watergate, and whether it is good or bad to accept a sense of limits on America's national power. Such questions are crucial not only for understanding the 1970s and 1980s, but also for assessing what policies are appropriate for the 1990s, and the twenty-first century.

Watergate

Jonathan Schell

If the decade of the 1960s is remembered for the war in Vietnam and civil rights, the decade of the 1970s will inevitably be associated with Watergate. Through a bizarre series of events, the Nixon administration found itself in a situation where, in order to cover up high-level involvement in a burglary, it created a set of circumstances that brought down the entire administration. The ironies of the situation were endless. Nixon had such a commanding lead over his opponents that virtually no one could challenge him, yet in order to gain a still greater edge, he, or his associates, authorized a break-in at Democratic national headquarters. Even with the evidence turned up by journalists and congressional hearings, Nixon would probably have remained in office, yet the taping system he himself had installed in order to preserve history tripped him up. Perhaps appropriately, the man who sought office in order to "bring us together again" ended up accomplishing his purpose by uniting the country in revulsion against his unconstitutional actions. Jonathan Schell presents here a vivid portrait of how and why the Watergate episode occurred, revealing in the process the dangers inherent in what Arthur Schlesinger, Jr., has called "the imperial presidency."

At some point back at the beginning of the Vietnam war, long before Richard Nixon became President, American history had split into two streams. One flowed aboveground, the other underground. At first, the underground stream was only a trickle of

Excerpted from Jonathan Schell, *A Time of Illusion* (New York: Alfred A. Knopf, 1975). Reprinted by permission of Random House.

events. But during the nineteen sixties—the period mainly described in the Pentagon Papers—the trickle grew to a torrent, and
a significant part of the record of foreign affairs disappeared
from public view. In the Nixon years, the torrent flowing underground began to include events in the domestic sphere, and soon
a large part of the domestic record, too, had plunged out of sight.
By 1972, an elaborate preelection strategy—the Administration
strategy of dividing the Democrats—was unfolding in deep secrecy. And this strategy of dividing the Democrats governed not
only a program of secret sabotage and espionage but the formation of Administration policy on the most important issues facing
the nation. Indeed, hidden strategies for consolidating Presidential authority had been governing expanding areas of Administration policy since 1969, when it first occurred to the President to
frame policy not to solve what one aide called "real problems" but
to satisfy the needs of public relations. As more and more events
occurred out of sight, the aboveground, public record of the period became impoverished and misleading. It became a carefully
smoothed surface beneath which many of the most significant
events of the period were being concealed. In fact, the split between the Administration's real actions and policies was largely
responsible for the new form of government that had arisen in
the Nixon White House—a form in which images consistently
took precedence over substance, and affairs of state were ruled by
what the occupants of the White House called scenarios. The
methods of secrecy and the techniques of public relations were
necessary to one another, for the people, lacking access to the
truth, had to be told something, and it was the public-relations
experts who decided what that something would be.

When the President made his trip to Russia, some students of
government who had been worried about the crisis of the American Constitutional system allowed themselves to hope that the
relaxation of tensions in the international sphere would spread to
the domestic sphere. Since the tensions at home had grown out of
events in the international sphere in the first place, it seemed
reasonable to assume that an improvement in the mood abroad
would give some relief in the United States, too. These hopes
were soon disappointed. In fact, the President's drive to expand
his authority at home was accelerated; although the nation didn't
know it, this was the period in which White House operatives

advanced from crimes whose purpose was the discovery of national-security leaks to crimes against the domestic political opposition. The Presidential Offensive had not been called off; it had merely been routed underground. The President spoke incessantly of peace, and had arranged for his public-relations men to portray him as a man of peace, but there was to be no peace— not in Indo-China, and not with a constantly growing list of people he saw as his domestic "enemies." Detente, far from relaxing tensions at home, was seen in the White House as one more justification for its campaign to crush the opposition and seize absolute power.

On Sunday, June 18, 1972, readers of the front page of the *Times* learned, among other things, that heavy American air strikes were continuing over North Vietnam, that the chairman of President Nixon's Council of Economic Advisers, Herbert Stein, had attacked the economic proposals of Senator George McGovern, who in less than a month was to become the Presidential nominee of the Democratic Party, and that the musical "Fiddler on the Roof" had just had its three-thousand-two-hundred-and-twenty-fifth performance on Broadway. Readers of page 30 learned, in a story not listed in the "News Summary and Index," that five men had been arrested in the headquarters of the Democratic National Committee, in the Watergate office building, with burglary tools, cameras, and equipment for electronic surveillance in their possession. In rooms that the men had rented, under aliases, in the adjacent Watergate Hotel, thirty-two hundred-dollar bills were found, along with a notebook containing the notation "E. Hunt" (for E. Howard Hunt, as it turned out) and, next to that, the notation "W. H." (for the White House). The men were members of the Gemstone team, a White House undercover group, which had been attempting to install bugging devices in the telephones of Democrats.

Most of the high command of the Nixon Administration and the Nixon reelection committee were out of town when the arrests were made. The President and his chief of staff, H. R. Halderman, were on the President's estate in Key Biscayne, Florida. The President's counsel, John Dean, was in Manila, giving a lecture on drug abuse. John Mitchell, the former Attorney General, who was then director of the Committee for the Re-Election of the President, and Jeb Magruder, a former White House aide, who had become the committee's assistant director, were in California. In the hours and days immediately following the arrests, there was a flurry of activity at the headquarters of the committee, in a Washington office building; in California; and at the White House. Magruder called his assistant in Washington and had him remove certain papers—what later came to be publicly known as Gemstone materials—from his files. Gordon Liddy, by then the chief counsel of the Finance Committee to Re-Elect the President, went into the headquarters himself, removed from his files other materials having to do with the break-in, including other hundred-dollar bills, and shredded them. At the White House, Gordon Strachan, an aide to Haldeman, shredded a number of papers having to do with the setting up of the reelection committee's undercover operation, of which the break-in at the headquarters of the Democratic National Committee was an important part. Liddy, having destroyed all the evidence in his possession, offered up another piece of potential evidence for destruction: himself. He informed Dean that if the White House wished to have him assassinated he would stand at a given street corner at an appointed time to make things easy. E. Howard Hunt went to his office in the Executive Office Building, took from a safe ten thousand dollars in cash he had there for emergencies, and used it to hire an attorney for the burglars. In the days following, Hunt's name was expunged from the White House telephone directory. On orders from John Ehrlichman, the President's chief domestic-affairs adviser, his safe was opened and his papers were removed. At one point, Dean—also said to have been acting under instructions from Ehrlichman—gave an order for Hunt to leave the country, but then the order was rescinded. Hunt's payment to an attorney for the burglars was the first of many. The President's personal attorney, Herbert Kalmbach, was instructed by Dean and, later, by Ehrlichman, Haldeman, and Mitchell to keep on making payments, and he, in turn, delegated the task to Anthony Ulasewicz, a retired New York City policeman who had been hired to conduct covert political investigations for the White House. Theirs was a hastily improvised operation. Kalmbach and Ulasewicz spoke to each other from phone booths. (Phone booths apparently had a strong attraction for Ulasewicz. He attached a change-maker to his belt to be sure to have enough coins for his calls, and he chose to make several of his "drops" of the payoff money in them.) He and

Kalmbach used aliases and code language in their conversations. Kalmbach became Mr. Novak and Ulasewicz became Mr. Rivers—names that seem to have been chosen for no specific reason. Hunt, who had some forty mystery stories published, was referred to as "the writer," and Haldeman, who wore a crewcut, as "the brush." The payoff money became "the laundry," because when Ulasewicz arrived at Kalmbach's hotel room to pick up the first installment he put it in a laundry bag. The burglars were "the players," and the payoff scheme was "the script." Apparently, the reason the White House conspirators spoke to one another from phone booths was that they thought the Democrats might be wiretapping them, just as they had wiretapped the Democrats. In late June, the President himself said to Haldeman, of the Democrats, "When they start bugging us, which they have, our little boys will not know how to handle it. I hope they will, though." Considerations like these led Kalmbach, Ulasewicz, and others working for the White House to spend many unnecessary hours in phone booths that summer.

All these actions were of the sort that any powerful group of conspirators might take upon the arrest of some of their number. Soon, however, the White House was taking actions that were possible only because the conspirators occupied high positions in the government, including the highest position of all—the Presidency. For almost four years, the President had been "reorganizing" the executive branch of the government with a view to getting the Cabinet departments and the agencies under his personal control, and now he undertook to use several of these agencies to cover up crimes committed by his subordinates. In the early stages of the coverup, his efforts were directed toward removing a single evidentiary link: the fact that the Watergate burglars had been paid with funds from his campaign committee. There was a vast amount of other information that needed to be concealed—information concerning not just the Watergate break-in but the whole four-year record of the improper and illegal activities of the White House undercover operators, which stretched from mid-1969, when the warrantless wiretaps were placed, to the months in 1972 when the secret program for dividing the Democrats was being carried out—but if this one fact could somehow be suppressed, then the chain of evidence would be broken, and the rest of it might go undetected. On June 23rd, the President met with

Haldeman and ordered him to have the C.I.A. request that the F.B.I. halt its investigation into the origin of the Watergate burglars' funds, on the pretext that C.I.A. secrets might come to light if the investigation went forward. The problem, Haldeman told the President, was that "the F.B.I. is not under control, because Gray doesn't exactly know how to control it." Patrick Gray was Acting Director of the F.B.I. "The way to handle this now," he went on, "is for us to have Walters call Pat Gray and just say, 'Stay to hell out of this.' " The reference was to Vernon Walters, Deputy Director of the C.I.A. A moment later, Haldeman asked the President, concerning the F.B.I., "And you seem to think the thing to do is get them to stop?" "Right, fine," the President answered. But he wanted Haldeman to issue the instructions. "I'm not going to get that involved," he said. About two hours later, Haldeman and Ehrlichman met with C.I.A. Director Richard Helms and Deputy Director Walters, and issued the order.

The maneuver gave the White House only a temporary advantage. Six days later, on June 29th, Gray did cancel interviews with two people who could shed light on the origin of the burglars' funds. (On the twenty-eighth, Ehrlichman and Dean had handed him all the materials taken from Hunt's safe, and Dean had told him that they were never to "see the light of day." Gray had taken them home, and later he burned them.) But soon a small rebellion broke out among officials of the F.B.I. and the C.I.A. Meetings were held, and at one point Gray and Walters told each other they would rather resign than submit to the White House pressure and compromise their agencies. Several weeks after the request was made, the F.B.I. held the interviews after all. The rebellion in the ranks of the federal bureaucracy was not the first to break out against the Nixon White House. As early as 1969, some members of the Justice Department had fought Administration attempts to thwart the civil-rights laws. In 1970, members of the State Department and members of the Office of Education, in the Department of Health, Education, and Welfare, had protested the invasion of Cambodia. In 1970, too, J. Edgar Hoover had refused to go along with a White House scheme devised by a young lawyer named Tom Huston for illegal intelligence-gathering. The executive bureaucracy was one source of the President's great power, but it was also acting as a check on his power. In some ways, it served this function more effectively than the checks provided by the

Constitution, for, unlike the other institutions of government, it at least had some idea of what was going on. But ultimately it was no replacement for the Constitutional checks. A President who hired and fired enough people could in time bring the bureaucracy to heel. And although a Gray, a Walters, or a Helms might offer some resistance to becoming deeply involved in White House crimes, they would do nothing to expose the crimes. Moreover, the bureaucracy had no public voice, and was therefore powerless to sway public opinion. Politicians of all persuasions could—and did—heap abuse on "faceless," "briefcase-toting" bureaucrats and their "red tape," and the bureaucracy had no way to reply to this abuse. It had only its silent rebellions, waged with the passive weapons of obfuscation, concealment, and general foot-dragging. Decisive opposition, if there was to be any, had to come from without.

With respect to the prosecutorial arm of the Justice Department, the White House had aims that were less ambitious than its aims with respect to the F.B.I. and the C.I.A., but it was more successful in achieving them. Here, on the whole, the White House men wished merely to keep abreast of developments in the grand-jury room of the U.S. District Court, where officials of the Committee for the Re-Election of the President were testifying on Watergate, and this they accomplished through the obliging cooperation of Henry Petersen, the chief of the Criminal Division, who reported regularly to John Dean and later to the President himself. Dean subsequently described the cooperation to the President by saying, "Petersen is a soldier. He played—he kept me informed. He told me when we had problems, where we had problems, and the like. Uh, he believes in, in, in you. He believes in this Administration. This Administration had made him." What happened in the grand-jury room was further controlled by the coordinating of perjured testimony from White House aides and men working for the campaign committee. As for the prosecutors, a sort of dim-wittedness—a failure to draw obvious conclusions, a failure to follow up leads, a seeming willingness to construe the Watergate case narrowly—appeared to be enough to keep them from running afoul of the White House.

While all these moves were being made, the public was treated to a steady stream of categorical denials that the White House or the President's campaign committee had had anything to do with the break-in or with efforts to cover up the origins of the crime. The day after the break-in, Mitchell, in California, described James McCord, one of the burglars, as "the proprietor of a private security agency who was employed by our Committee months ago to assist with the installation of our security system." Actually, McCord was the committee's chief of security at the moment when he was arrested. Mitchell added, "We want to emphasize that this man and the other people involved were not operating either in our behalf or with our consent. . . . There is no place in our campaign or in the electoral process for this type of activity, and we will not permit nor condone it." On June 19th, two days after the break-in, Ronald Ziegler, the President's press secretary, contemptuously dismissed press reports of White House involvement. "I'm not going to comment from the White House on a third-rate burglary attempt," he said. On June 20th, when Lawrence O'Brien, the chairman of the Democratic Party, revealed that the Party had brought a one-million-dollar civil-damages suit against the Committee for the Re-Election of the President and the five burglary suspects, charging invasion of privacy and violation of the civil rights of the Democrats, Mitchell stated that the action represented "another example of sheer demagoguery on the part of Mr. O'Brien." Mitchell said, "I reiterate that this committee did not authorize and does not condone the alleged actions of the five men apprehended there."

Among the nation's major newspapers, only one, the Washington *Post*, consistently gave the Watergate story prominent headlines on the front page. Most papers, when they dealt with the story at all, tended to treat it as something of a joke. All in all, the tone of the coverage was not unlike the coverage of the Clifford Irving affair the previous winter, and the volume of the coverage was, if anything, less. "Caper" was the word that most of the press settled upon to describe the incident. A week after the break-in, for instance, the *Times* headlined its Watergate story "WATERGATE CAPER." When another week had passed, and Howard Hunt's connection with the break-in had been made known, *Time* stated that the story was "fast stretching into the most provocative caper of 1972, an extraordinary bit of bungling of great potential advantage to the Democrats and damage to the Republicans in this election year." In early August, the *Times* was still running headlines like "THE PLOT THICKENS IN WATERGATE WHODUNIT" over accounts of the repercussions of the burglary. "Above all, the purpose of the break-in seemed obscure," the *Times* said. "But these details are never explained until the last chapter." The President held a news conference six weeks after the break-in, and by then the story was of such small interest to newsmen that not one question was asked concerning it.

Disavowals such as those made by Mitchell and Ziegler carried great weight in the absence of incontrovertible evidence refuting them. The public had grown accustomed to deception and evasion in high places, but not yet to repeated, consistent, barefaced lying at all levels. The very boldness of the lies raised the cost of contradicting them, for to do so would be to call high officials outright liars. Another effective White House technique was to induce semi-informed or wholly uninformed spokesmen to deny charges. One of these spokemen was Clark MacGregor, a former member of Congress from Minnesota, who became reelection-campaign director early in July, when John Mitchell resigned, pleading family difficulties. A few weeks later, when Senator McGovern described the break-ins as "the kind of thing you expect under a person like Hitler," MacGregor called McGovern's remark "character assassination." The practice of using as spokesmen officials who were more or less innocent of the facts was one more refinement of the technique of dissociating "what we say" from "what we do." In this manner, honest men could be made to lend the weight of their integrity to untruths. They spoke words without knowing whether the words were true or false. Such spokesmen lent their vocal cords to the campaign but left their brains behind, and confused the public with words spoken by nobody.

On September 15th, the five men who had been caught in the Democratic National Committee headquarters were indicted—together with E. Howard Hunt and G. Gordon Liddy, who were elsewhere in the Watergate complex at the time of the break-in—for the felonies of burglary, conspiracy, and wiretapping. A few days later, the seven defendants pleaded not guilty. As the case stood at that moment, their crimes were officially motiveless. The prosecutors had not been able to suggest who might have asked employees of the Committee for the Re-Election of the President to wiretap the Democratic headquarters, or why a check belonging to that committee should have found its way into the bank account of Bernard Barker. That afternoon, the President met with Haldeman and Dean, and congratulated Dean on his work. "Well," he said, "the whole thing is a can of worms. . . . But the, but the way you, you've handled it, it seems to me, has been very skillful, because you—putting your fingers in the dikes every time that leaks have sprung here and sprung there." Representative Wright Patman, the chairman of the House Banking and Currency Committee, was planning to hold hearings on the Watergate break-in, and the President, Dean, and Haldeman went on to discuss ways of "turning that off," as Dean put it. Dean reported to the two others that he was studying the possibility of blackmailing members of the Patman committee with damaging information about their own campaigns, and then the President suggested that Gerald Ford, the minority leader of the House, would be the man to pressure Patman into dropping the hearings. Ford should be told that "he's got to get at this and screw this thing up while he can," the President said. Two and a half weeks later, a majority of the members of the committee voted to deny Patman the power to subpoena witnesses. But Patman made the gesture of carrying on anyway for a while, and asked questions of an empty chair.

At the end of September—more than a month before the election—the Washington *Post* reported that John Mitchell had had control of a secret fund for spying on the Democrats. Throughout October, denials continued to pour out from the Administration. As before, some were outright lies by men who knew the facts, and others were untruths spoken by men who were simply repeating what they had been told. On October 2nd, Acting Director Gray of the F.B.I. said that it was unreasonable to believe that the President had deceived the nation about Watergate. "Even if some of us [in federal law enforcement agencies] are crooked, there aren't that many that are. I don't believe everyone is a Sir Galahad, but there's not been one single bit of pressure put on me or any of my special agents." In reality, of course, Gray had once considered resigning because the pressure from the White House to help with the coverup had been so intense, and even as he spoke he was keeping the contents of E. Howard Hunt's safe in a drawer of a dresser at his home in Connecticut. Gray went on to say, "It strains the credulity that the President of the United States—if he had a mind to—could have done a con job on the whole American people." Gray added, "He would have to control the United States."

In the months since the election, the issue of Watergate had faded, and the papers had devoted their front pages to other news. Shortly after the trial began, however, the front-page news was that all the defendants but two had pleaded guilty. In the courtroom, Judge John Sirica, who presided, found himself dissatisfied with the questioning of witnesses by the government prosecutors. The prosecutors now had a suggestion as to the burglars' motive. They suggested that it might be blackmail. They did not say of whom or over what. At the trial, the key prosecution witness, the former F.B.I. agent Alfred Baldwin, related that on one occasion he had taken the logs of the Watergate wiretaps to the headquarters of the Committee for the Re-Election of the President. But this suggested nothing to the Justice Department, one of whose spokesmen had maintained when the indictment was handed up in September that there was "no evidence" showing that anyone except the defendants was involved. Sirica demurred. "I want to know where the money comes from," he said to the defendant Bernard Barker. "There were hundred-dollar bills floating around like coupons." When Barker replied that he had simply received the money in the mail in a blank envelope and had no idea who might have sent it, Sirica commented, "I'm sorry, but I don't believe you." When the defense lawyers protested Sirica's questioning, he said, "I don't think we should sit up here like nincompoops. The function of a trial is to search for the truth."

All the Watergate defendants but one were following the White House scenario to the letter. The exception was James McCord. He was seething with scenarios of his own. He hoped to have the charges against him dismissed, and, besides, he had been angered by what he understood as a suggestion from one of his lawyers that the blame for the Watergate break-in be assigned to the C.I.A., his old outfit, to which he retained an intense loyalty. There was some irony in the fact that McCord's anger had been aroused by an Administration plan to involve the C.I.A. in its crimes. McCord believed that Nixon's removal of C.I.A. director Richard Helms, in December of 1972—at the very time that McCord himself was being urged to lay the blame for Watergate at the door of the C.I.A.—was designed to pave the way for an attempt by the Administration itself to blame the break-in on the agency and for a takeover of the agency by the White House. He had worked for the White House, but he did not see the reorganizational wars from the White House point of view. He saw them from the bureaucrats' point of view; in his opinion, President Nixon was attempting to take over the C.I.A. in a manner reminiscent of attempts by Hitler to take control of German intelligence agencies before the Second World War. The White House, that is, belatedly discovered that it had a disgruntled "holdover" on its hands. And this particular holdover really was prepared to perform sabotage; he was prepared, indeed, to sabotage not just the President's policies but the President himself, and, what was more, he had the means to do it. McCord was putting together a scenario that could destroy the Nixon Administration. In a letter delivered to his White House contact, the undercover operative John Caulfield, McCord pronounced a dread warning: If the White House continued to try to have the C.I.A. take responsibility for the Watergate burglary, "every tree in the forest will fall," and "it will be a scorched desert." Piling on yet another metaphor of catastrophe, he wrote, "Pass the message that if they want it to blow, they are on exactly the right course. I am sorry that you will get hurt in the fallout." McCord was the first person in the Watergate conspiracy to put in writing exactly what the magnitude of the Watergate scandal was. Many observers had been amazed at the extreme hard line that the President had taken since his landslide reelection—the firings in the bureaucracies, the incomprehensible continuation of the attacks on Senator McGovern, the renewed attacks on the press, the attacks on Congress's power of the purse, the bombing of Hanoi. They could not know that at the exact moment when President Nixon was wreaking devastation on North Vietnam, James McCord was threatening to wreak devastation on him.

On February 7th, the Senate, by a vote of seventy-seven to none, established a Select Committee on Presidential Campaign Activities, to look into abuses in the Presidential campaign of 1972, including the Watergate break-in; and the Democratic leadership appointed Senator Sam Ervin, of North Carolina, the author of the resolution to establish the Select Committee, to be its chairman. Three days later, the Administration secretly convened a Watergate committee of its own, in California—at the La

Costa Resort Hotel and Spa, not far from the President's estate in San Clemente, with John Dean, H. R. Haldeman, John Ehrlichman, and Richard Moore, a White House aide, in attendance. The meeting lasted for two days. Its work was to devise ways of hampering, discrediting, and ultimately blocking the Ervin committee's investigation.

The President's drive to take over the federal government was going well. By the end of March those legislators who were worried about the possibility of a collapse of the Constitutional system were in a state of near-hopelessness. It seemed that the President would have his will, and Congress could not stop him; as for the public, it was uninterested in Constitutional matters. Senator Muskie had now joined Senator McGovern in warning against the dangers of "one-man rule," and he said that the Administration's proposal for preventing the release of "classified" information, no matter how arbitrarily the "classified" designation had been applied, could impose "the silence of democracy's graveyard." Senator William Fulbright, of Arkansas, had expressed fear that the United States might "pass on, as most of the world had passed on, to a totalitarian system." In the press, a new feeling seemed to be crystallizing that Congress had had its day as an institution of American life. Commentators of all political persuasions were talking about Congress as though it were moribund. Kevin Phillips, a political writer who had played an important role in formulating "the Southern strategy," and who had once worked in John Mitchell's Justice Department, wrote, in an article in *Newsweek* called "Our Obsolete System," that "Congress's separate power is an obstacle to modern policy-making." He proposed a "fusion of powers" to replace the Constitution's separation of powers. "In sum," he wrote, "we may have reached a point where separation of powers is doing more harm than good by distorting the logical evolution of technology-era government." In *The New Republic*, the columnist TRB, who, like Senator McGovern and Senator Muskie, was worried that "one-man rule" was in prospect, wrote, "President Nixon treats Congress with contempt which, it has to be admitted, is richly deserved. We have a lot of problems—the economy, inflation, the unfinished war, Watergate—but in the long run the biggest problem is whether Congress can be salvaged, because if it can't our peculiar 18th-century form of government, with separation of powers, can't be salvaged," And he wrote, "A vacuum has to be filled. The authority of Congress has decayed till it is overripe and rotten. Mr. Nixon has merely proclaimed it." At the Justice Department, Donald Santarelli, who was shortly to become head of the Law Enforcement Assistance Administration, told a reporter, "Today, the whole Constitution is up for grabs." These observers took the undeniable fact that the Congress was impotent as a sign that the Congress was obsolete. And the executive branch, having helped reduce the Congress to helplessness, could now point to that helplessness as proof that the Congress was of no value.

The coverup and the takeover had merged into a single project. For four years, the President's anger at his "enemies" had been growing. As his anger had grown, so had that clandestine repressive apparatus in the White House whose purpose was to punish and destroy his enemies. And as this apparatus had grown, so had the need to control the Cabinet departments and the agencies; and the other branches of government, because they might find out about it—until, finally, the coverup had come to exceed in importance every other matter facing the Administration. For almost a year now, the coverup had been the motor of American politics. It had safeguarded the President's reelection, and it had determined the substance and the mood of the Administration's second term so far. In 1969, when President Nixon launched his Presidential Offensive, he had probably not foreseen that the tools he was developing then would one day serve him in a mortal struggle between his Administration and the other powers of the Republic; but now his assault on the press, the television networks, the Congress, the federal bureaucracy, and the courts had coalesced into a single, coordinated assault on the American Constitutional democracy. Either the Nixon Administration would survive in power and the democracy would die or the Administration would be driven from power and the democracy would have another chance to live. If the newly reelected President should be able to thwart investigations by the news media, the agencies of federal law enforcement, the courts, and Congress, he would be clear of all accountability, and would be above the law; on the other hand, if the rival institutions of the Republic should succeed in laying bare the crimes of his Administration and in bringing the criminals to justice, the Administration would be destroyed.

In the latter part of March, the pace of events in this area of the coverup quickened. Under the pressure of the pending sentences, ·two of the conspirators were breaking ranks: James McCord and Howard Hunt. McCord, who had been threatening the White House with exposure since December, now wrote a letter to Judge Sirica telling what he knew of the coverup. Hunt, for his part, was angry because he and the other defendants and their lawyers had not been paid as much money as they wanted in return for their silence. In November, 1972, he called Charles Colson to remind him that the continuation of the coverup was a "two-way street," and shortly after the middle of March he told Paul O'Brien, an attorney for the reelection committee, that if more funds weren't forthcoming immediately he might reveal some of the "many things" he had done for John Haldeman—an apparent reference to the break-in at the office of Daniel Ellsberg's psychiatrist. Shortly thereafter, O'Brien informed Dean of Hunt's demand. These events on one edge of the coverup had an immediate influence on the chemistry of the whole enterprise. On March 21st, John Dean, convinced now that the coverup could not be maintained, met with the President and told him the story of it as he knew it from beginning to end. The President's response was to recommend that the blackmail money be paid to Hunt. "I think you should handle that one pretty fast," he said. And later he said, "But at the moment don't you agree that you'd better get the Hunt thing? I mean, that's worth it, at the moment." And he said, "That's why, John, for your immediate thing you've got no choice with Hunt but the hundred and twenty or whatever it is. Right?" The President was willing to consider plans for limited disclosure, and the meeting ended with a suggestion from Haldeman, who had joined the two other men: "We've got to figure out where to turn it off at the lowest cost we can, but at whatever cost it takes."

The defection of Hunt and McCord had upset the delicate balance of roles demanded by the coverup. Information that had to be kept secret began to flow in a wide loop through the coverup's various departments. Not only Hunt and McCord but Dean and Magruder began to tell their stories to the prosecutors. The prosecutors, in turn, relayed the information to Attorney General Kleindienst and Assistant Attorney General Petersen, who then relayed it to the President, who then relayed it to Haldeman and

Ehrlichman, who in this period were desperately attempting to avoid prosecution, and were therefore eager to know what was happening in the Grand Jury room. Any defections placed the remaining conspirators in an awkward position. In order to get clear of the collapsing coverup, they had to become public inquisitors of their former subordinates and collaborators. Such a transformation, however, was not likely to sit well with the defectors, who were far from eager to shoulder the blame for the crimes of others, and who, furthermore, were in possession of damaging information with which to retaliate.

Notwithstanding these new tensions, the President sought to continue the coverup. In the weeks following his meeting with Dean on March 21st, his consistent strategy was what might be called the hors d'oeuvre strategy. The President described the strategy to Haldeman and Ehrlichman after a conversation with Dean on April 14th by saying, "Give 'em an hors d'oeuvre and maybe they won't come back for the main course." His hope was that by making certain public revelations and by offering a certain number of victims to the prosecutors he could satisfy the public's appetite, so that it would seek no more revelations and no more victims. (This technique, which Ehrlichman, on another occasion, called a "modified limited hang-out," was also what Haldeman had had in mind when he suggested that they should "turn it off at the lowest cost" they could.) Hors d'oeuvres of many kinds came under consideration. Some were in the form of scapegoats to be turned over to the prosecutors, and others were in the form of incomplete or false reports to be issued to the public. By now, the country's appetite for revelations was well developed, and in the White House it was decided that no less a man than Mitchell was needed to satisfy it.

As Ehrlichman explained the new plan to the President, Mitchell would be induced to make a statement saying, "I am both morally and legally responsible."

"How does it redound to our advantage?" the President asked.

"That you have a report from me based on three weeks' work," Ehrlichman replied, "that when you got it, you immediately acted to call Mitchell in as the provable wrongdoer, and you say, 'My God, I've got a report here. And it's clear from this report that you are guilty as hell. Now John . . . go on in there and do what you should.' "

That way, the President could pose as the man who had cracked the conspiracy.

Shortly thereafter, Mitchell was called down to the White House, and Ehrlichman proposed the plan. Mitchell did not care for it. He not only maintained his innocence but suggested that the guilt lay elsewhere; namely, in the White House. Ehrlichman told the President when Mitchell had left that Mitchell had "lobbed, uh, mud balls at the White House at every opportunity." Faced with Mitchell's refusal to play the scapegoat, the President, Haldeman, and Ehrlichman next invited Dean to step into the role. Soon after Ehrlichman's unsatisfactory experience with Mitchell, the President met with Dean and attempted to induce him to sign a letter of resignation because of his implication in the scandal.

The President approached the subject in an offhand manner. "You know, I was thinking we ought to get the odds and ends, uh . . . we talked, and, uh, it was confirmed that—you remember we talked about resignations and so forth," he said.

"Uh huh," Dean replied.

"But I should have in hand something, or otherwise they'll say, 'What the hell did you—after Mr. Dean told you all of this, what did you do?' " the President went on.

Again Dean answered "Uh huh."

The President then related that even Henry Petersen had been concerned about "this situation on Dean," and Dean once more answered with an "uh huh."

"See what I mean?" the President asked the uncommunicative Dean.

"Are we talking Dean, or are we talking Dean, Ehrlichman, and Haldeman?" Dean finally asked.

"Well, I'm talking Dean," the President answered.

But Dean, like Mitchell before him, was talking Ehrlichman and Haldeman, too, and would not resign unless they also resigned. He did not want to be an hors d'oeuvre any more than Mitchell did. And since Dean was in possession of highly detailed information that implicated not only Haldeman and Ehrlichman but the President as well, the President was unable to "bite the Dean bullet," as he put it, until he also was willing to let Haldeman and Ehrlichman go. Their turn came quickly. By now the President was under intense pressure to act soon. If he did not, he could hardly pose as the man who had cracked the case. On April 17th, the day after the unproductive conversation with Dean, the President said to Haldeman and Ehrlichman. "Let me say this. . . . It's a hell of a lot different [from] John Dean. I know that as far as you're concerned, you'll go out and throw yourselves on a damned sword. I'm aware of that. . . . The problem we got here is this. I do not want to be in a position where the damned public clamor makes, as it did with Eisenhower, with Adams, makes it necessary or calls—to have Bob come in one day and say, 'Well, Mr. President, the public—blah, blah, blah—I'm going to leave.' " But Ehrlichman was not willing to throw himself on a sword. The person he was willing to throw on a sword was Dean. "Let me make a suggestion," he responded. It was that the President give Dean a leave of absence and then defer any decision on Ehrlichman and Haldeman until the case had developed further. However, the President pursued the point, seeming at times to favor Haldeman's and Ehrlichman's resignation, and finally Ehrlichman did what McCord, Hunt, Mitchell, and Dean had done before him. He lobbed mud balls at the White House—which in this case meant the President.

If he and Haldeman should resign, Ehrlichman observed, "we are put in a position of defending ourselves." And he went on, "The things that I am going to have to say about Dean are: basically that Dean was the sole proprietor of this project, that he reported to the President, he reported to me only incidentally."

" 'Reported to the President'?" the President inquired.

A moment later, speaking in his own defense, the President said, "You see the problem you've got there is that Dean does have a point there which you've got to realize. He didn't see me when he came out to California. He didn't see me until the day you said, 'I think you ought to talk to John Dean.'

At this point, Ehrlichman retreated into ambiguity, and said, "But you see I get into a very funny defensive position then vis-à-vis you and vis-à-vis him, and it's very damned awkward. And I haven't thought it clear through. I don't know where we come out."

On April 17th, the President made a short statement saying simply that there had been "major developments in the case concerning which it would be improper to be more specific now." He was unable to offer any diversionary reports or propitiatory victims to deflect the public's wrath at the forthcoming disclosures. He and his aides had talked over countless schemes, but all of them had foundered on the unwillingness of any of the aides to sacrifice themselves for him—or for "the Presidency," as he had asked them to do. The coverup was all one piece, and it cohered in exposure just as it had cohered in concealment.

The President had become adept at recollecting whatever was needed at a particular moment. By April of 1973, he and his aides were spending most of their time making up history out of whole cloth to suit the needs of each moment. Unfortunately for them, the history they were making up was self-serving history, and by April their individual interests had grown apart. Each of them had begun to "recollect" things to his own advantage and to the detriment of the others. As their community of interests dissolved under the pressure of the investigation, each of them was retreating into his own private, self-interested reality. The capacity for deception which had once divided them from the country but united them with one another now divided them from one another as well.

In the White House, the fabric of reality had disintegrated altogether. What had got the President into trouble from the start had been his remarkable capacity for fantasy. He had begun by imagining a host of domestic foes. In retaliating against them, he had broken the law. Then he had compounded his lawbreaking by concealing it. And, finally, in the same way that he had broken the law although breaking it was against his best interests, he was bringing himself to justice even as he thought he was evading justice. For, as though in anticipation of the deterioration of his memory, he had installed another memory in the Oval Office, which was more nearly perfect than his own, or anyone else's merely human equipment: he had installed the taping system. The Watergate coverup had cast him in the double role of conspirator and investigator. Though the conspirator in him worked hard to escape the law, it was the investigator in him that gained the upper hand in the end. While he was attempting to evade the truth, his machines were preserving it forever.

At the moment when the President announced "major developments" in the Watergate case, the national process that was the investigation overwhelmed the national process that was the coverup. The events that followed were all the more astounding to

the nation because, at just the moment when the coverup began to
explode, the President, in the view of many observers, had been
on the point of strangling the "obsolete" Constitutional system
and replacing it with a Presidential dictatorship. One moment, he
was triumphant and his power was apparently irresistible; the
next moment, he was at bay. For in the instant the President made
his announcement, the coverup cracked—not just the Watergate
coverup but the broader coverup, which concealed the underground history of the last five years—and the nation suffered an
inundation of news. The newspaper headlines now came faster
and thicker than ever before in American history. The stories ran
backward in time, and each day's newspaper told of some event a
little further in the past as reporters traced the underground
history to the early days of the Administration, and even into the
terms of former Administrations. With the history of half a decade pouring out all at once, the papers were stuffed with more
news than even the most diligent reader could absorb, Moreover,
along with the facts, non-facts proliferated as the desperate men
in the White House put out one false or distorted statement after
another, so that each true fragment of the story was all but lost in
a maze of deceptions, and each event, true or false, came up
dozens of times, in dozens of versions, until the reader's mind was
swamped. And, as if what was in the newspapers were not already
too much, television soon started up, and, in coverage that was
itself a full-time job to watch, presented first the proceedings of
the Ervin committee and then the proceedings of the House Judiciary Committee, when it began to weigh the impeachment of the
President. And, finally, in a burst of disclosure without anything
close to a precedent in history, the tapes were revealed—and not
just once but twice. The first set of transcripts was released by the
White House and was doctored, and only the second set, which
was released by the Judiciary Committee, gave an accurate account of the President's conversations.

As the flood of information flowed into the public realm, over-
turning the accepted history of recent years, the present scene was
also transformed. The Vice-President was swept from office when
his bribe-taking became known, but so rapid was the pace of
events that his departure was hardly noticed. Each of the institutions of the democracy that had been menaced by the President—
and all had been menaced—was galvanized into action in its turn:

the press, the television networks, the Senate, the House of Representatives, and, finally, in a dispute over release of the tapes, the Supreme Court. The public, too, was at last awakened, when the President fired the Special Prosecutor whom he had appointed to look into the White House crimes. In an outpouring of public sentiment that, like so much else that happened at the time, had no precedent in the nation's history, millions of letters and telegrams poured in to Congress protesting the President's action. The time of letters sent by the President to himself was over, and the time of real letters from real people had come. No one of the democracy's institutions was powerful enough by itself to remove the President; the efforts of all were required—and only when those efforts were combined was he forced from office.

America's Crisis of Confidence

Jimmy Carter

Very early in his campaign for the presidency, Jimmy Carter established a new and successful mode of relating to the American people. Speaking partly as a moralist, partly a preacher, partly a friend, he communicated a sense of caring deeply about the underlying values of the American people. When Carter came to Washington, he discovered that the same style did not work with government bureaucrats or Congressional leaders. Frustrated by his failure to win support for his plans to solve the energy crisis, Carter returned to the style of his campaign and reached over the heads of Congress to the American people. Retreating to Camp David in the Maryland mountains, Carter asked religious leaders, historians, poets, and psychiatrists to journey to Camp David and tell him what was wrong with America. The result was the speech that follows. Significantly, it traces all of America's problems to an underlying "crisis of confidence," a disease of the soul. The speech reveals both Carter's greatest strength and his greatest weakness. He successfully identifies a pervasive feeling of uncertainty and unease in the population. Yet, he failed to translate his insight into effective policy. Carter the preacher and therapist was a success. Carter, the politician, was a failure.

This is a special night for me. Exactly three years ago on July 15, 1976, I accepted the nomination of my party to run for President of the United States. I promised to you a President who is not isolated from the people, who feels your pain and shares your dreams and who draws his strength and his wisdom from you.

Excerpted from *The New York Times*, July 16, 1979.

During the past three years, I've spoken to you on many occasions about national concerns: the energy crisis, reorganizing the Government, our nation's economy and issues of war, and especially peace. But over those years the subjects of the speeches, the talks and the press conferences have become increasingly narrow, focused more and more on what the isolated world of Washington thinks is important.

Ten days ago I had plans to speak to you again about a very important subject—energy. For the fifth time I would have described the urgency of the problem and laid out a series of legislative recommendations to the Congress, but as I was preparing to speak I began to ask myself the same question that I now know has been troubling many of you: Why have we not been able to get together as a nation to resolve our serious energy problem?

It's clear that the true problems of our nation are much deeper—deeper than gasoline lines or energy shortages. Deeper, even, than inflation or recession. And I realize more than ever that as President I need your help, so I decided to reach out and to listen to the voices of America. I invited to Camp David people from almost every segment of our society: business and labor; teachers and preachers; governors, mayors and private citizens.

And then I left Camp David to listen to other Americans. Men and women like you. It has been an extraordinary 10 days and I want to share with you what I heard.

ADVICE FROM THE PEOPLE

First of all, I got a lot of personal advice. Let me quote a few of the typical comments that I wrote down.

This from a Southern Governor: "Mr. President, you're not leading this nation, you're just managing the Government."

"You don't see the people enough anymore."

"Some of your Cabinet members don't seem loyal. There's not enough discipline among your disciples."

Many people talked about themselves and about the condition of our nation. This from a young woman in Pennsylvania: "I feel so far from government. I feel like ordinary people are excluded from political power." And this from a young Chicano: "Some of us have suffered from recession all our lives. Some people have wasted energy but others haven't had anything to waste." And this from a religious leader: "No material shortage can touch the important things like God's love for us or our love for one another."

Several of our discussions were on energy, and I have a notebook full of comments and advice. I'll read just a few.

"We can't go on consuming 40 percent more energy than we produce. When we import oil, we are also importing inflation plus unemployment. We've got to use what we have. The Middle East has only 5 percent of the world's energy, but the United States has 24 percent."

And this is one of the most vivid statements: "Our neck is stretched over the fence and OPEC has the knife."

These 10 days confirmed my belief in the decency and the strength and the wisdom of the American people, but it also bore out some of my long-standing concerns about out nation's underlying problems. I know, of course, being President, that Government actions and legislation can be very important.

That's why I've worked hard to put my campaign promises into law, and I have to admit with just mixed success. But after listening to the American people I have been reminded again that all the legislatures in the world can't fix what's wrong with America.

A FUNDAMENTAL THREAT

So I want to speak to you tonight about a subject even more serious than energy or inflation. I want to talk to you right now about a fundamental threat to American democracy.

I do not mean our political and civil liberties. They will endure. And I do not refer to the outward strength of America—the nation that is at peace tonight everywhere in the world with unmatched economic power and military might. The threat is nearly invisible in ordinary ways. It is a crisis of confidence. It is a crisis that strikes at the very heart and soul and spirit of our national will.

We can see this crisis in the growing doubt about the meaning of our own lives and in the loss of a unity of purpose for our nation.

The erosion of our confidence in the future is threatening to destroy the social and the political fabric of America. The confidence that we have always had as a people is not simply some romantic dream or a proverb in a dusty book that we read just on the Fourth of July. It is the idea which founded our nation and which has guided our development as a people. Confidence in the future has supported everything else—public institutions and private enterprise, our own families and the very Constitution of the United States. Confidence has defined our course and has served as a link between generations.

We've always believed in something called progress. We've always had a faith that the days of our children would be better than our own.

CLOSING THE DOOR ON OUR PAST

Our people are losing that faith. Not only in Government itself, but in their ability as citizens to serve as the ultimate rulers and shapers of our democracy. As a people, we know our past and we are proud of it. Our progress has been part of the living history of America, even the world. We always believed that we were part of a great movement of humanity itself called democracy, involved in the search for freedom. And that belief has always strengthened us in our purpose. But just as we are losing our confidence in the future, we are also beginning to close the door on our past.

In a nation that was proud of hard work, strong families, close-knit communities and our faith in God, too many of us now tend to worship self-indulgence and consumption. Human identity is no longer defined by what one does but by what one owns.

But we've discovered that owning things and consuming things does not satisfy our longing for meaning.

We have learned that piling up material goods cannot fill the emptiness of lives which have no confidence or purpose. The symptoms of this crisis of the American spirit are all around us. For the first time in the history of our country a majority of our people believe that the next five years will be worse than that past five years. Two-thirds of our people do not even vote. The productivity of American workers is actually dropping and the willingness of Americans to save for the future has fallen below that of all other people in the Western world.

As you know there is a growing disrespect for Government and for churches and for schools, the news media and other institutions. This is not a message of happiness or reassurance but it is the truth. And it is a warning. These changes did not happen overnight. They've come upon us gradually over the last generation. Years that were filled with shocks and tragedy.

We were sure that ours was a nation of the ballot, not of the bullet, until the murders of John Kennedy and Robert Kennedy and Martin Luther King, Jr. We were taught that our armies were always invincible and our causes were always just only to suffer the agony of Vietnam. We respected the Presidency as a place of honor until the shock of Watergate. We remember when the phrase "sound as a dollar" was an expression of absolute dependability until 10 years of inflation began to shrink our dollar and our savings. We believed that our nation's resources were limitless until 1973, when we had to face a growing dependence on foreign oil.

These wounds are still very deep. They have never been healed.

ISOLATION OF GOVERNMENT

Looking for a way out of this crisis, our people have turned to the Federal Government and found it isolated from the mainstream of our nation's life. Washington, D.C., has become an island. The gap between our citizens and our Government has never been so wide. The people are looking for honest answers, not easy answers, clear leadership, not false claims and evasiveness and politics as usual. What you see too often in Washington and elsewhere around the country is a system of government that seems incapable of action.

You see a Congress twisted and pulled in every direction by hundreds of well-financed and powerful special interests. You see every extreme position defended to the last vote, almost to the last breath, by one unyielding group or another.

Often you see paralysis and stagnation and drift. You don't like it.

And neither do I.

What can we do? First of all, we must face the truth and then we can change our course. We simply must have faith in each other. Faith in our ability to govern ourselves and faith in the future of this nation. Restoring that faith and that confidence to America is now the most important task we face.

TURNING POINT IN HISTORY

Our fathers and mothers were strong men and women who shaped the new society during the Great Depression, who fought world wars and who carved out a new charter of peace for the world. We ourselves are the same Americans who just 10 years ago put a man on the moon. We are the generation that dedicated our society to the pursuit of human rights and equality.

And we are the generation that will win the war on the energy problem, and in that process rebuild the unity and confidence of America. We are at a turning point in our history. There are two paths to choose. One is the path I've warned about tonight—the path that leads to fragmentation and self-interest. Down that road lies a mistaken idea of freedom.

All the traditions of our past, all the lessons of our heritage, all the promises of our future point to another path: the path of common purpose and the restoration of American values. That path leads to true freedom for our nation and ourselves. We can take the first steps down that path as we begin to solve our energy problem. Energy will be the immediate test of our ability to unite this nation.

You know we can do it. We have the natural resources. We have more oil in our shale alone than several Saudi Arabias. We have more coal than any nation on earth. We have the world's highest level of technology. We have the most skilled work force, with innovative genius.

And I firmly believe we have the national will to win this war.

"The Second American Revolution"

Ronald W. Reagan

Whether political observers are hostile or friendly to Ronald Reagan, nearly every political commentator agrees that Reagan possessed extraordinary skill in articulating his point of view and rallying support for it. Although Reagan retained a level of popular backing usually reserved for "consensus" politicians of a moderate persuasion, he presented, and argued effectively for, a singularly partisan definition of America's purpose and goals. Reagan had clear ideas, many of them in deep conflict with the direction of American government and policies since the New Deal. He wished to dismantle the "welfare state," cut taxes severely, restore a laissez-faire economy, and simultaneously construct a huge new military machine. In fact, Reagan did seek a new American revolution, one that would alter dramatically the shape and substance of American politics. Here in his State of the Union Address in 1985, the dimensions of that revolution are outlined, suggesting the degree to which Reagan sought publicly to build support for his strong ideas.

Mr. Speaker, Mr. President, distinguished members of the Congress, honored guests and fellow citizens. I come before you to report on the state of our union. And I am pleased to report that, after four years of united effort, the American people have brought forth a nation renewed—stronger, freer and more secure than before.

Four years ago, we began to change—forever, I hope—our assumptions about government and its place in our lives. Out of that change has come great and robust growth—in our confidence, our economy and our role in the world. . . .

Four years ago, we said we would invigorate our economy by giving people greater freedom and incentives to take risks, and letting them keep more of what they earned.

We did what we promised, and a great industrial giant is reborn. Tonight we can take pride in 25 straight months of economic growth, the strongest in 34 years: a three-year inflation average of 3.9 percent the lowest in 17 years; and 7.3 million new jobs in two years, with more of our citizens working than ever before. . . .

We have begun well. But it's only a beginning. We are not here to congratulate ourselves on what we have done, but to challenge ourselves to finish what has not yet been done.

We are here to speak for millions in our inner cities who long for real jobs, safe neighborhoods and schools that truly teach. We are here to speak for the American farmer, the entrepreneur and every worker in industries fighting to modernize and compete. And, yes, we are here to stand, and proudly so, for all who struggle to break free from totalitarianism; for all who know in their hearts that freedom is the one true path to peace and human happiness. . . .

We honor the giants of our history not by going back, but forward to the dreams their vision foresaw. My fellow citizens, this nation is poised for greatness. The time has come to proceed toward a great new challenge—a Second American Revolution of hope and opportunity; a revolution carrying us to new heights of progress by pushing back frontiers of knowledge and space; a revolution of spirit that taps the soul of America, enabling us to summon greater strength than we have ever known; and, a revolution that carries beyond our shores the golden promise of human freedom in a world at peace.

Let us begin by challenging conventional wisdom: There are no constraints on the human mind, no walls around the human spirit, no barriers to our progress except those we ourselves erect. Already, pushing down tax rates has freed our economy to vault forward to record growth.

In Europe, they call it "the American Miracle." Day by day, we are shattering accepted notions of what is possible. . . .

We stand on the threshold of a great ability to produce more, do more, be more. Our economy is not getting older and weaker, it's getting younger and stronger; it doesn't need rest and supervi-

sion, it needs new challenge, greater freedom. And that word—
freedom—is the key to the Second American Revolution we
mean to bring about.

Let us move together with an historic reform of tax simplification for fairness and growth. Last year, I asked then-Treasury
Secretary Regan to develop a plan to simplify the tax code, so all
taxpayers would be treated more fairly, and personal tax rates
could come further down.

We have cut tax rates by almost 25 percent, yet the tax system
remains unfair and limits our potential for growth. Exclusions
and exemptions cause similar incomes to be taxed at different
levels. Low-income families face steep tax barriers that make hard
lives even harder. The Treasury Department has produced an
excellent reform plan whose principles will guide the final proposal we will ask you to enact.

One thing that tax reform will not be is a tax increase in disguise. We will not jeopardize the mortgage interest deduction
families need. We will reduce personal tax rates as low as possible
by removing many tax preferences. We will propose a top rate of
no more than 35 percent, and possibly lower. And we will propose
reducing corporate rates while maintaining incentives for capital
formation. . . .

Tax simplification will be a giant step toward unleashing the
tremendous pent-up power of our economy. But a Second American Revolution must carry the promise of opportunity for all. It is
time to liberate the spirit of enterprise in the most distressed areas
of our country.

This government will meet its responsibility to help those in
need. But policies that increase dependency, break up families
and destroy self-respect are not progressive, they are reactionary.
Despite our strides in civil rights, blacks, Hispanics and all minorities will not have full and equal power until they have full economic powers. . . .

Let us resolve that we will stop spreading dependency and start
spreading opportunity; that we will stop spreading bondage and
start spreading freedom.

There are some who say that growth initiatives must await final
action on deficit reductions. The best way to reduce deficits is
through economic growth. More business will be started, more
investments made, more jobs created and more people will be on

payrolls paying taxes. The best way to reduce government spending is to reduce the need for spending by increasing prosperity. . . .

To move steadily toward a balanced budget we must also lighten government's claim on our total economy. We will not do this by raising taxes. We must make sure that our economy grows faster than growth in spending by federal government. In our fiscal year 1986 budget, overall government program spending will be frozen at the current level; it must not be one dime higher than fiscal year 1985. And three points are key:

First, the social safety net for the elderly, needy, disabled and unemployed will be left intact. Growth of our major health care programs, Medicare and Medicaid, will be slowed, but protections for the elderly and needy will be preserved.

Second, we must not relax our efforts to restore military strength just as we near our goal of a fully equipped, trained and ready professional corps. National security is government's first responsibility, so, in past years, defense spending took about half the federal budget. Today it takes less than a third.

We have already reduced our planned defense expenditures by nearly $100 billion over the past four years, and reduced projected spending again this year. You know, we only have a military industrial complex until a time of danger. Then it becomes the arsenal of democracy. Spending for defense is investing in things that are priceless: peace and freedom.

Third, we must reduce or eliminate costly government subsidies. For example, deregulation of the airline industry has led to cheaper airfares, but on Amtrak taxpayers pay about $35 per passenger every time an Amtrak train leaves the station. It's time we ended this huge federal subsidy.

Our farm program costs have quadrupled in recent years. Yet I know from visiting farmers, many in great financial distress, that we need an orderly transition to a market-oriented farm economy. We can help farmers best, not by expanding federal payments, but by making fundamental reforms, keeping interest rates heading down and knocking down foreign trade barriers to American farm exports. . . .

In the long run, we must protect the taxpayers from government. And I ask again that you pass, as 32 states have now called for, an amendment mandating the federal government spend no more than it takes in. And I ask for the authority used responsibly by 43 governors to veto individual items in appropriations bills. . . .

Nearly 50 years of government living beyond its means has brought us to a time of reckoning. Ours is but a moment in history. But one moment of courage, idealism and bipartisan unity can change American history forever. . . .

Every dollar the federal government does not take from us, every decision it does not make for us, will make our economy stronger, our lives more abundant, our future more free. . . .

There is another great heritage to speak of this evening. Of all the changes that have swept America the past four years, none brings greater promise than our rediscovery of the value of faith, freedom, family, work and neighborhood.

We see signs of renewal in increased attendance in places of worship: renewed optimism and faith in our future; love of country rediscovered by our young who are leading the way. We have rediscovered that work is good in and of itself; that it ennobles us to create and contribute no matter how seemingly humble our jobs. We have seen a powerful new current from an old and honorable tradition—American generosity. . . .

I thank the Congress for passing equal access legislation giving religious groups the same right to use classrooms after school that other groups enjoy. But no citizen need tremble, nor the world shudder, if a child stands in a classroom and breathes a prayer. We ask you again—give children back a right they had for a century-and-a-half or more in this country.

The question of abortion grips our nation. Abortion is either the taking of human life, or it isn't; and if it is—and medical technology is increasingly showing it is—it must be stopped. . . .

Of all the changes in the past 20 years, none has more threatened our sense of national well-being than the explosion of violent crime. One does not have to have been attacked to be a victim. The woman who must run to her car after shopping at night is a victim; the couple draping their door with locks and chains are victims; as is the tired, decent cleaning woman who can't ride a subway home without being afraid.

We do not seek to violate rights of defendants, but shouldn't we feed more compassion for victims of crime than for those who commit crime? For the first time in 20 years, the crime index has fallen two years in a row; we've convicted over 7,400 drug offenders, and put them, as well as leaders of organized crime, behind bars in record numbers.

But we must do more. I urge the House to follow the Senate and enact proposals permitting use of all reliable evidence that police officers acquire in good faith. These proposals would also reform the *habeas corpus* laws and allow, in keeping with the will of the overwhelming majority of Americans, the use of the death penalty where necessary.

There can be no economic revival in ghettos when the most violent among us are allowed to roam free. It is time we restored domestic tranquility. And we mean to do just that. . . .

Tonight I have spoken of great plans and great dreams. They are dreams we can make come true. Two hundred years of American history should have taught us that nothing is impossible. . . . Anything is possible in American if we have the faith, the will and the heart.

History is asking us, once again, to be a force for good in the world. Let us begin—in unity, with justice and love.

Thank you and God bless you.

The "New Right"

Alan Crawford

Throughout the political history of postwar America, pundits have commented on the periodic emergence of right-wing groups seeking to mobilize mass opinion behind a variety of stances. In the late forties and fifties, anti-communism provided the rallying cry. Attacks against the welfare state and "big" government characterized the Goldwater movement of the '60s. But conservatism achieved a new power in American politics during the 1970s, with the development of the "New Right,' a multifaceted coalition of political forces that drew on the anti-communism and individualism of previous movements, yet added to these a powerful, emotion-based appeal closely connected to evangelical Christianity and moral exhortations to defend traditional morality and the sanctity of the family. According to various New Right leaders, America's most cherished values were being subverted by a combination of "liberal," secular forces. The only way to combat such forces, the New Right argued, was to go to the people, galvanize their anger, and seize political power on behalf of old-fashioned values and virtues. In this series of excerpts from his book Thunder on the Right, *Alan Crawford delineates the salient characteristics of the New Right, shows how direct-mail fund-raising techniques and electronic evangelism have fueled the movement, and demonstrates the power of singling out specific pro-family issues as vehicles for achieving political clout for conservatism.*

Many Americans are fearful of crime. They are distressed by rising taxes and double-digit inflation. Still others worry that their

Excerpted from Alan Crawford, *Thunder on the Right: The "New Right" and the Politics of Resentment* (New York: Pantheon, 1981), Reprinted by permission of Random House.

schools will be destroyed by busing. The list of code words that refer to the object of their fears seems endless: forced busing, abortion, gun control, permissiveness, gay rights, women's lib, the surrender of the Panama Canal, reverse discrimination, and on and on. . . .

Rising to address—and exploit—these anxieties is a new set of self-appointed leaders, men and women of the New Right. One Republican political professional estimated in 1977 that the New Right now constitutes the "fourth most powerful political force in America," behind the two major parties and organized labor. These leaders and the organizations they represent seek radical social and political change, and, unlike previous radicals of the Right, they have built a political and organizational network through which to further those aims. . . .

By the 1970s, the Right had been transformed into an institutionalized, disciplined, well-organized, and well-financed movement of loosely knit affiliates. Collecting millions of dollars in small contributions from blue-collar workers and housewives, the New Right feeds on discontent, anger, insecurity, and resentment, and flourishes on backlash politics. Through its interlocking network, it seeks to veto whatever it perceives to threaten its way of life—busing, women's liberation, gay rights, pornography, loss of the Panama Canal—and promotes a beefed-up defense budget, lower taxes, and reduced federal regulation of small business. Moreover, the New Right exploits social protest and encourages class hostility by trying to fuel the hostilities of lower-middle-class Americans against those above and below them on the economic ladder. Wholly bipartisan, though predominantly Republican, the New Right network supports whoever shares its desire for radical political change and its resentments of the status quo. As such, the New Right is anything but conservative.

The clout of the New Right is a result of their expertise in the field of direct-mail solicitation, an art they have been refining for years and have only recently employed for specifically political purposes. "Direct mail has allowed conservatives to by-pass the liberal media, and go directly into the homes of the conservatives in this country," Richard Viguerie said to the 1977 Conservative Political Action Conference. "There really is a silent majority in this country, and the New Right now has learned how to identify them and communicate with them and mobilize them." "It's our best way to offset the unions' lavishly financed political organizations," Huck Walther of the National Right to Work Committee told *Conservative Digest,* explaining his group's reliance on direct mail. Since 1978, the conservative PACs have actually been raising vastly more money than organized labor.

Having already amassed a small fortune from his advertising business, Viguerie now maintains a staff of 300 nonunion employees in the offices of the Richard A. Viguerie Co. (RAVCO) in Falls Church, Virginia, a Washington suburb. His apparatus sends out 100 million pieces of mail a year from some 300 mailing lists that contain the names of 25 million Americans. His inner sanctum is guarded by two different security systems, and even Viguerie himself must produce proper identification before guards will let him in. In his office are 3,000 reels of magnetic computer tape containing the names and addresses of more than 10 percent of the population of the United States. Two giant computers, leased for $2,700 per month, operate twenty-four hours a day; high-speed printers and tape units churn out the letters, which are packaged and mailed from various Viguerie businesses in northern Virginia.

The mailing lists accummulated by the fundraisers and their clients are often exchanged—usually bought or sold but sometimes loaned. In 1977, for example, State Senator John Briggs of Orange County, California, crusader against homosexuals, used the mailing list built by Anita Bryant's fundraiser to support Proposition 6, his anti-gay rights ballot measure. As Marvin Leibman told me: "Ever since [the direct-mail business] took off, there's been an entire army of hustlers emerge—list brokers, public affairs consultants, copywriters, mailing house operators . . . an entire army!" George Will has referred to the right-wing pen pals as "quasi-political entrepreneurs who have discovered commercial opportunities in merchandising discontent. . . ."

The key to all of these appeals is anger and fear. As Terry Dolan of the National Conservative Political Action Committee told me, his organization's fund-raising letters try to "make them angry" and "stir up hostilities." The "shriller you are," he said, the easier it is to raise funds. "That's the nature of our beast," he explained. The fund-raising letters of the New Right groups depict a world gone haywire, with liberal villains poised to destroy

the American Way of Life. After reciting a list of horrors about to
be perpetrated, the signatory—often a prominent right-wing activist or politician—asks for "help" from the recipient, frequently
requesting his participation in a survey or poll; then he is asked to
contribute and told how his $5 or $10 contribution will be used to
further the counterattack on the liberals. In the case of a political
campaign, almost invariably launched to defeat some "radical"
incumbent, the donor is told that his $10 will be used, for ex-
ample, to maintain a phonebank for a given period of time. The
more specific they can be, the fundraisers have learned, the more
likely they will be to receive a contribution. They try to get the
donor involved—or at least get him to feel that he is involved.

From Americans for LIFE signed by Ohio state representative
Donald E. "Buz" Lukens:

> Dear Friend:
>   Please take a second right now to look at the outrageous pro-
> abortion political propaganda I've enclosed.
>   And then help me STOP THE BABY KILLERS by signing and mail-
> ing the enclosed anti-abortion postcards to your U.S. Senators.
> (You'll find a list of all U.S. Senators on the back of that sickening
> baby killer propaganda.)
>   These anti-life Baby Killers are already organizing, working and
> raising money to re-elect pro-abortionists like George McGovern,
> South Dakota . . . Congressman Robert Drinan, Massachusetts . . .
> Senators John Culver, Iowa . . . Frank Church, Idaho . . . Birch
> Bayh, Indiana . . . men who apparently think it's perfectly OK to
> slaughter unborn infants by abortion. . . .
>   Abortion means killing a living baby, a tiny human being with a
> beating heart and little fingers . . . killing a baby boy or girl with
> burning deadly chemicals or a powerful machine that sucks and
> tears the little infant from its mother's womb.

While the men of the New Right symbolically guard the frontier
from external threats, exercising their energies on *macho* issues
like gun ownership, national defense, law and order, and "free-
market" economics, the women—with some help from sympathetic male politicians and preachers—protect hearth and home
from threats to their way of life. Like the women of the Old West,
they work with the school and church to safeguard the home and
neighborhood. Their struggles over textbook selection, busing,
abortion, gay rights, and the Equal Rights Amendment have pro-

duced charismatic political leaders and cult figures like Phyllis Schlafly, Anita Bryant, and the Reverend Jerry Falwell. They have become a political force of awesome power, with a potential of becoming more powerful still, given their zeal and numbers.

At stake, as they see it, is nothing less than the future of society itself and the values that will prevail in it. On one side, threatening traditional values, are the feminists, the liberals, the university communities, minorities, residents of the urban centers, and the media. On the other—side of the angels—are the "pro-family" forces, the leadership of the New Right and its disgruntled constituents, plus a growing political movement of fundamentalist evangelical ministers speaking from their television and radio pulpits in support of right-wing politics. Both sides are competing for the soul of America.

The New Right women, with the help of the fundamentalist ministers, are determined to reassert control of the culture, to further not only specific political goals, but to assure that the values they believe in are allowed to survive—and prevail. No better summary of their fear exists, perhaps, than this fund-raising letter from Christian Voice, a fundamentalist political lobby:

THIS LETTER WILL MAKE YOU ANGRY!
But I'm Going To Tell
You The Truth About . . .
. . . Militant gays
. . . Liberal Educators
. . . Cruel Atheists
. . . And Godless Politicians

Dear Friend:
   I am rushing you this urgent letter because the children in your neighborhood are in danger.
How would you feel if tomorrow your child . . .
. . . was taught by a practicing homosexual?
. . . was bused 20 to 30 miles away to school every morning?
. . . was forced to attend classes in a school where all religion is banned?
If you think this could never happen . . .
. . . you are in for a shock!

The rest of the letter, signed by the Reverend Robert G. Grant, head of Christian Voice, said that the drive for homosexual rights, busing, the ban on prayer in public schools, and other related issues are *"just a fraction of a master plan to destroy everything that is good and moral here in America."*

This "master plan" is orchestrated by "godless militant gays, liberal educators and vicious atheists" who—unless stopped—"will tell you how your children will be educated." They will, that is, determine America's future by shaping the minds and hearts of youth, by undermining the values instilled in the home. . . .

The Equal Rights Amendment perhaps most of all is viewed by the New Right women as an attempt to undermine the family by withdrawing privileges that keep the family together by protecting the woman in her traditional role within the family, and without which the family—they believe—would disintegrate.

The revolt of the New Right women is, clearly, a rear-guard action to arrest the society's growing acceptance of views more liberal than their own. It is, in this sense, a status revolt, growing out of deep anxieties on the part of those Americans who, in Ben Wattenberg's words, are "unyoung, unpoor and unblack," "middle-aged, middle-income and middle-minded," who fear that the culture is being controlled, more and more, by "new morality" liberals. These Americans resent the fact that many of the relevant social questions are being resolved by others. They sense a loss of their own social status, resulting in attitudes which Friedrich Nietzsche described in the late nineteenth century as *ressentiment,* a term now used to explain the social behavior of persons frustrated by their roles in society.

Important allies of the New Right women in protecting hearth and home, school and community from the liberal onslaught are certain fundamentalist ministers who are becoming increasingly involved in right-wing politics.

Their following is immense, and the power they wield from the television and radio pulpits may well make them a political force of enormous impact in the 1980s. Benefiting from the growth of the fundamentalist churches and the decline in membership in liberal Protestant churches—the Southern Baptist Convention alone gained almost two million members, from 10.77 million in 1965 to 12.51 million in 1974—these ministers represent a revolt against the move toward "relevance" and "secularism" in the churches. As the Reverend Jerry Falwell, the most prominent of the new right-wing evangelists, said of his own militancy: "Jesus was not a pacifist. He was not a sissy." Falwell, a fundmentalist from Lynchburg, Virginia, services his growing flock from his Old Time Gospel Hour, which airs on 325 television stations and 300 radio stations each week, netting roughly $1 million to the coffers of his Thomas Road Baptist Church in Lynchburg and its affiliated colleges and schools. During the days of the civil rights movement, Falwell spoke out against clergymen who were involved in politics, a position he has since reversed, on the grounds that the church is now being "assaulted" and "attacked." The result is his far-reaching "Clean Up America Crusade" and a political organization, Moral Majority. As Falwell explained in a Capitol Hill rally in April 1979, the time has come to "fight the pornography, obscenity, vulgarity, profanity that under the guise of sex education and 'values clarification' literally pervades the literature" that children read in the public schools. Falwell is alarmed also by homosexuality and bids his followers to send their dollars to fight these and related evils. "We are very much trying to create emotional involvement in these issues," he said. . . . "We are going to single out those people in government who are against what we consider to be the Bible, moralist positon, and we're going to inform the public. . . ."

Other right-wing fundamentalist ministers also owe much to "the electronic church," the vast radio and television operations run by the fundamentalists. It is immense, with thirty-six wholly religious television channels, 1,300 religious radio stations, and dozens of gospel television shows that buy time on commercial stations, reaching an estimated 100 million Americans each week. The flagship of the new evangelical talkshows is the "700 Club" of the Christian Broadcasting Network, which operates out of a $20 million facility in Virginia Beach. "700 Club" host Pat Robertson, a genial graduate of Yale Law School and son of a U.S. senator, in 1979 spoke out against "the humanistic/atheistic/hedonistic influence on American government," which he said was the result of control by the "Trilateral Commission and the Council on Foreign Relations," also a bogeyman of the John Birch Society. Of growing stature is the Reverend James Robison, a fiery Dallas evangelist who was dropped from a local commercial station in Dallas but reinstated after 12,000 fans turned out to express their support for a controversial sermon against homosexuality which had temporarily cost Robison his air-time.

Their constituency is estimated to consist of roughly 50 million "born-again" Christians, mostly Protestant, plus 30 million "morally conservative" Roman Catholics and a few million Mormons and Jews. As Pat Robertson put it. "We have enough votes to run the country. And when the people say, 'We've had enough,' we are going to take over. . . ."

Like Carl McIntyre and other right-wing ·evangelists of the 1950s and 1960s, the "electronic churchmen" of the 1970s and 1980s are stressing political concerns, determined, as Falwell put it, to "turn this into a Christian nation." One manifestation of the close association between the fundamentalists' and the right-wingers' shared anxieties over school busing and textbooks is the emergence of hundreds of Christian private schools, estimated by *The Wall Street Journal* to be a $2-billion-a-year industry. Supporters include Senators Helms of North Carolina, Paul Laxalt of Nevada, Gordon Humphrey of New Hampshire, and Congressman Robert K. Dornan of California—all of whom attended Falwell's Capitol Hill rally.

The growing political clout of the "born-again" lobby was felt in 1978, as the "moral majority" constituency claimed credit for blocking the Equal Rights Amendment, for denying election to liberal Iowa Senator Dick Clark, and for repealing, by referenda, gay rights ordinances. Politicians are beginning to pay heed. In mid-1979, Republican presidential hopeful John Connally held a private meeting at his ranch with top religious broadcasters and activists, including Falwell and Billings, and, as one participant told *U.S. News and World Report,* "At the end of the meeting, some of those guys were ready to carry Connally out of there on their shoulders." A second presidential aspirant, Illinois Congressman Philip Crane, a "born-again" Christian, was asked to appear on the "700 Club."

The cherished goal of the New Right, repeated throughout its literature, is to forge a "new majority," a grand coalition which, no longer encumbered by sentimental allegiances to such presumably outmoded institutions as the Republican and Democratic parties, can sweep the New Right to power. There exist, the Right contends, millions of Americans who are New Rightists by instinct, waiting for the opportunity to be liberated from their traditional loyalties and ignorant of the choice for freedom the Right offers.

Much of the New Right's activities in the late-1970s were devoted to forging this "new majority."

New Rightists had already made inroads in the traditional conservative domain of the GOP. Key to the new effort is the invasion or infiltration of the Democratic party.

The right-wing constituency is those whom political scientist Donald Warren has called "the Radical Center"—those "alienated," "forgotten," "angry," "troubled" Americans who are ripe to engage in backlash politics, and distinguished from the rest of society by their suspicion and distrust of it, by the belief that others are engaged in a conspiracy against them. These are Americans uniquely unable to make common cause within the established system, ill-equipped to engage in the give-and-take politics of cooperation and compromise that coalition-building requires, more attuned to social protest than to the complex process of governing, deeply distrustful of the very nature of coalitions. They put "principle above party." But if the alienated can *become* the society the core becomes the majority. So New Right leaders hope.

The "new majority" has been described by William Rusher as a union of economic conservatism, "the dominant secular faith of the American middle class," and of social conservatism, "predominantly a movement of the lower middle class and portions of what would be the American 'proletariat' if its behavior warranted that Marxist term."

The implications of this transition on the Right from Republicans to Democrats (or democratists) are immense. What is at stake is nothing short of what kind of democracy is to prevail in America. The constitutional democracy as envisioned by the Founding Fathers—and here there was little disagreement between Hamilton and Jefferson, Adams and Madison—is at issue. As conceived by the Founders, democracy was limited, restrained by a complex system of safeguards and restrictions. The work of government would be carried forth regularly, routinely, and calmly by constitutionally designated agencies, each as important as the next, each restrained yet accountable to the citizens. The Congress would be a deliberative body, a representative assembly, and on few occasions, indeed, were the people—in the sense of a mass—to become directly involved in the governing process. These included regular election of representatives and constitutional conventions. But even in the latter, the people would work their will through designated representatives.

The checks and balances of the American system are intended to preserve the process of translating the popular will into public opinion and public policy; representative bodies, dealing with issues by protracted negotiation, filter the popular voice,

> which ensures that moral issues are not frivolously decided, especially by the whim of some majority of the moment.
> If one tried to govern a country by the decisions in referenda, that country would be in a ceaseless state of moral strife and indignation.

A country in which highly sensitive questions are settled by continual referenda would be one of constant moral contention. The New Rightists seem to prefer the fanatics and demagogues—the Anita Bryants, Howard Jarvises, and John Briggses—to the reasoned, responsible leadership associated with classic conservatism. Already such sensitive personal questions as abortion and homosexual rights are put to the public for its approval. We are entering a period when biological discoveries will force many difficult and vital decisions of public policy to be made by the society and the state. When the kind of fury that is aroused by busing or by homosexuality, or—sixty years ago—by Prohibition,

> is let loose on issues of life and death, we will have reason to quail. The thought of unfiltered popular voice playing around with genetics is terrifying. Then indeed we will be able to say that *vox populi* has become *vox dei*, the voice of the people has become the voice of God.

Nothing less is at stake, as the American Right moves from a traditional conservative defense of representative government against the onslaughts of direct democracy into a celebration of government by rabble-rousing, by adding machine, by majorities of the moment.

Part Nine

WHERE DO WE GO FROM HERE?

As America enters the last decade of this century, issues that developed as an outgrowth of World War II continue to dominate our national agenda. In foreign policy we need to work out stable relationships with other superpowers as well as to cooperate effectively with developing nations. The world cannot afford a nuclear war. Yet as the capacity to make nuclear weapons proliferates, it becomes more and more difficult to prevent that possibility from becoming a reality. If the United States and the Soviet Union are not able to reduce their own armaments and prevent the development of nuclear weapons in countries like Libya and South Africa, it may be impossible to hold back the threat of a world-wide nuclear holocaust.

Within our own society, major problems continue in the areas of race and sex discrimination, economic productivity, and maldistribution of wealth and resources. It is difficult for the United States to be a place of equal opportunity unless people from different races and backgrounds begin from relatively the same place. Yet that cannot happen as long as the top 5 percent of the population controls nearly 53 percent of the wealth, and the bottom 20 percent of the population has less than half of 1 percent of the wealth. Many people believe that each American must be treated as an individual, equal before the law, if we are to hold on to our traditional values. Others, however, insist that we need to recognize the importance of group differences in setting social policy. If women and black Americans have suffered through most of our history because they have belonged to a specific gender or racial group, is it not necessary to use these same categories in order to overcome past oppression and bring members of these groups into the mainstream of American society?

Domestic problems and international issues come together around such problems as energy. The rich industrial societies of the world have only a small portion of the world's population, yet use the vast majority of energy resources. At least some observers believe that the only way to prevent a north-south world civil war is to redistribute the world's wealth to the poverty-stricken areas of the south. But can we embark on such policies without their having a significant impact on the way we organize our lives at home?

The following selections deal with these issues. McGeorge Bundy offers an analysis of why affirmative action may be necessary for the next generation if America is to come to grips with its legacy of racial oppression. According to Bundy, fairness requires that those who have borne the brunt of injustice in the past now be given aid toward achieving a position of equality. Kevin Phillips, by contrast, insists that such encouragement of group identification will eventually tear apart the society and destroy its possibility for homogeneity. Michael Harrington shows how the "new poverty" in America reflects international economic developments, as well as structural problems of inequality within America. Finally, George Kennan—one of those most involved in defining the rationale for our opposition to communism in the Cold War—presents a moving argument for retreating from the brink of nuclear destruction. His assessment of where we are and what we need to do in order to prevent annihilation of the universe is a powerful and fitting place for this book to end.

The Issue before the Court: Who Gets Ahead in America?

McGeorge Bundy

There are few domestic issues that have been more perplexing than affirmative action. After the 1964 Civil Rights Act prohibited discrimination on the basis of race or sex, the Johnson administration ordered executive agencies to take "affirmative action" to guarantee civil rights. Initially, the words were interpreted simply to mean recruiting minority candidates for job openings. Over time, however, more explicit rules were established, designed to correct past injustices. In one Southern state, for example, only 3.6 percent of the employees in a state agency were black, all of them janitors. Although it was likely that more blacks would be hired for a variety of jobs after the 1964 Act, it was improbable that an equitable proportion would be employed as long as hiring took place on an individual basis. Hence the need for affirmative action plans which mandated preferential employment to overcome past injustices.

To some people, such practices seemed like "reverse discrimination"—denying equal protection before the law to white individuals. The controversy over affirmative action came to a head with the Bakke case in 1978. There, the issue was whether a percentage of places at the University of California Medical School at Davis should be set aside for minorities. Although nearly everyone agreed that this particular case was not totally representative of the problem (the Davis Medical School, for example, was new and so had no historical record of discrimination against minorities), it became the focal point for Supreme Court action. Subsequent Supreme Court decisions appear to have upheld affirmative action, but the concept remains controversial. The following article by McGeorge Bundy, then president of the Ford Foundation, argues the case for affirmative action.

Bundy, a former Dean at Harvard and National Security Advisor to Presidents Kennedy and Johnson, became an active proponent of social reform during his tenure as president of the Ford Foundation. Here, he places the question of affirmative action in an historical context, contending that only through such programs will it be possible for the United States to achieve in practice, as well as in theory, the principle of racial equality.

The struggle for racial equality is old, but the constitutional questions presented by special admissions to colleges and graduate schools are new. Through the 1930s and 1940s the cases that rose to the Supreme Court were concerned with the exclusion of blacks from segregated professional schools. In the 1950s and 1960s the Court was occupied first with its great decision in *Brown,* declaring segregation in the public schools unconstitutional, and then with a long series of cases in which it was presented with one effort after another to evade the import of that decision. It did not confront problems like those of Allan Bakke because programs like the one to which he objects did not exist. In the early 1970s, a quite similar case, that of Marco DeFunis against the Law School of the University of Washington, was never decided because DeFunis was eventually admitted to the Law School and had almost finished by the time the Supreme Court was ready. The DeFunis case had great consequences in arousing feelings and stirring reflection, but it did nothing to clarify the constitutional standing of special admissions.

Large-scale attempts to increase the numbers of minorities in selective colleges and professional schools have a short history. In medical schools, for example, the effort became general less than ten years ago. These initial actions were compelled neither by government nor by courts. They were the product rather of the recognition, by whites as well as blacks, that the barriers to educational opportunity did not tumble in a day after the civil rights victories of the 1950s and early 1960s. Black demand, white awareness, riots in the cities, and the death of Martin Luther King, Jr. were all a part of what brought the change, but its deeper and more durable cause was the growing conviction that there was a fundamental contradiction between an asserted opposition to racism and the maintenance, by whatever process of selection, of essentially all-white col-

Excerpted from McGeorge Bundy, "The Issue Before the Court: Who Gets Ahead in America?" *The Atlantic Monthly,* November 1978. Reprinted by permission of the author.

leges and professional schools. Law schools, medical schools, graduate schools, and selective colleges all across the country began to recognize a direct responsibility to find and make room for larger numbers of qualified nonwhites.

Many legitimate purposes have animated those engaged in this effort, but the deepest and most general objective—toward which any one school or college can do only a little—has been to ensure full and fair access to all parts of our social, economic, and professional life for nonwhite Americans. Of course *all* kinds of Americans deserve such access, and it is right to remember from the outset that no past injustice permits us to set any one group above any other. But there can be no blinking the enormous and unique set of handicaps which our whole history, right up to the present, has imposed on those who are not white. It is not the fault of today's laws or of the present Supreme Court that racism should be our most destructive inheritance. But that reality makes the effort to overcome it a matter of the most compelling interest.

The essence of this new enterprise, whether at the college or the graduate level, has been the making of special attempts to find, attract, enroll, and support students who are members of disadvantaged racial minorities. So far this has meant mainly blacks, and in this discussion I shall often refer to them alone, simply to shorten matters. But the programs are directed also at Hispanic students and native Americans, and often at Americans of Asian origin. They include one or all of the following elements: active recruitment, targets or goals or even quotas for numbers enrolled, high levels of financial aid, and special courses or other academic arrangements when they are needed to help the student succeed. In all these programs attention to race, indeed special attention *because* of race, has been essential.

These new programs, in medical schools and elsewhere, have not yet been comprehensively and comparatively studied, and even if we knew more about them than we do, we could not know enough for confident judgment of their effects. The first medical students to enter by special admissions have not yet had time to prove themselves as practicing physicians, and in any case the programs of the medical schools have changed in shape while the number of minority students admitted has been growing, from less than 300 in 1968 to 1400 in 1976. Such evidence as we have— much of it oral and informal—suggests that most medical schools have had a great deal to learn in this short time about judging minority candidates, about helping them to come to terms with their own environment, and about treading the narrow and necessary path between sympathetic recognition of difficulties and cynical or condescending acceptance of unsatisfactory performance. Many minority students have had much to learn about these same matters. . . .

Racial mistrust and misunderstanding have not been exorcised by these programs, and sensitive observers know that all concerned, white and nonwhite alike, have a long way to go. But there is a clear and positive relation between effort and success in these programs, and much evidence that they are working better now than when they began. . . .

The moral and intellectual standing of those who complain against special admissions is not in doubt. When we find on the same side men as different as Justice Douglas and the late Alexander Bickel of Yale, and when a Court that has earned respect and even criticism for its liberalism comes down as hard as has the Supreme Court of California, we must understand what troubles them so much.

The first and strongest of their contentions is simply that both in the law and in common feeling there has developed a heavy suspicion of any program, whatever its motive, which gives members of one race any advantage over members of another on account of race alone. Ironically but understandably, the most sweeping and eloquent expressions of this sentiment may have come from the leaders in the battle for black civil rights.

In 1947 Thurgood Marshall himself, then the director of the Legal Defense and Educational Fund of the NAACP, denounced the classification by race under which the laws of Texas deprived Herman Sweatt of admission to law school: "There is no understandable factual basis for classfication by race, and under a long line of decisions by the Supreme Court, not on the question of Negroes, but on the Fourteenth Amendment, all courts agree that if there is no rational basis for the classification, it is flat in the teeth of the Fourteenth Amendment." As we shall see, the defenders of special admissions programs argue strongly today that the use of racial classifications in those programs is not only rational but necessary for compelling purposes; but what deserves emphasis first is that it is easy to relate both the logic and the feeling of Thurgood Marshall's outburst in Texas to the reaction of those who feel that when it comes to choosing who shall be a doctor, there is no rational basis for using color as a test.

A closely related objection to special admissions is that they seem to many to require the use of racial quotas. There has been much haggling about the difference between goals and quotas, and I shall argue that the distinction is not trivial, but when in fact a fixed number of places is reserved for qualified minorities (the situation at Davis), it becomes hard to deny that some spaces that would otherwise be open to all are now closed off to whites. One cannot miss the fervor in the opinion of Justice Mosk for the California court: "No college admission policy in history has been as thoroughly discredited in contemporary times as the use of racial percentages. Originated as a means of exclusion of racial and religious minorities from higher education, a quota becomes no less offensive when it seems to exclude a racial majority." The fervor is underlined, if anything, by the rhetorical excess of the suggestion that a majority that has a full and open chance at 84 percent of the places available is "excluded."

Not surprisingly, it is Professor Bickel who is most eloquent of all. Nothing in the briefs supporting Mr. Bakke's claim is as strong as the argument Bickel put forth in *DeFunis*. He tells us flatly that it is quite simply wrong

> to require the employment or the admission to a school or to any other position of unqualified or less qualified persons solely on the basis of their race. When this is done, a cost is paid in loss of efficiency and in injustice . . . [I]n a society in which men and women expect to succeed by hard work and to better themselves by making themselves better, it is no trivial moral wrong to proceed systematically to defeat this expectation; the more so as for some groups that do not now benefit from affirmative action programs prejudice has only recently been overcome, and the expectation that members of such groups might rise by merit has just begun to be fully met . . . [T]o reject an applicant who meets established, realistic, and unchanged qualifications in favor of a less qualified candidate is morally wrong, and in the aggregate, practically disastrous.

Driven by convictions like these, Justice Douglas (in a separate opinion on the merits in *DeFunis*) reached the conclusion that any admissions program must fail unless it is handled in a *"racially neutral way"* (his italics). Sharing this judgment, and quoting liberally from the Douglas opinion, the California Supreme Court reached the same conclusion: Whatever the processes of admission, they must be racially neutral. Whatever methods and standards are used, they must be "applied without regard to race."

To the average reader, all this may seem fair enough. Why then is it so shocking to the institutions that would be principally affected? The reason is simple, if also painful: the gaps in social, economic, educational, and cultural advantage between racial minorities and the white majority are still so wide that *there is no racially neutral process of choice that will produce more than a handful of minority students in our competitive colleges and professional schools.*

Let us stay with medical schools and blacks alone and look back at 1967–1968, the last year before special admissions began to be significant. In that year there were 735 blacks in medical schools, but 71 percent of them had been admitted by ways that were far from racially neutral: they were at Howard and Meharry, then and now the country's two predominantly black medical schools. Out in the broad white world of a hundred other medical schools, the 211 blacks enrolled in all four classes were only 0.6 percent of the total, though blacks are about 12 percent of the total population. Today, as a consequence of a nation-wide ten-year effort, there are some 3000 blacks, 5 percent of the total, in the mainly white medical schools. It is an extraordinary transformation. And what most close observers believe is that if these same mainly white medical schools were driven back to "racially neutral" admissions, the number of blacks would slide back close to where it was in 1968. A parallel impact would be felt in other professional schools and in selective colleges. The consequences of such a backsliding, both to the aspirations of racial minorities and to the honorable efforts of whites, are mildly described by the word catastrophic. The message would go out, to something like one sixth of our nation, that all the words of a generation since *Brown* are hollow—that the educational doors are to be neutrally open, but only to an overcrowded staircase on which nearly all of those with a head start will be white.

The reasons for this conclusion are both multiple and simple. First, we must agree that selective colleges and professional schools do want entering students who are not merely qualified but highly qualified. They have learned that when other things are equal, the applicant with the better academic record and the better test scores is more likely to succeed. Records and scores must be handled with care, and it is easy to make too much or too little of them. It is much less easy to deny the reality they tend to reflect: that developed capacity for certain kinds of analysis, familiarity with certain kinds of knowledge, successful experience of certain kinds of mental effort, and natural exposure to a social environment in which those things are encouraged are all strongly relevant to a person's promise. In America today disadvantaged racial minorities are still greatly underrepresented among those best qualified on these criteria alone. The burden of centuries has not been lifted in the short and stressful decades since *Brown*. Selective colleges and professional schools admitting students as they admitted them fifteen years ago would soon be nearly lily-white again. . . .

Among those who have worked hardest and longest on this matter the agreement is overwhelming. If you want to enlarge the numbers of minority students in selective colleges and professional schools you simply *must* make race a factor in your work. You must target blacks and Hispanics and others in your recruiting; you must assess their promise in the light of the specific disadvantage that their race itself still carries. If you wish to attract well-qualified candidates you must earn a reputation for real accessibility; you must become known as a place that accepts minorities in more than token numbers. You must then spend time and money well beyond your normal standards in helping them survive and succeed. Precisely because it is not yet "racially neutral" to be black in America, a racially neutral standard will not lead to equal opportunity for blacks. . . .

So far we may have established the importance of action to increase minority enrollment, and we may even have made good our claim that this simply cannot be done in a racially neutral way. But the two hurdles we recognized at the outset remain: Is it not somehow wrong to admit "less qualified" people because of race, and is it not doubly wrong to reserve space for them at the inescapable expense of others in the competition? . . .

The weight of the evidence available suggests that a steadily growing percentage of the men and women of minority origin who are admitted to selective colleges, law schools, medical schools, and graduate schools are "making it." Schools are choosing with more skill and giving better support to those who enroll. Some fail or drop out, as some (but relatively fewer) whites do. But the rates of minority attrition are now reported to be roughly comparable to the failure and dropout rate of white males some thirty or forty years ago. Middle-aged men who received their own professional training at about that time can fairly be asked to consider whether a class with records as good as their own should be considered as underqualified.

I labor this point because both logic and sentiment suggest that it may be central to the thinking of a great many Americans, however little it may appear in records and arguments. *No one is arguing for the admission of the unqualified, and there is no finding in* Bakke *that such admissions have occurred.* Indeed, there is not in *Bakke* any serious legal challenge to the generally accepted proposition that the elemental decision on whether a candidate is qualified for medical school must be left to the professional judgment of faculties and their agents. . . .

We are near the center of the matter. Let us recognize the reality: in affirmative action to admit more members of racial minorities, there are and will be measurable differences, among those admitted, between the average test scores and academic records of minorities and those of whites. The scores and records of blacks and other minorities are such that this result is inescapable, at least for the present. A similar relative weakness in test scores has existed in other groups in the past and has been gradually overcome. There is also a clear relation between low scores and low socioeconomic status, which hits racial minorities with particular force. Of course not all members of racial minorities have low scores or poor records, just as not all are culturally or economically disadvantaged. There is indeed a growing pool of applicants who are black or brown and bright by any test. Nonetheless, the average scores for most racial minorities are lower than the comparable scores for whites.

But does it follow, as Professor Bickel seems to have thought, that to admit such lower-scoring minority applicants is "morally wrong" and "practically disastrous"? Does a difference in such "established, realistic, and unchanged qualifications" mean that those who fall short on these measurements are "less qualified"? Or does it mean only that when one prefers a candidate who is weaker in such relatively measurable qualifications, one must have some good and solid reason? Race for a moment aside, the latter standard is clearly the right one. Sensitive admissions officers agree that while scores and records can tell you a lot at the upper and lower margins, they give little guidance in the hard cases of choice among those who are academically qualified but not extraordinary. . . .

Even where records and tests have been used most mechanically it has been only because of their *relative* advantage; among thoughtful admissions officers it has always been agreed that when time permitted and educational need required, it was right to look at other things. I put the point most gently. Especially at the undergraduate level, most admissions officers will say that mechanical reliance on any such measurement is what would be "morally wrong" and "practically disastrous." Recognizing their fallibility, knowing they will make mistakes and commit unfairness, they nonetheless reach out to try to identify promise and quality of all sorts. They look at other things, not only for help at the margins, but because they think these other things are critical to the quality of the student body as a whole.

Now we are right at the heart of it. Is race itself permissibly such another thing to look at? If I am a qualified black (in the basic sense already discussed), may not my blackness perhaps make me *more* qualified? Have I had something extra to go through? If I score 550 where a middle-class white scores 650, have I shown as much or more of what is so critical to success in learning—a *determination* to learn? Can I bring a different and needed perspective? Is there a special need for people like me in courts and hospitals and on college faculties? May the profession itself be better if more people of my race are in it? Can my presence and participation as a student enlarge the educational experience of others? Does the whole society somehow have a need for me in this profession that it simply does not have, today, for one more white? If the answer to these questions, or some of them, is yes, are not my qualifications by that much improved, and improved precisely by my blackness? If so, at some point it becomes right that I should be admitted; I am not "less qualified" when all things are considered.

I put this case by questions because I wish to emphasize that it is not necessary here to be dogmatic in response to dogma. It is quite enough to argue that it would be a dangerous and sweeping business, in the present state of our knowledge and experience, to answer all these questions in the negative. Yet that is precisely what Professor Bickel's argument and the opinion of the California court would require. . . .

But what about quotas, or even goals? Are they not arbitrary and discriminatory? Certainly they could be, if unqualified candidates were admitted or if their numbers went beyond the compelling needs of the profession or the state. There is no such claim in *Bakke;* at Davis about one sixth of the places were held for qualified members of minorities, who make up about a quarter of the state's population. Even if it really was the minority entrants who beat Bakke out, and even though his scores were better than theirs, still, as long as one grants that to be black or Chicano can be in itself a qualification, the program does not seem excessive. Indeed, it is not the sixteen places that are denounced by Bakke and his supporters—it is the award of any admission *at all* on grounds even partly related to race. It is not the size of the space reserved, or even its existence, that is the ultimate basis of the invocation of "equal protection." What Bakke and his friends assert is that race must play *no* part in selective admissions, and they may feel themselves forced to this argument because no other will justify their appeal for constitutional protection.

Thus Bakke and the California court are asserting an absolute claim when what we really face here is conflicting values which have to be compared in weight. There can be no doubt at all that if the number of nonwhites goes up in selective schools and colleges, the number of whites will go down. Some will be rejected who would otherwise have been accepted. But what needs attention is the magnitude of this consequence.

Set Bakke himself to one side for a moment and consider the net damage to disappointed white applicants, as a group, arising from the nationwide admission of racial minorities to medical schools. (This is a reasonable course even in considering Bakke as an individual, because he applied not only to Davis, with its relatively large and rigid goal for minorities, but to a number of other medical schools with other kinds of programs. He wants to be a doctor, not a Davis graduate.) In 1975–1976, there were just under 35,000 white applicants for medical school, and 22,000 of them were not accepted. In the same year the total number of minority candidates accepted and enrolled was 1400. If not one minority candidate had been accepted, the entering classes throughout the country could have accommodated less than 7 percent of the disappointed whites. In this raw statistical sense, at least 93 percent of the majority's problem lies in something else.

The most important "something else" is a simple excess of demand over supply. More people of all sorts want to be doctors than ever before, and for powerful reasons. In the last ten years the number of formal applicants has increased by 130 percent, while the number of places available has increased by only 66 percent. . . .

Most of the competition the white males face comes from other white males, but it is interesting that even if one persists in pitting white males against others, their most dangerous rivals, quantitatively, are not specially admitted black or Hispanic males, but women of all races. Since 1968 the number of women entering medical schools has risen from 8 percent to 25 percent of the total. . . . The 4000 young women who have entered medical school this year have a lot more to do with the rejection of men like Bakke than any special admissions program for minorities.

But let us return to Bakke: it is not statistics alone that suggest the fault assignable to minority admissions programs in his case is small. It is evident in the history of his effort, if not in the appellate arguments, that his central trouble was his age. He was ten years older than the ordinary candidate for admission. Medical education is a prolonged affair at best, and the profession has been troubled for years by the fact that even if a student proceeds promptly along all the usual tracks—college, medical school, internship, and often specialty boards—he or she can be well in the thirties before being fully prepared for practice. Bakke would have been over forty at best, and rightly or wrongly this fact was a considerable handicap to him.

Conversely, what is most impressive about Bakke is not his scores but his determination. It seems at least possible, from the admittedly fragmentary evidence, that the authorities at Davis would have made a better judgment to admit Allan Bakke precisely because he so clearly cared so much; moreover, his health and energy levels appear to be high enough to justify some flexibility in considering his age. And it can be argued today that whether he wins or loses his legal case, he has made sacrifices in fighting it which somehow ought to win for him even now what he has wanted most in life—a chance to be a doctor.

Both Bakke's age and his determination are largely absent from the legal arguments. Constitutionally they do not seem to count. But they are what really mattered in his case. Together they are a powerful concrete demonstration of the difficulty of the art of choice among those qualified.

Thus both general and specific evidence, not reached by the legal arguments, combine to suggest that any hurt sustained by whites in general or Bakke in particular is only doubtfully and marginally related to special admission of minorities. Moreover, there is no way of avoiding some such displacement if in fact there are to be more nonwhites in medical schools. Since everyone except perhaps Bakke himself appears to agree that more qualified nonwhites are in fact needed, there is a flavor of Catch-22 about the arguments of his friends and the California court. They want more blacks, and that means fewer whites, but any program that produces more blacks by considering blackness in any way is by that very fact unconstitutionally unfair! Can this kind of thinking lead to sound constitutional law? . . .

Through most of [our] history, most institutions of higher learning, like the rest of America, have been blatantly racist; the exceptions have been as few as they have been honorable. For only about ten years out of our two centuries as a nation has there been a serious nationwide attempt to make room in the higher reaches of this world for those who have been held back so long. The results so far are uncertain, but the achievement is real, while the asserted dangers are hypothetical. If the process is not yet as open and skillful as it should be, it is much more open and skillful than it was. Faculties still insist on their responsibilities, but they are more and more aware that there are constituencies all around them that have a right to an accounting. Their efforts to meet competing claims do not proceed in a vacuum. The whole process is incomparably broader than the narrow chains of legal reasoning which are offered to the Court, and members of the white majority are hardly powerless in that process. Whatever is selective will always be imperfectly equitable, but in the absence of a

persuasive showing of any grave or general damage to basic constitutional rights, it would seem genuinely tragic to block this
great new effort at racial fairness just as it begins. . . .

I repeat that this effort is young, difficult, and hopeful. What
most needs emphasis is its youth. In the lives of the races, the
professions, and the universities, ten years are but a moment.
Some of those who defend affirmative action sometimes speak as
if it could be a relatively short matter. If we measure in generations, they may be right. It seems fair to hope that we can have
decisive progress by the time the children of today's children are
of college age. But that single generation takes us well beyond the
year 2000. For the rest of the working lives of those who are now
concerned with these matters, persistence will be the name of the
game.

No one can deny that special admissions programs, even at
their best, have costs and dangers; the grievances of Allan Bakke
and others may be overstated and even misdirected, but they are
deeply felt. Racial preference can arouse racial antagonism, and
the general rule that judgment should be based on personal merit
alone has its high claims. Still, it seems clear that to take race into
account today is better than to let the doors swing almost shut
because of the head start of others. We must hope and believe
that in the long run our effort for equal opportunity will put the
need for special programs behind us. In that deep sense there is
no conflict between special admissions and every other form of
action to help the disadvantaged, white and nonwhite alike. But
what special admissions, and only special admissions, can do today
is to make access to the learned professions a reality for nonwhites. To get past racism, we must here take account of race.
There is no other present way. In the words of Alexander Heard
of Vanderbilt, "To treat our black students equally, we have to
treat them differently.". . .

My own last thought is this: It is right to ask of the Court in this
case that it should find its way to a result which somehow respects
the reality that the world of American higher learning is at last
embarked upon a long-delayed and indispensable effort to do its
part to deal with our most deeply rooted social evil, one which was
the proximate cause of the Fourteenth Amendment itself. To
read the words of that amendment in ways that would cripple that
effort would seem a cruel irony. What is worse, it would be to

assert that in the learned professions the equal protection clause somehow requires the perpetuation of de facto white supremacy. Worst of all, it would place the great moral authority of the Court on the wrong side of a fundamental issue, on which it has a hard-won right to speak for the national conscience.

In asking whether the equal protection clause really requires all this, I have found myself rereading two of the most famous of all judicial comments on the Constitution—what it is and what it permits. They both came from the pen of John Marshall in 1819.

> In considering this question, then, we must never forget, that it is *a constitution* we are expounding.

And later in the same opinion:

> Let the end be legitimate, let it be within the scope of the constitution, and all means which are appropriate, which are plainly adapted to the end, but consist with the letter and spirit of the constitution, are constitutional.

If the Constitution is read in this grand manner, can it truly be *unconstitutional* to make room for qualified members of racial minorities on the staircase to the professions?

The Balkanization of America

Kevin Phillips

Many Americans have seen affirmative action as but one example of a growing tendency toward disintegration in American society, posing one group over against another, and destroying any sense of our common identity as Americans. In the following selection, Kevin Phillips—a political consultant, writer, and former government official—contends that traditional American values of individualism are profoundly threatened by this revitalization of group assertiveness. Thus, instead of America being seen as a melting pot, various ethnic, regional, religious, and racial groups are pitted against each other, with no consensus on shared values.

Ironically, Phillips himself was the architect in the 1960s of the so-called Southern strategy, arguing that the Republican Party could win significant gains by appealing to regional political and economic interests. Phillips also helped to popularize the notion of the Sun Belt as a political and geographic entity. Here, he contends that whatever the short-term benefits derived from such identification, the long-range interests of American society require a higher allegiance to common values which de-emphasize class, racial, or sectional differences.

They are wrong, or too superficial, these people who calibrate the alleged decline of the United States by the decreasing relative hitting power stored in North American missile silos or by the second-place number of ship miles logged by the U.S. Navy in the

Indian Ocean. Would that our national problem were such a simple matter of matériel and logistics. Unhappily for us all, the larger crisis of spirit engaging the United States has relatively little to do with the too-few and too-old destroyers in the Persian Gulf or the too-old and too-few heavy bombers expected to reach Novosibirsk in a Maximum Alert. One can argue—and I will—that the Union of the United States (both as an idea and as a matter of domestic political geography) is unraveling in more fundamental ways. This is no small irony: that even as modern American technology has learned to package instant steel-bonding cyanoacrylate in a dimestore tube, the bonds of American society itself should be weakening or dissolving.

All too many examples suggest themselves: the congealing of the melting pot and the re-emergence of ethnicity; the proliferation of sexual preferences and religious cults; the new political geography of localism and neighborhoods; the substitution of causes for political parties; the narrowing of loyalties; the fragmentation of government; the twilight of authority. Some months back, Energy Secretary James Schlesinger, who had not yet ascended to that dismal eminence, suggested that the well-known and much-dreaded energy crisis might bring about the "Balkanization" of America. Fair enough: The parochial politics of energy *do* smack enough of Bulgarian or Serbian bickering circa 1911 to make the term "Balkanization" reasonably appropriate. In a larger perspective, however, the trend that Schlesinger feared *already* has established itself as a fact of national life. As the politics of natural-gas pipelines resemble the plots and counterplots of Zagreb and Sofia, so also one can find just as much social Balkanization in the rise of feminism or "gay rights," or in the "Red Power" demands of American Indians—for tribal sovereignty and the return of former Indian lands—from Maine to California. For the past several years the symptoms of decomposition have appeared throughout the body politic—in the economic, geographic, ethnic, religious, cultural, biological sectors of society. Small loyalties are replacing larger ones. Small outlooks are also replacing larger ones. . . .

In such a context, then, the Balkanization of America is closely related to what Andrew Hacker has called "the end of the American era." Can it be coincidental that U.S. political and social decomposition has accelerated in tandem with Vietnam and the end of Pax Americana, the concurrent failure of the Great Society, the end of energy abundance, the downfall of cultural optimism, and—of course—Watergate and public loss of confidence in the U.S. political system? On the contrary, the breakdown of these unities, hopes, and glories has been enough to send Americans, too, scrambling after a variety of lesser combinations and self-identifications: ethnicities, regions, selfish economic interests, sects, and neighborhoods.

At this point, let me admit that regionalism, separatism, fragmentation, and rampant ethnicity are hardly new in the United States. On the contrary, they are as old as Jamestown, New Amsterdam, and Plymouth. But the critical historical distinction must lie in the tidal flow and ebb: From George Washington's day through the Trajan-like imperial high-water mark of the early 1960s, Americans retrospectively can see ethnicity, regionalism, and states' rights yield before growing concepts of global optimism, the melting pot, equality, homogeneity, and centralization of (benign federal) power. Since that time, however, the reemergence of ethnicity, regionalism, states' rights, and political splintering has occurred in a very different psychological climate—amidst the *end* of optimism, the *collapse* of Manifest Destiny, the *failure* of the Great Society, the *failure* of the melting pot, and of all the other hopes and slogans of America's national rise. Credit this distinction, and today's social Balkanization process takes on a significance little rebutted by invocations of ethnicity circa 1880, regionalism circa 1896, feminism circa 1912, or states' rights circa 1948. Only the pre-Civil War period raises some parallel.

SUN BELT VERSUS FROST BELT

Let's begin with the most frequently discussed example of the phenomenon, which in many ways is also the pivot: Sun Belt versus Frost Belt. To be sure, regional conflict has been a staple of American history—as late as 1948, Harry Truman was declaiming that the Northeast treated the South and the West like colonies. What *is* new is the first regional attempt in over a century to remove national leadership from the Northeast. Ten years ago, when I coined the term "Sun Belt," it seemed like a good phrase for a boom region owing its ascendance to the shining of the sun—tourism, retirement, irrigated agribusiness, year-round military facilities. But over the past decade, the term has come to represent a phenomenon of much greater importance.

Competition for natural and energy resources is one major factor in the increasingly high-voltage regional rivalries. By and large, the Sun Belt states, which contain most of the country's oil and natural gas, favor energy deregulation and progrowth economic development. The most intense demand for energy regulation, allocation, and conservation, meanwhile, is centered in the North. Mutual suspicion characterizes the attitudes of both factions. The Washington lobbyist for the state of Louisiana told an interviewer last year that "the attitudes today are the same as those preceding the Civil War. The North wants everything its own way. This time, it won't get it."

The point hardly need be dwelt upon for anyone who has seen Texas's bumper stickers ("Drive fast, freeze a Yankee") or who has noticed hostile alignments of Sun Belt and Frost Belt political organizations and lobby groups. Less well known is the extent of squabbles over water and energy at the state level. Virginia and North Carolina are fighting over water from the Roanoke and Chowan rivers; Arizona and California are fighting over the Colorado River. . . .

Economic and geographic Balkanization is at once confirmed and, if anything, surpassed by the biological fragmentation overtaking the United States. Five biological denominators currently lend themselves to civil-rights campaigns and the assertion of group identities: sex, sexual preference, age, race, and ethnic origin. Rising egocentrism is a related development.

Fragmentation of American society by sex and sexual-preference group need not be greatly elaborated here, given the (excessive) extent to which it has been dwelt upon elsewhere. Escalating definitions of "rights" produce at least two unfortunate results: group categorization and militance. Feminism has gone far beyond Susan B. Anthony. Certainly the organization, cohesion, and civil-rights militance of homosexuals is a new phenomenon in American society—"Gay Power" has as much political weight in San Francisco (and maybe Manhattan) as does the steel caucus in Ohio's Mahoning Valley.

Age is yet another denominator. The group awareness of senior citizens—"Gray Power"—is a considerable phenomenon in Florida, Arizona, and California. At the other end of the age chart, more and more legal rights are being defined for children. Even second- and third-trimester fetuses have had their own bio-political Balkan army marshalled for them in the right-to-life movement.

The concept of racial Balkanization is open to argument. On one hand, pre-1960s segregation resulted in what was in effect two nations—one white, one black. Against *that* backdrop, desegregation has increased racial unity. Yet in another sense, the last few years have seen a definite resegregation in many cities, coupled with a growth of black sentiment to go it alone. Today's trend toward predominantly nonwhite central cities raises critical questions, as does official fondness for the racial-quota system. Indeed, the use of either quotas or "affirmative action" programs verging on quotas is tantamount to an official recognition of Balkanization—acceptance of the notion that equality can be pursued only by racial and ethnic group categorization.

Therein lies the problem. The consequence of the attempt to *proscribe* discrimination may be to *prescribe* opportunity by various biological categories. Officially mandated quotas and preferences for nonwhites have already produced a variety of unfortunate practices. In Queens County, New York, parents claiming a certain racial background in order to get their children assigned to a local school must present themselves at a Board of Education racial-inspection office. Under the signature of the Honorable Bert Lance, the federal Office of Management and Budget last May promulgated guidelines for collecting uniform racial and ethnic data. Central or South American antecedents put you in a minority group; Middle East antecedents do not. The classification is elaborate and likely to become more so. Daniel P. Moynihan (Dem.-N.Y.) has invoked the specter of Germany's Nuremberg race laws.

There will be those who say, quite correctly, that such criteria are nothing new to America, that through the 1960s many state statutes included definitions of Negroes as persons of one-eighth or even one-thirty-second Negro ancestry. Such classifications were indisputably the stuff of cultural apartheid. The point is that we had seemed to be getting away from such racial measurements for a decade or so, but now they are reemerging, together with official prescriptions for housing, education, and employment eligibility. . . .

Meanwhile, ethnic consciousness certainly is resurgent. Rev. Jesse Jackson, currently a black favorite of the white media, preaches a gospel of self-determination—"for us, by us, of us." In Joliet, Illinois, black parents have set up their own school rather than let their children be bused to predominantly white schools. From Eastport and Nantucket to Palm Springs, Indians are asserting Red Power and seeking tribal sovereignty. What's more, the melting pot is rehardening for northwestern Europeans—even for the basic "Anglo-Saxon American" H.L. Mencken loathed so much. Dozens of Midwestern German towns have begun celebrating *Oktoberfest* again, and Pan American World Airways has been running commercials reminding white Anglo-Saxons of their British-American heritage to get them to fly back to *their* "old country" the way Italians and Norwegians do.

All in all, there's virtually no facet of human biology—sex, color, age, ethnic heritage—that isn't currently gaining strength as a denominator of social fragmentation. That phenomenon may not be without precedent, but I don't know of one. . . .

FURTHER SPLINTERING

If biological and cultural Balkanization illustrates the breadth of our impetus for national fragmentation, potentially more important symptoms are visible in the decomposition of the American polity. Only ten to fifteen years ago, it seemed that states' rights would be stripped away by a benign centralism, that the flow of public opinion was toward federal authority, with less and less of a role for local government, education, and customs. On a more exalted plane, the Presidency was gaining ground, its imperial promise accredited by no less a prophet than Prof. Arthur Schlesinger, Jr. If anything, the expectation was for further universality—for the onset of metropolitan government in our cities, for racial integration, for the withering away of state lines, and even for the possible loss of national identity to a new world order.

Instead, over the past few years, the tide has begun running strongly in the other direction. Far from becoming an effective world federation, the United Nations is being made less and less useful by the rise (and U.N. admission) of dozens of small states and mini-states. . . . Resurgent parochialism is the theme. Scotland flies its Red Lion once again, and Wales its Dragon. Belgium is dissolving into Flemings and Walloons. Brittany and Corsica would like to detach themselves from France. Nearer home, Quebec threatens to secede from Canada.

Too few Americans realize the extent to which we have similar problems. As Rep. Lloyd Meeds (Dem.-Wash.) has put it, the growing demand of American Indian tribes for "sovereignty" over their reservation lands presents the prospect of *two hundred and sixty* Quebecs. . . .

Demographers also have begun to draw attention to the huge and fast-growing U.S. Hispanic minority. In a generation, Hispanics will outnumber blacks. Each year, the Southwestern states increase their percentage of Spanish-speaking residents. Many are legal residents; many are not. In Texas and California the gathering of huge Hispanic populations (and the prospect that Mexico's poverty and birthrate can only spur more emigration) has prompted regional talk of a *reconquista*—literally a Spanish reconquest of the once-Spanish Southwest. . . .

Turning from the geographical to the institutional aspect of U.S. political Balkanization, one best begins in Washington, D.C. Over the past fifteen years, the executive and legislative branches of the federal government have staffed-up in a new kind of rivalry. Congressional staffs have multiplied to enable Representatives and Senators to entrench themselves institutionally as well as electorally. If the White House has a Budget Office (or a National Security Council or a Science/Technology Office), well then, so must the Congress. For years, much of this intellectual-political arms race was attributed to the 1969–76 desire of a Democratic Congress to match the resources of the GOP White House. But now, with Democrat Jimmy Carter in the Presidency, it's clear that the institutional Balkanization of Washington has a life of its own.

The phenomenon is a long way from being harmless or quaint. Richard Nixon was infuriated by his inability to control the government from the White House, and his frustration brought him much of the way to Watergate. In his book *The Ends of Power*, H.R. Haldeman, former White House chief of staff, explains how, as of 1972–73, the "four major power blocs in Washington"—the press, the bureaucracy, the Congress, the intelligence community—were "under threat" by a President who hoped to use various reorganization techniques to break the independent, unresponsive authority of the bureaucracy and the Cental Intelligence Agency. Likewise, Haldeman sees the critical Watergate events of the spring of 1973 not as the unfolding of justice but as a coup d'état by the threatened interests. To be sure, most Americans will disagree with Haldeman's effort to transform Watergate into a multi-institutional power play. It's an interesting analysis, however; one at least touched with truth (if not permeated by it), and worth pondering with regard to a larger question: How can any President deal with these same power blocs? . . .

Further evidence of Balkanization can be found *within* the several branches of government. If the Executive has rival bureaucracies, Congress, for its part, has been divided by new subgroups and special-interest mechanisms. A recent article in *Roll Call,* the weekly newspaper of Capitol Hill, mentioned an almost feudal arrangement: "Subcommittee staffs have grown which no longer feel responsible to the committee chairman, central authority and discipline have eroded, and lobbyists have learned how to take advantage of this situation by playing one committee against another, or as one veteran put it, 'playing one Balkan prince against another Balkan prince.'" From yet another perspective, the early ideological subgroupings that took shape in Congress during the 1960s paralleled and respected party divisions—the Democratic Study Group for party liberals, the Republican Study Group for GOP conservatives, the Wednesday Club for GOP liberals. Over the past few years, a new set of caucuses is growing up to promote special interests across party lines. And Sun Belt and Frost Belt forces are already marching up and down the aisles of Congress, turning debate after debate into a display of comparative and combative economic geography.

Arguably, these nonparty mechanisms have come into being in part because the 120-year-old Republican-Democratic party system is no longer an effective arbiter of regional, cultural, and economic differences (just as its predecessor during the 1850s wasn't). Indeed, talk of a breakdown in the two-party system and/or the need for new parties is a recurrent staple of political discussion. There is nothing unusual about this; we have had splinter movements before, usually absorbed by one of the major parties in periodic realignments. What *is* unusual is the way the party mechanisms thus far have been unable or unwilling to respond to public desires. Many Americans have either loosened their affiliation, begun to put ideology ahead of party, or simply decided not to vote. Issues like abortion, gun control, the right to work, taxes, busing, feminism, and "gay" liberation appear to be superseding parties as the basis of political mobilization. The obvious description is: *ideological* Balkanization. . . .

A NATION DIVIDED

The United States has been divided and fragmented before, but—save for the Civil War—with the underlying trend pointing in the direction of unity, fraternity, and increasing federal authority. Now American society seems determined to pursue smaller loyalties—regional, economic, political, ethnic, and even sexual—rather than larger ones. Unless the trend reverses in the next few years, and no such prospect is apparent, it bespeaks a fundamental reversal in the American experience. The heterogeneity of America will become a burden, the constitutional separation of powers crippling, the economy threatened, the cohesion of society further diminished. Which brings us to the unhappy question: is American Balkanization a sign of national decline?

I think it is such a sign, despite the optimism and relevance of counterarguments perceiving strength, not weakness, in the renewed closeness of Americans to neighborhood, ethnic, and regional roots. The overall hypothesis of decline is too well supported by the great theories of biological, psychological, and historical-cultural evolution. Progress has always flowed in a movement from the limited, the parochial, to the more general and universal. This is true whether one cites Charles Darwin on the evolution of species, Sigmund Freud's analyses of personality, or Arnold Toynbee's theories of history. A species, a personality, or an empire—they all grow or rise from the parochial to the general and then, as their hour or role passes, *reparochialize*. Progress flows toward the universal, but when that impetus expires, the particularisms and subdivisions—of function, personality, culture, or politics—reassert themselves. "Parochial" and

"clannish" may be negative concepts, but we recognize basic human nature much less pejoratively with terms like "grass roots,"
"homeland," "kinfolk," and even "bedrock."

Given the imperial, political, and societal nature of my dis-
course on the Balkanization of America, Toynbee's analysis is perhaps the most relevant, linking the advent of a great nation to its
élan vital and the leadership of a creative minority able to define
national values and goals. But that growth period does not last
forever. Sooner or later, there comes a failure of creativity and an
end to mass inspiration. At this point, in Toynbee's words,

> the loss of harmony between elements which had formerly coex-
> isted in a society as an integral whole leads inevitably to an outbreak
> of social discord. The broken-down society is rent in two different
> dimensions simultaneously by the social schisms in which this dis-
> cord is expressed. There are "vertical" schisms between geographi-
> cally segregated communities and "horizontal" schisms between
> geographically intermingled but socially segregated classes.

Overschematized, perhaps, but true. The "articulation of society into a number of parochial states" that Toynbee posited describes all too well the process overtaking the contemporary
United States. Different kinds of vertical and horizontal schisms
are apparent all around us. Less apparent to most upper-middle-
income Americans, however, is the deepening socioeconomic disillusionment of the poorer third of the American population. Con-
sumer-confidence surveys illustrate a marked attitudinal disparity.
Upper-middle-income professionals may be buying imported
cheese at $4.50 a pound, but low-income and lower-middle-
income Americans are losing economic hope. The American
Dream is slipping away. A few pollsters such as Louis Harris play
down such attitudes, saying that people are developing a new
nonmaterialist outlook. Perhaps. If Harris isn't correct, though,
economically and socially disillusioned "Middle America" may
represent the "internal proletariat" that Toynbee found characteristic of every disintegrating major civilization.

As for another of Toynbee's measurements—unproductive
elite leadership by a "dominant minority" that has lost its earlier
creativity—we have to look at our current national leadership
elites. The "Eastern Establishment" that imposed Pax Americana

on the post-World War II world has now given way to a "Parody Establishment," wearing the same tailored suits and bench-made shoes but lacking the élan of their predecessors in the 1940s, 1950s, and even in the 1960s. The national media elite is no better. Indeed, today's American Balkanization in large measure represents the failure of these leadership elites to understand the simple facts of race, ethnicity, territory, greed, and inequality.

Approached from yet another direction, the failures of the Sixties and Seventies have helped bring on what conservative sociologist Robert Nisbet has called "the twilight of authority." Nisbet's thesis: The United States has lost its sense of authority and common purpose—more or less what Toynbee called *élan vital* and the Romans call *civitas*. The crumbling of authority is certainly clear enough, not just in polls measuring popular attitudes toward leading institutions but in the events of the past decade and a half. Yesterday's "Eastern Establishment" has been partially displaced by provincial centers of power—regional, cultural, and institutional—but none of these has had the energy to assume effective national command. . . .

From a different perspective, the sexual and religious Balkanization of America offers another glum thought. In an interview, Will Durant, coauthor with his wife Ariel of the eleven-volume *Story of Civilization,* expressed concern that

> we're in the stage in which Greece was when the gods ceased to be gods and became mere poetry, and therefore exercised no element of order or command upon human behavior. There was the development of city life, of science and philosophy, and the result was a period of pagan license—say around 200 B.C. to 100 A.D.—in which morals floundered in an ocean of competing religions, just as you have a flotsam and jetsam of religions today. By the time of Caesar, you had a permissive society and a pagan society in the sense of sexual enjoyment with a minimal moral restraint. Now . . . we shall have to wait for a new religion, the way the Greeks and Romans did, because . . . what happened was the old civilization decayed to a point where it cried out for a new religion, for something to worship and obey.

Of course, Balkanization is not all bad. No doubt cheerful things can be said about the new commitment to neighborhood, the new individual fulfillment of accepting (even trumpeting) ethnicity rather than cowering before the melting pot, the resurging attention to states' rights, the renewed concern with family and church. Yet much of the new localism seems essentially romantic—the obverse of the last decade's romantic universalism. Too many of the same naive people who were for global unity a decade or two ago are now saying "Small is beautiful," ecstasizing over self-governing Vermont communes and renovated central-city blocks of brownstones. The trouble is that these regional, ethnic, and local forces now seem to be recurring in a U.S. context of societal fragmentation and decomposition, rather than (as in 1800 or 1900) as grass-roots evidence of cultural vigor and functioning political federalism. *Decomposition is just not the same thing as revitalized diversity.* Moreover, in the present-day context of U.S. and world affairs, small-is-beautiful is likely to be overshadowed by small-is-divisive or even small-is-dangerous. An ineffective 1978 U.S. political system is not like a loose, immature 1878 U.S. political system. Under current circumstances, a Balkanized United States is likely to lose headway externally, in the world of nuclear missiles and global oil supplies, as well as internally, in the minds of the American people.

And the future? Just as nature abhors a vacuum, history abhors fragmentation. Some sort of new, sweeping force—a charismatic politics or a religious revival—could emerge out of America's contemporary muddle. A new universalism may yet unite our political, geographic, religious, biological, and economic factions. In the meantime, policies that do not recognize U.S. Balkanization are probably doomed to further promote it.

The New American Poverty

Michael Harrington

As Michael Harrington shows in this article, Americans believed that they had effectively attacked the problem of poverty in the 1960s, when during the Great Society, Lyndon Johnson declared war on poverty and pledged an end to a society where any significant group of people would be excluded from the good life of equal opportunity and material comfort. But twenty years later, approximately one out of six Americans was still poor. The difference was that this time, the poverty that existed was harder to attack, more deeply rooted in the structure of America's economic position vis-à-vis the rest of the world, and more clearly correlated with being female, black, and a single parent. No longer, Harrington says, can we conclude optimistically that a growing economy will solve all problems. Rather, a new war on poverty must focus in concerted fashion on planning for full employment, since only an economy based on that premise can fulfill conservative self-interest as well as liberal hopes and values. Here, Harrington both exposes the flaws of earlier anti-poverty programs (many of them based on his own earlier book, The Other America*) and illuminates the structural obstacles that must be overcome if such spectres as development of a permanent underclass are to be avoided.*

The poor are still there.

Two decades after the President of the United States declared an "unconditional" war on poverty, poverty does not simply continue to exist; worse, we must deal with structures of misery, with a new poverty much more tenacious than the old.

Structures of misery. The idea was a commonplace when one thought of Appalachia a generation ago. An economy controlled by absentee corporations neglected basic investments, which eroded the physical and social infrastructure as well as the tax base. People fled this impossible situation, so there were even fewer human resources, which made further investment unlikely. That in turn further eroded the physical and social infrastructure as well as the tax base. Under such conditions, poverty is not merely an episode or the fault of some heartless Scrooge, but the ongoing product of the organization of disorganization.

Now there are new structures of misery. In the winter of our national discontent in 1982–83, when there were more jobless Americans than at any other time in almost half a century, a young worker walked through the milling, sometimes menacing men on East Third Street in Manhattan and asked the City of New York for a bed at the Municipal Shelter. One of the reasons he was there was that there are steel mills in South Korea. That is, the poor—and the entire American economy—are caught up in a crisis which is literally global. Yet one cannot simply blame changes in the way the world is run for what is happening on East Third Street, or in the *barrios* of Los Angeles, the steel towns of the Monongahela Valley, and the backwoods of Maine.

The great, impersonal forces have indeed created a context in which poverty is much more difficult to abolish than it was twenty years ago. But it is not the South Koreans—or the Japanese, the West Germans, or anyone else—who have decided that the human costs of this wrenching transition should be borne by the most vulnerable Americans. We have done that to ourselves.

One reason is that this economic upheaval did not simply strike at the poor. It had an enormous impact on everyone else and, among many other things, changed the very eyes of the society. In the sixties there was economic growth, political and social movement hope. What was shocking was that poverty existed at all, and the very fact that it did was an incitement to abolish it. I simplify, of course. Even then, as I pointed out in *The Other America,* suburbanization was removing the middle class from daily contact with the poor. In our geography, as in our social structure, we were becoming two nations.

Moreover, the optimistic sixties often overlooked the systemic nature of its own poverty. I remember a quintessential political cocktail party of those times. It was during the 1964 Presidential campaign at the Dakota, perhaps the most chic apartment building in New York City. A leading trade unionist was talking to some of the intellectual elite. We are going to the moon, he said. Why can't we put an end to the slums? He, and almost everyone else there, knew that our capacities were boundless, that we could deal with ghettos as well as outer space. But there are no people on the moon, no landlords, no silk-stocking districts reluctant to welcome the ex-poor into affluent neighborhoods. Lunar exploration posed technical problems; abolishing poverty raised issues of power and wealth.

Few people realized this in 1964, so there was a social war without a human enemy. The opposing forces were abstractions: hunger, illiteracy, bad housing, inadequate motivation, and the like. It was innocently assumed that ending the outrage of poverty was in everyone's interest. It was not until the seventies, during the debate over Richard Nixon's Family Assistance Plan, that a Southern congressman bluntly stated the more complex truth. If the government provided a minimum income to everyone, "Who," he asked, "will iron my shirts and rake the yard?"

But even if there were more than a few illusions in the sixties, they facilitated some very real gains. There were many of the working poor who, in a decade of falling unemployment, fought their way out of poverty. The aging made dramatic gains through Medicare and increased, indexed social security benefits. Blacks successfully eradicated legal Jim Crow; Chicanos and Filipinos created a union in the fields; even Appalachia registered some grains. If the antipoverty program turned out to be a skirmish rather than an unconditional war, it nonetheless made some significant advances.

In the eighties it is not simply that structural economic change has created new poverties and given old poverties a new lease on life. That very same process has impaired the national vision; misery has simultaneously become more intractable and more difficult to see.

In the seventies and the early eighties, we had both inflation and recession, which subverted the established liberal wisdom; the highest unemployment rates since the Great Depression; and a consequent loss of political and social nerve. Crises, particularly at first, do not make people radical or compassionate. They are frightening, and most people concentrate on saving themselves. Thoughts of "brothers" or "sisters," who are moral kin but not one's blood relatives, are a luxury many cannot afford. It was not an accident that the Economic Opportunity Act of 1964 proclaimed that its goal was "to eliminate the paradox of poverty in the midst of plenty." It is somewhat more problematic to summon the average American to such a struggle in the midst of declining real wages and chronic unemployment. . . .

The poverty of the eighties is different from all those poverties that preceded it.

Around 1970, the United States joined the global economy for the first time and the American poor began to suffer from the international division of labor in unprecedented ways. Of course, this country had been involved in foreign trade from the earliest days of the Republic. But if America had long been important for the world, the world was not too important for America. We were the technological pioneers, the inventors of the second industrial revolution of steel and mass production, as well as of the third, electronic industrial revolution. After all, we had an internal market so much larger than any other that it was not especially crucial for us to be concerned about foreigners. Even today, after more than a decade of relative decline, the gross national product (GNP) of the United States is six times that of France, four times that of West Germany, three times that of Japan, and twice as big as that of the Soviet Union.

But this country rebuilt the European and Japanese economies after World War II, made a handsome profit in the process, and did the job too well. Our former clients in West Germany and Japan became fierce competitors. At the same time, trade became more important for the United States than ever before. In the seventies, exports almost doubled (from 9 percent to 17 percent) and the imported portion of the internal market more than doubled (from 9 percent to 21 percent). The West Germans and the Japanese, however, proceeded to sell "turnkey" plants—complete factories ready to start up—to South Korea and other Third World countries. With the spread of multinationals—corporations without a country to be loyal to—there was an unprecedented internationalization of the economy.

Suddenly the industrial geography of a good part of the United States—its mass-production heartland—no longer made as much sense as it once had. That did not simply menace the traditional working class with a new poverty, but by beginning to reshape the occupational structure of the United States, it also threatened a new, mainly immigrant working class and undercut the struggle of blacks, Hispanics, and other minorities who suffered from the effects of an institutional economic racism.

. . . This multifaceted internationalization of poverty occurred at the same time as a technological revolution also restructured America from within. In the auto industry, for instance, it is well known by everyone that a significant portion of the men and women laid off during the 1982–83 recession will never get their jobs back. The companies, like many other corporations, had found a certain utility in the recession. It allowed them to shut down obsolete plants, which also meant destroying living communities, and to plan for more efficient, robotized, automated production. This process is still very much in progress. It has transformed agriculture and the factory, and it is now invading the office.

In his State of the Union Message of 1964, Lyndon B. Johnson declared an "unconditional war on poverty."

The problem was that many Americans heard the President's rhetoric and did not notice that reality contradicted it. They thought the nation was doing so much because they had it on the highest authority—only the highest authority was wrong. Daniel Patrick Moynihan commented in the early seventies that the program was "oversold and underfinanced to the point that its failure was almost a matter of design." That is right if one understands that what "failed" was an original plan that was never implemented. But the overselling of a good cause had serious—and bad—consequences. First, when things did not get dramatically better for the poor in the second half of the sixties, there was frustration, rage, and even violence because of broken promises. And, second, when things became problematic for everyone in the seventies, people could say. "If only we had not been so foolishly generous to the poor, this would not have happened." The savior that never was became the scapegoat that is.

There is a rhythm in federal innovations. A new idea is

broached—say, social security or food stamps—and a principle is adopted. In the first year or so, not much money is spent as plans are laid, guidelines established. Then there is a steady increase in expenditures as the program goes into effect—the food stamp program cost Washington $577 million in 1970, an estimated $10.9 billion in 1984, even after the Reagan cuts. Put simply but not at all unfairly, the OEO never got much beyond the first stage. In its glory days, it received about $800 million in the first fiscal year, and a total of less than $6 billion between 1965 and 1968. . . .

Vietnam was why. I had long imagined a conversation between Sargent Shriver and Lyndon Johnson. When I talked to Shriver in the fall of 1982, he confirmed that it had actually taken place. In 1966, Shriver, obviously assuming that the standard federal pattern was going to prevail, drew up an ambitious, long-range budget for the OEO that would allow it to fulfil its promise. He went to see the President in Texas in the early autumn and was told that because of the expenditures for Vietnam, there was not enough money to fulfill his request.

Why not raise taxes? Shriver asked Johnson. That, he was told, can't be done to the Democrats in Congress on the eve of an election. The President then went on to say that Secretary McNamara had assured him that the war would be over by the end of the year. In 1967 there would be no problems.

Of course, when light did finally come at the end of the Vietnam tunnel, it illuminated an American defeat, occurring at a time when the economy was already malfunctioning badly and under the administration of a Republican President who wanted to dismantle, not expand, the OEO. There were other problems with the War on Poverty, but Vietnam, it should never be forgotten was terminal.

In the sixties, the number of poor families headed by a full-time worker declined dramatically as the falling joblessness rates of the Kennedy-Johnson years made themselves felt. In the seventies, the poverty population was on the same roller coaster as the economy, going up, going down. And in the eighties, the numbers of the poor did not simply increase, which would be bad enough, but since the achievement of full employment had now become much more difficult than anyone had ever dreamed in the sixties, the abolition of poverty became that much more problematic.

As is so often the case, politics lagged behind economics. There was not a direct legislative attack on the poor in the seventies, not the least because the poverty program had acquired some bureaucratic constituents in the city halls of the nation, who were more effective advocates than the unregistered voters in the slums and backwoods. But the economy turned savagely upon the other America long before Ronald Reagan became President. Between 1973 and 1981, the real value of food stamps fell by 12 percent, and AFDC [Aid to Families with Dependent Children] benefits, measured in constant dollars, declined by 28 percent between 1972 and 1981. Indeed, an AFDC family of four, with no earnings and food stamps, had 4 percent less buying power than an AFDC family in 1969, before food stamps became available.

These trends resulted in countless private tragedies, but something more sinister and public was taking place at the same time, preparing a mass audience to accept Reagan's cruel oversimplifications and outright distortions in the 1980s. In the sixties, Kennedy and Johnson had persuaded the people that social justice was smart economics. Johnson, in particular, emphasized how rebuilding the cities and educating the poor would create jobs, profits, and increased productivity. The economy, it was said, was no longer a "zero-sum game" where winners pay losers and someone's gain must be another person's loss. Now America was playing a "positive-sum game" in which, if no one group got too demanding, all would be satisfied from the dividends of endless growth, and a social revolution would take place without the inconvenience of changing any institutions.

All that was the euphoric overgeneralization of a decade of growth, but it was also potent politics. But as the seventies lurched from economic crisis to economic crisis, a contrary and much grander oversimplification took over: It was social spending, all that money lavished on the poor and the minorities, that had caused the drop in productivity and even corrupted the very moral fiber of the society. If only those funds had been invested in machines, if only the rich had been given money to put into factories, all would be better, even for the poor. Where the sixties believed that justice was good economics, the seventies, in a desperate search for a scapegoat for a "stagflation" no one had predicted and few understood, asserted that meanness was good economics.

So it was that there was little public protest when, in 1981, the new President imposed 60 percent of his budget cuts upon the poor: AFDC was reduced by 11.7 percent, food stamps by 18.8 percent, other food programs by 13.3 percent. There was considerable administration talk about a "safety net," but this really meant that the White House had courageously declared that it would not challenge programs with strong political backing, like social security.

These were some of the reasons why an Urban Institute study discovered that between 1979 and 1984, income inequality grew significantly. The bad times had lowered the incomes of the richest fifth by .5 percent and that of the poorest fifth by 9.4 percent. Most shocking of all, taxes for the bottom quintile went up from 9.7 percent of income in 1979 to 11.9 percent in 1984, while the rates of the richest fifth *declined* by .5 percent.

Thus, America under Ronald Reagan turned savagely against a gigantic antipoverty boondoggle that never took place. And, for a complex series of reasons—their own economic insecurity first and foremost—decent people who had welcomed the War on Poverty now supported the war on the poor.

... There is no way to go back to the strategies of another, easier time and place. So this history ultimately teaches us that we are back at Square One, or, rather, that we have advanced to a Square One with a much bleaker prospect than in 1964.

If we have learned anything from this past, we now know that the antipoverty movement of the rest of this century must be internationalist. It was the wrong and bloody war in Southeast Asia that undercut the right and nonviolent war in the United States. And it is the international economy that is now one of the main reasons that the plight of the poor is much more problematic than it was when Johnson committed the nation to end poverty. We also know that the next time around it is a matter of life and death to include the organized workers and the middle class in a coalition with the poor. And that is not done by declaring it to be desirable or necessary, but by developing programs that are in the interests of all three constituencies. . . .

One of the new structures of misery in the United States—is the "feminization" of poverty.

In 1960, 8.1 percent of white households and 20.9 percent of black households were headed by a woman. In 1981, the white percentage had risen to 11.9, the black to 41.7. Between 1950 and

1979, the number of children born out of wedlock in the United States quadrupled for both blacks and whites. In that same year, more than half of the black births in the United States were out of wedlock (the white figure was 17.1 percent). Among black women, teenagers accounted for 44 percent of those pregnancies out of wedlock. . . .

The problems of the family life of the poor are a particularly cruel, exaggerated example of a larger trend that is transforming the family structure of all social classes. In 1980, the Census found that less than 20 percent of the households in Philadelphia conformed to the supposedly "normal" pattern of a husband-wife couple with children. In San Francisco the figure was 13 percent.

These matters are obviously difficult to discuss. On the one hand, this society still outrageously stigmatizes children born out of wedlock as "illegitimate," even though it is rather obvious that it was not the baby who engaged in pre- or extramarital sex. Coupled with this is the fact that here, as in the case of crime, there is a higher rate of black family breakdown (even when the figures are corrected for some very important simplifications to be discussed in a moment) than white. Such a statistic is clearly very easy to use in a racist argument, and that makes people wary of it for understandable reasons.

All of those families headed by a woman were not poor. As a matter of fact, 70 percent of them were not, only 30 percent were. Even so, the decline in intact families, the epidemic of unmarried teenage poverty, the growing number of families headed by a poor woman, significantly changed the structure of poverty in the United States. In 1960, on the basis of the official figures, 65 percent of poor families were headed by a man under sixty-five years of age, 21.2 percent were headed by a woman (13.8 percent of the families were headed by either a man or a woman over sixty-five). By 1979, the percentage of male heads had dropped to 42.4, and of female heads had risen to 43.7. Adding in the fact that the aging poor are predominantly female, the feminine percentage of the adult poverty population had doubled in the years after the declaration of war on poverty!

Women in the United States occupy about the same economic position as blacks and other minorities. They, like the minorities, receive about 60 percent of the dominant (white male) workers' income. This result is not normally a consequence of overt sexual discrimination, i.e., a woman being paid less than a man working at the very same job. Rather, it is the result of the very structure of "women's work" in the United States. The vast increase in the percentage of working women took place after World War II (and, to a considerable measure, *because* of World War II, a period when it was necessary to recruit females to replace drafted males in the war industries). Mainly they took typically "female" jobs: typists, clerks, workers in the service sector.

The "female" jobs were almost always less well paid than the male, even when, as was often the case, the qualifications required were the same in both. But then, even when women did get professional positions, they were not paid as much as men. In part, this was because they tended to be segregated in the professions themselves. They were pediatricians, gynecologists, and psychotherapists when they got an M.D., not surgeons. These specialties, it will be noted, are appropriately "feminine," involving taking care of children, women, and emotional problems, rather than the "masculine" functions of repairing broken bodies or performing miraculous transplants. Women are also much more likely to be part time workers than are men: In 1980, 67.3 percent of white males were full-timers all year, but only 43.3 percent of white women (the respective figures for blacks are 59.3 percent and 47.2 percent).

The plight of the female poor is to occupy a disadvantaged position within an already disadvantaged occupational structure for women. Take that enormous number of teenage pregnancies. Those young women will, in almost every case, become single parents and will receive little or nothing from the fathers of their children. That happens to them before they are even out of high school, and they therefore come into that women's labor market with much less training than anyone else. Some of them will despair of ever finding a job—not an irrational response—and will simply drop out altogether, becoming welfare cases. The "lucky" ones will find a menial, poorly paid job somewhere.

The Chinese ideograph for crisis is composed of the symbols for two words: danger and hope.

That accurately describes these times. The old poverty—the pace of social and economic time is accelerated and I am talking of the ancient days twenty and thirty years ago—seemed to be an

THE NEW AMERICAN POVERTY

exception to the basic trends of the society. Everyone was progressing steadily; a minority had been left behind. Therefore it would be a rather simple matter to deduct some few billions as they poured out of our industrial cornucopia and to use them to abolish the "pockets" of poverty. But the new poverty I have described in this book is quite different. It is, in complex ways, precisely the extreme consequence of tendencies that are transforming the entire society. To repeat, one reason why young men in the winter of 1983 had to ask New York City for beds for the night was that there were steel mills in South Korea, a fact that also menaced relatively well-paid trade unionists and even corporate executives.

This is the great danger confronting the new poor. If their plight is not an anomaly of the affluent society but the outcome of massive economic trends, why will the majority undertake the fairly radical changes that are needed in order to help a minority that is either not seen, despised, or feared? In the sixties, people thought that the struggle against poverty was going to be a lovely little war. But if, in the eighties, the poor and their friends explain that it is going to be a difficult and arduous struggle, who will respond, particularly when everyone is concerned about how it will affect him personally?

In that very real danger there is also hope. The majority of the people of the United States cannot possibly make themselves secure unless they also help the poor. That is, the very measures that will most benefit the working people and the middle class—the rich will take care of themselves, as they always have—will also strike a blow against poverty. That is by no means an automatic process; there are specific measures that have to be worked out to deal with particular problems of the poor. But basically the programs that are in the self-interest of the majority are always in the special interest of the poor.

But how is it that justice and self-interest are, in this miraculous case, in harmony with each other?

Full employment is good for almost everyone. That is a critical reason.

In the sixties, one of the most significant accomplishments of the decade came not from the War on Poverty as such, but from the fact that unemployment declined, with one insignificant exception, in every year of the Kennedy and Johnson administrations. So it was that the working poor constituted one of the two groups (the aging were, of course, the other) who made the greatest progress in the struggle to get out of poverty. And the harmony of justice and self-interest being asserted here as a possible future was a fact then. In a mere ten years the real buying power of production workers went up by more than 15 percent. In 1980, by stark contrast, the weekly wage had declined in real buying power to 1962 levels.

Would these patterns of escape from poverty in the sixties still hold in the eighties? Not for everyone; poor women are, we shall see, a special and very important case. But blacks, Hispanics, and other minorities, whether members of a marginalized underclass or part of the working poor, would gain. So would immigrants, and the question of undocumented workers would be put into a context in which decency would be an economic possibility as well as a moral imperative. The newness of much of the new poverty is precisely a function of an occupational structure that has destroyed many of the rungs of social mobility, the traditional escape routes from poverty. If a full-employment economy would begin to restore some of those possibilities, it would have a major and positive impact on these groups of the new poor.

Moreover, a full-employment economy is probably more effective at job counseling than are some psychiatrists and social workers. When it becomes the norm for everyone to work, people who were "unemployable" only yesterday suddenly turn out to be quite useful. World War II demonstrated this when it took women, blacks, and the long-term unemployed and put them to work in the arms plants; so did the European postwar boom, which showed that Greek and Yugoslavian peasants could do useful work in a sophisticated West German economy. Motivation is often not a matter of individual will but of social atmosphere. Full employment motivates work.

Full employment would even help reduce the levels of crime and violence in America. I am not proposing a strawman here, i.e., I am not suggesting that we disband the police and wait for jobs to abolish crime. I am saying, to frightened people as well as to the conservative cynics who tend that strawman and think they have actually done serious intellectual work, that a radical drop in the jobless rate will appreciably lower the number of muggings

and assaults. There are other things that have to be done to protect society from violence. But this is certainly the most humane
way of fighting crime.

Full employment would help a great number of the new poor;
and it would benefit the nonpoor as well.

When the official figures admitted to more than eleven million
unemployed and almost two million "discouraged workers" driven
out of the labor market in 1983, that was obviously disastrous for
those who had lost their jobs. But it also made things much worse
for those who were still at work. The existence of a huge pool of
idle people makes those with jobs fearful and helps drive wages
down. It also sets off that vicious cycle where people clutch at
every possibility and take jobs for which they are overqualified,
and those they replace do the same until the least qualified at the
bottom suffer the most. As a result, a pervasive sense of insecurity
saps any spirit of militancy. It was not an accident that members
of the United Automobile Workers turned against concessions to
the companies almost the minute the economy improved a bit in
1983. So it is that a full-employment economy would not simply
help the least paid, or the unemployed; it would set in motion a
virtuous cycle that would improve the lot of everyone in the labor
force.

The forces that are reshaping the American economy and
society are extremely radical and will not respond to unrelated
reforms on the fringes of massive problems. We have no choice
but to redefine the nature of work, because if we don't do it
consciously and in the name of specific values, it will be done for
us from on high, in the worst possible way, with a new joblessness rather than a new leisure. In that case, the greatest costs will
be imposed upon the most vulnerable, a response to the crisis
that is already under way.

An antipoverty politics must be coalitional, with full employment as a central goal, and must awaken the latent moral idealism
of the nation in the service of a very specific program.

Will it happen? The danger that it will not is great; the structures of misery are much more menacing today than they were in
the sixties. There could be a revolution without revolutionaries,
an unwitting transformation of the conditions of human existence
that would preserve the worst of the past in a fantasy future.
There would be custodial care for the suffering of increasing

numbers of superfluous people, and electronic security would become a growth industry, protecting the elite from the sporadic, unorganized violence of a disconsolate, demoralized stratum at the bottom of the society. The gulf between the two nations—that of the rich and that of the poor—would deepen, since there would be an occupational void in what had once been the middle ground of the economy.

The pattern would be international—but then it already is. In Europe, there are immigrants of the second generation now, young people who have lost their parents' homeland but have not been allowed to find their own. Unemployment threatens the gains of welfare states much more generous than our own. There is homelessness and aimlessness. The dirty jobs are being sent to the Third World, the high technology is reserved for the rich countries, and Africans starve while Americans spend billions to create an artificial food scarcity as a way of maintaining farm income. The danger in that Chinese ideograph of crisis is palpable, already here.

But there is reason for hope. In the sixties, the best people thought they were doing something for "them"—the blacks, the Appalachians, the truly *other* Americans. But now, more and more people are discovering that they, too, are "them." I do not mean to imply for a moment that the majority of Americans have become poor or will do so in the near future. I merely but emphatically insist that there is a growing sense of insecurity in the society, and for good reason. The very trends that have helped to create the new structure of misery for the poor are the ones that bewilder that famous middle of the American society, the traditional bastion of our complacency. And perhaps that middle will learn one of the basic lessons this book has tried to impart: A new campaign for social decency is not simply good and moral, but is also a necessity if we are to solve the problems that bedevil not just the poor, but almost all of us.

If we do understand that point, perhaps we will do something more profound than simply to discover an enlightened self-interest. Perhaps in the process we will discover a new vision of ourselves that rises above our individual needs and unites us in a common purpose. Perhaps that pilgrimage toward the fullness of our humanity will begin once again.

Ways To Turn Back
the Nuclear Tide

George Kennan

In 1946 and 1947 George Kennan played a critical role in shaping American foreign policy regarding the Soviet Union. As a veteran of years in the American Embassy in Moscow, Kennan had the opportunity to experience first hand the difficulties of dealing with Russian politics and culture. At the time, he concluded that Russian suspicions of the West, together with Soviet commitment to world-wide revolution, made it incumbent on the United States to "contain" Soviet aggression. Kennan's eight-thousand-word telegram to the State Department in 1946 helped to crystallize the thinking of the Truman administration toward the Cold War, and his famous "Mr. X" article in Foreign Policy *in 1947 provided an explicit intellectual justification for that policy. (The Clifford memorandum reprinted here in Part I is largely a recapitulation of Kennan's 1946 telegram.) Almost immediately, however, Kennan began to regret the way in which his words were used. In particular, he opposed the military aspects of the Truman Doctrine, and warned against the rigid polarization that resulted from a Cold War mentality that saw every event in the world as either pro-Russian or pro-American. Here, in a speech given in 1981, Kennan asks us to reconsider some of the assumptions that have guided our foreign policy during the past thirty-five years. With passion, he urges that we have the courage to entertain new thoughts—about nuclear armament, our attitudes toward the Soviet Union, and our responsibility toward future generations of humankind.*

The recent growth and gathering strength of the antinuclear-war movement here and in Europe is to my mind the most striking

Excerpted from George Kennan, "Ways To Turn Back the Nuclear Tide," reprinted from *Christian Science Monitor*.

phenomenon of this beginning decade of the 1980s. It is all the more impressive because it is so extensively spontaneous. It has already achieved dimensions which will make it impossible for the respective governments to ignore it. It will continue to grow until something is done to meet it.

This movement against nuclear armaments and nuclear war may be ragged and confused and disorganized; but at the heart of it lie some very fundamental, reasonable, and powerful motivations: among them a growing appreciation by many people for the true horrors of a nuclear war; a determination not to see their children deprived of life, and their civilization destroyed by a holocaust of this nature; and finally, as Grenville Clark said, a very real exasperation with their governments for the rigidity and traditionalism that causes those governments to ignore the fundamental distinction between conventional weapons and the weapons of mass destruction and prevents them from finding, or even seriously seeking, ways of escape from the fearful trap into which the nuclear ones are leading us.

Such considerations are not the reflections of communist propaganda. They are not the products of some sort of timorous neutralism. They are the expression of a deep instinctive insistence, if you don't mind, on sheer survival—on survival as individuals, as parents, and as members of a civilization.

What is involved for us in the effort to turn these things around is a fundamental and extensive change in our prevailing outlooks on a number of points, and an extensive restructuring of our entire defense posture.

What would this change consist of?

We would have to begin by accepting the validity of two very fundamental appreciations. The first is that there is no issue at stake in our political relations with the Soviet Union—no hope, no fear, nothing to which we aspire, nothing we would like to avoid—which could conceivably be worth a nuclear war, which could conceivably justify the resort to nuclear weaponry. And the second is that there is no way in which nuclear weapons could conceivably be employed in combat that would not involve the possibility—and indeed the prohibitively high probability—of escalation into a general nuclear disaster.

If we can once get these two truths into our heads, then the next thing we shall have to do is to abandon the option of the first use of nuclear weapons in any military encounter.

We might, so long as others retained such weapons, have to retain them ourselves for purposes of deterrence and reassurance to our people. But we could no longer rely on them for any positive purpose even in the case of reverses on the conventional battlefield; and our forces would have to be trained and equipped accordingly.

But there is something else, too, that will have to be altered, in my opinion, if we are to move things around and take a more constructive posture. . . . I find the view of the Soviet Union that prevails today in our governmental and journalistic establishments so extreme, so subjective, so far removed from what any sober scrutiny of external reality would reveal, that it is not only ineffective but dangerous as a guide to political action.

This endless series of distortions and oversimplifications; this systematic dehumanization of the leadership of another great country; this routine exaggeration of Moscow's military capabilities and of the supposed iniquity of Soviet intentions; this monotonous misrepresentation of the nature and the attitudes of another great people—and a long-suffering people at that, sorely tried by the vicissitudes of this past century; this ignoring of their pride, their hopes—yes, even of their illusions (for they have their illusions, just as we have ours; and illusions, too, deserve respect); this reckless application of the double standard to the judgment of Soviet conduct and our own; this failure to recognize, finally, the communality of many of their problems and ours as we both move inexorably into the modern technological age; and this corresponding tendency to view all aspects of the relationship in terms of a supposed total and irreconcilable conflict of concerns and of aims: these, believe me, are not the marks of the maturity and discrimination one expects of the diplomacy of a great power; they are the marks of an intellectual primitivism and naïveté unpardonable in a great government. I use the word naïveté, because there is a naïveté of cynicism and suspicion just as there is a naïveté of innocence.

And we shall not be able to turn these things around as they should be turned, on the plane of military and nuclear rivalry, until we learn to correct these childish distortions—until we correct our tendency to see in the Soviet Union only a mirror in which we look for the reflection of our own virtue—until we consent to see there another great people, one of the world's greatest, in all its complexity and variety, embracing the good with the bad—a people whose life, whose views, whose habits, whose fears and aspirations, whose successes and failures, are the products, just as ours are the products, not of any inherent iniquity but of the relentless discipline of history, tradition, and national experience. Above all, we must learn to see the behavior of the leadership of that country as partly the reflection of our own treatment of it. If we insist on demonizing these Soviet leaders—on viewing them as total and incorrigible enemies, consumed only with their fear or hatred of us and dedicated to nothing other than our destruction—that, in the end, is the way we shall assuredly have them—if for no other reason than that our view of them allows for nothing else—either for them or for us.

Suggestions for Further Reading

The best one-volume work on the sources of the Cold War is J. L. Gaddis, *The United States and the Origins of the Cold War, 1941–1947* (1972). Gaddis' most recent book, *Strategies of Containment, A Critical Appraisal of Postwar American National Security Policy* (1982), assesses America's Cold War policies through the 1970s. Provocative interpretations of the Cold War are found in S. Ambrose, *Rise to Globalism: American Foreign Policy, 1938–1980* (1983); H. Feis, *From Trust to Terror: The Onset of the Cold War, 1945–1950* (1971); G. Kolko's *The Politics of War* (1968) and *The Limits of Power* (1972); W. LaFeber, *American, Russia, and the Cold War* (1980); T. Paterson, *On Every Front: The Making of the Cold War* (1979); A. Ulam's *Containment and Coexistence* (1967) and *Expansion and Coexistence* (1974); B. Weisberger, *Cold War, Cold Peace* (1984); and D. Yergin, *A Shattered Peace: The Origins of the Cold War and the National Security State* (1977). D. Acheson offers a first-person perspective in *Present at the Creation: My Years In the State Department* (1969), as does G. Kennan in his *Memoirs: 1925–1950* (1967) and *Memoirs: 1950–1963* (1972). Excellent discussions of the economic issues dividing the Soviet Union from the United States are contained in G. Herring, *Aid to Russia, 1941–1946: Strategy, Diplomacy, The Origins of the Cold War* (1973), and T. Paterson, *Soviet-American Confrontation: Postwar Reconstruction and the Origins of the Cold War* (1973). M. Sherwin's *A World Destroyed: The Atomic Bomb and the Grand Alliance* (1975) should be compared with two conflicting assessments of the decision to drop the atomic bombs: G. Alperovitz, *Atomic Diplomacy: Hiroshima and Potsdam* (1965), and H. Feis, *The Atomic Bomb and the End of World War II* (1966). Also see G. Herken, *The Winning Weapon: The Atomic Bomb in the Cold War,*

1945–1950 (1982), and a stimulating analysis of the impact of the atomic bomb on American culture and thought, P. Boyer, *By the Bomb's Early Light* (1985).

R. Rovere, *Senator Joe McCarthy* (1960), is a pungent account, and D. M. Oshinsky, *A Conspiracy So Immense: The World of Joe McCarthy* (1983), and T. C. Reeves, *The Life and Times of Joe McCarthy: A Biography* (1982) are full-scale examinations. Key monographs are R. Fried, *Men Against McCarthy* (1976); A. Harper, *The Politics of Loyalty: The White House and the Communist Issue, 1946–1952* (1970); and E. Latham, *The Communist Controversy in Washington: From the New Deal to McCarthy* (1966). Their interpretations clash with those of D. Caute, *The Great Fear: The Anti-Communist Purge Under Truman and Eisenhower* (1978); S. I. Kutler, *The American Inquisition: Justice and Injustice in the Cold War* (1982); M. Rogin, *The Intellectuals and McCarthy: The Radical Specter* (1967); and A. Theoharis, *Seeds of Repression: Harry S. Truman and the Origins of McCarthyism* (1971). American Communism is fairly treated by V. Gornick, *The Romance of American Communism* (1977), and J. Starobin, *American Communism in Crisis 1943–1957* (1972). HUAC's probes are dissected by L. Ceplair and S. Englund, *The Inquisition in Hollywood: Politics in the Film Community 1930–1960* (1980); V. Navasky, *Naming Names* (1980); and A. Weinstein, *Perjury: The Hiss-Chambers Case* (1978).

A. Hamby, *Beyond the New Deal: Harry S. Truman and American Liberalism* (1973) is a solid introduction to postwar domestic politics. Insight into specific presidencies is provided by R. Donovan, *Conflict and Crisis: The Presidency of Harry S Truman, 1945–1948* (1977); R. H. Ferrell, *Harry S. Truman and the Modern American Presidency* (1983); D. R. McCoy, *The Presidency of Harry S. Truman* (1984); C. Alexander, *Holding the Line: The Eisenhower Era, 1952–61* (1975); S. Ambrose, *Eisenhower: The President* (1984); F. I. Greenstein, *The Hidden-Hand Presidency* (1982); H. Fairlie, *The Kennedy Promise* (1973); H. Parmet, *JFK: The Presidency of John F. Kennedy* (1983); G. Wills, *The Kennedy Imprisonment* (1982); R. Dugger, *The Politician: The Life and Times of Lyndon Johnson* (1982); E. Goldman, *The Tragedy of Lyndon Johnson* (1969); and D. Kearns, *Lyndon Johnson and the American Dream* (1976). Revealing are H. Truman, *Memoirs* (2 vols., 1958); D. Eisenhower, *Mandate for*

Change (1963) and *Waging Peace* (1965); and L. Johnson, *The Vantage Point* (1971). Also see O. Graham, Jr., *Toward a Planned Society: From Roosevelt to Nixon* (1976); S. Levitan and R. Taggart, *The Promise of Greatness* (1976); and J. Sundquist, *Politics and Policy: The Eisenhower, Kennedy, and Johnson Years* (1968). Especially illuminating are E. Dale, *Conservatives in Power* (1960); S. Lubell, *The Future of American Politics* (1956); C. Wright Mills, *The Power Elite* (1956); H. Eulay, *Class and Party in the Eisenhower Years* (1962); and R. Wood, *Suburbia: Its People and Their Politics* (1959).

The literature on the Black struggle is particularly rich. Legal developments culminating in the *Brown* decision are brilliantly described in R. Kluger, *Simple Justice: The History of Brown v. Board of Education and Black America's Struggle for Equality* (1976). H. Sitkoff presents a comprehensive overview of the civil rights movement in *The Struggle for Black Equality* (1981), while individual organizations are analyzed by C. Carson, *In Struggle: SNCC and the Black Awakening of the 1960s* (1981); A. Meier and E. Rudwick, *CORE* (1975); and H. Zinn, *SNCC: The New Abolitionists* (1964). The best biography of Martin Luther King, Jr. is D. Lewis, *King: A Critical Biography* (1970). It should be augmented by D. Garrow, *The FBI and Martin Luther King* (1980), and S. B. Oates, *Let the Trumpet Sound: The Life of Martin Luther King, Jr.* (1982). Key monographs include W. H. Chafe, *Civilities and Civil Rights: Greensboro, North Carolina, and the Black Struggle for Freedom* (1980); D. Garrow, *Protest at Selma* (1978); and M. A. Rothschild, *A Case of Black and White: Northern Volunteers and Southern Freedom Summers, 1964–1965* (1982). S. Carmichael and C. Hamilton, *Black Power: The Politics of Liberation in America* (1967), and J. Lester, *Look Out Whitey! Black Power's Gon' Get Your Mama!* (1968) are enlightening explanations of this divisive phenomenon. Revealing first-person accounts are Malcolm X, *The Autobiography of Malcolm X* (1964); J. Forman, *The Making of Black Revolutionaries* (1972); and C. Sellers, *River of No Return* (1973). Powerful oral histories are H. Raines, *My Soul is Rested* (1977), and J. L. Gwaltney, *Drylongso* (1980).

W. H. Chafe, *The American Woman: Her Changing Social, Political, and Economic Roles, 1920–1970* (1972) offers an overview of changes in the status of women during the twentieth century, as does L. Banner, *Women in the 20th Century* (1974); S. Rothman,

Woman's Proper Place: A History of Changing Ideals and Practices, 1870 to the Present (1978); and M. Ryan, *Womanhood in America* (1975); and N. Woloch, *Women and the American Experience* (1984). G. Lerner, *The Majority Finds its Past* (1980) presents a collection of articles on women's history, as well as a theoretical interpretation of the study of women. S. Evens, *Personal Politics: The Roots of Women's Liberation in the Civil Rights Movement and the New Left* (1979) is the best study of the origins of the women's liberation movement, while J. Freeman, *The Politics of Women's Liberation* (1975), B. Deckard, *The Women's Movement* (1979), E. Klein, *Gender Politics* (1984), and K. Luker, *Abortion and the Politics of Motherhood* (1984) are important political analyses. Much of the more brilliant literature on women's experience appears in anthologies of writings by and about women, particularly A. Koedt, E. Levine, and A. Rapone, eds., *Radical Feminism* (1973); B. Moran and V. Gornick, eds., *Woman in Sexist Society* (1971); R. Morgan, ed., *Sisterhood is Powerful* (1970); and S. Ruth, ed., *Issues in Feminism: A First Course in Women's Studies* (1980). A. Walker's novel, *Meridian* (1976) discusses the experience of women in the civil rights movement, and M. Wallace focuses specifically on black women in *Black Macho and the Myth of the Superwoman* (1979). Also see B. Ehrenreich, *The Hearts of Men: American Dreams and the Flight from Commitment* (1983), and B. C. Mossberg, *Backstage of the American Dream* (1986).

The Pentagon Papers (1971) is the indispensable source on the causes and conduct of American intervention in Vietnam, and the best single-volume history of the conflict is G. Herring, *America's Longest War: The United States and Vietnam 1950–1975* (1979). Varied explanations for the deepening involvement of the United States are offered by F. Fitzgerald, *Fire in the Lake* (1972); D. Halberstam, *The Making of a Quagmire* (1965) and *The Best and the Brightest* (1972); R. Shaplan, *The Road from War: Vietnam 1965–1971* (1971); A. Schlesinger, Jr., *Bitter Heritage: Vietnam and American Democracy* (1967); and G. Lewy, *America in Vietnam* (1978). The escalation of the war is analyzed in D. Bloodworth, *An Eye for the Dragon: Southeast Asia Observed, 1954–1970* (1970), and E. Weintal and C. Bartlett, *Facing the Brink: An Intimate Study of Crisis Diplomacy* (1967). Some of the tragic consequences are chillingly told in F. Harvey, *Air War—Vietnam* (1967); R. Hammer, *One Morning in* the War: The Tragedy at Son My (1971); S. Hersh, My Lai 4: A Report on the Massacre and its Aftermath (1970); J. Schell, The Military Half: An Account of Destruction in Quang Ngai and Quang Tin (1968); and M. Herr, Dispatches (1977). Also see G. Emerson's absorbing Winners and Losers (1977); P. Caputo's personal A Rumor of War (1977); and a former State Department official's insider account, C. Cooper, The Lost Crusade: America in Vietnam (1970). N. Podhoretz, Why We Were In Vietnam (1982) and W. W. Rostow, The Diffusion of Power (1972) strongly defend America's involvement in the war, while vital questions about the way Americans fought the war are raised by H. G. Summers, Jr., On Strategy: A Critical Analysis of the Vietnam War (1982). The opposition to the war is chronicled in N. Zaroulis and G. Sullivan, Who Spoke Up? American Protests Against the War in Vietnam, 1963–1975 (1984). T. J. Lomperis, The War Everyone Lost—and Won (1984), M. MacPherson, Long Time Passing: Vietnam and the Haunted Generation (1984), and H. E. Salisbury, ed., Vietnam Reconsidered (1984) assess the lessons and legacies of the conflict.

The student revolt of the 1960s is the subject of S. Lipset and S. Wolin, eds., The Berkeley Student Revolt (1965); P. Jacobs and S. Landau, eds., The New Radicals (1966); S. Lipset and P. Altbach, eds., Students in Revolt (1969); K. Sale, SDS (1973); and I. Unger, The Movement: A History of the American New Left, 1959–1972 (1974). K. Kenniston's The Uncommitted (1965) and Young Radicals (1968) offer a sympathetic analysis of the revolt by the young. More penetrating are W. Breines, Community and Organization in the New Left (1983) and S. Rothman and S. R. Lichter, Roots of Radicalism (1982). The most important works on the counterculture include T. Roszak, The Making of a Counter-Culture (1969); P. Slater, Pursuit of Loneliness (1970); C. Riech, The Greening of America (1979); and L. Yablonsky, The Hippie Trip (1968). The connections between culture and radicalism are analyzed quite differently by R. Berman, America in the Sixties (1968) and M. Dickstein, Gates of Eden: American Culture in the Sixties (1977). T. Gitlin, The Whole World is Watching: The Mass Media in the Making and Unmaking of the New Left (1980) and M. Viorst, America in the 1960's (1980) offer stimulating explanations on the demise of the revolt. The backlash is chronicled in R. Lemons, The Troubled American (1970). Two perceptive anthologies are M. Friedman, ed., Over-

coming Middleclass Rage (1971) and L. K. Howe, ed., *The White Majority* (1970). They should be compared with A. J. Matusow, *The Unraveling of America: A History of Liberalism in the 1960s* (1984) and C. Murray, *Losing Ground: American Social Policy 1950–1980* (1984).

Indispensable for understanding the Watergate crimes are the President's memoirs, *Six Crises* (1962) and *RN: The Memoirs of Richard Nixon* (1978), and those of his co-conspirators, especially J. Dean, *Blind Ambition: The White House Years* (1976); H. R. Haldeman, *The Ends of Power* (1978); and M. Stans, *The Terrors of Justice: The Untold Side of Watergate* (1979). The prosecution's story is best told by L. Jaworski, *The Right and the Power: The Prosecution of Watergate* (1976), and J. Sirica, *To Set the Record Straight: The Break-in, the Tapes, the Conspirators, the Pardon* (1979). Stimulating speculations on the causes and meaning of Watergate are J. Houghan, *Secret Agenda: Watergate, Deep Throat and the CIA* (1984); J. Lukas, *Nightmare: The Underside of the Nixon Years* (1976); and J. Schell, *The Time of Illusion* (1976). Changing political trends in the 1970s are discussed by A. Crawford, *Thunder on the Right: The "New Right" and the Politics of Resentment* (1980); E. Ladd, Jr., *Transformations of the American Party System: Political Coalitions from the New Deal to the 1970s* (1978); R. C. Liebman and R. Wuthnow, eds., *The New Christian right* (1983); G. Peele, *Revival and Reaction: The Right in Contemporary America* (1984); K. Sale, *Power Shift: The Rise of the Southern Rim and Its Challenge to the Eastern Establishment* (1975); P. Steinfels, *The Neoconservatives: The Men Who Are Changing America's Politics* (1979); and D. Warren, *The Radical Center: Middle America and the Politics of Alienation* (1976). Also see R. Dallek, *Ronald Reagan: The Politics of Symbolism* (1984) and L. A. Shoup, *The Carter Presidency and Beyond* (1980).

The debate on the meaning of equality in America can be traced through the following: J. Rawls, *Theory of Justice* (1971); H. Gans, *More Equality* (1973); N. Glazer, *Affirmative Discrimination: Ethnic Inequality and Public Policy* (1976); and A. Okum, *Equality and Efficiency* (1976). On class, race, and ethnicity see S. Aronowitz, *False Promises: The Shaping of American Working Class Consciousness* (1973); K. Auletta, *The Underclass* (1982); J. Crewden, *The Tarnished Door: The New Immigrants and the Transformation of America*

(1983); M. Harrington, *The New American Poverty* (1984); and R. Polenberg, *One Nation Divisible* (1980). B. Wattenberg, *In Search of the Real America: A Challenge to the Chaos of Failure and Guilt* (1976); C. Lasch, *The Culture of Narcissism: American Life in an Age of Diminishing Expectations* (1979); and L. Jones, *Great Expectations* (1980) are divergent efforts to explain contemporary predicaments.

The major environmental questions are raised by B. Commoner, *The Closing Circle* (1971); F. Graham, Jr., *Since Silent Spring* (1970); and J. Lash, *A Season of Spoils: The Story of the Reagan Administration's Attack on the Environment* (1984). Useful guides to the maze of contemporary disputes over nuclear weaponry are W. M. Arkin and R. Fieldhouse, *Nuclear Battlefields* (1985); F. Kaplan, *Dubious Specter, A Skeptical Look at the Soviet Nuclear Threat* (1980); R. Scheer, *With Enough Shovels: Reagan, Bush and Nuclear War* (1983); and S. Talbott, *Deadly Gambits* (1984). Also see D. Calleo, *Imperious Economy* (1982); R. L. Garthoff, *Detente and Confrontation: American-Soviet Relations from Nixon to Reagan* (1985); D. F. Noble, *Forces of Production: A Social History of Industrial Automation* (1984); and R. L. Heilbroner and L. C. Thurow, *Five Economic Challenges* (1983).